.NET Application Architecture Guide, 2nd Edition

patterns & practices

ISBN: 9780735627109

Contents

Chapter 5: Layered Application Guidelines   55

Chapter 6: Presentation Layer Guidelines   67

Chapter 9: Service Layer Guidelines   115

Chapter 10: Component Guidelines   135

Chapter 15: Designing Data Components   181

Chapter 16: Quality Attributes   191

Chapter 17: Crosscutting Concerns   205

Chapter 18: Communication and Messaging   227

Chapter 22: Designing Rich Client Applications   297

Chapter 23: Designing Rich Internet Applications   319

Chapter 24: Designing Mobile Applications   339

Appendices   435

Foreword by S. Somasegar

In using our own technologies to build Microsoft products, and working with customers and partners every day, we have developed practical guidance on applying best practices for application architecture and design patterns and principles using our technologies. This guidance is valuable to both the developer and to the solution architect. We have built the *Microsoft Application Architecture Guide* to consolidate guidance that we have gathered from our internal practices, external experts, customers, and others in the community in order to share it with you.

The purpose of the guide is to help solution architects and developers to design and build applications on the Microsoft platform that are more effective, to support key decision making at the early stages of a new project, as well as providing topic-specific content to help architects and developers improve their existing solutions. This guidance incorporates the contributions and reviews from more than 25 external experts and customers.

By thinking about solutions in terms of architectural patterns and principles, quality attributes, and crosscutting concerns, you can very quickly determine a baseline application architecture and the relevant technologies, patterns, and guidance assets that will help you build your solution. You can then use the guide to identify key areas of your application architecture so you can refine them for your scenario.

The guide includes reference application architectures for common application types, such as Web, rich client, RIA, mobile, and services applications; guidelines for quality attributes and crosscutting concerns; and guidelines on design approaches that can help you to design and refine your solution architecture.

We are confident that the *Microsoft Application Architecture Guide 2nd Edition* will help you choose the right architecture, the right technologies, and the relevant patterns that will help you make more effective design decisions.

Sincerely,
S. Somasegar
Senior Vice President of Developer Division
Microsoft

Foreword by Scott Guthrie

Application architecture is a challenging topic, as evidenced by the wide variety of books, articles, and white papers on the subject. It is still too hard for developers and architects to understand architecture and best practice design for the Microsoft platform. The original *Application Architecture for .NET: Designing Applications and Services* guide did a great job of covering this topic, but it was written in 2002.

To deal with the many technology additions since then, J. D. Meier, David Hill, and their team from Microsoft patterns & practices have created a new application architecture guide to provide insightful guidance for designing applications and services that run on the Microsoft platform based on the latest best practices and technologies. The outcome is *Microsoft Application Architecture Guide 2nd Edition*, a guide targeted to help solution architects and developers design effective applications on the Microsoft platform. While the guide provides an overview of the .NET Framework, the Microsoft platform, and the main technologies and capabilities within them, it also provides platform-independent, pattern-oriented, principles-based guidance that will help you design your applications on a solid foundation.

The guide is based on a number of key architecture and design principles that provide structure. It includes guidelines for identifying and dealing with key engineering decisions, and an explanation of the quality attributes, crosscutting concerns, and capabilities that shape your application architecture; such as performance, security, scalability, manageability, deployment, communication, and more.

The guide also describes, at a meta-level, the tiers and layers that a solution architect should consider. Each tier/layer is described in terms of its focus, function, capabilities, common design patterns, and technologies. Using these as a backdrop, the guide then overlays relevant principles, patterns, and practices. Finally, the guide provides canonical application archetypes to illustrate common application types. Each archetype is described in terms of the target scenarios, technologies, patterns, and infrastructure it contains.

The guidance as a whole is based on the combined experience and knowledge of Microsoft experts, Microsoft partners, customers, and others in the community. It will help you understand our platform, choose the right architecture and the right technologies, and build applications using proven practices and lessons learned.

Sincerely,
Scott Guthrie
Corporate Vice President of .NET Developer Platform
Microsoft

Preface by David Hill

There is an old joke, told amongst mischievous developers, that in order to be considered an architect you just need to answer every technical question with "it depends"—Q: What's the best way to implement authentication and authorization in my solution? —A: It depends; Q: How should I implement my data access layer?—A: It depends; Q: Which technology should I use for my solution's UI?—A: It depends. Q: How can I make my application scalable?—A: It depends. You get the general idea.

The truth is, of course, that it really does depend. Ultimately, every solution is different and there are many factors, both technical and non-technical, that can significantly affect the architecture and design of a solution at both the small and the large scales. The role of the developer and solution architect is to balance the (frequently contradictory) requirements and constraints imposed by the business, the end user, the organization's IT environment and management infrastructure, the economic environment, and of course the technologies and tools that are used to build the solution.

And, to make life really interesting, these requirements and constraints are constantly evolving as new opportunities arise or as new demands are imposed on the system. Changes to business rules or the emergence of new business areas can affect both new and existing applications. Over time, users expect richer, more consistent and more highly integrated user experiences. New compliance requirements might emerge. Or new IT infrastructure technologies might appear that can reduce costs or improve availability or scalability. And, of course new technologies, frameworks, and tools are being released all the time with promises to reduce development costs, or to enable scenarios that were previously difficult to implement.

Clearly, making sense of all of this and at the same time delivering an effective solution on budget and to schedule is not an easy task. It requires that the developer or solution architect have to account for a whole host of competing and overlapping factors (some of which are non-technical) and strike a pragmatic balance between them all. Trying to account for too many factors can result in over-engineered, complex solutions that take a long time to build and nevertheless fail to deliver on promises of improved longevity or flexibility. On the other hand, consideration of too few factors can result in constrained, inflexible, and improvised solutions that are difficult to evolve or that do not scale well. In other words, developers and solution architects often have to walk the path between a "golden solution" on the one hand, and a "point-in-time solution" on the other.

This, to me, is what application architecture is all about—it's about using today's tools and technologies to create as much business value as possible whilst keeping one eye on the requirements and constraints imposed by the business today, and one eye looking to tomorrow to maximize ongoing value through scalability, flexibility and maintainability. A good understanding of architectural principles and patterns allows the developer or solution architect to understand and factor into the overall design process the important design issues that can have a big impact on the overall success of their solution. Armed with this knowledge, they can make more informed decisions, better balance competing or overlapping requirements and constraints, and make sure that the solution not only meets or exceeds its business goals but it does so in way that is cost effective and scalable, maintainable and flexible.

You'll notice that I refer to both developers and solution architects. I believe that both can benefit greatly from a solid understanding of the architectural patterns and principles outlined in this guide. Some might argue that the implementation details are less important than the overall design. In my experience this is not the case. Small decisions accumulate over time. Implementation-level details can have a very large impact on the overall solution architecture and on its scalability, maintainability, and flexibility, so a solid understanding by both developers and solution architects is essential. In addition, a shared understanding leads to better communication between developers and architects, which is a good thing.

This guide aims to provide an overview of the application architecture and design principles and patterns that will help you make better decisions and build more successful solutions. The guide is structured in a way that allows you to read it from start to finish, or use as a reference resource so you can jump directly to the most relevant sections. The first half of the guide is focused on generally applicable architecture and design principles and apply to any type of solution. The last half is focused on common application types—such as Web applications, rich client application, or mobile applications—and describes the typical architecture and key design considerations for each. It's likely that your particular solution won't map directly to these, but they can serve to provide a baseline architecture that you can take and evolve for your particular situation. The guide provides advice on how to identify the key elements of your architecture so you can refine it over time.

There is a particular focus throughout the guide on developing solutions on the Microsoft platform with the .NET Framework so the guide contains references to articles and resources that provide details on relevant technologies and tools. You'll find though that the underlying principles and patterns are generally applicable to any platform. It is also worth noting that the guide is not meant to be a complete and comprehensive reference to every aspect of application architecture and design—that would require either a much larger guide, or multiple volumes—so the guide aims to provide a pragmatic overview of the most important topics along with links to more detailed guidance or in-depth material.

The field of application architecture and design is dynamic and constantly evolving. The foundations on which successful solutions have been built in the past will continue to serve us well into the foreseeable future, but we should also expect that the pace of innovation, in both technologies and new design approaches, will not decrease. The Microsoft platform and the .NET Framework and the range of technologies and scenarios that they support are both deep and wide, and getting deeper and wider all the time. On the other hand, we don't need to wait for what might be. We can build compelling valuable solutions right now, and hopefully this guide will help you do just that.

David Hill
patterns and practices
September 2009

Introducing the Guide

The goal of this guide is to help developers and solution architects build effective, high quality applications on the Microsoft platform and the .NET Framework more quickly and with less risk by leveraging tried and trusted architecture and design principles and patterns.

The guide provides an overview of the underlying principles and patterns that provide a solid foundation for good application architecture and design. On top of this foundation, the guide provides generally applicable guidance for partitioning an application's functionality into layers, components, and services. It goes on to provide guidance on identifying and addressing the key design characteristics of the solution and the key quality attributes (such as performance, security, and scalability) and crosscutting concerns (such as caching and logging). The guide builds still further and provides guidance that is more specific on the architecture and design of the most common application types, such as Web, rich Internet applications (RIA), rich client, services, and mobile applications.

The guidance is presented in parts that correspond to major architecture and design focus points. It is designed to be used as a reference resource, or it can be read from beginning to end.

The guide will help you to:

- Understand the underlying architecture and design principles and patterns for developing successful solutions on the Microsoft platform.
- Identify appropriate strategies and design patterns that will help you design your solution's layers, components, and services.
- Identify and address the key engineering decision points for your solution.
- Identify and address the key quality attributes and crosscutting concerns for your solution.
- Choose the right technologies for your solution.
- Create a candidate baseline architecture for your solution.
- Identify patterns & practices solution assets and further guidance that will help you to implement your solution.

Note that while the guide is extensive, it is should not be considered a complete and comprehensive treatise on the field of application architecture and design. The guide is intended to serve as a practical and convenient overview of and reference to the general principles of architecture and design on the Microsoft platform and the .NET Framework.

In particular, the guide does not try to provide a definitive or authoritative solution architecture for any particular scenario. Rather, it provides a concise overview of the principles and patterns that underpin good architecture and design, and highlights and provides recommendations for some of the most important issues you might encounter.

The bulk of the guide is technology-agnostic and principled-based, and can be applied to any platform or technology. However, we have added specific Microsoft and .NET Framework technology considerations where we think it helps you to choose amongst available technologies, or to make the most of them in a particular situation.

Audience

This guide is primarily written for developers and solution architects who are looking for guidance on architecting and designing applications on the Microsoft platform and the .NET Framework.

However, this guide will benefit any technologist who is generally interested in the field of application architecture and design, wishes to understand the underlying patterns and principles behind good application design on the .Microsoft platform or the .NET Framework, or is new to the Microsoft platform or the .NET Framework.

How to Use This Guide

This guide is not a step-by-step tutorial for application architecture and design, but rather an overview and a reference. The guide is divided into four main sections, each containing a number of chapters:

- The first section of the guide, "Software Architecture and Design," provides a summary of the underlying principles and patterns that provide the foundation for good application architecture and design and a suggested approach for creating your architecture design. If you are using the guide to learn about the fundamentals of application architecture, start with this section and then work through the remaining parts to learn about layered design, components, quality attributes, crosscutting concerns, communication, deployment, and common application types.

- The second section of the guide, "Design Fundamentals," provides generally applicable guidance for designing a solution's layers, components, and services; and guidance on addressing quality attributes and crosscutting concerns. It also covers communication and deployment topics. If you want to learn about the layered approach to application architecture and design, or the design of specific components and services, start with this section and then explore the following sections to see how to take account of quality attributes and how to design a physical deployment strategy.

- The third section of the guide, "Application Archetypes," provides specific guidance on the architecture and design of typical application types, such as Web, RIA, rich client, mobile, and services applications. If you have some prior experience with application architecture and design and want to learn about the architecture and major design features of common types of application and the specific guidance for each type, start with this section and then use the remaining sections to expand and verify your knowledge.

- Finally, the Appendices provide an overview of the Microsoft platform and .NET Framework technologies and their capabilities. This section also provides a summary of common design patterns, and references to additional resources and materials. If you are new to the .NET Framework, or want to learn about the technologies available on the Microsoft platform, use this section to get an overview of the .NET Framework and platform services, see the major technology matrices, and read descriptions of patterns & practices assets such as Enterprise Library and the patterns & practices design pattern library.

Depending on your experience and requirements, you can refer directly to the specific section(s) that best address your needs. Alternatively, if you are looking for an extensive overview of design and architecture on the Microsoft platform and the .NET Framework, you can read the guide from start to finish. It will help you to understand the architecture and design approach. You can work the guidance into your application development life cycle and processes, and use it as a training tool.

Feedback and Support

We have made every effort to ensure the accuracy of this guide. However, we welcome feedback on any topics it contains. This includes technical issues specific to the recommendations, usefulness and usability issues, and writing and editing issues. To more easily access the various Web resources, see the online version of the bibliography at: http://www.microsoft.com/architectureguide.

If you have comments on this guide, please visit the Application Architecture Guide community site at http://www.codeplex.com/AppArchGuide.

Technical Support

Technical support for the Microsoft products and technologies referenced in this guidance is provided by Microsoft Product Support Services (PSS). For product support information, please visit the Microsoft Product Support Web site at: http://support.microsoft.com.

Community and Newsgroup Support

You can also obtain community support, discuss this guide, and provide feedback by visiting the Microsoft MSDN® Newsgroups site at http://msdn.microsoft.com/en-us/subscriptions/aa974230.aspx.

The Team Who Brought You This Guide

This guide was produced by the following .NET architecture and development specialists:

- J.D. Meier
- David Hill
- Alex Homer
- Jason Taylor
- Prashant Bansode
- Lonnie Wall
- Rob Boucher Jr.
- Akshay Bogawat

Contributors and Reviewers

Many thanks to the contributors and reviewers:

- **Test Team.** Rohit Sharma; Praveen Rangarajan
- **Edit Team.** Dennis Rea
- **External Contributors and Reviewers.** Adwait Ullal; Andy Eunson; Brian Sletten; Christian Weyer; David Guimbellot; David Ing; David Weller; David Sussman; Derek Greer; Eduardo Jezierski; Evan Hoff; Gajapathi Kannan; Jeremy D. Miller; John Kordyback; Keith Pleas; Kent Corley; Mark Baker; Paul Ballard; Peter Oehlert; Norman Headlam; Ryan Plant; Sam Gentile; Sidney G Pinney; Ted Neward; Udi Dahan; Oren Eini aka Ayende Rahien; Gregory Young
- **Microsoft Contributors and Reviewers.** Ade Miller; Amit Chopra; Anna Liu; Anoop Gupta; Bob Brumfield; Brad Abrams; Brian Cawelti; Bhushan Nene; Burley Kawasaki; Carl Perry; Chris Keyser; Chris Tavares; Clint Edmonson; Dan Reagan; David Hill; Denny Dayton; Diego Dagum; Dmitri Martynov; Dmitri Ossipov; Don Smith; Dragos Manolescu; Elisa Flasko; Eric Fleck; Erwin van der Valk; Faisal Mohamood; Francis Cheung; Gary Lewis; Glenn Block; Gregory Leake; Ian Ellison-Taylor; Ilia Fortunov; J.R. Arredondo; John deVadoss; Joseph Hofstader; Kashinath TR; Koby Avital; Loke Uei Tan; Luke Nyswonger; Manish Prabhu; Meghan Perez; Mehran Nikoo; Michael Puleio; Mike Francis; Mike Walker; Mubarak Elamin; Nick Malik; Nobuyuki Akama; Ofer Ashkenazi; Pablo Castro; Pat Helland; Phil Haack; Rabi Satter; Reed Robison; Rob Tiffany; Ryno Rijnsburger; Scott Hanselman; Seema Ramchandani; Serena Yeoh; Simon Calvert; Srinath Vasireddy; Tom Hollander; Vijaya Janakiraman; Wojtek Kozaczynski

Tell Us About Your Success

If this guide helps you, we would like to know. Tell us by writing a short summary of the problems you faced and how this guide helped you out. Submit your summary by e-mail to MyStory@Microsoft.com.

Software Architecture and Design

This section of the guide contains a series of topics that will help you to understand the fundamentals of architecture and design. It starts by describing what is software architecture is, why is it important. It discusses the general issues you must consider, such as requirements and constraints and the intersection between the user, the business, and the system on which the application will run. This is followed by a description of the key design principles, and the architectural patterns and styles in common use today. Finally, this section provides an insight into the approach you should follow when designing your architecture. For more information, see the following chapters:

- Chapter 1, "What is Software Architecture?"
- Chapter 2, "Key Principles of Software Architecture"
- Chapter 3, "Architectural Patterns and Styles"
- Chapter 4, "A Technique for Architecture and Design"

1

What Is Software Architecture?

Software application architecture is the process of defining a structured solution that meets all of the technical and operational requirements, while optimizing common quality attributes such as performance, security, and manageability. It involves a series of decisions based on a wide range of factors, and each of these decisions can have considerable impact on the quality, performance, maintainability, and overall success of the application.

Philippe Kruchten, Grady Booch, Kurt Bittner, and Rich Reitman derived and refined a definition of architecture based on work by Mary Shaw and David Garlan (Shaw and Garlan 1996). Their definition is:

> "Software architecture encompasses the set of significant decisions about the organization of a software system including the selection of the structural elements and their interfaces by which the system is composed; behavior as specified in collaboration among those elements; composition of these structural and behavioral elements into larger subsystems; and an architectural style that guides this organization. Software architecture also involves functionality, usability, resilience, performance, reuse, comprehensibility, economic and technology constraints, tradeoffs and aesthetic concerns."

In *Patterns of Enterprise Application Architecture*, Martin Fowler outlines some common recurring themes when explaining architecture. He identifies these themes as:

> "The highest-level breakdown of a system into its parts; the decisions that are hard to change; there are multiple architectures in a system; what is architecturally significant can change over a system's lifetime; and, in the end, architecture boils down to whatever the important stuff is."

> [http://www.pearsonhighered.com/educator/academic/product/0,3110,0321127420,00.html]

In *Software Architecture in Practice (2nd edition)*, Bass, Clements, and Kazman define architecture as follows:

> "The software architecture of a program or computing system is the structure or structures of the system, which comprise software elements, the externally visible properties of those elements, and the relationships among them. Architecture is concerned with the public side of interfaces; private details of elements—details having to do solely with internal implementation—are not architectural."

> [http://www.aw-bc.com/catalog/academic/product/0,4096,0321154959,00.html]

Why Is Architecture Important?

Like any other complex structure, software must be built on a solid foundation. Failing to consider key scenarios, failing to design for common problems, or failing to appreciate the long term consequences of key decisions can put your application at risk. Modern tools and platforms help to simplify the task of building applications, but they do not replace the need to design your application carefully, based on your specific scenarios and requirements. The risks exposed by poor architecture include software that is unstable, is unable to support existing or future business requirements, or is difficult to deploy or manage in a production environment.

Systems should be designed with consideration for the user, the system (the IT infrastructure), and the business goals. For each of these areas, you should outline key scenarios and identify important quality attributes (for example, reliability or scalability) and key areas of satisfaction and dissatisfaction. Where possible, develop and consider metrics that measure success in each of these areas.

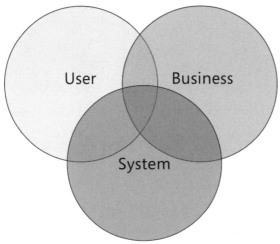

Figure 1
User, business, and system goals

Tradeoffs are likely, and a balance must often be found between competing requirements across these three areas. For example, the overall user experience of the solution is very often a function of the business and the IT infrastructure, and changes in one or the other can significantly affect the resulting user experience. Similarly, changes in the user experience requirements can have significant impact on the business and IT infrastructure requirements. Performance might be a major user and business goal, but the system administrator may not be able to invest in the hardware required to meet that goal 100 percent of the time. A balance point might be to meet the goal only 80 percent of the time.

Architecture focuses on how the major elements and components within an application are used by, or interact with, other major elements and components within the application. The selection of data structures and algorithms or the implementation details of individual components are design concerns. Architecture and design concerns very often overlap. Rather than use hard and fast rules to distinguish between architecture and design, it makes sense to combine these two areas. In some cases, decisions are clearly more architectural in nature. In other cases, the decisions are more about design, and how they help you to realize that architecture.

By following the processes described in this guide, and using the information it contains, you will be able to construct architectural solutions that address all of the relevant concerns, can be deployed on your chosen infrastructure, and provide results that meet the original aims and objectives.

Consider the following high level concerns when thinking about software architecture:

- How will the users be using the application?
- How will the application be deployed into production and managed?
- What are the quality attribute requirements for the application, such as security, performance, concurrency, internationalization, and configuration?
- How can the application be designed to be flexible and maintainable over time?
- What are the architectural trends that might impact your application now or after it has been deployed?

The Goals of Architecture

Application architecture seeks to build a bridge between business requirements and technical requirements by understanding use cases, and then finding ways to implement those use cases in the software. The goal of architecture is to identify the requirements that affect the structure of the application. Good architecture reduces the business risks associated with building a technical solution. A good design is sufficiently flexible to be able to handle the natural drift that will occur over time in hardware and software technology, as well as in user scenarios and requirements. An architect must consider the overall effect of design decisions, the inherent trade-offs between quality attributes (such as performance and security), and the tradeoffs required to address user, system, and business requirements.

Keep in mind that the architecture should:

- Expose the structure of the system but hide the implementation details.
- Realize all of the use cases and scenarios.
- Try to address the requirements of various stakeholders.
- Handle both functional and quality requirements.

The Architectural Landscape

It is important to understand the key forces that are shaping architectural decisions today, and which will change how architectural decisions are made in the future. These key forces are driven by user demand, as well as by business demand for faster results, better support for varying work styles and workflows, and improved adaptability of software design.

Consider the following key trends:

- **User empowerment.** A design that supports user empowerment is flexible, configurable, and focused on the user experience. Design your application with appropriate levels of user personalization and options in mind. Allow the user to define how they interact with your application instead of dictating to them, but do not overload them with unnecessary options and settings that can lead to confusion. Understand the key scenarios and make them as simple as possible; make it easy to find information and use the application.

- **Market maturity.** Take advantage of market maturity by taking advantage of existing platform and technology options. Build on higher level application frameworks where it makes sense, so that you can focus on what is uniquely valuable in your application rather than recreating something that already exists and can be reused. Use patterns that provide rich sources of proven solutions for common problems.

- **Flexible design.** Increasingly, flexible designs take advantage of loose coupling to allow reuse and to improve maintainability. Pluggable designs allow you to provide post-deployment extensibility. You can also take advantage of service orientation techniques such as SOA to provide interoperability with other systems.

- **Future trends.** When building your architecture, understand the future trends that might affect your design after deployment. For example, consider trends in rich UI and media, composition models such as mashups, increasing network bandwidth and availability, increasing use of mobile devices, continued improvement in hardware performance, interest in community and personal publishing models, the rise of cloud-based computing, and remote operation.

The Principles of Architecture Design

Current thinking on architecture assumes that your design will evolve over time and that you cannot know everything you need to know up front in order to fully architect your system. Your design will generally need to evolve during the implementation stages of the application as you learn more, and as you test the design against real world requirements. Create your architecture with this evolution in mind so that it will be able to adapt to requirements that are not fully known at the start of the design process.

Consider the following questions as you create an architectural design:

- What are the foundational parts of the architecture that represent the greatest risk if you get them wrong?
- What are the parts of the architecture that are most likely to change, or whose design you can delay until later with little impact?
- What are your key assumptions, and how will you test them?
- What conditions may require you to refactor the design?

Do not attempt to over engineer the architecture, and do not make assumptions that you cannot verify. Instead, keep your options open for future change. There will be aspects of your design that you must fix early in the process, which may represent significant cost if redesign is required. Identify these areas quickly and invest the time necessary to get them right.

Key Architecture Principles

Consider the following key principles when designing your architecture:

- **Build to change instead of building to last.** Consider how the application may need to change over time to address new requirements and challenges, and build in the flexibility to support this.
- **Model to analyze and reduce risk.** Use design tools, modeling systems such as Unified Modeling Language (UML), and visualizations where appropriate to help you capture requirements and architectural and design decisions, and to analyze their impact. However, do not formalize the model to the extent that it suppresses the capability to iterate and adapt the design easily.
- **Use models and visualizations as a communication and collaboration tool.** Efficient communication of the design, the decisions you make, and ongoing changes to the design, is critical to good architecture. Use models, views, and other visualizations of the architecture to communicate and share your design efficiently with all the stakeholders, and to enable rapid communication of changes to the design.

- **Identify key engineering decisions.** Use the information in this guide to understand the key engineering decisions and the areas where mistakes are most often made. Invest in getting these key decisions right the first time so that the design is more flexible and less likely to be broken by changes.

Consider using an incremental and iterative approach to refining your architecture. Start with a baseline architecture to get the big picture right, and then evolve candidate architectures as you iteratively test and improve your architecture. Do not try to get it all right the first time—design just as much as you can in order to start testing the design against requirements and assumptions. Iteratively add details to the design over multiple passes to make sure that you get the big decisions right first, and then focus on the details. A common pitfall is to dive into the details too quickly and get the big decisions wrong by making incorrect assumptions, or by failing to evaluate your architecture effectively. When testing your architecture, consider the following questions:

- What assumptions have I made in this architecture?
- What explicit or implied requirements is this architecture meeting?
- What are the key risks with this architectural approach?
- What countermeasures are in place to mitigate key risks?
- In what ways is this architecture an improvement over the baseline or the last candidate architecture?

For more information about the key principles of software architecture design, see Chapter 2, "Key Principles of Software Architecture."

For information about the incremental and iterative approach to architecture, baseline and candidate architectures, and representing and communicating the design, see Chapter 4, "A Technique for Architecture and Design."

Additional Resources

Bass, Len, Paul Clements, and Rick Kazman. *Software Architecture in Practice, 2nd ed.* Addison-Wesley Professional, 2003.

Fowler, Martin. *Patterns of Enterprise Application Architecture*. Addison-Wesley, 2002.

2

Key Principles of Software Architecture

Overview

In this chapter, you will learn about the key design principles and guidelines for software architecture. Software architecture is often described as the organization or structure of a system, where the system represents a collection of components that accomplish a specific function or set of functions. In other words, architecture is focused on organizing components to support specific functionality. This organization of functionality is often referred to as grouping components into "areas of concern." Figure 1 illustrates common application architecture with components grouped by different areas of concern.

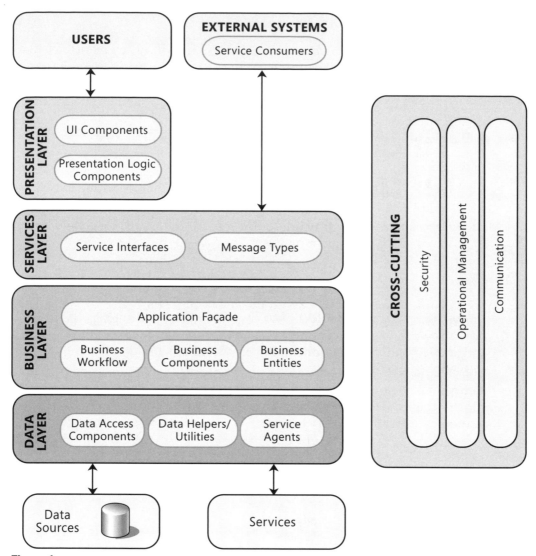

Figure 1
Common application architecture

In addition to the grouping of components, other areas of concern focus on interaction between the components and how different components work together. The guidelines in this chapter examine different areas of concern that you should consider when designing the architecture of your application.

Key Design Principles

When getting started with your design, keep in mind the key principles that will help you to create an architecture that adheres to proven principles, minimizes costs and maintenance requirements, and promotes usability and extendibility. The key principles are:

- **Separation of concerns.** Divide your application into distinct features with as little overlap in functionality as possible. The important factor is minimization of interaction points to achieve high cohesion and low coupling. However, separating functionality at the wrong boundaries can result in high coupling and complexity between features even though the contained functionality within a feature does not significantly overlap.

- **Single Responsibility principle.** Each component or module should be responsible for only a specific feature or functionality, or aggregation of cohesive functionality.

- **Principle of Least Knowledge** (also known as the Law of Demeter or LoD). A component or object should not know about internal details of other components or objects.

- **Don't repeat yourself (DRY).** You should only need to specify intent in one place. For example, in terms of application design, specific functionality should be implemented in only one component; the functionality should not be duplicated in any other component.

- **Minimize upfront design.** Only design what is necessary. In some cases, you may require upfront comprehensive design and testing if the cost of development or a failure in the design is very high. In other cases, especially for agile development, you can avoid big design upfront (BDUF). If your application requirements are unclear, or if there is a possibility of the design evolving over time, avoid making a large design effort prematurely. This principle is sometimes known as YAGNI ("You ain't gonna need it").

When designing an application or system, the goal of a software architect is to minimize the complexity by separating the design into different areas of concern. For example, the user interface (UI), business processing, and data access all represent different areas of concern. Within each area, the components you design should focus on that specific area and should not mix code from other areas of concern. For example, UI processing components should not include code that directly accesses a data source, but instead should use either business components or data access components to retrieve data.

However, you must also make a cost/value determination on the investment you make for an application. In some cases, you may need to simplify the structure to allow, for example, UI data binding to a result set. In general, try to consider the functional boundaries from a business viewpoint as well. The following high level guidelines will help you to consider the wide range of factors that can affect the ease of designing, implementing, deploying, testing, and maintaining your application.

Design Practices

- **Keep design patterns consistent within each layer.** Within a logical layer, where possible, the design of components should be consistent for a particular operation. For example, if you choose to use the Table Data Gateway pattern to create an object that acts as a gateway to tables or views in a database, you should not include another pattern such as Repository, which uses a different paradigm for accessing data and initializing business entities. However, you may need to use different patterns for tasks in a layer that have a large variation in requirements, such as an application that contains business transaction and reporting functionality.

- **Do not duplicate functionality within an application.** There should be only one component providing a specific functionality—this functionality should not be duplicated in any other component. This makes your components cohesive and makes it easier to optimize the components if a specific feature or functionality changes. Duplication of functionality within an application can make it difficult to implement changes, decrease clarity, and introduce potential inconsistencies.

- **Prefer composition to inheritance.** Wherever possible, use composition over inheritance when reusing functionality because inheritance increases the dependency between parent and child classes, thereby limiting the reuse of child classes. This also reduces the inheritance hierarchies, which can become very difficult to deal with.

- **Establish a coding style and naming convention for development.** Check to see if the organization has established coding style and naming standards. If not, you should establish common standards. This provides a consistent model that makes it easier for team members to review code they did not write, which leads to better maintainability.

- **Maintain system quality using automated QA techniques during development.** Use unit testing and other automated Quality Analysis techniques, such as dependency analysis and static code analysis, during development. Define clear behavioral and performance metrics for components and sub-systems, and use automated QA tools during the build process to ensure that local design or implementation decisions do not adversely affect the overall system quality.

- **Consider the operation of your application.** Determine what metrics and operational data are required by the IT infrastructure to ensure the efficient deployment and operation of your application. Designing your application's components and sub-systems with a clear understanding of their individual operational requirements will significantly ease overall deployment and operation. Use automated QA tools during development to ensure that the correct operational data is provided by your application's components and sub-systems.

Application Layers

- **Separate the areas of concern.** Break your application into distinct features that overlap in functionality as little as possible. The main benefit of this approach is that a feature or functionality can be optimized independently of other features or functionality. In addition, if one feature fails, it will not cause other features to fail as well, and they can run independently of one another. This approach also helps to make the application easier to understand and design, and facilitates management of complex interdependent systems.

- **Be explicit about how layers communicate with each other.** Allowing every layer in an application to communicate with or have dependencies upon all of the other layers will result in a solution that is more challenging to understand and manage. Make explicit decisions about the dependencies between layers and the data flow between them.

- **Use abstraction to implement loose coupling between layers.** This can be accomplished by defining interface components such as a façade with well known inputs and outputs that translate requests into a format understood by components within the layer. In addition, you can also use Interface types or abstract base classes to define a common interface or shared abstraction (dependency inversion) that must be implemented by interface components.

- **Do not mix different types of components in the same logical layer.** Start by identifying different areas of concern, and then group components associated with each area of concern into logical layers. For example, the UI layer should not contain business processing components, but instead should contain components used to handle user input and process user requests.

- **Keep the data format consistent within a layer or component.** Mixing data formats will make the application more difficult to implement, extend, and maintain. Every time you need to convert data from one format to another, you are required to implement translation code to perform the operation and incur a processing overhead.

Components, Modules, and Functions

- **A component or an object should not rely on internal details of other components or objects.** Each component or object should call a method of another object or component, and that method should have information about how to process the request and, if appropriate, how to route it to appropriate subcomponents or other components. This helps to create an application that is more maintainable and adaptable.

- **Do not overload the functionality of a component.** For example, a UI processing component should not contain data access code or attempt to provide additional functionality. Overloaded components often have many functions and properties providing business functionality mixed with crosscutting functionality such as logging and exception handling. The result is a design that is very error prone and difficult to maintain. Applying the single responsibility and separation of concerns principles will help you to avoid this.

- **Understand how components will communicate with each other.** This requires an understanding of the deployment scenarios your application must support. You must determine if all components will run within the same process, or if communication across physical or process boundaries must be supported— perhaps by implementing message-based interfaces.

- **Keep crosscutting code abstracted from the application business logic as far as possible.** Crosscutting code refers to code related to security, communications, or operational management such as logging and instrumentation. Mixing the code that implements these functions with the business logic can lead to a design that is difficult to extend and maintain. Changes to the crosscutting code require touching all of the business logic code that is mixed with the crosscutting code. Consider using frameworks and techniques (such as aspect oriented programming) that can help to manage crosscutting concerns.

- **Define a clear contract for components.** Components, modules, and functions should define a contract or interface specification that describes their usage and behavior clearly. The contract should describe how other components can access the internal functionality of the component, module, or function; and the behavior of that functionality in terms of pre-conditions, post-conditions, side effects, exceptions, performance characteristics, and other factors.

Key Design Considerations

This guide describes the major decisions that you must make, and which help to ensure that you consider all of the important factors as you begin and then iteratively develop your architecture design. The major decisions, briefly described in the following sections, are:

- Determine the Application Type
- Determine the Deployment Strategy
- Determine the Appropriate Technologies
- Determine the Quality Attributes
- Determine the Crosscutting Concerns

For a more detailed description of the design process, see Chapter 4, "A Technique for Architecture and Design."

Determine the Application Type

Choosing the appropriate application type is the key part of the process of designing an application. Your choice is governed by your specific requirements and infrastructure limitations. Many applications must support multiple types of client, and may make use of more than one of the basic archetypes. This guide covers the following basic application types:

- Applications designed for mobile devices.
- Rich client applications designed to run primarily on a client PC.
- Rich Internet applications designed to be deployed from the Internet, which support rich UI and media scenarios.
- Service applications designed to support communication between loosely coupled components.
- Web applications designed to run primarily on the server in fully connected scenarios.

In addition, it provides information and guidelines for some more specialist application types. These include the following:

- Hosted and cloud-based applications and services.
- Office Business Applications (OBAs) that integrate Microsoft Office and Microsoft server technologies.
- SharePoint Line of Business (LOB) applications that provide portal style access to business information and functions.

For more information about application archetypes, see Chapter 20, "Choosing an Application Type."

Determine the Deployment Strategy

Your application may be deployed in a variety of environments, each with its own specific set of constraints such as physical separation of components across different servers, a limitation on networking protocols, firewall and router configurations, and more. Several common deployment patterns exist, which describe the benefits and considerations for a range of distributed and non-distributed scenarios. You must balance the requirements of the application with the appropriate patterns that the hardware can support, and the constraints that the environment exerts on your deployment options. These factors will influence your architecture design.

For more information about deployment issues, see Chapter 19, "Physical Tiers and Deployment."

Determine the Appropriate Technologies

When choosing technologies for your application, the key factors to consider are the type of application you are developing and your preferred options for application deployment topology and architectural styles. Your choice of technologies will also be governed by organization policies, infrastructure limitations, resource skills, and so on. You must compare the capabilities of the technologies you choose against your application requirements, taking into account all of these factors before making decisions.

For more information about technologies available on the Microsoft platform, see Appendix A, "The Microsoft Application Platform."

Determine the Quality Attributes

Quality attributes—such as security, performance, and usability—can be used to focus your thinking on the critical problems that your design should solve. Depending on your requirements, you might need to consider every quality attribute covered in this guide, or you might only need to consider a subset. For example, every application design must consider security and performance, but not every design needs to consider interoperability or scalability. Understand your requirements and deployment scenarios first so that you know which quality attributes are important for your design. Keep in mind that quality attributes may conflict; for example, security often requires a tradeoff against performance or usability.

When designing to accommodate quality attributes, consider the following guidelines:

- Quality attributes are system properties that are separate from the functionality of the system.
- From a technical perspective, implementing quality attributes can differentiate a good system from a bad one.
- There are two types of quality attributes: those that are measured at run time, and those that can only be estimated through inspection.
- Analyze the tradeoffs between quality attributes.

Questions you should ask when considering quality attributes include:

- What are the key quality attributes required for your application? Identify them as part of the design process.
- What are the key requirements for addressing these attributes? Are they actually quantifiable?
- What are the acceptance criteria that will indicate that you have met the requirements?

For more information about quality attributes, see Chapter 16, "Quality Attributes."

Determine the Crosscutting Concerns

Crosscutting concerns represent key areas of your design that are not related to a specific layer in your application. For example, you should consider implementing centralized or common solutions for the following:

- A logging mechanism that allows each layer to log to a common store, or log to separate stores in such a way that the results can be correlated afterwards.
- A mechanism for authentication and authorization that passes identities across multiple layers to permit granting access to resources.
- An exception management framework that will work within each layer, and across the layers as exceptions are propagated to the system boundaries.
- A communication approach that you can use to communicate between the layers.
- A common caching infrastructure that allows you to cache data in the presentation layer, the business layer, and the data access layer.

The following list describes some of the key crosscutting concerns that you must consider when architecting your applications:

- **Instrumentation and logging.** Instrument all of the business-critical and system-critical events, and log sufficient details to recreate events in your system without including sensitive information.
- **Authentication.** Determine how to authenticate your users and pass authenticated identities across the layers.
- **Authorization.** Ensure proper authorization with appropriate granularity within each layer, and across trust boundaries.
- **Exception management.** Catch exceptions at functional, logical, and physical boundaries; and avoid revealing sensitive information to end users.
- **Communication.** Choose appropriate protocols, minimize calls across the network, and protect sensitive data passing over the network.
- **Caching.** Identify what should be cached, and where to cache, to improve your application's performance and responsiveness. Ensure that you consider Web farm and application farm issues when designing caching.

For more information about crosscutting concerns, see Chapter 17, "Crosscutting Concerns."

3

Architectural Patterns and Styles

Overview

This chapter describes and discusses high level patterns and principles commonly used for applications today. These are often referred to as the architectural styles, and include patterns such as client/server, layered architecture, component-based architecture, message bus architecture, and service-oriented architecture (SOA). For each style, you will find an overview, key principles, major benefits, and information that will help you choose the appropriate architectural styles for your application. It is important to understand that the styles describe different aspects of applications. For example, some architectural styles describe deployment patterns, some describe structure and design issues, and others describe communication factors. Therefore, a typical application will usually use a combination of more than one of the styles described in this chapter.

What Is an Architectural Style?

An architectural style, sometimes called an architectural pattern, is a set of principles—a coarse grained pattern that provides an abstract framework for a family of systems. An architectural style improves partitioning and promotes design reuse by providing solutions to frequently recurring problems. You can think of architecture styles and patterns as sets of principles that shape an application. Garlan and Shaw define an architectural style as:

> "…a family of systems in terms of a pattern of structural organization. More specifically, an architectural style determines the vocabulary of components and connectors that can be used in instances of that style, together with a set of constraints on how they can be combined. These can include topological constraints on architectural descriptions (e.g., no cycles). Other constraints—say, having to do with execution semantics—might also be part of the style definition."

> [David Garlan and Mary Shaw, January 1994, CMU-CS-94-166, see *"An Introduction to Software Architecture"* at http://www.cs.cmu.edu/afs/cs/project/able/ftp/intro_softarch/intro_softarch.pdf]

An understanding of architectural styles provides several benefits. The most important benefit is that they provide a common language. They also provide opportunities for conversations that are technology agnostic. This facilitates a higher level of conversation that is inclusive of patterns and principles, without getting into specifics. For example, by using architecture styles, you can talk about client/server versus *n*-tier. Architectural styles can be organized by their key focus area. The following table lists the major areas of focus and the corresponding architectural styles.

Category	Architecture styles
Communication	Service-Oriented Architecture (SOA), Message Bus
Deployment	Client/Server, N-Tier, 3-Tier
Domain	Domain Driven Design
Structure	Component-Based, Object-Oriented, Layered Architecture

Summary of Key Architectural Styles

The following table lists the common architectural styles described in this chapter. It also contains a brief description of each style. Later sections of this chapter contain more details of each style, as well as guidance to help you choose the appropriate ones for your application.

Architecture style	Description
Client/Server	Segregates the system into two applications, where the client makes requests to the server. In many cases, the server is a database with application logic represented as stored procedures.
Component-Based Architecture	Decomposes application design into reusable functional or logical components that expose well-defined communication interfaces.
Domain Driven Design	An object-oriented architectural style focused on modeling a business domain and defining business objects based on entities within the business domain.
Layered Architecture	Partitions the concerns of the application into stacked groups (layers).
Message Bus	An architecture style that prescribes use of a software system that can receive and send messages using one or more communication channels, so that applications can interact without needing to know specific details about each other.
N-Tier / 3-Tier	Segregates functionality into separate segments in much the same way as the layered style, but with each segment being a tier located on a physically separate computer.
Object-Oriented	A design paradigm based on division of responsibilities for an application or system into individual reusable and self-sufficient objects, each containing the data and the behavior relevant to the object.
Service-Oriented Architecture (SOA)	Refers to applications that expose and consume functionality as a service using contracts and messages.

Combining Architectural Styles

The architecture of a software system is almost never limited to a single architectural style, but is often a combination of architectural styles that make up the complete system. For example, you might have a SOA design composed of services developed using a layered architecture approach and an object-oriented architecture style.

A combination of architecture styles is also useful if you are building a public facing Web application, where you can achieve effective separation of concerns by using the layered architecture style. This will separate your presentation logic from your business logic and your data access logic. Your organization's security requirements might force you to deploy the application using either the 3-tier deployment approach, or a deployment of more than three tiers. The presentation tier may be deployed to the perimeter network, which sits between an organization's internal network and an external network. On your presentation tier, you may decide to use a separated presentation pattern (a type of layered design style), such as Model-View-Controller (MVC), for your interaction model. You might also choose a SOA architecture style, and implement message-based communication, between your Web server and application server.

If you are building a desktop application, you may have a client that sends requests to a program on the server. In this case, you might deploy the client and server using the client/server architecture style, and use the component-based architecture style to decompose the design further into independent components that expose the appropriate communication interfaces. Using the object-oriented design approach for these components will improve reuse, testability, and flexibility.

Many factors will influence the architectural styles you choose. These factors include the capacity of your organization for design and implementation; the capabilities and experience of your developers; and your infrastructure and organizational constraints. The following sections will help you to determine the appropriate styles for your applications.

Client/Server Architectural Style

The client/server architectural style describes distributed systems that involve a separate client and server system, and a connecting network. The simplest form of client/server system involves a server application that is accessed directly by multiple clients, referred to as a 2-Tier architectural style.

Historically, client/server architecture indicated a graphical desktop UI application that communicated with a database server containing much of the business logic in the form of stored procedures, or with a dedicated file server. More generally, however, the client/server architectural style describes the relationship between a client and one or more servers, where the client initiates one or more requests (perhaps using a graphical UI), waits for replies, and processes the replies on receipt. The server typically authorizes the user and then carries out the processing required to generate the result. The server may send responses using a range of protocols and data formats to communicate information to the client.

Today, some examples of the client/server architectural style include Web browser–based programs running on the Internet or an intranet; Microsoft Windows® operating system–based applications that access networked data services; applications that access remote data stores (such as e-mail readers, FTP clients, and database query tools); and tools and utilities that manipulate remote systems (such as system management tools and network monitoring tools).

Other variations on the client/server style include:

- **Client-Queue-Client systems.** This approach allows clients to communicate with other clients through a server-based queue. Clients can read data from and send data to a server that acts simply as a queue to store the data. This allows clients to distribute and synchronize files and information. This is sometimes known as a passive queue architecture.

- **Peer-to-Peer (P2P) applications.** Developed from the Client-Queue-Client style, the P2P style allows the client and server to swap their roles in order to distribute and synchronize files and information across multiple clients. It extends the client/server style through multiple responses to requests, shared data, resource discovery, and resilience to removal of peers.

- **Application servers.** A specialized architectural style where the server hosts and executes applications and services that a thin client accesses through a browser or specialized client installed software. An example is a client executing an application that runs on the server through a framework such as Terminal Services.

The main benefits of the client/server architectural style are:

- **Higher security.** All data is stored on the server, which generally offers a greater control of security than client machines.

- **Centralized data access.** Because data is stored only on the server, access and updates to the data are far easier to administer than in other architectural styles.

- **Ease of maintenance.** Roles and responsibilities of a computing system are distributed among several servers that are known to each other through a network. This ensures that a client remains unaware and unaffected by a server repair, upgrade, or relocation.

Consider the client/server architectural style if your application is server based and will support many clients, you are creating Web-based applications exposed through a Web browser, you are implementing business processes that will be used by people throughout the organization, or you are creating services for other applications to consume. The client/server architectural style is also suitable, like many networked styles, when you want to centralize data storage, backup, and management functions, or when your application must support different client types and different devices.

However, the traditional 2-Tier client/server architectural style has numerous disadvantages, including the tendency for application data and business logic to be closely combined on the server, which can negatively impact system extensibility and scalability, and its dependence on a central server, which can negatively impact system reliability. To address these issues, the client-server architectural style has evolved into the more general 3-Tier (or N-Tier) architectural style, described below, which overcomes some of the disadvantages inherent in the 2-Tier client-server architecture and provides additional benefits.

Component-Based Architectural Style

Component-based architecture describes a software engineering approach to system design and development. It focuses on the decomposition of the design into individual functional or logical components that expose well-defined communication interfaces containing methods, events, and properties. This provides a higher level of abstraction than object-oriented design principles, and does not focus on issues such as communication protocols and shared state.

The key principle of the component-based style is the use of components that are:

- **Reusable.** Components are usually designed to be reused in different scenarios in different applications. However, some components may be designed for a specific task.

- **Replaceable.** Components may be readily substituted with other similar components.

- **Not context specific.** Components are designed to operate in different environments and contexts. Specific information, such as state data, should be passed to the component instead of being included in or accessed by the component.

- **Extensible.** A component can be extended from existing components to provide new behavior.

- **Encapsulated.** Components expose interfaces that allow the caller to use its functionality, and do not reveal details of the internal processes or any internal variables or state.

- **Independent.** Components are designed to have minimal dependencies on other components. Therefore components can be deployed into any appropriate environment without affecting other components or systems.

Common types of components used in applications include user interface components such as grids and buttons (often referred to as *controls*), and helper and utility components that expose a specific subset of functions used in other components. Other common types of components are those that are resource intensive, not frequently accessed, and must be activated using the just-in-time (JIT) approach (common in remoting or distributed component scenarios); and queued components whose method calls may be executed asynchronously using message queuing and store and forward.

Components depend upon a mechanism within the platform that provides an environment in which they can execute, often referred to as *component architecture*. Examples are the component object model (COM) and the distributed component object model (DCOM) in Windows; and Common Object Request Broker Architecture (CORBA) and Enterprise JavaBeans (EJB) on other platforms. Component architectures manage the mechanics of locating components and their interfaces, passing messages or commands between components, and—in some cases—maintaining state.

However, the term component is often used in the more basic sense of *a constituent part, element, or ingredient*. The Microsoft .NET Framework provides support for building applications using such a component based approach. For example, this guide discusses business and data components, which are commonly code classes compiled into .NET Framework assemblies. They execute under the control of the .NET Framework runtime, and there may be more than one such component in each assembly.

The following are the main benefits of the component-based architectural style:

- **Ease of deployment.** As new compatible versions become available, you can replace existing versions with no impact on the other components or the system as a whole.
- **Reduced cost.** The use of third-party components allows you to spread the cost of development and maintenance.
- **Ease of development.** Components implement well-known interfaces to provide defined functionality, allowing development without impacting other parts of the system.
- **Reusable.** The use of reusable components means that they can be used to spread the development and maintenance cost across several applications or systems.
- **Mitigation of technical complexity.** Components mitigate complexity through the use of a component container and its services. Example component services include component activation, lifetime management, method queuing, eventing, and transactions.

Design patterns such as the Dependency Injection pattern or the Service Locator pattern can be used to manage dependencies between components, and promote loose coupling and reuse. Such patterns are often used to build composite applications that combine and reuse components across multiple applications.

Consider the component-based architectural style if you already have suitable components or can obtain suitable components from third-party suppliers; your application will predominantly execute procedural-style functions, perhaps with little or no data input; or you want to be able to combine components written in different code languages. Also, consider this style if you want to create a pluggable or composite architecture that allows you to easily replace and update individual components.

Domain Driven Design Architectural Style

Domain Driven Design (DDD) is an object-oriented approach to designing software based on the business domain, its elements and behaviors, and the relationships between them. It aims to enable software systems that are a realization of the underlying business domain by defining a domain model expressed in the language of business domain experts. The domain model can be viewed as a framework from which solutions can then be rationalized.

To apply Domain Driven Design, you must have a good understanding of the business domain you want to model, or be skilled in acquiring such business knowledge. The development team will often work with business domain experts to model the domain. Architects, developers, and subject matter experts have diverse backgrounds, and in many environments will use different languages to describe their goals, designs and requirements. However, within Domain Driven Design, the whole team agrees to only use a single language that is focused on the business domain, and which excludes any technical jargon.

As the core of the software is the domain model, which is a direct projection of this shared language, it allows the team to quickly find gaps in the software by analyzing the language around it. The creation of a common language is not merely an exercise in accepting information from the domain experts and applying it. Quite often, communication problems within development teams are due not only to misunderstanding the language of the domain, but also due to the fact that the domain's language is itself ambiguous. The Domain Driven Design process holds the goal not only of implementing the language being used, but also improving and refining the language of the domain. This in turn benefits the software being built, since the model is a direct projection of the domain language.

In order to help maintain the model as a pure and helpful language construct, you must typically implement a great deal of isolation and encapsulation within the domain model. Consequently, a system based on Domain Driven Design can come at a relatively high cost. While Domain Driven Design provides many technical benefits, such as maintainability, it should be applied only to complex domains where the model and the linguistic processes provide clear benefits in the communication of complex information, and in the formulation of a common understanding of the domain.

The following are the main benefits of the Domain Driven Design style:

- **Communication.** All parties within a development team can use the domain model and the entities it defines to communicate business knowledge and requirements using a common business domain language, without requiring technical jargon.

- **Extensible.** The domain model is often modular and flexible, making it easy to update and extend as conditions and requirements change.

- **Testable.** The domain model objects are loosely coupled and cohesive, allowing them to be more easily tested.

Consider DDD if you have a complex domain and you wish to improve communication and understanding within your development team, or where you must express the design of an application in a common language that all stakeholders can understand. DDD can also be an ideal approach if you have large and complex enterprise data scenarios that are difficult to manage using other techniques.

For a summary of domain driven design techniques, see *"Domain Driven Design Quickly"* at http://www.infoq.com/minibooks/domain-driven-design-quickly. Alternatively, see *"Domain-Driven Design: Tackling Complexity in the Heart of Software"* by Eric Evans (Addison-Wesley, ISBN: 0-321-12521-5) and *"Applying Domain-Driven Design and Patterns"* by Jimmy Nilsson (Addison-Wesley, ISBN: 0-321-26820-2).

Layered Architectural Style

Layered architecture focuses on the grouping of related functionality within an application into distinct layers that are stacked vertically on top of each other. Functionality within each layer is related by a common role or responsibility. Communication between layers is explicit and loosely coupled. Layering your application appropriately helps to support a strong separation of concerns that, in turn, supports flexibility and maintainability.

The layered architectural style has been described as an *inverted pyramid of reuse* where each layer aggregates the responsibilities and abstractions of the layer directly beneath it. With strict layering, components in one layer can interact only with components in the same layer or with components from the layer directly below it. More relaxed layering allows components in a layer to interact with components in the same layer or with components in any lower layer.

The layers of an application may reside on the same physical computer (the same tier) or may be distributed over separate computers (*n*-tier), and the components in each layer communicate with components in other layers through well-defined interfaces. For example, a typical Web application design consists of a presentation layer (functionality related to the UI), a business layer (business rules processing), and a data layer (functionality related to data access, often almost entirely implemented using high-level data access frameworks). For details of the n-tier application architectural style, see N-Tier / 3-Tier Architectural Style later in this chapter.

Common principles for designs that use the layered architectural style include:

- **Abstraction.** Layered architecture abstracts the view of the system as whole while providing enough detail to understand the roles and responsibilities of individual layers and the relationship between them.

- **Encapsulation.** No assumptions need to be made about data types, methods and properties, or implementation during design, as these features are not exposed at layer boundaries.

- **Clearly defined functional layers.** The separation between functionality in each layer is clear. Upper layers such as the presentation layer send commands to lower layers, such as the business and data layers, and may react to events in these layers, allowing data to flow both up and down between the layers.

- **High cohesion.** Well-defined responsibility boundaries for each layer, and ensuring that each layer contains functionality directly related to the tasks of that layer, will help to maximize cohesion within the layer.

- **Reusable.** Lower layers have no dependencies on higher layers, potentially allowing them to be reusable in other scenarios.

- **Loose coupling.** Communication between layers is based on abstraction and events to provide loose coupling between layers.

Examples of layered applications include line-of-business (LOB) applications such as accounting and customer-management systems; enterprise Web-based applications and Web sites, and enterprise desktop or smart clients with centralized application servers for business logic.

A number of design patterns support the layered architectural style. For example, **Separated Presentation** patterns encompass a range of patterns that the handling of the user's interactions from the UI, the presentation and business logic, and the application data with which the user works. Separated Presentation allows graphical designers to create a UI while developers generate the code to drive it. Dividing the functionality into separate roles in this way provides increased opportunities to test the behavior of individual roles. The following are the key principles of the Separated Presentation patterns:

- **Separation of concerns.** Separated Presentation patterns divide UI processing concerns into distinct roles; for example, MVC has three roles: the Model, the View, and the Controller. The Model represents data (perhaps a domain model that includes business rules); the View represents the UI; and the Controller handles requests, manipulates the model, and performs other operations.

- **Event-based notification.** The Observer pattern is commonly used to provide notifications to the View when data managed by the Model changes.

- **Delegated event handling.** The controller handles events triggered from the UI controls in the View.

Other examples of Separated Presentation patterns are the Passive View pattern and the Supervising Presenter (or Supervising Controller) pattern.

The main benefits of the layered architectural style, and the use of a Separated Presentation pattern, are:

- **Abstraction.** Layers allow changes to be made at the abstract level. You can increase or decrease the level of abstraction you use in each layer of the hierarchical stack.

- **Isolation.** Allows you to isolate technology upgrades to individual layers in order to reduce risk and minimize impact on the overall system.

- **Manageability.** Separation of core concerns helps to identify dependencies, and organizes the code into more manageable sections.

- **Performance.** Distributing the layers over multiple physical tiers can improve scalability, fault tolerance, and performance.

- **Reusability.** Roles promote reusability. For example, in MVC, the Controller can often be reused with other compatible Views in order to provide a role specific or a user-customized view on to the same data and functionality.

- **Testability.** Increased testability arises from having well-defined layer interfaces, as well as the ability to switch between different implementations of the layer interfaces. Separated Presentation patterns allow you to build mock objects that mimic the behavior of concrete objects such as the Model, Controller, or View during testing.

Consider the layered architectural style if you have existing layers that are suitable for reuse in other applications, you already have applications that expose suitable business processes through service interfaces, or your application is complex and the high-level design demands separation so that teams can focus on different areas of functionality. The layered architectural style is also appropriate if your application must support different client types and different devices, or you want to implement complex and/or configurable business rules and processes.

Consider a Separated Presentation pattern if you want improved testability and simplified maintenance of UI functionality, or you want to separate the task of designing the UI from the development of the logic code that drives it. These patterns are also appropriate when your UI view does not contain any request processing code, and does not implement any business logic.

Message Bus Architectural Style

Message bus architecture describes the principle of using a software system that can receive and send messages using one or more communication channels, so that applications can interact without needing to know specific details about each other. It is a style for designing applications where interaction between applications is accomplished by passing messages (usually asynchronously) over a common bus. The most common implementations of message bus architecture use either a messaging router or a Publish/Subscribe pattern, and are often implemented using a messaging system such as Message Queuing. Many implementations consist of individual applications that communicate using common schemas and a shared infrastructure for sending and receiving messages. A message bus provides the ability to handle:

- **Message-oriented communications.** All communication between applications is based on messages that use known schemas.

- **Complex processing logic.** Complex operations can be executed by combining a set of smaller operations, each of which supports specific tasks, as part of a multi-step itinerary.

- **Modifications to processing logic.** Because interaction with the bus is based on common schemas and commands, you can insert or remove applications on the bus to change the logic that is used to process messages.

- **Integration with different environments.** By using a message-based communication model based on common standards, you can interact with applications developed for different environments, such as Microsoft .NET and Java.

Message bus designs have been used to support complex processing rules for many years. The design provides a pluggable architecture that allows you to insert applications into the process, or improve scalability by attaching several instances of the same application to the bus. Variations on the message bus style include:

- **Enterprise Service Bus (ESB).** Based on message bus designs, an ESB uses services for communication between the bus and components attached to the bus. An ESB will usually provide services that transform messages from one format to another, allowing clients that use incompatible message formats to communicate with each other.

- **Internet Service Bus (ISB).** This is similar to an enterprise service bus, but with applications hosted in the cloud instead of on an enterprise network. A core concept of ISB is the use of Uniform Resource Identifiers (URIs) and policies to control the routing of logic through applications and services in the cloud.

The main benefits of the message-bus architectural style are:

- **Extensibility.** Applications can be added to or removed from the bus without having an impact on the existing applications.
- **Low complexity.** Application complexity is reduced because each application only needs to know how to communicate with the bus.
- **Flexibility.** The set of applications that make up a complex process, or the communication patterns between applications, can be changed easily to match changes in business or user requirements, simply through changes to the configuration or parameters that control routing.
- **Loose coupling.** As long as applications expose a suitable interface for communication with the message bus, there is no dependency on the application itself, allowing changes, updates, and replacements that expose the same interface.
- **Scalability.** Multiple instances of the same application can be attached to the bus in order to handle multiple requests at the same time.
- **Application simplicity.** Although a message bus implementation adds complexity to the infrastructure, each application needs to support only a single connection to the message bus instead of multiple connections to other applications.

Consider the message bus architectural style if you have existing applications that interoperate with each other to perform tasks, or you want to combine multiple tasks into a single operation. This style is also appropriate if you are implementing a task that requires interaction with external applications, or applications hosted in different environments.

N-Tier / 3-Tier Architectural Style

N-tier and 3-tier are architectural deployment styles that describe the separation of functionality into segments in much the same way as the layered style, but with each segment being a tier that can be located on a physically separate computer. They evolved through the component-oriented approach, generally using platform specific methods for communication instead of a message-based approach.

N-tier application architecture is characterized by the functional decomposition of applications, service components, and their distributed deployment, providing improved scalability, availability, manageability, and resource utilization. Each tier is completely independent from all other tiers, except for those immediately above and below it. The nth tier only has to know how to handle a request from the n+1th tier, how to forward that request on to the n-1th tier (if there is one), and how to handle the results of the request. Communication between tiers is typically asynchronous in order to support better scalability.

N-tier architectures usually have at least three separate logical parts, each located on a separate physical server. Each part is responsible for specific functionality. When using a layered design approach, a layer is deployed on a tier if more than one service or application is dependent on the functionality exposed by the layer.

An example of the N-tier/3-tier architectural style is a typical financial Web application where security is important. The business layer must be deployed behind a firewall, which forces the deployment of the presentation layer on a separate tier in the perimeter network. Another example is a typical rich client connected application, where the presentation layer is deployed on client machines and the business layer and data access layer are deployed on one or more server tiers.

The main benefits of the N-tier/3-tier architectural style are:

- **Maintainability.** Because each tier is independent of the other tiers, updates or changes can be carried out without affecting the application as a whole.
- **Scalability.** Because tiers are based on the deployment of layers, scaling out an application is reasonably straightforward.
- **Flexibility.** Because each tier can be managed or scaled independently, flexibility is increased.
- **Availability.** Applications can exploit the modular architecture of enabling systems using easily scalable components, which increases availability.

Consider either the N-tier or the 3-tier architectural style if the processing requirements of the layers in the application differ such that processing in one layer could absorb sufficient resources to slow the processing in other layers, or if the security requirements of the layers in the application differ. For example, the presentation layer should not store sensitive data, while this may be stored in the business and data layers. The N-tier or the 3-tier architectural style is also appropriate if you want to be able to share business logic between applications, and you have sufficient hardware to allocate the required number of servers to each tier.

Consider using just three tiers if you are developing an intranet application where all servers are located within the private network; or an Internet application where security requirements do not restrict the deployment of business logic on the public facing Web or application server. Consider using more than three tiers if security requirements dictate that business logic cannot be deployed to the perimeter network, or the application makes heavy use of resources and you want to offload that functionality to another server.

Object-Oriented Architectural Style

Object-oriented architecture is a design paradigm based on the division of responsibilities for an application or system into individual reusable and self-sufficient objects, each containing the data and the behavior relevant to the object. An object-oriented design views a system as a series of cooperating objects, instead of a set of routines or procedural instructions. Objects are discrete, independent, and loosely coupled; they communicate through interfaces, by calling methods or accessing properties in other objects, and by sending and receiving messages. The key principles of the object-oriented architectural style are:

- **Abstraction.** This allows you to reduce a complex operation into a generalization that retains the base characteristics of the operation. For example, an abstract interface can be a well-known definition that supports data access operations using simple methods such as Get and Update. Another form of abstraction could be metadata used to provide a mapping between two formats that hold structured data.

- **Composition.** Objects can be assembled from other objects, and can choose to hide these internal objects from other classes or expose them as simple interfaces.

- **Inheritance.** Objects can inherit from other objects, and use functionality in the base object or override it to implement new behavior. Moreover, inheritance makes maintenance and updates easier, as changes to the base object are propagated automatically to the inheriting objects.

- **Encapsulation.** Objects expose functionality only through methods, properties, and events, and hide the internal details such as state and variables from other objects. This makes it easier to update or replace objects, as long as their interfaces are compatible, without affecting other objects and code.

- **Polymorphism.** This allows you to override the behavior of a base type that supports operations in your application by implementing new types that are interchangeable with the existing object.

- **Decoupling.** Objects can be decoupled from the consumer by defining an abstract interface that the object implements and the consumer can understand. This allows you to provide alternative implementations without affecting consumers of the interface.

Common uses of the object-oriented style include defining an object model that supports complex scientific or financial operations, and defining objects that represent real world artifacts within a business domain (such as a customer or an order). The latter is a process commonly implemented using the more specialized domain driven design style, which takes advantage of the principles of the object-oriented style. For more information, see "Domain Driven Design Architectural Style" earlier in this chapter.

The main benefits of the object-oriented architectural style are that it is:

- **Understandable.** It maps the application more closely to the real world objects, making it more understandable.

- **Reusable.** It provides for reusability through polymorphism and abstraction.

- **Testable.** It provides for improved testability through encapsulation.

- **Extensible.** Encapsulation, polymorphism, and abstraction ensure that a change in the representation of data does not affect the interfaces that the object exposes, which would limit the capability to communicate and interact with other objects.

- **Highly Cohesive.** By locating only related methods and features in an object, and using different objects for different sets of features, you can achieve a high level of cohesion.

Consider the object-oriented architectural style if you want to model your application based on real world objects and actions, or you already have suitable objects and classes that match the design and operational requirements. The object-oriented style is also suitable if you must encapsulate logic and data together in reusable components or you have complex business logic that requires abstraction and dynamic behavior.

Service-Oriented Architectural Style

Service-oriented architecture (SOA) enables application functionality to be provided as a set of services, and the creation of applications that make use of software services. Services are loosely coupled because they use standards-based interfaces that can be invoked, published, and discovered. Services in SOA are focused on providing a schema and message-based interaction with an application through interfaces that are application scoped, and not component or object-based. An SOA service should not be treated as a component-based service provider.

The SOA style can package business processes into interoperable services, using a range of protocols and data formats to communicate information. Clients and other services can access local services running on the same tier, or access remote services over a connecting network.

The key principles of the SOA architectural style are:

- **Services are autonomous.** Each service is maintained, developed, deployed, and versioned independently.

- **Services are distributable.** Services can be located anywhere on a network, locally or remotely, as long as the network supports the required communication protocols.

- **Services are loosely coupled.** Each service is independent of others, and can be replaced or updated without breaking applications that use it as long as the interface is still compatible.

- **Services share schema and contract, not class.** Services share contracts and schemas when they communicate, not internal classes.
- **Compatibility is based on policy.** Policy in this case means definition of features such as transport, protocol, and security.

Common examples of service-oriented applications include sharing information, handling multistep processes such as reservation systems and online stores, exposing industry specific data or services over an extranet, and creating mashups that combine information from multiple sources.

The main benefits of the SOA architectural style are:

- **Domain alignment.** Reuse of common services with standard interfaces increases business and technology opportunities and reduces cost.
- **Abstraction.** Services are autonomous and accessed through a formal contract, which provides loose coupling and abstraction.
- **Discoverability.** Services can expose descriptions that allow other applications and services to locate them and automatically determine the interface.
- **Interoperability.** Because the protocols and data formats are based on industry standards, the provider and consumer of the service can be built and deployed on different platforms.
- **Rationalization.** Services can be granular in order to provide specific functionality, rather than duplicating the functionality in number of applications, which removes duplication.

Consider the SOA style if you have access to suitable services that you wish to reuse; can purchase suitable services provided by a hosting company; want to build applications that compose a variety of services into a single UI; or you are creating Software plus Services (S+S), Software as a Service (SaaS), or cloud-based applications. The SOA style is suitable when you must support message-based communication between segments of the application and expose functionality in a platform independent way, when you want to take advantage of federated services such as authentication, or you want to expose services that are discoverable through directories and can be used by clients that have no prior knowledge of the interfaces.

Additional Resources

To more easily access Web resources, see the online version of the bibliography at: http://www.microsoft.com/architectureguide.

Evans, Eric. *Domain-Driven Design: Tackling Complexity in the Heart of Software.* Addison-Wesley, 2004.

Nilsson, Jimmy. *Applying Domain-Driven Design and Patterns: With Examples in C# and NET.* Addison-Wesley, 2006.

For more information about architectural styles, see the following resources:

- *"An Introduction To Domain-Driven Design"* at http://msdn.microsoft.com/en-us/magazine/dd419654.aspx.
- *"Domain Driven Design and Development in Practice"* at http://www.infoq.com/articles/ddd-in-practice.
- *"Fear Those Tiers"* at http://msdn.microsoft.com/en-us/library/cc168629.aspx.
- *"Layered Versus Client-Server"* at http://msdn.microsoft.com/en-us/library/bb421529.aspx.
- *"Message Bus"* at http://msdn.microsoft.com/en-us/library/ms978583.aspx.
- *"Microsoft Enterprise Service Bus (ESB) Guidance"* at http://www.microsoft.com/biztalk/solutions/soa/esb.mspx.
- *"Separated Presentation"* at http://martinfowler.com/eaaDev/SeparatedPresentation.html.
- *"Services Fabric: Fine Fabrics for New-Era Systems"* at http://msdn.microsoft.com/en-us/library/cc168621.aspx.

Design Fundamentals

This section of the guide contains a series of topics that will help you to understand the fundamentals of layered architecture, and provide practical guidance for some of the typical layers used by most applications, such as presentation, business, data, and service layers. This section contains the following chapters:

- Chapter 5, "Layered Application Guidelines"
- Chapter 6, "Presentation Layer Guidelines"
- Chapter 7, "Business Layer Guidelines"
- Chapter 8, "Data Layer Guidelines"
- Chapter 9, "Service Layer Guidelines"

Typically, each layer will contain of number of components. As you design the components in each layer, you must consider a range of factors that will affect the overall success of your design. This section of the guide contains guidance to help you design your components to avoid the commonly found issues, and to follow best practice. For more details, see the following chapters:

- Chapter 10, "Component Guidelines"
- Chapter 11, "Designing Presentation Components"
- Chapter 12, "Designing Business Components"
- Chapter 13, "Designing Business Entities"
- Chapter 14, "Designing Workflow Components"
- Chapter 15, "Designing Data Components"

The overall quality and the subsequent success and of your application design depends on how well it addresses a range of quality attributes such as security, reusability, performance, and maintainability. In addition, your application is likely to contain crosscutting functionality such as exception handling, caching, and logging. This section contains guidance on how you should address quality attributes and design for crosscutting concerns in your applications. See the following chapters for more information:

- Chapter 16, "Quality Attributes"
- Chapter 17, "Crosscutting Concerns"

When designing an application, particularly a distributed application, designing an appropriate communication infrastructure is a key to the success of the design. This section of the guide will also help you to understand communication requirements and implement designs that provide the appropriate levels of decoupling, security, and performance. For more information, see Chapter 18, "Communication and Messaging."

Finally, you must consider how you will deploy your application, and take into account any constraints implied by the physical infrastructure, networking, and other facilities that will support the application at runtime. The final chapter in this section discusses physical deployment scenarios, and describes some of the issues you will encounter, such as security, when employing a multi-tiered deployment model. For more information, see Chapter 19, "Physical Tiers and Deployment."

4

A Technique for Architecture and Design

Overview

This chapter describes an iterative technique that you can use to think about and sketch out your potential architecture. It will help you to bring together the key decisions discussed in this guide; including quality attributes, architecture styles, application types, technologies, and deployment decisions.

The technique includes a series of five main steps, each of which breaks down into individual considerations explained throughout the remainder of the guide. The iterative process will help you to produce candidate solutions that you can further refine by repeating the steps, finally creating an architecture design that best fits your application. At the end of the process, you can review and communicate your architecture to all interested parties.

Depending on your organization's approach to software development, you may revisit your architecture many times during the lifetime of a project. You can use this technique to refine your architecture further, building on what you have learned in the intervening period of spiking, prototyping, and actual development.

It is also important to realize that this is just one possible approach. There are many other more formal approaches to defining, reviewing, and communicating your architecture. Some are discussed briefly at the end of this chapter.

Inputs, Ouyputs, and Design Steps

The inputs to your design can help you to formalize the requirements and constraints that your architecture must accommodate. Common inputs are use cases and usage scenarios, functional requirements, non-functional requirements (including quality attributes such as performance, security, reliability, and others), technological requirements, the target deployment environment, and other constraints.

During the design process, you will create a list of the architecturally significant use cases, the architecture issues that require special attention, and the candidate architecture solutions that satisfy the requirements and constraints defined in the design process. A common technique for refining the design over time, until it satisfies all of the requirements and adheres to all of the constraints, is an iterative technique consisting of the five major stages shown in Figure 1.

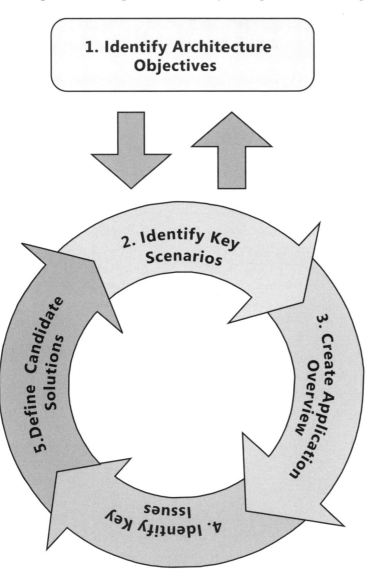

Figure 1
The iterative steps for core architecture design activities

The steps, described in more detail in the following sections, are:

1. **Identify Architecture Objectives.** Clear objectives help you to focus on your architecture and on solving the right problems in your design. Precise objectives help you to determine when you have completed the current phase, and when you are ready to move to the next phase.

2. **Key Scenarios.** Use key scenarios to focus your design on what matters most, and to evaluate your candidate architectures when they are ready.

3. **Application Overview.** Identify your application type, deployment architecture, architecture styles, and technologies in order to connect your design to the real world in which the application will operate.

4. **Key Issues.** Identify key issues based on quality attributes and crosscutting concerns. These are the areas where mistakes are most often made when designing an application.

5. **Candidate Solutions.** Create an architecture spike or prototype that evolves and improves the solution and evaluate it against your key scenarios, issues, and deployment constraints before beginning the next iteration of your architecture.

This architectural process is meant to be an iterative and incremental approach. Your first candidate architecture will be a high-level design that you can test against key scenarios, requirements, known constraints, quality attributes, and the architecture frame. As you refine your candidate architecture, you will learn more details about the design and will be able to further expand key scenarios, your application overview, and your approach to issues.

Note: When taking an iterative approach to architecture, it is often tempting to iterate on horizontal slices (layers) of the application rather than vertical slices that require you to think about functionality across layers that comprise a complete feature (use case) for users. If you fail to iterate vertically, you run the risk of implementing a great deal of functionality before your users can validate it.

You should not try to build your architecture in a single iteration. Each iteration should add more detail. Do not get lost in the details, but instead focus on the major steps and build a framework on which you can base your architecture and design. The following sections provide guidelines and information on each of the steps.

Identify Architecture Objectives

Architecture objectives are the goals and constraints that shape your architecture and design process, scope the exercise, and help you determine when you are finished. Consider the following key points as you identify your architecture objectives:

- **Identify your architecture goals at the start.** The amount of time you spend in each phase of architecture and design will depend on these goals. For example, are you building a prototype, testing potential paths, or embarking on a long-running architectural process for a new application?

- **Identify who will consume your architecture.** Determine if your design will be used by other architects, or made available to developers and testers, operations staff, and management. Consider the needs and experience of your audience to make your resulting design more accessible to them.

- **Identify your constraints.** Understand your technology options and constraints, usage constraints, and deployment constraints. Understand your constraints at the start so that you do not waste time or encounter surprises later in your application development process.

Scope and Time

Based on the high-level goals for your architecture, you can scope the amount of time to spend on each of your design activities. For example, a prototype might only require a few days to design, while a complete and fully detailed architecture for a complex application could potentially take months to complete—and may involve architecture and design over many iterations. Use your understanding of the objectives to determine how much time and energy to spend on each step, to gain an understanding of what the outcome will look like, and to define clearly the purpose and priorities of your architecture. Possible purposes might include:

- Creating a complete application design.
- Building a prototype.
- Identifying key technical risks.
- Testing potential options.
- Building shared models to gain an understanding of the system.

Each of these will result in a different emphasis on design, and a varying time commitment. For example, if you want to identify key risks in your authentication architecture, you will spend much of your time and energy identifying authentication scenarios, constraints on your authentication architecture, and possible authentication technology choices. However, if you are in the early stages of considering the overall architecture for an application, authentication will be only one of many other concerns for which you address and document solutions.

Some examples of architecture activities are building a prototype to get feedback on the order-processing UI for a Web application, testing different ways to map location data to search results, building a customer order-tracking application, and designing the authentication and authorization architecture for an application in order to perform a security review.

Key Scenarios

In the context of architecture and design, a *use case* is a description of a set of interactions between the system and one or more actors (either a user or another system). A *scenario* is a broader and more encompassing description of a user's interaction with the system, rather than a path through a use case. When thinking about the architecture of your system, the goal should be to identify several key scenarios that will help you to make decisions about your architecture. The goal is to achieve a balance between the user, business, and system goals (as shown in Figure 1 of Chapter 1 "What is Software Architecture?").

Key scenarios are those that are considered the most important scenarios for the success of your application. Key scenarios can be defined as any scenario that meets one or more of the following criteria:

- It represents an issue—a significant unknown area or an area of significant risk.
- It refers to an architecturally significant use case (described in the following section).
- It represents the intersection of quality attributes with functionality.
- It represents a tradeoff between quality attributes.

For example, your scenarios covering user authentication may be key scenarios because they are an intersection of a quality attribute (security) with important functionality (how a user logs into your system). Another example would be a scenario that centered on an unfamiliar or new technology.

Architecturally Significant Use Cases

Architecturally significant use cases have an impact on many aspects of your design. These use cases are especially important in shaping the success of your application. They are important for the acceptance of the deployed application, and they must exercise enough of the design to be useful in evaluating the architecture. Architecturally significant use cases are:

- **Business Critical.** The use case has a high usage level or is particularly important to users or other stakeholders when compared to other features, or it implies high risk.
- **High Impact.** The use case intersects with both functionality and quality attributes, or represents a crosscutting concern that has an end-to-end impact across the layer and tiers of your application. An example might be a Create, Read, Update, Delete (CRUD) operation that is security-sensitive.

After you have determined the architecturally significant use cases for your application, you can use them as a way to evaluate the success or failure of candidate architectures. If the candidate architecture addresses more use cases, or addresses existing use cases more effectively, it will help usually indicate that this candidate architecture is an improvement over the baseline architecture. For a definition of the term *use case*, see *"What is a Use Case?"* at http://searchsoftwarequality.techtarget.com/sDefinition/0,,sid92_gci334062,00.html.

A good use case will intersect the user view, the system view, and the business view of the architecture. Use these scenarios and use cases to test your design and determine where any issues may be. Consider the following when thinking about your use cases and scenarios:

- Early in the project, reduce risk by creating a candidate architecture that supports architecturally significant end-to-end scenarios that exercise all layers of the architecture.

- Using your architecture model as a guide, make changes to your architecture, design, and code to meet your scenarios, functional requirements, technological requirements, quality attributes, and constraints.

- Create an architecture model based on what you know at the time, and define a list of questions that must be addressed in subsequent stories and iterations.

- After you make sufficient significant changes to the architecture and design, consider creating a use case that reflects and exercises these changes.

Application Overview

Create an overview of what your application will look like when it is complete. This overview serves to make your architecture more tangible, connecting it to real-world constraints and decisions. An application overview consists of the following activities:

1. **Determine your application type.** First, determine what type of application you are building. Is it a mobile application, a rich client, a rich Internet application, a service, a Web application, or some combination of these types? For more details of the common application archetypes, see Chapter 20, "Choosing an Application Type."

2. **Identify your deployment constraints.** When you design your application architecture, you must take into account corporate policies and procedures, together with the infrastructure on which you plan to deploy your application. If the target environment is fixed or inflexible, your application design must reflect restrictions that exist in that environment. Your application design must also take into account Quality-of-Service (QoS) attributes such as security and reliability. Sometimes you must make design tradeoffs due to protocol restrictions and network topologies. By identifying the requirements and constraints

that exist between the application architecture and infrastructure architecture early in the design process, you can choose an appropriate deployment topology and resolve conflicts between the application and the target infrastructure. For more information about deployment scenarios, see Chapter 19, "Physical Tiers and Deployment."

3. **Identify important architecture design styles.** Determine which architecture styles you will be using in your design. An architecture style is a set of principles. You can think of it as a coarse-grained pattern that provides an abstract framework for a family of systems. Each style defines a set of rules that specify the kinds of components you can use to assemble a system, the kinds of relationships used in their assembly, constraints on the way they are assembled, and assumptions about the meaning of how you put them together. An architecture style improves partitioning and promotes design reuse by providing solutions to frequently recurring problems. Common architectural styles are Service Oriented Architecture (SOA), client/server, layered, message-bus, and domain-driven design. Applications will often use a combination of styles. For more information about the architectural styles in common use today, see Chapter 3, "Architectural Patterns and Styles."

4. **Determine relevant technologies.** Finally, identify the relevant technology choices based on your application type and other constraints, and determine which technologies you will use in your design. Key factors to consider are the type of application you are developing, and your preferred options for application deployment topology and architectural styles. The choice of technologies will also be governed by organization policies, infrastructure limitations, resource skills, and so on. The following section describes some of the common Microsoft technologies for each type of application.

Relevant Technologies

When choosing the technologies you will use in your design, consider which will help you to support your chosen architectural styles, your chosen application type, and the key quality attributes for your application. For example, for the Microsoft platform, the following list will help you understand which presentation, implementation, and communication technologies are most suited to each type of application:

- **Mobile Applications.** You can use presentation-layer technologies such as the .NET Compact Framework, ASP.NET for Mobile, and Silverlight for Mobile to develop applications for mobile devices.

- **Rich Client Applications.** You can use combinations of Windows Presentation Foundation (WPF), Windows Forms, and XAML Browser Application (XBAP) presentation-layer technologies to develop applications with rich UIs that are deployed and run on the client.

- **Rich Internet Client Applications (RIA).** You can use the Microsoft Silverlight™ browser plug-in, or Silverlight combined with AJAX, to deploy rich UI experiences within a Web browser.

- **Web Applications.** You can use ASP.NET Web Forms, AJAX, Silverlight controls, ASP.NET MVC, and ASP.NET Dynamic data to create Web applications.
- **Service Applications.** You can use Windows Communication Foundation (WCF) and ASP.NET Web services (ASMX) to create services that expose functionality to external systems and service consumers.

For more details about the technologies available for different types of applications, see the following topics in the appendices at the end of this guide:

- The Microsoft Application Platform
- Presentation Technology Matrix
- Data Access Technology Matrix
- Integration Technology Matrix
- Workflow Technology Matrix

Whiteboard Your Architecture

It is important that you are able to whiteboard your architecture. Whether you share your whiteboard on paper, slides, or through another format, the key is to show the major constraints and decisions in order to frame and start conversations. The value is actually twofold. If you cannot whiteboard the architecture then it suggests that it is not well understood. If you can provide a clear and concise whiteboard diagram, others will understand it and you can communicate details to them more easily.

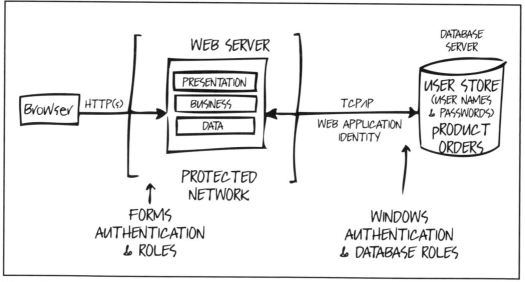

Figure 2
Example of an architecture whiteboard showing a high-level design for a Web application indicating the protocols and authentication methods it will use.

Key Issues

Identify the issues in your application architecture to understand the areas where mistakes are most likely to be made. Potential issues include the appearance of new technologies, and critical business requirements. For example, "Can I swap from one third party service to another?," "Can I add support for a new client type?," "Can I quickly change my business rules relating to billing?," and "Can I migrate to a new technology for X?" While these factors are extremely generalized, they (and other areas of risk) generally map in implementation terms to *quality attributes* and *crosscutting concerns*.

Quality Attributes

Quality attributes are the overall features of your architecture that affect run-time behavior, system design, and user experience. The extent to which the application possesses a desired combination of quality attributes such as usability, performance, reliability, and security indicates the success of the design and the overall quality of the software application. When designing applications to meet any of these qualities, it is necessary to consider the impact on other requirements; you must analyze the tradeoffs between multiple quality attributes. The importance or priority of each quality attribute differs from system to system; for example, in a line-of-business (LOB) system, performance, scalability, security, and usability will be more important than interoperability. Interoperability is likely to be far more important in a shrink-wrap application than in a LOB application.

Quality attributes represent areas of concern that have the potential for application-wide impact across layers and tiers. Some attributes are related to the overall system design, while others are specific to run-time, design-time, or user-centric issues. Use the following list to help you organize your thinking about the quality attributes, and to understand which scenarios they are most likely to affect:

- **System qualities.** The overall qualities of the system when considered as a whole; such as supportability and testability.
- **Run-time qualities.** The qualities of the system directly expressed at run-time; such as availability, interoperability, manageability, performance, reliability, scalability, and security.
- **Design qualities.** The qualities reflecting the design of the system; such as conceptual integrity, flexibility, maintainability, and reusability.
- **User qualities.** The usability of the system.

For more information about ensuring that your design implements the appropriate quality attributes, see Chapter 16 "Quality Attributes."

Crosscutting Concerns

Crosscutting concerns are the features of your design that may apply across all layers, components, and tiers. These are also the areas in which high-impact design mistakes are most often made. Examples of crosscutting concerns are:

- **Authentication and Authorization.** How you choose appropriate authentication and authorization strategies, flow identity across layers and tiers, and store user identities.

- **Caching.** How you choose an appropriate caching technology, determine what data to cache, where to cache the data, and a suitable expiration policy.

- **Communication.** How you choose appropriate protocols for communication across layers and tiers, design loose coupling across layers, perform asynchronous communication, and pass sensitive data.

- **Configuration Management.** How you determine what information must be configurable, where and how to store configuration information, how to protect sensitive configuration information, and how to handle configuration information in a farm or cluster.

- **Exception Management.** How you handle and log exceptions, and provide notification when required.

- **Logging and Instrumentation.** How you determine which information to log, how to make the logging configurable, and determine what level of instrumentation is required.

- **Validation.** How you determine where and how to perform validation; the techniques you choose for validating on length, range, format, and type; how you constrain and reject input invalid values; how you sanitize potentially malicious or dangerous input; and how you can define and reuse validation logic across your application's layers and tiers.

For more information about ensuring that your design correctly handles crosscutting concerns, see Chapter 17 "Crosscutting Concerns."

Designing for Issue Mitigation

By analyzing quality attributes and crosscutting concerns in relation to your design requirements, you can focus on specific areas of concern. For example, the quality attribute Security is obviously a vital factor in your design, and applies at many levels and areas of the architecture. The relevant crosscutting concerns for security provide guidance on specific areas where you should focus your attention. You can use the individual crosscutting categories to divide your application architecture for further analysis, and to help you identify application vulnerabilities. This approach leads to a design that optimizes security aspects. Questions you might consider when examining the crosscutting concerns for security are:

- **Auditing and Logging.** Who did what and when? Is the application operating normally? Auditing refers to how your application records security-related events. Logging refers to how your application publishes information about its operation.

- **Authentication.** Who are you? Authentication is the process where one entity definitively establishes the identity of another entity, typically with credentials such as a username and password.

- **Authorization.** What can you do? Authorization refers to how your application controls access to resources and operations.

- **Configuration Management.** What context does your application run under? Which databases does it connect to? How is your application administered? How are these settings protected? Configuration management refers to how your application handles these operations and issues.

- **Cryptography.** How are you handling secrets (confidentiality)? How are you tamper-proofing your data or libraries (integrity)? How are seeding random values that must be cryptographically strong? Cryptography refers to how your application enforces confidentiality and integrity.

- **Exception Management.** When a method call in your application fails, what does your application do? How much information does it reveal? Does it return friendly error messages to end users? Does it pass valuable exception information back to the calling code? Does it fail gracefully? Does it help administrators to perform root cause analysis of the fault? Exception management refers to how you handle exceptions within your application.

- **Input and Data Validation.** How do you know that the input your application receives is valid and safe? Does it constrain input through entry points and encode output through exit points. Can it trust data sources such as databases and file shares? Input validation refers to how your application filters, scrubs, or rejects input before additional processing.

- **Sensitive data.** How does your application handle sensitive data? Does it protect confidential user and application data? Sensitive data refers to how your application handles any data that must be protected either in memory, over the network, or in persistent stores.

- **Session Management.** How does your application handle and protect user sessions? A session refers to a set of related interactions between a user and your application.

You can use these questions and answers to make key security design decisions for your application, and document these are part of your architecture. For example, Figure 3 shows the security issues identified in a typical Web application architecture.

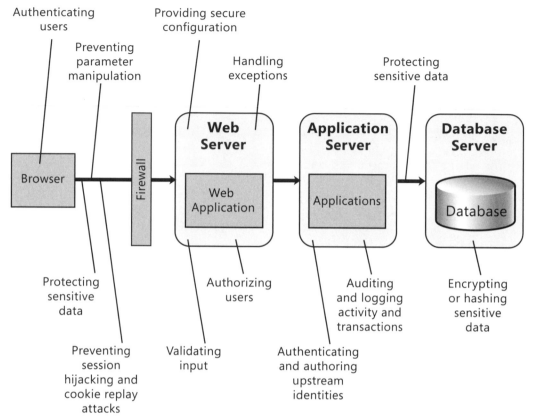

Figure 3
Security issues identified in a typical Web application architecture.

Candidate Solutions

After you define the key issues, you can create your initial baseline architecture and then start to fill in the details to produce a candidate architecture. Along the way, you may use architectural spikes to explore specific areas of the design or to validate new concepts. You then validate your new candidate architecture against the key scenarios and requirements you have defined, before iteratively following the cycle and improving the design.

Note: It is important, especially if your design and development is following an agile process, that your iteration encompass both architecture and development activities. This avoids the *big design up front* approach.

Baseline and Candidate Architectures

A *baseline architecture* describes the existing system —it is how your system looks today. If this is a new architecture, your initial baseline is the first high-level architectural design from which candidate architectures will be built. A candidate architecture includes the application type, the deployment architecture, the architectural style, technology choices, quality attributes, and crosscutting concerns.

As you evolve the design, ensure that at each stage you understand the key risks and adapt your design to reduce them, optimize for effective and efficient communication of design information, and build your architecture with flexibility and refactoring in mind. You may need to modify your architecture a number of times, through several iterations, candidate architectures, and by using multiple architectural spikes. If the candidate architecture is an improvement, it can become the baseline from which new candidate architectures can be created and tested.

This iterative and incremental approach allows you to get the big risks out of the way first, iteratively render your architecture, and use architectural tests to prove that each new baseline is an improvement over the last. Consider the following questions to help you test a new candidate architecture that results from an architectural spike:

- Does this architecture succeed without introducing any new risks?
- Does this architecture mitigate more known risks than the previous iteration?
- Does this architecture meet additional requirements?
- Does this architecture enable architecturally significant use cases?
- Does this architecture address quality attribute concerns?
- Does this architecture address additional crosscutting concerns?

Architectural Spikes

An *architectural spike* is a test implementation of a small part of the application's overall design or architecture. The purpose is to analyze a technical aspect of a specific piece of the solution in order to validate technical assumptions, choose between potential designs and implementation strategies, or sometimes to estimate implementation timescales.

Architectural spikes are often used as part of agile or extreme programming development approaches but can be a very effective way to refine and evolve a solution's design regardless of the development approach adopted. By focusing on key parts of the solution's overall design, architectural spikes can be used to resolve important technical challenges and to reduce overall risk and uncertainty in the solution's design.

What to Do Next

After you complete the architecture-modeling activity, you can begin to refine the design, plan tests, and communicate the design to others. Keep in mind the following guidelines:

- If you capture your candidate architectures and architectural test cases in a document, keep the document lightweight so that you can easily update it. Such a document may include details of your objectives, application type, deployment topology, key scenarios and requirements, technologies, quality attributes, and tests.

- Use the quality attributes to help shape your design and implementation. For example, developers should be aware of anti-patterns related to the identified architectural risks, and use the appropriate proven patterns to help address the issues.

- Communicate the information you capture to relevant team members and other stakeholders. This may include your application development team, your test team, and your network and system administrators.

Reviewing Your Architecture

Reviewing the architecture for your application is a critically important task in order to reduce the cost of mistakes and to find and fix architectural problems as early as possible. Architecture review is a proven, cost-effective way of reducing project costs and the chances of project failure. Review your architecture frequently: at major project milestones, and in response to other significant architectural changes. Build your architecture with common review questions in mind, both to improve your architecture and to reduce the time required for each review.

The main goal of an architecture review is to determine the feasibility of your baseline and candidate architectures, and verify that the architecture correctly links the functional requirements and the quality attributes with the proposed technical solution. Additionally, it helps you to identify issues and recognize areas for improvement.

Scenario-Based Evaluations

Scenario-based evaluations are a powerful method for reviewing an architecture design. In a scenario-based evaluation, the focus is on the scenarios that are most important from the business perspective, and which have the greatest impact on the architecture. Consider using one of the following common review methodologies:

- **Software Architecture Analysis Method (SAAM).** SAAM was originally designed for assessing modifiability, but later was extended for reviewing architecture with respect to quality attributes such as modifiability, portability, extensibility, integratability, and functional coverage.

- **Architecture Tradeoff Analysis Method (ATAM).** ATAM is a refined and improved version of SAAM that helps you review architectural decisions with respect to the quality attributes requirements, and how well they satisfy particular quality goals.

- **Active Design Review (ADR).** ADR is best suited for incomplete or in-progress architectures. The main difference is that the review is more focused on a set of issues or individual sections of the architecture at a time, rather than performing a general review.

- **Active Reviews of Intermediate Designs (ARID).** ARID combines the ADR aspect of reviewing in-progress architecture with a focus on a set of issues, and the ATAM and SAAM approach of scenario-based review focused on quality attributes.

- **Cost Benefit Analysis Method (CBAM).** This CBAM focuses on analyzing the costs, benefits, and schedule implications of architectural decisions.

- **Architecture Level Modifiability Analysis (ALMA).** ALMA evaluates the modifiability of architecture for business information systems (BIS).

- **Family Architecture Assessment Method (FAAM).** FAAM evaluates information system family architectures for interoperability and extensibility.

For information about techniques for analyzing and reviewing architecture designs, see *"Evaluating Software Architectures: Methods and Case Studies (SEI Series in Software Engineering)"* by Paul Clements, Rick Kazman, and Mark Klein (Addison-Wesley Professional , ISBN-10: 020170482X, ISBN-13: 978-0201704822)

Representing and Communicating Your Architecture Design

Communicating your design is critical for architecture reviews, as well as to ensure it is implemented correctly. You must communicate your architectural design to all the stakeholders including the development team, system administrators and operators, business owners, and other interested parties.

One way to think of an architectural view is as a map of the important decisions. The map is not the terrain; instead, it is an abstraction that helps you to share and communicate the architecture. There are several well-known methods for describing architecture to others, including the following:

- **4+1.** This approach uses five views of the complete architecture. Four of the views describe the architecture from different approaches: the logical view (such as the object model), the process view (such as concurrency and synchronization aspects), the physical view (the map of the software layers and functions onto the distributed hardware infrastructure), and the development view. A fifth view shows the scenarios and use cases for the software. For more information, see *"Architectural Blueprints—The "4+1" View Model of Software Architecture"* at http://www.cs.ubc.ca/~gregor/teaching/papers/4+1view-architecture.pdf.

- **Agile Modeling.** This approach follows the concept that content is more important than representation. This ensures that the models created are simple and easy to understand, sufficiently accurate, and consistent. The simplicity of the document ensures that there is active stakeholder participation in the modeling of the artifact. For more information, see *"Agile Modeling: Effective Practices for eXtreme Programming and the Unified Process"* by Scott Ambler (J. Wiley, ISBN-10: 0471202827, ISBN-13: 978-0471202820).

- **IEEE 1471.** IEEE 1471 is the short name for a standard formally known as ANSI/IEEE 1471-2000, which enhance the content of an architectural description; in particular giving specific meaning to context, views, and viewpoints. For more information, see *"Recommended Practice for Architecture Description of Software-Intensive Systems"* at http://standards.ieee.org/reading/ieee/std_public/description/se/1471-2000_desc.html.

- **Unified Modeling Language (UML).** This approach represents three views of a system model. The functional requirements view (functional requirements of the system from the point of view of the user, including use cases); the static structural view (objects, attributes, relationships, and operations including class diagrams); and the dynamic behavior view (collaboration among objects and changes to the internal state of objects, including includes sequence, activity, and state diagrams). For more information, see *"UML Distilled: A Brief Guide to the Standard Object Modeling Language"* by Martin Fowler (Addison-Wesley Professional, ISBN-10: 0321193687, ISBN-13: 978-0321193681)

Additional Resources

Ambler, Scott. *Agile Modeling: Effective Practices for eXtreme Programming and the Unified Process.* J. Wiley, 2002.

Clements, Paul, Rick Kazman, and Mark Klein. *Evaluating Software Architectures: Methods and Case Studies (SEI Series in Software Engineering).* Addison-Wesley Professional, 2001.

Fowler, Martin. *UML Distilled: A Brief Guide to the Standard Object Modeling Language.* Addison-Wesley Professional, 2003.

5

Layered Application Guidelines

Overview

This chapter discusses the overall structure for applications in terms of the logical grouping of components into separate layers that communicate with each other and with other clients and applications. Layers are concerned with the logical division of components and functionality, and do not take into account the physical location of components. Layers can be located on different tiers, or they may reside on the same tier. In this chapter, you will learn how to divide your applications into separate logical parts, how to choose an appropriate functional layout for your applications, and how applications can support multiple client types. You will also learn about services that you can use to expose logic in your layers.

Note: It is important to understand the distinction between layers and tiers. *Layers* describe the logical groupings of the functionality and components in an application; whereas *tiers* describe the physical distribution of the functionality and components on separate servers, computers, networks, or remote locations. Although both layers and tiers use the same set of names (presentation, business, services, and data), remember that only tiers imply a physical separation. It is quite common to locate more than one layer on the same physical machine (the same tier). You can think of the term tier as referring to physical distribution patterns such as two-tier, three-tier, and *n*-tier. For more information about physical tiers and deployment, see Chapter 19, "Physical Tiers and Deployment."

Logical Layered Design

Irrespective of the type of application that you are designing, and whether it has a user interface or it is a services application that only exposes services (not to be confused with services layer of an application), you can decompose the design into logical groupings of software components. These logical groupings are called layers. Layers help to differentiate between the different kinds of tasks performed by the components, making it easier to create a design that supports reusability of components. Each logical layer contains a number of discrete component types grouped into sub layers, with each sub layer performing a specific type of task.

By identifying the generic types of components that exist in most solutions, you can construct a meaningful map of an application or service, and then use this map as a blueprint for your design. Dividing an application into separate layers that have distinct roles and functionalities helps you to maximize maintainability of the code, optimize the way that the application works when deployed in different ways, and provides a clear delineation between locations where certain technology or design decisions must be made.

Presentation, Business, and Data Layers

At the highest and most abstract level, the logical architecture view of any system can be considered as a set of cooperating components grouped into layers. Figure 1 shows a simplified, high level representation of these layers and their relationships with users, other applications that call services implemented within the application's business layer, data sources such as relational databases or Web services that provide access to data, and external or remote services that are consumed by the application.

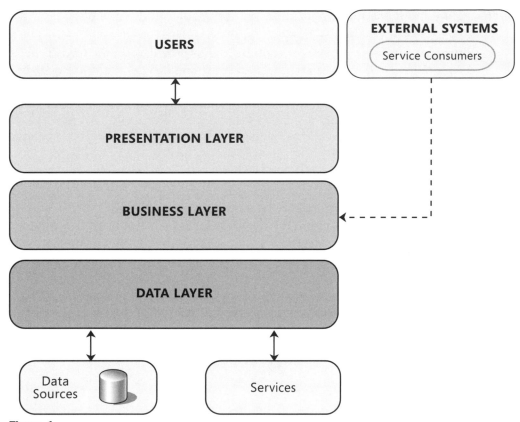

Figure 1
The logical architecture view of a layered system

These layers may be located on the same physical tier, or may be located on separate tiers. If they are located on separate tiers, or separated by physical boundaries, your design must accommodate this. For more information, see Design Steps for a Layered Structure later in this chapter.

As shown in Figure 1, an application can consist of a number of basic layers. The common three-layer design shown in Figure 1 consists of the following layers:

- **Presentation layer.** This layer contains the user oriented functionality responsible for managing user interaction with the system, and generally consists of components that provide a common bridge into the core business logic encapsulated in the business layer. For more information about designing the presentation layer, see Chapter 6, "Presentation Layer Guidelines." For more information about designing presentation components, see Chapter 11, "Designing Presentation Components."

- **Business layer.** This layer implements the core functionality of the system, and encapsulates the relevant business logic. It generally consists of components, some of which may expose service interfaces that other callers can use. For more information about designing the business layer, see Chapter 7, "Business Layer Guidelines." For more information about designing business components, see Chapter 12, "Designing Business Components."

- **Data layer.** This layer provides access to data hosted within the boundaries of the system, and data exposed by other networked systems; perhaps accessed through services. The data layer exposes generic interfaces that the components in the business layer can consume. For more information about designing the data layer, see Chapter 8, "Data Layer Guidelines." For more information about designing data components, see Chapter 15, "Designing Data Components."

Services and Layers

From a high level perspective, a service-based solution can be seen as being composed of multiple services, each communicating with the others by passing messages. Conceptually, the services can be seen as components of the overall solution. However, internally, each service is made up of software components, just like any other application, and these components can be logically grouped into presentation, business, and data layers. Other applications can make use of the services without being aware of the way they are implemented. The layered design principles discussed in the previous section apply equally to service-based solutions.

Services Layer

When an application must provide services to other applications, as well as implementing features to support clients directly, a common approach is to use a services layer that exposes the business functionality of the application, as shown in Figure 2. The services layer effectively provides an alternative view that allows clients to use a different channel to access the application.

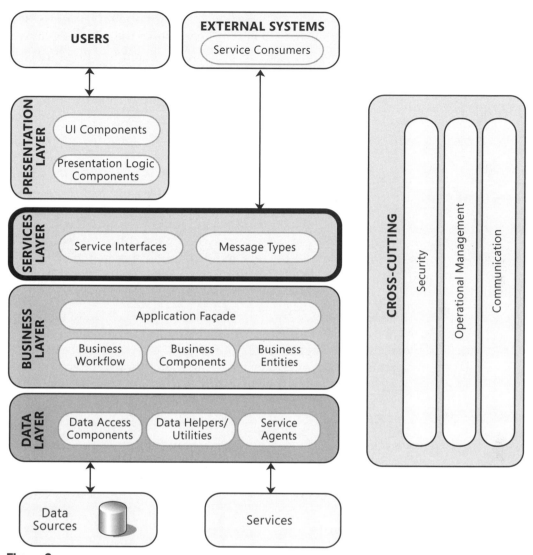

Figure 2
Incorporating a services layer in an application

In this scenario, users can access the application through the presentation layer, which communicates either directly with the components in the business layer; or through an application façade in the business layer if the communication methods require composition of functionality. Meanwhile, external clients and other systems can access the application and make use of its functionality by communicating with the business layer through service interfaces. This allows the application to better support multiple client types, and promotes re-use and higher level composition of functionality across applications.

In some cases, the presentation layer may communicate with the business layer through the services layer. However, this is not an absolute requirement. If the physical deployment of the application locates the presentation layer and the business layer on the same tier, they may communicate directly. For more information about designing the services layer, see Chapter 9, "Service Layer Guidelines." For more information about communication between layers, see Chapter 18, "Communication and Messaging."

Design Steps for a Layered Structure

When starting to design an application, your first task is to focus on the highest level of abstraction and start by grouping functionality into layers. Next, you must define the public interface for each layer, which depends on the type of application you are designing. Once you have defined the layers and interfaces, you must determine how the application will be deployed. Finally, you choose the communication protocols to use for interaction between the layers and tiers of the application. Although your structure and interfaces may evolve over time, especially if you use agile development, these steps will ensure that you consider the important aspects at the start of the process. A typical series of design steps is the following:

- Step 1 – Choose Your Layering Strategy
- Step 2 – Determine the Layers You Require
- Step 3 – Decide How to Distribute Layers and Components
- Step 4 – Determine If You Need to Collapse Layers
- Step 5 – Determine Rules for Interaction between Layers
- Step 6 – Identify Cross Cutting Concerns
- Step 7 – Define the Interfaces between Layers
- Step 8 – Choose Your Deployment Strategy
- Step 9 – Choose Communication Protocols

Step 1 – Choose Your Layering Strategy

Layering represents the logical separation of an application's components into groups that represent distinct roles and functionality. Using a layered approach can improve the maintainability of your application and make it easier to scale out when necessary to improve performance. There are many different ways to group related functionality into layers. However, separating an application into too few or too many layers can add unnecessary complexity; and can decrease the overall performance, maintainability, and flexibility. Determining the granularity of layering appropriate for your application is a critical first step in determining your layering strategy.

You must also consider whether you are implementing layering in order to achieve purely logical separation of functionality, or in order to potentially achieve physical separation as well. Crossing layer boundaries imposes a local performance overhead, especially for boundaries between physically remote components. However, the overall increase in the scalability and flexibility of your application can far outweigh this performance overhead. In addition, layering can make it easier to optimize the performance of individual layers without affecting adjacent layers.

In the case of logical layering, interacting application layers will be deployed on the same tier and operate within the same process, which allows you to take advantage of higher performance communication mechanisms such as direct calls through component interfaces. However, in order to maintain the advantages of logical layering and ensure flexibility for the future, you must be careful to maintain encapsulation and loose coupling between the layers.

For layers that are deployed to separate tiers (separate physical machines), communication with adjacent layers will occur over a connecting network, and you must ensure that the design you choose supports a suitable communication mechanism that takes account of communication latency and maintains loose coupling between layers.

Determining which of your application layers are likely to be deployed to separate tiers, and which are likely to be deployed to the same tier, is also an important part of your layering strategy. To maintain flexibility, always ensure that interaction between layers is loosely coupled. This allows you to take advantage of the higher performance available when layers are located on the same tier, while allowing you to deploy them to multiple tiers if and when required.

Adopting a layered approach can add some complexity, and may increase initial development time, but if implemented correctly will significantly improve the maintainability, extensibility, and flexibility of your application. You must consider the trade off of reusability and loose coupling that layers provide against their impact on performance and the increase in complexity. Carefully considering how your application is layered, and how the layers will interact with each other, will ensure a good balance between performance and flexibility. In general, the gain in flexibility and maintainability provided by a layered design far outweighs the marginal improvement in performance that you might gain from a closely coupled design that does not use layers.

For a description of the common types of layers, and guidance on deciding which layers you need, see the section "Logical Layered Design" earlier in this chapter.

Step 2 – Determine the Layers You Require

There are many different ways to group related functionality into layers. The most common approach in business applications is to separate presentation, services, business, and data access functionality into separate layers. Some applications also introduce reporting, management, or infrastructure layers.

Be careful when adding additional layers, and do not add them if they do not provide a logical grouping of related components that manifestly increases the maintainability, scalability, or flexibility of your application. For example, if your application does not expose services, a separate service layer may not be required and you may just have presentation, business, and data access layers.

Step 3 – Decide How to Distribute Layers and Components

You should distribute layers and components across separate physical tiers only where this is necessary. Common reasons for implementing distributed deployment include security policies, physical constraints, shared business logic, and scalability.

- In Web applications, if your presentation components access your business components synchronously, consider deploying the business layer and presentation layer components on the same physical tier to maximize performance and ease operational management, unless security restrictions require a trust boundary between them.

- In rich client applications, where the UI processing occurs on the desktop, you may prefer to deploy the business components in a physically separate business tier for security reasons, and to ease operational management.

- Deploy business entities on the same physical tier as the code that uses them. This may mean deploying them in more than one place; for example, placing copies on a physically separated presentation tier or data tier where that logic makes use of or references the business entities. Deploy service agent components on the same tier as the code that calls the components, unless security restrictions require a trust boundary between them.

- Consider deploying asynchronous business components, workflow components, and services that have similar load and I/O characteristics on a separate physical tier so that you can fine tune that infrastructure to maximize performance and scalability.

Step 4 – Determine If You Need to Collapse Layers

In some cases, it makes sense to collapse or relax layers. For example, an application with very limited business rules, or one that uses rules mainly for validation, might implement both the business and presentation logic in a single layer. In an application that pulls data from a Web service and displays that data, it may make sense to simply add a Web service references directly to the presentation layer and consume the Web service data directly. In this case, you are logically combining the data access and presentation layers.

These are just some examples of where it might make sense to collapse layers. However, the general rule is that you should always group functionality into layers. In some cases, one layer may act as a proxy or pass-through layer that provides encapsulation and loose coupling without providing a great deal of functionality. However, by separating that functionality, you can extend it later with little or no impact on other layers in the design.

Step 5 – Determine Rules for Interaction Between Layers

When it comes to a layering strategy, you must define rules for how the layers will interact with each other. The main reasons for specifying interaction rules are to minimize dependencies and eliminate circular references. For example, if two layers each have a dependency on components in the other layer you have introduced a circular dependency. As a result, a common rule to follow is to allow only one way interaction between the layers using one of the following approaches:

- **Top-down interaction.** Higher level layers can interact with layers below, but a lower level layer should never interact with layers above. This rule will help you to avoid circular dependencies between layers. You can use events to make components in higher layers aware of changes in lower layers without introducing dependencies.

- **Strict interaction.** Each layer must interact with only the layer directly below. This rule will enforce strict separation of concerns where each layer knows only about the layer directly below. The benefit of this rule is that modifications to the interface of the layer will only affect the layer directly above. Consider using this approach if you are designing an application that will be modified over time to introduce new functionality and you want to minimize the impact of those changes, or you are designing an application that may be distributed across different physical tiers.

- **Loose interaction.** Higher level layers can bypass layers to interact with lower level layers directly. This can improve performance, but will also increase dependencies. In other words, modification to a lower level layer can affect multiple layers above. Consider using this approach if you are designing an application that you know will not be distributed across physical tiers (for example, a stand-alone rich client application), or you are designing a small application where changes that affect multiple layers can be managed with minimal effort.

Step 6 – Identify Cross Cutting Concerns

After you define the layers, you must identify the functionality that spans layers. This functionality is often described as *crosscutting concerns*, and includes logging, caching, validation, authentication, and exception management. It is important to identify each of the crosscutting concerns in your application, and design separate components to manage these concerns where possible. This approach helps you to achieve of better reusability and maintainability.

Avoid mixing the crosscutting code with code in the components of each layer, so that the layers and their components only make calls to the crosscutting components when they must carry out an action such as logging, caching, or authentication. As the functionality must be available across layers, you must deploy crosscutting components in such a way that they are accessible to all the layers—even when the layers are located on separate physical tiers.

There are different approaches to handling crosscutting functionality, from common libraries such as the patterns & practices Enterprise Library to Aspect Oriented Programming (AOP) methods where metadata is used to insert crosscutting code directly into the compiled output. For more information about crosscutting concerns, see Chapter 17, "Crosscutting Concerns."

Step 7 – Define the Interfaces between Layers

When you define the interface for a layer, the primary goal is to enforce loose coupling between layers. What this means is that a layer should not expose internal details on which another layer could depend. Instead, the interface to a layer should be designed to minimize dependencies by providing a public interface that hides details of the components within the layer. This hiding is called *abstraction*, and there are many different ways to implement it. The following design approaches can be used to define the interface to a layer:

- **Abstract interface.** This can be accomplished by defining an abstract base class or code interface class that acts as a type definition for concrete classes. The type defines a common interface that all consumers of the layer use to interact with the layer. This approach also improves testability, because you can use test objects (sometimes referred to as mock objects) that implement the abstract interface.

- **Common design type.** Many design patterns define concrete object types that represent an interface into different layers. These object types provide an abstraction that hides details related to the layer. For example, the Table Data Gateway pattern defines object types that represent tables in a database and are responsible for implementing the SQL queries required to interact with the data. Consumers of the object have no knowledge of the SQL queries, or the details of how the object connects to the database and executes commands. Many design patterns are based on abstract interfaces but some are based on concrete classes instead, and most of the appropriate patterns such as Table Data Gateway are well documented in this respect. Consider using common design types if you want a fast and easy way to implement the interface to your layer, or if you are implementing a design pattern for the interface to your layer.

- **Dependency inversion.** This is a programming style where abstract interfaces are defined external to, or independent of, any layers. Instead of one layer being dependent on another, both layers depend upon common interfaces. The Dependency Injection pattern is a common implementation of dependency inversion. With dependency injection, a container defines mappings that specify how to locate components that another component may depend upon, and the container can create and inject these dependent components automatically. The dependency inversion approach provides flexibility and can help to implement a pluggable design because the dependencies are composed through configuration rather than code. It also maximizes testability because you can easily inject concrete test classes into different layers of the design.

- **Message-based.** Instead of interacting directly with components in other layers by calling methods or accessing properties of these objects, you can use message-based communication to implement interfaces and provide interaction between layers. There are several messaging solutions such as Windows Communication Foundation, Web services, and Microsoft Message Queuing that support interaction across physical and process boundaries. However, you can also combine abstract interfaces with a common message type used to define data structures for the interaction. The key difference with a message-based interface is that the interaction between layers uses a common structure that encapsulates all the details of the interaction. This structure can define operations, data schemas, fault contracts, security information, and many other structures related to communication between layers. Consider using a message-based approach if you are implementing a Web application and defining the interface between the presentation layer and business layer, you have an application layer that must support multiple client types, or you want to support interaction across physical and process boundaries. Also, consider a message-based approach if you want to formalize the interaction with a common structure, or you want to interact with a stateless interface where state information is carried with the message.

To implement the interaction between the presentation layer of a Web application and the business logic layer, the recommendation is to use a message-based interface. If the business layer does not maintain state between calls (in other words, each call between the presentation layer and business layer represents a new context), you can pass context information along with the request and provide a common model for exception and error handling in the presentation layer.

Step 8 – Choose Your Deployment Strategy

There are several common patterns that represent application deployment structures found in most solutions. When it comes to determining the best deployment solution for your application, it helps to first identify the common patterns. Once you have a good understanding of the different patterns, you then consider scenarios, requirements, and security constraints to choose the most appropriate pattern or patterns. For more information on deployment patterns, see Chapter 19, "Physical Tiers and Deployment."

Step 9 – Choose Communication Protocols

The physical protocols used for communication across layers or tiers in your design play a major role in the performance, security, and reliability of the application. The choice of communication protocol is even more important when considering distributed deployment. When components are located on the same physical tier, you can often rely on direct communication between these components. However, if you deploy components and layers on physically separate servers and client machines—as is likely in most scenarios—you must consider how the components in these layers will communicate with each other efficiently and reliably. For more information on communication protocols and technologies, see Chapter 18, "Communication and Messaging."

6

Presentation Layer Guidelines

Overview

This chapter describes the key guidelines for designing the presentation layer of an application. It will help you to understand how the presentation layer fits into the typical layered application architecture, the components it usually contains, and the key issues you face when designing the presentation layer. You will see guidelines for design, the recommended design steps, relevant design patterns, and technology options.

The presentation layer contains the components that implement and display the user interface and manage user interaction. This layer includes controls for user input and display, in addition to components that organize user interaction. Figure 1 shows how the presentation layer fits into a common application architecture.

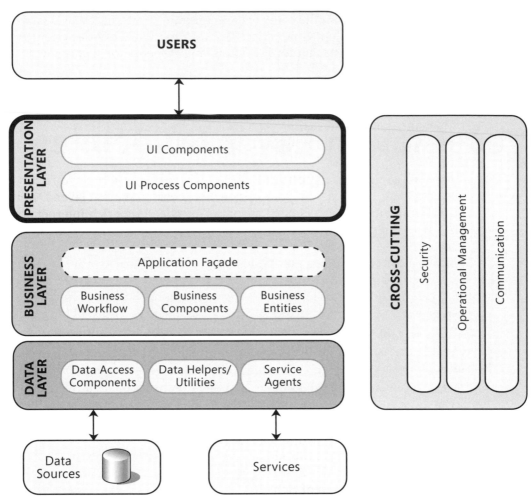

Figure 1
A typical application showing the presentation layer and the components it may contain

The presentation layer will usually include the following:

- **User Interface components.** These are the application's visual elements used to display information to the user and accept user input.

- **Presentation Logic components.** Presentation logic is the application code that defines the logical behavior and structure of the application in a way that is independent of any specific user interface implementation. When implementing the Separated Presentation pattern, the presentation logic components may include Presenter, Presentation Model, and ViewModel components. The presentation layer may also include Presentation Layer Model components that encapsulate the data from your business layer, or Presentation Entity components that encapsulate business logic and data in a form that is easily consumable by the presentation layer.

For more information about the components commonly used in the presentation layer, see Chapter 10, "Component Guidelines." For information about designing presentation layer components, see Chapter 11, "Designing Presentation Components."

General Design Considerations

There are several key factors that you should consider when designing your presentation layer. Use the following principles to ensure that your design meets the requirements for your application, and follows best practices:

- **Choose the appropriate application type.** The application type you choose will have considerable impact on your options for the presentation layer. Determine if you will implement a rich (smart) client, a Web client, or a rich Internet application (RIA). Base your decision on application requirements, and on organizational and infrastructure constraints. For information on the main application archetypes, and their benefits and liabilities, see Chapter 20, "Choosing an Application Type."

- **Choose the appropriate UI technology.** Different application types provide different sets of technologies that you can use to develop the presentation layer. Each technology type has distinct advantages that can affect your ability to create a suitable presentation layer design. For information on the technologies available for each application type, see Appendix B "Presentation Technology Matrix."

- **Use the relevant patterns.** Review the presentation layer patterns (listed at the end of this chapter) for proven solutions to common presentation problems. Keep in mind that not all patterns apply equally to all archetypes. However, the general pattern of Separated Presentation, which separates presentation specific concerns from the underlying application logic, applies to all application types. Specific patterns such as MVC, MVP, and Supervising Presenter are commonly used in presentation layer design of rich client applications and RIAs. Variants of the Model-View-Controller (MVC) and Model-View-Presenter (MVP) patterns can be used in Web applications.

- **Design for separation of concerns.** Use dedicated UI components that focus on rendering, display, and user interaction. Consider using dedicated presentation logic components to manage the processing of user interaction where this is complex or where you want to be able to unit test it. Also, consider using dedicated presentation entities to represent your business logic and data in a form that is easily consumable by your UI and presentation logic components. Presentation entities encapsulate within the presentation layer the business logic and data from your business layer, for use in much the same way as business entities are used in the business layer. For more information about the different types of presentation layer components you may use, see Chapter 11, "Designing Presentation Components."

- **Consider human interface guidelines.** Implement your organization's guidelines for UI design, including factors such as accessibility, localization, and usability when designing the presentation layer. Review established UI guidelines for interactivity, usability, system compatibility, conformance, and relevant UI design patterns based on the client type and the technologies that you choose, and apply those applicable to your application design and requirements.
- **Adhere to user driven design principles.** Before designing your presentation layer, understand your customer. Use surveys, usability studies, and interviews to determine the best presentation design to meet your customer's requirements.

Specific Design Issues

There are several common issues that you must consider as your develop your design. These issues can be categorized into specific areas of the design. The following sections provide guidelines for the common areas where mistakes are most often made:

- Caching
- Communication
- Composition
- Exception Management
- Navigation
- User Experience
- User Interface
- Validation

Caching

Caching is one of the best mechanisms you can use to improve application performance and UI responsiveness. You can use data caching in the presentation layer to optimize data lookups and avoid network round trips, and to store the results of expensive or repetitive processes to avoid unnecessary duplicated processing. Consider the following guidelines when designing your caching strategy:

- Choose the appropriate location for your cache, such as in memory or on disk. If your application is deployed in Web farm, avoid using local caches that must be synchronized. In general, for Web and application farm deployments, consider using a transactional resource manager such as Microsoft SQL Server®, or a product that supports distributed caching such as the Danga Interactive "Memcached" technology or the Microsoft "Velocity" caching mechanism. However, if the variation between individual servers is not critical, or the data changes very slowly, in-memory caching may be appropriate.

- Consider caching data in a ready to use format when working with an in-memory cache. For example, use a specific object instead of caching raw database data. However, avoid caching volatile data as the cost of caching may exceed that of recreating or fetching the data again if it constantly changes.

- Do not cache sensitive data unless you encrypt it.

- Do not depend on data still being in your cache; it may have been removed. Also, consider that the cached data may be stale. For example, when conducting a business transaction, you may want to fetch the most recent data to apply to the transaction rather than use what is in the cache.

- Consider authorization rights for cached data. Only cache data for which you can apply appropriate authorization if users in different roles may access the data.

- If you are using multiple threads, ensure that all access to the cache is thread-safe.

For more information on caching techniques, see Chapter 17, "Crosscutting Concerns."

Communication

Handle long-running requests with user responsiveness in mind, as well as code maintainability and testability. Consider the following guidelines when designing request processing:

- Consider using asynchronous operations or worker threads to avoid blocking the UI for long-running actions in Windows Forms and WPF applications. In ASP.NET, consider using AJAX to perform asynchronous requests. Provide feedback to the user on the progress of the long running action. Consider allowing the user to cancel the long running action.

- Avoid mixing your UI processing and rendering logic.

- When making expensive calls to remote sources or layers, such as when calling Web services or querying a database, consider if it makes more sense to make these calls *chatty* (many smaller requests) or *chunky* (one large request). If the user requires a large volume of data to complete a task, consider retrieving just what is required for display and to get started, then incrementally retrieve the additional data on a background thread or as the user requires it (data paging and UI virtualization are examples of this approach). Consider using larger, chunky calls when the user does not have to wait for the call to complete.

Composition

Consider whether your application will be easier to develop and maintain if the presentation layer uses independent modules and views that are composed at run time. UI composition patterns support the creation of views and the presentation layout at run time. These patterns also help to minimize code and library dependencies that would otherwise force recompilation and redeployment of a module when the dependencies change. Composition patterns help you to implement sharing, reuse, and replacement of presentation logic and views. Consider the following guidelines when designing your UI composition strategy:

- Avoid dependencies between components. For example, use abstraction patterns when possible to avoid issues with maintainability. Consider patterns that support run-time dependency injection.

- Consider creating templates with placeholders. For example, use the Template View pattern to compose dynamic Web pages in order to ensure reuse and consistency.

- Consider composing views from reusable modular parts. For example, use the Composite View pattern to build a view from modular, atomic component parts. Consider decoupling for your application by using separate modules that can be added easily.

- Be cautious when using layouts generated dynamically at run time, which can be difficult to load and maintain. Investigate patterns and third-party libraries that support dynamic layout and injection of views and presentation at runtime.

- When communicating between presentation components, consider using loosely coupled communication patterns such as Publish/Subscribe. This will lower the coupling between the components and improve testability and flexibility.

Exception Management

Design a centralized exception management mechanism for your application that catches and manages unexpected exceptions (exceptions that you cannot recover from locally) in a consistent way. Pay particular attention to exceptions that propagate across layer or tier boundaries, as well as exceptions that cross trust boundaries. Consider the following guidelines when designing your exception management strategy:

- Provide user friendly error messages to notify users of errors in the application, but ensure that you avoid exposing sensitive data in error pages, error messages, log files, and audit files. Attempt to leave the application in a consistent state if possible, or consider terminating it if this is not possible.

- Ensure that you catch exceptions that will not be caught elsewhere (such as in a global error handler), and clean up resources and state after an exception occurs. A global exception handler that displays a global error page or an error message is useful for all unhandled exceptions. Unhandled exceptions generally likely indicate that the system is in an inconsistent state and may need to be gracefully shut down.

- Differentiate between system exceptions and business errors. In the case of business errors, display a user friendly error message and allow the user to retry the operation. In the case of system exceptions, check to see if an issue such as a service or database failure caused the exception, display a user friendly error message, and log the error message to assist in troubleshooting.

- Only catch exceptions that you can handle, and avoid the use of custom exceptions when not necessary. Do not use exceptions to control application logic flow.

For more information on exception management techniques, see Chapter 17, "Crosscutting Concerns."

Navigation

Design your navigation strategy so that users can navigate easily through your screens or pages, and so that you can separate navigation from presentation and UI processing. Ensure that you display navigation links and controls in a consistent way throughout your application to reduce user confusion and to hide application complexity. Consider the following guidelines when designing your navigation strategy:

- Design toolbars and menus to help users find functionality provided by the UI.
- Consider using wizards to implement navigation between forms in a predictable way, and determine how you will preserve navigation state between sessions if this is necessary.
- Avoid duplication of logic for navigation event handlers, and avoid hard-coding navigation paths where possible. Consider using the Command pattern to handle common actions from multiple sources.

User Experience

Good user experience can make the difference between a usable and unusable application. Perceived performance is much more important than actual performance and so expectation management and knowledge of the patterns of user interaction are essential. For example, users might not mind waiting longer for a page to load if they get feedback on when the page is likely to be loaded, and this wait time does not interfere with their activities. In other situations, a very short delay—even fractions of a second for some UI actions—can make the application feel unresponsive. Consider conducting usability studies, surveys, and interviews to understand what users require and expect from your application, and design to achieve an efficient UI with these results in mind. Consider the following guidelines when designing for user experience:

- Do not design overloaded or over complex interfaces. Provide a clear path through the application for each key user scenario, and consider using colors and noninvasive animations to draw the user's attention to important changes in the UI, such as state changes.
- Provide helpful and informative error messages, without exposing sensitive data.
- For actions that might take longer to complete, try to avoid blocking the user. At a minimum, provide feedback on the progress of the action, and consider if the user should be able to cancel the process.
- Consider empowering the user by providing flexibility and customization of the UI through configuration and, where appropriate, personalization.

- Consider how you will support localization and globalization, even if this is not a primary requirement in the initial design. Attempting to add support for localization and globalization once the design is complete can involve a great deal of rework and refactoring.

User Interface

Design a suitable user interface to support your data input and data validation requirements. For maximum usability, follow the established guidelines defined by your organization, and the many established industry usability guidelines that are based on years of user research into input design and mechanisms. When choosing a layout strategy for your user interface, consider whether you will have a separate team of designers building the layout, or whether the development team will create the UI. If designers will be creating the UI, choose a layout approach that does not require code or the use of development focused tools. Consider the following guidelines when designing your user interface:

- Consider using a Separated Presentation pattern such as MVP to separate the layout design from interface processing. Use templates to provide a common look and feel to all of the UI screens, and maintain a common look and feel for all elements of your UI to maximize accessibility and ease of use. Avoid over complex layouts.

- Consider using forms-based input controls for data collection tasks, a document-based input mechanism for collecting more free form input such as text or drawing documents, or a wizard-based approach for more sequenced or workflow driven data collection tasks.

- Avoid using hard-coded strings, and using external resources for text and layout information (for example, to support right-to-left languages), especially if your application will be localized.

- Consider accessibility in your design. You should consider users with disabilities when designing your input strategy; for example, implement text-to-speech software for blind users, or enlarge text and images for users with poor sight. Support keyboard-only scenarios where possible for users who cannot manipulate a pointing device.

- Take into account different screen sizes and resolutions, and different device and input types such as mobile devices, touch screens, and pen and ink–enabled devices. For example, with touch screen input you will typically use larger buttons with more spacing between them than you would in a UI designed only for mouse and keyboard input. When building a Web application, consider using Cascading Style Sheets (CSS) for layout. This will improve rendering performance and maintainability.

Validation

Designing an effective input and data validation strategy is critical for the security and correct operation of your application. Determine the validation rules for user input as well as for business rules that exist in the presentation layer. Consider the following guidelines when designing your input and data validation strategy:

- Input validation should be handled by the presentation layer, whilst business rule validation should be handled by the business layer. However, if your business and presentation layers are physically separated, business rule validation logic should be mirrored in the presentation layer to improve usability and responsiveness. This can be achieved using meta-data or by using common validation rule components in both layers.

- Design your validation strategy to constrain, reject, and sanitize malicious input. Investigate design patterns and third party libraries that can assist in implementing validation. Identify business rules that are appropriate for validation, such as transaction limits, and implement comprehensive validation to ensure that these rules are not compromised.

- Ensure that you correctly handle validation errors, and avoid exposing sensitive information in error messages. In addition, ensure that you log validation failures to assist in the detection of malicious activity.

For more information on validation techniques, see Chapter 17, "Crosscutting Concerns."

Technology Considerations

For the Microsoft platform, the following guidelines will help you to choose an appropriate implementation technology for the presentation layer. These guidelines also suggest common patterns that are useful for specific types of applications and technologies.

Mobile Applications

Consider the following guidelines when designing a mobile application:

- If you want to build full-featured connected, occasionally connected, or disconnected executable applications that run on a wide range of Microsoft Windows–based devices, consider using the Microsoft Windows Compact Framework.

- If you want to build connected applications that support a wide variety of mobile devices, or require Wireless Application Protocol (WAP), compact HTML (cHTML), or similar rendering formats, consider using ASP.NET for Mobile.

Rich Client Applications

Consider the following guidelines when designing a rich client application:

- If you want to build rich media and graphics capable applications, consider using Windows Presentation Foundation (WPF).
- If you want to build applications that are downloaded from a Web server and execute on a Windows client, consider using XAML Browser Applications (XBAP).
- If you want to build applications that are predominantly document-based, or are used for reporting, consider designing a Microsoft Office Business Application (OBA).
- If you want to take advantage of the extensive range of third party controls, and rapid application development tools, consider using Windows Forms. If you decide to use Windows Forms and you are designing a composite application, consider using the patterns & practices Smart Client Software Factory.
- If you decide to build an application using WPF, consider the following:
  - For composite applications, consider using the patterns & practices Composite Client Application Guidance.
  - Consider using the Presentation Model (Model-View-ViewModel) pattern, which is a variation of Model-View-Controller (MVC) tailored for modern UI development platforms where the View is the responsibility of a designer rather than a classic developer. You can achieve this by implementing DataTemplates over User Controls to give designers more control. Also, consider using WPF Commands to communicate between your View and your Presenter or ViewModel.

Rich Internet Applications

Consider the following guidelines when designing a Rich Internet Application (RIA):

- If you want to build browser-based, connected applications that have broad cross-platform reach, are highly graphical, and support rich media and presentation features, consider using Silverlight.
- If you decide to build an application using Silverlight, consider the following:
  - Consider using the Presentation Model (Model-View-ViewModel) pattern as described earlier in this chapter.
  - If you are designing an application that must last and change, consider using the patterns & practices Composite Client Application Guidance.

Web Applications

Consider the following guidelines when designing a Web application:

- If you want to build applications that are accessed through a Web browser or specialist user agent, consider using ASP.NET.
- If you decide to build an application using ASP.NET, consider the following:
  - Consider using master pages to simplify development and implement a consistent UI across all pages.
  - For increased interactivity and background processing, with fewer page reloads, consider using AJAX with ASP.NET Web Forms.
  - If you want to include islands of rich media content and interactivity, consider using Silverlight controls with ASP.NET.
  - If you want to improve the testability of your application, or implement a more clear separation between your application user interface and business logic, consider using the ASP.NET MVC Framework. This framework supports a model-view-controller based approach to Web application development.

For information on the patterns & practices Smart Client Software Factory and Composite Client Application Guidance, see "patterns & practices Offerings" later in this chapter.

Performance Considerations

Consider the following guidelines to maximize the performance of your presentation layer:

- Design your presentation layer carefully so that it contains the functionality required to deliver a rich and responsive user experience. For example, ensure that your presentation layer is able to validate user input in a responsive way without requiring cross-tier communication. This may require business layer data validation rules to be represented in the presentation layer, perhaps by using meta-data or shared components.
- Interaction between the presentation layer and the business or services layer of the application should be asynchronous. This avoids the possibility of high latency or intermittent connectivity adversely affecting the usability and responsiveness of the application.
- Consider caching data in the presentation layer that will be displayed to the user. For example, you can cache the historical information that is displayed in a stock ticker.

- In general, avoid maintaining session data or caching per-user data unless the number of users is limited, or the total size of the data relatively small. However, if users tend to be active for a while, caching per user data for short periods may be an appropriate technique. Be aware of affinity issues in Web or application farms when storing or caching session data or per user data.

- Always use data paging when querying for information. Do not rely on queries that may return an unbounded volume of data, and use a data page size that is appropriate for the amount of data you will display. Use client-side paging only when absolutely necessary.

- In ASP.NET, use view state cautiously because it increases the volume of data included in each round trip, and can reduce the performance of the application. Consider configuring pages to use read-only sessions, or to not maintain sessions at all, where this is appropriate.

Design Steps for the Presentation Layer

The following steps describe a suggested process for designing the presentation layer of your application. This approach will ensure that you consider all of the relevant factors as you develop your architecture. The steps are:

1. **Identify your client type.** Choose a client type that satisfies your requirements and adheres to the infrastructure and deployment constraints of your organization. For instance, if your users are equipped with mobile devices, and will be connected intermittently to the network, a mobile client is probably the best choice. For information that will help you choose the appropriate type of client, see Chapter 20, "Choosing an Application Type."

2. **Choose your presentation layer technology.** Identify the functionality for your UI and the presentation layer in general and choose a UI technology that meets these requirements and is available for the type of client you have chosen. At this point, if the available technologies are not suitable, you may need to reconsider your choice of client type. For information on the technologies available for each application type, see Appendix B "Presentation Technology Matrix."

3. **Design your user interface.** Consider if you want your UI to be modular, and identify how you will enforce separation of concerns in your presentation layer. Consider separated presentation patterns such as Presentation Model, MVC, and MVP. Use the guidelines in the sections on Composition, Navigation, User Experience, and User Interface earlier in this chapter to ensure that you design a suitable UI that meets your requirements. For details of the types of components that you may choose to use in your design, see Chapter 11, "Designing Presentation Components."

4. **Determine your data validation strategy.** Use data validation techniques to protect your system from untrusted input. Also, determine an appropriate strategy for exception handling and logging. For more details of implementing appropriate strategies for validation, exception handling, and logging see Chapter 17, "Crosscutting Concerns."

5. **Determine your business logic strategy.** Factor out your business logic to decouple it from your presentation layer code. This will improve the maintainability of your application, making it easier to modify your business logic without affecting the presentation layer. The technique you choose depends on the complexity of your application; the following are the common approaches:

   - **UI Validation.** For simple applications where the business logic is used only to validate user input, you may decide to locate the business logic in the UI components. However, be careful not to mix any business logic not concerned with validation within your UI components.

   - **Business Process Components.** For applications that are more complex, applications that support transactions, or applications that contain basic business logic that extends beyond UI validation, consider locating the business logic in separate components that are used by the UI components.

   - **Domain Model.** For complex enterprise applications, where the business logic is shared among multiple applications, consider separating the business components into their own logical layer. This allows you to deploy the business layer onto a separate physical tier to improve scalability and support reuse by other applications.

   - **Rules Engine.** In applications that must support complex validation, process orchestrations, and domain logic, consider placing your business logic in a rules engine such as Microsoft BizTalk® Server.

6. **Determine your strategy for communication with other layers.** If your application has multiple layers, such as a data access layer and a business layer, determine a strategy for communication between your presentation layer and other layers. If you have a separate business layer, your presentation layer will communicate with the business layer. If you do not have a business layer, your presentation layer will communicate directly with the data access layer. Use the following techniques to access other layers:

   - **Direct method calls.** If the layer with which you are communicating is on the same physical tier as the presentation layer, you can make direct method calls.

   - **Web services.** Use a Web service interface if you want to share the data access or business logic with other applications, if the business layer or data access layer are deployed on a separate tier from presentation layer, or if decoupling is important. Consider WCF using the TCP protocol if your business logic or data access logic will be consumed by the presentation layer within your intranet. Consider WCF using the HTTP protocol if your business logic or data access logic will be consumed by your presentation layer across the Internet. Consider asynchronous communication using WCF and message queuing if your business logic or data access logic performs long-running calls.

   For more details of implementing appropriate communication strategies, see Chapter 18, "Communication and Messaging."

Relevant Design Patterns

Key patterns for the presentation layer are organized by categories as detailed in the following table. Consider using these patterns when making design decisions.

Category	Relevant patterns
Caching	**Cache Dependency.** Use external information to determine the state of data stored in a cache. **Page Cache.** Improve the response time for dynamic Web pages that are accessed frequently, but change less often and consume a large amount of system resources to construct.

Category	Relevant patterns
Composition and Layout	**Composite View.** Combine individual views into a composite representation. **Presentation Model.** (Model-View-ViewModel) pattern. A variation of Model-View-Controller (MVC) tailored for modern UI development platforms where the View is the responsibility of a designer rather than a classic developer. **Template View.** Implement a common template view, and derive or construct views using this template view. **Transform View.** Transform the data passed to the presentation tier into HTML for display in the UI. **Two-Step View.** Transform the model data into a logical presentation without any specific formatting, and then convert that logical presentation to add the actual formatting required.
Exception Management	**Exception Shielding.** Prevent a service from exposing information about its internal implementation when an exception occurs.
Navigation	**Application Controller.** A single point for handling screen navigation. **Front Controller.** A Web only pattern that consolidates request handling by channeling all requests through a single handler object, which can be modified at run time with decorators. **Page Controller.** Accept input from the request and handle it for a specific page or action on a Web site. **Command.** Encapsulate request processing in a separate command object with a common execution interface.
User Experience	**Asynchronous Callback.** Execute long-running tasks on a separate thread that executes in the background, and provide a function for the thread to call back into when the task is complete. **Chain of Responsibility.** Avoid coupling the sender of a request to its receiver by giving more than one object a chance to handle the request.

For more information on the Page Cache pattern, see "*Enterprise Solution Patterns Using Microsoft .NET*" at http://msdn.microsoft.com/en-us/library/ms998469.aspx.

For more information on the Application Controller, Front Controller, Page Controller, Template View, Transform View, and Two-Step View patterns, see Fowler, Martin. *Patterns of Enterprise Application Architecture*. Addison-Wesley, 2002. Or at http://martinfowler.com/eaaCatalog.

For more information on the Composite View and Presentation Model patterns, see "*Patterns in the Composite Application Library*" at http://msdn.microsoft.com/en-us/library/dd458924.aspx.

For more information on the Chain of Responsibility pattern, see "*Patterns in Practice*" at http://msdn.microsoft.com/en-us/magazine/cc546578.aspx.

For more information on the Command pattern, see Chapter 5, "Behavioral Patterns" in Gamma, Erich, Richard Helm, Ralph Johnson, and John Vlissides. *Design Patterns: Elements of Reusable Object-Oriented Software.* Addison Wesley Professional, 1995.

For more information on the Asynchronous Callback pattern, see *"Creating a Simplified Asynchronous Call Pattern for Windows Forms Applications"* at http://msdn.microsoft.com/en-us/library/ms996483.aspx.

For more information on the Exception Shielding and Entity Translator patterns, see *"Useful Patterns for Services"* at http://msdn.microsoft.com/en-us/library/cc304800.aspx.

patterns & practices Offerings

For more information on relevant offerings available from the Microsoft patterns & practices group, see the following resources:

- *"Composite Client Application Guidance"* at http://msdn.microsoft.com/en-us/library/cc707819.aspx.
- *"Smart Client Software Factory"* at http://msdn.microsoft.com/en-us/library/aa480482.aspx.
- *"Web Client Software Factory"* at http://msdn.microsoft.com/en-us/library/bb264518.aspx.

Additional Resources

To more easily access Web resources, see the online version of the bibliography at: http://www.microsoft.com/architectureguide.

- *"Choosing the Right Presentation Layer Architecture"* at http://msdn.microsoft.com/en-us/library/aa480039.aspx.
- *""memcached"* distributed memory object caching system at http://www.danga.com/memcached/.
- *"Microsoft Inductive User Interface Guidelines"* at http://msdn.microsoft.com/en-us/library/ms997506.aspx.
- *"Microsoft Project Code Named Velocity"* at http://msdn.microsoft.com/en-us/data/cc655792.aspx.
- *"User Interface Text Guidelines"* at http://msdn.microsoft.com/en-us/library/bb158574.aspx.
- *"Design and Implementation Guidelines for Web Clients"* at http://msdn.microsoft.com/en-us/library/ms978631.aspx.
- *"Web Presentation Patterns"* at http://msdn.microsoft.com/en-us/library/ms998516.aspx.

7

Business Layer Guidelines

Overview

This chapter describes the key guidelines for designing the business layer of an application. It will help you to understand how the business layer fits into the typical layered application architecture, the components it usually contains, and the key issues you face when designing the business layer. You will see guidelines for design, the recommended design steps, relevant design patterns, and technology options. Figure 1 shows how the business layer fits into a typical application architecture.

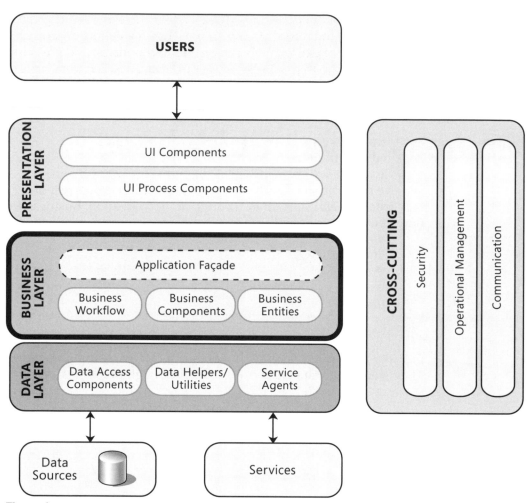

Figure 1
A typical application showing the business layer and the components it may contain

The business layer will usually include the following:

- **Application façade.** This optional component typically provides a simplified interface to the business logic components, often by combining multiple business operations into a single operation that makes it easier to use the business logic. It reduces dependencies because external callers do not need to know details of the business components and the relationships between them.

- **Business Logic components.** Business logic is defined as any application logic that is concerned with the retrieval, processing, transformation, and management of application data; application of business rules and policies; and ensuring data consistency and validity. To maximize reuse opportunities, business logic components should not contain any behavior or application logic that is specific to a use case or user story. Business logic components can be further subdivided into the following two categories:

    - **Business Workflow components.** After the UI components collect the required data from the user and pass it to the business layer, the application can use this data to perform a business process. Many business processes involve multiple steps that must be performed in the correct order, and may interact with each other through an orchestration. Business workflow components define and coordinate long running, multistep business processes, and can be implemented using business process management tools. They work with business process components that instantiate and perform operations on workflow components. For more information on business workflow components, see Chapter 14, "Designing Workflow Components."

    - **Business Entity components.** Business entities, or—more generally—business objects, encapsulate the business logic and data necessary to represent real world elements, such as Customers or Orders, within your application. They store data values and expose them through properties; contain and manage business data used by the application; and provide stateful programmatic access to the business data and related functionality. Business entities also validate the data contained within the entity and encapsulate business logic to ensure consistency and to implement business rules and behavior. For more information about business entity components, see Chapter 13, "Designing Business Entities."

For more information about the components commonly used in the business layer, see Chapter 10, "Component Guidelines."

For more information about designing components for the business layer, see Chapter 12, "Designing Business Components."

General Design Considerations

When designing a business layer, the goal of the software architect is to minimize complexity by separating tasks into different areas of concern. For example, logic for processing business rules, business workflows, and business entities all represent different areas of concern. Within each area, the components you design should focus on the specific area, and should not include code related to other areas of concern. Consider the following guidelines when designing the business layer:

- **Decide if you need a separate business layer.** It is always a good idea to use a separate business layer where possible to improve the maintainability of your application. The exception may be applications that have few or no business rules (other than data validation).

- **Identify the responsibilities and consumers of your business layer.** This will help you to decide what tasks the business layer must accomplish, and how you will expose your business layer. Use a business layer for processing complex business rules, transforming data, applying policies, and for validation. If your business layer will be used by your presentation layer and by an external application, you may choose to expose your business layer through a service.

- **Do not mix different types of components in your business layer.** Use a business layer to avoid mixing presentation and data access code with business logic code, to decouple business logic from presentation and data access logic, and to simplify testing of business functionality. Also, use a business layer to centralize common business logic functions and promote reuse.

- **Reduce round trips when accessing a remote business layer.** If the business layer is on a separate physical tier from layers and clients with which it must interact, consider implementing a message-based remote application façade or service layer that combines fine-grained operations into a smaller number of coarse-grained operations. Consider using coarse-grained packages for data transported over the network, such as Data Transfer Objects (DTOs).

- **Avoid tight coupling between layers.** Use the principles of abstraction to minimize coupling when creating an interface for the business layer. Techniques for abstraction include using public object interfaces, common interface definitions, abstract base classes, or messaging. For Web applications, consider a message-based interface between the presentation layer and the business layer. For more details, see Chapter 5, "Layered Application Guidelines."

Specific Design Issues

There are several common issues that you must consider as your develop your design. These issues can be categorized into specific areas of the design. The following sections provide guidelines for the common areas where mistakes are most often made:

- Authentication
- Authorization
- Caching
- Coupling and Cohesion
- Exception Management
- Logging, Auditing, and Instrumentation
- Validation

Authentication

Designing an effective authentication strategy for your business layer is important for the security and reliability of your application. Failure to do so can leave your application vulnerable to spoofing attacks, dictionary attacks, session hijacking, and other types of attacks. Consider the following guidelines when designing an authentication strategy:

- Avoid authentication in the business layer if it will be used only by a presentation layer or by a service layer on the same tier within a trusted boundary. Flow the caller's identity to the business layer only if you must authenticate or authorize based on the original caller's ID.

- If your business layer will be used in multiple applications, using separate user stores, consider implementing a single sign-on mechanism. Avoid designing custom authentication mechanisms; instead, make use of the built-in platform mechanisms whenever possible.

- If the presentation and business layers are deployed on the same machine and you must access resources based on the original caller's access control list (ACL) permissions, consider using impersonation. If the presentation and business layers are deployed to separate machines and you must access resources based on the original caller's ACL permissions, consider using delegation. However, use delegation only when necessary due to the increased use of resources, and additionally, because many environments do not support it. If your security requirements allow, consider authenticating the user at the boundary and using the trusted subsystem approach for calls to lower layers. Alternatively, consider using a claims-based security approach (especially for service-based applications) that takes advantage of federated identity mechanisms and allows target system to authenticate the user's claims.

Authorization

Designing an effective authorization strategy for your business layer is important for the security and reliability of your application. Failure to do so can leave your application vulnerable to information disclosure, data tampering, and elevation of privileges. Consider the following guidelines when designing an authorization strategy:

- Protect resources by applying authorization to callers based on their identity, account groups, roles, or other contextual information. For roles, consider minimizing the granularity of roles as far as possible to reduce the number of permission combinations required.

- Consider using role-based authorization for business decisions; resource-based authorization for system auditing; and claims-based authorization when you need to support federated authorization based on a mixture of information such as identity, role, permissions, rights, and other factors.

- Avoid using impersonation and delegation where possible because it can significantly affect performance and scaling opportunities. It is generally more expensive to impersonate a client on a call than to make the call directly.

- Do not mix authorization code and business processing code in the same components.

- As authorization is typically pervasive throughout the application, ensure that your authorization infrastructure does not impose any significant performance overhead.

Caching

Designing an appropriate caching strategy for your business layer is important for the performance and responsiveness of your application. Use caching to optimize reference data lookups, avoid network round trips, and avoid unnecessary and duplicated processing. As part of your caching strategy, you must decide when and how to load the cache data. To avoid client delays, load the cache asynchronously or by using a batch process. Consider the following guidelines when designing a caching strategy:

- Consider caching static data that will be reused regularly within the business layer, but avoid caching volatile data. Consider caching data that cannot be retrieved from the database quickly and efficiently, but avoid caching very large volumes of data that can slow down processing. Cache only the minimum required.

- Consider caching data in a ready to use format within your business layer.

- Avoid caching sensitive data if possible, or design a mechanism to protect sensitive data in the cache.
- Consider how Web farm deployment will affect the design of your business layer caching solution. If any server in the farm can handle requests from the same client, your caching solution must support the synchronization of cached data.

For more information on caching techniques, see Chapter 17, "Crosscutting Concerns."

Coupling and Cohesion

When designing components for your business layer, ensure that they are highly cohesive, and implement loose coupling between layers. This helps to improve the scalability of your application. Consider the following guidelines when designing for coupling and cohesion:

- Avoid circular dependencies. The business layer should know only about the layer below (the data access layer), and not the layer above (the presentation layer or external applications that access the business layer directly).
- Use abstraction to implement a loosely coupled interface. This can be achieved with interface components, common interface definitions, or shared abstraction where concrete components depend on abstractions and not on other concrete components (the principle of Dependency Inversion). For more information, see the steps for designing a layered structure in Chapter 5, "Layered Application Guidelines."
- Design for tight coupling within the business layer unless dynamic behavior requires loose coupling.
- Design for high cohesion. Components should contain only functionality specifically related to that component. Always avoid mixing data access logic with business logic in your business components.
- Consider using message-based interfaces to expose business components to reduce coupling and allow them to be located on separate physical tiers if required.

Exception Management

Designing an effective exception management solution for your business layer is important for the security and reliability of your application. Failing to do so can leave your application vulnerable to Denial of Service (DoS) attacks, and may allow it to reveal sensitive and critical information about your application. Raising and handling exceptions is an expensive operation, so it is important that your exception management design takes into account the impact on performance. When designing an exception management strategy, consider following guidelines:

- Only catch internal exceptions that you can handle, or if you need to add information. For example, catch data conversion exceptions that can occur when trying to convert null values. Do not use exceptions to control business logic or application flow.

- Design an appropriate exception propagation strategy. For example, allow exceptions to bubble up to boundary layers where they can be logged and transformed as necessary before passing them to the next layer. Consider including a context identifier so that related exceptions can be associated across layers when performing root cause analysis of errors and faults.

- Ensure that you catch exceptions that will not be caught elsewhere (such as in a global error handler), and clean up resources and state after an exception occurs.

- Design an appropriate logging and notification strategy for critical errors and exceptions that logs sufficient detail from exceptions and does not reveal sensitive information.

For more information on exception management techniques, see Chapter 17, "Crosscutting Concerns."

Logging, Auditing, and Instrumentation

Designing a good logging, auditing, and instrumentation solution for your business layer is important for the security and reliability of your application. Failing to do so can leave your application vulnerable to repudiation threats, where users deny their actions. Log files may also be required to prove wrongdoing in legal proceedings. Auditing is generally considered most authoritative if the log information is generated at the precise time of resource access, and by the same routine that accesses the resource. Instrumentation can be implemented using performance counters and events. System monitoring tools can use this instrumentation, or other access points, to provide administrators with information about the state, performance, and health of an application. Consider the following guidelines when designing a logging and instrumentation strategy:

- Centralize the logging, auditing, and instrumentation for your business layer. Consider using a library such as patterns & practices Enterprise Library, or a third party solutions such as the Apache Logging Services "log4Net" or Jarosław Kowalski's "NLog," to implement exception handling and logging features.

- Include instrumentation for system critical and business critical events in your business components.

- Do not store business sensitive information in the log files.

- Ensure that a logging failure does not affect normal business layer functionality.

- Consider auditing and logging all access to functions within business layer.

Validation

Designing an effective validation solution for your business layer is important for the usability and reliability of your application. Failure to do so can leave your application open to data inconsistencies and business rule violations, and a poor user experience. In addition, it may leave your application vulnerable to security issues such as cross-site scripting attacks, SQL injection attacks, buffer overflows, and other types of input attacks. There is no comprehensive definition of what constitutes a valid input or malicious input. In addition, how your application uses input influences the risk of the exploit. Consider the following guidelines when designing a validation strategy:

- Validate all input and method parameters within the business layer, even when input validation occurs in the presentation layer.
- Centralize your validation approach to maximize testability and reuse.
- Constrain, reject, and sanitize user input. In other words, assume that all user input is malicious. Validate input data for length, range, format, and type.

Deployment Considerations

When deploying a business layer, you must consider performance and security issues within the production environment. Consider the following guidelines when deploying a business layer:

- Consider deploying the business layer on the same physical tier as the presentation layer in order to maximize application performance, unless you must use a separate tier due to scalability or security concerns.
- If you must support a remote business layer, consider using the TCP protocol to improve application performance.
- Consider using Internet Protocol Security (IPSec) to protect data passed between physical tiers.
- Consider using Secure Sockets Layer (SSL) encryption to protect calls from business layer components to remote Web services.

Design Steps for the Business Layer

When designing a business layer, you must also take into account the design requirements for the main constituents of the layer, such as business components, business entities, and business workflow components. This section briefly explains the main activities involved in designing the business layer itself. Perform the following key steps when designing your data layer:

1. **Create a high level design for your business layer.** Identify the consumers of your business layer, such as the presentation layer, a service layer, or other applications. This will help you to determine how to expose your business layer. Next, determine the security requirements for your business layer, and the validation requirements and validation strategy. Use the guidelines in the "Specific Design Issues" section earlier in this chapter to ensure that you consider all of the relevant factors when creating the high level design.

2. **Design your business components.** There are several types of business components you can use when designing and implementing an application. Examples of these components include business process components, utility components, and helper components. Different aspects of your application design, transactional requirements, and processing rules affect the design you choose for your business components. For more information, see Chapter 12, "Designing Business Components."

3. **Design your business entity components.** Business entities are used to contain and manage business data used by an application. Business entities should provide validation of the data contained within the entity. In addition, business entities provide properties and operations used to access and initialize data contained within the entity. For more information, see Chapter 13, "Designing Business Entities."

4. **Design your workflow components.** There are many scenarios where tasks must be completed in an ordered way based on the completion of specific steps, or coordinated through human interaction. These requirements can be mapped to key workflow scenarios. You must understand how requirements and rules affect your options for implementing workflow components. For more information, see Chapter 14, "Designing Workflow Components."

For more information about designing and using components in your applications, see Chapter 10, "Component Guidelines."

Relevant Design Patterns

Key patterns are organized by key categories, as detailed in the following table. Consider using these patterns when making design decisions for each category.

Category	Relevant patterns
Business Components	**Application Façade.** Centralize and aggregate behavior to provide a uniform service layer. **Chain of Responsibility.** Avoid coupling the sender of a request to its receiver by allowing more than one object to handle the request. **Command.** Encapsulate request processing in a separate command object with a common execution interface.
Business Entities	**Domain Model.** A set of business objects that represents the entities in a domain and the relationships between them. **Entity Translator.** An object that transforms message data types to business types for requests, and reverses the transformation for responses. **Table Module.** A single component that handles the business logic for all rows in a database table or view.
Workflows	**Data-Driven Workflow.** A workflow that contains tasks whose sequence is determined by the values of data in the workflow or the system. **Human Workflow.** A workflow that involves tasks performed manually by humans. **Sequential Workflow.** A workflow that contains tasks that follow a sequence, where one task is initiated after completion of the preceding task. **State-Driven Workflow.** A workflow that contains tasks whose sequence is determined by the state of the system.

For more information on the Façade pattern, see Chapter 4, "Structural Patterns" in Gamma, Erich, Richard Helm, Ralph Johnson, and John Vlissides. Design Patterns: Elements of Reusable Object-Oriented Software. Addison Wesley Professional, 1995.

For more information on the Chain of Responsibility pattern, see *"Patterns in Practice"* at http://msdn.microsoft.com/en-us/magazine/cc546578.aspx.

For more information on the Command pattern, see 5, "Behavioral Patterns" in Gamma, Erich, Richard Helm, Ralph Johnson, and John Vlissides. Design Patterns: Elements of Reusable Object-Oriented Software. Addison Wesley Professional, 1995.

For more information on the Entity Translator pattern, see *"Useful Patterns for Services"* at http://msdn.microsoft.com/en-us/library/cc304800.aspx.

For more information on the Data-Driven Workflow, Human Workflow, Sequential Workflow, and State-Driven Workflow, see *"Windows Workflow Foundation Overview"* at http://msdn.microsoft.com/en-us/library/ms734631.aspx and *"Workflow Patterns"* at http://www.workflowpatterns.com/.

patterns & practices Offerings

For more information on relevant offerings available from the Microsoft patterns & practices group, see the following resources:

- *"Enterprise Library"* at http://msdn.microsoft.com/en-us/library/cc467894.aspx.
- *"Unity"* (dependency injection mechanism) at http://msdn.microsoft.com/en-us/library/dd203101.aspx.

Additional Resources

To more easily access Web resources, see the online version of the bibliography at: http://www.microsoft.com/architectureguide.

For more information on integrating business layers, see *"Integration Patterns"* at http://msdn.microsoft.com/en-us/library/ms978729.aspx.

For more information on Apache Logging Services "log4Net," see http://logging.apache.org/log4net/index.html.

For more information on Jarosław Kowalski's "NLog," see http://www.nlog-project.org/introduction.html.

8

Data Layer Guidelines

Overview

This chapter describes the key guidelines for designing the data layer of an application. It will help you to understand how the data layer fits into the typical layered application architecture, the components it usually contains, and the key issues you face when designing the data layer. You will see guidelines for design, the recommended design steps, relevant design patterns, and technology options. Figure 1 shows how the data layer fits into a typical application architecture.

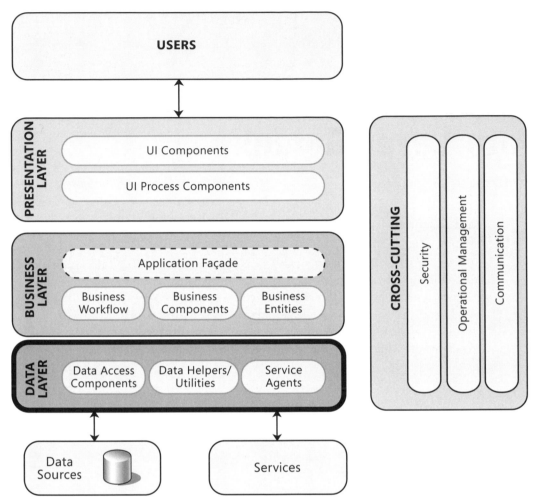

Figure 1
A typical application showing the data layer and the components it may contain

The data layer may include the following:

- **Data Access components.** These components abstract the logic required to access the underlying data stores. They centralize common data access functionality in order to make the application easier to configure and maintain. Some data access frameworks may require the developer to identify and implement common data access logic in separate reusable helper or utility data access components. Other data access frameworks, including many Object/Relational Mapping (O/RM) frameworks, implement such components automatically, reducing the amount of data access code that the developer must write.

- **Service agents.** When a business component must access data provided by an external service, you might need to implement code to manage the semantics of communicating with that particular service. Service agents implement data access components that isolate the varying requirements for calling services from your application, and may provide additional services such as caching, offline support, and basic mapping between the format of the data exposed by the service and the format your application requires.

For more information about the components commonly used in the data layer, see Chapter 10, "Component Guidelines." For more information about creating data access components, see Chapter 15, "Designing Data Components."

General Design Considerations

Your data access layer must meet the requirements of your application, perform efficiently and securely, and be easy to maintain and extend as business requirements change. When designing the data layer, consider the following general design guidelines:

- **Choose an appropriate data access technology.** The choice of data access technology depends on the type of data you must handle, and how you intent to manipulate that data within the application. Certain technologies are better suited to specific scenarios. The Appendix "Data Access Technology Matrix" at the end of this guide discusses these options and enumerates the benefits and considerations for each data access technology.

- **Use abstraction to implement a loosely coupled interface to the data access layer.** This can be accomplished by defining interface components, such as a gateway with well-known inputs and outputs, which translate requests into a format understood by components within the layer. In addition, you can use interface types or abstract base classes to define a shared abstraction that must be implemented by interface components. For more information about layer abstraction, see Chapter 5, "Layered Application Guidelines."

- **Encapsulate data access functionality within the data access layer.** The data access layer should hide the details of data source access. It should be responsible for managing connections, generating queries, and mapping application entities to data source structures. Consumers of the data access layer interact through abstract interfaces using application entities such as custom objects, Typed DataSets, and XML, and should have no knowledge of the internal details of the data access layer. Separating concerns in this way assists in application development and maintenance.

- **Decide how to map application entities to data source structures.** The type of entity you use in your application is the main factor in deciding how to map those entities to data source structures. Common design approaches follow the Domain Model or Table Module patterns or use Object/Relational Mapping (O/RM) frameworks, though you may implement business entities using different formats. You must identify a strategy for populating the business entities or data structures from the data source and making them available to the business layer or presentation layer of the application. For more information about the Domain Model or Table Module patterns, see the section "Relevant Design Patterns" near the end of this chapter. For more information about business entities and data formats, see Chapter 13, "Designing Business Entities."

- **Consider consolidating data structures.** If you are exposing data through services, consider using Data Transfer Objects (DTOs) to help you organize the data into unified structures. In addition, DTOs encourage coarse-grained operations while providing a structure that is designed to move data across different boundary layers. DTOs can also span business entities for aggregate operations. If you are using the Table Data Gateway or Active Record pattern, you may consider using a DataTable to represent the data.

- **Decide how you will manage connections.** As a rule, the data access layer should create and manage all connections to all data sources required by the application. You must choose an appropriate method for storing and protecting connection information, perhaps by encrypting sections of the configuration file or limiting storage of configuration information to the server, in order to conform to corporate security requirements. For more information, see Chapter 15, "Designing Data Components."

- **Determine how you will handle data exceptions.** The data access layer should catch and (at least initially) handle all exceptions associated with data sources and CRUD (Create, Read, Update, and Delete) operations. Exceptions concerning the data itself, and data source access and timeout errors, should be handled in this layer and passed to other layers only if the failures affect application responsiveness or functionality.

- **Consider security risks.** The data access layer should protect against attacks that try to steal or corrupt data, and protect the mechanisms used to gain access to the data source. For example, sanitize error and exception information so that data source information is not revealed, and use least privilege accounts to restrict privileges to only those needed to perform the operations required by the application. Even if the data source itself has the ability to limit privileges, security should be implemented in the data access layer as well as in the data source. Database access should be through parameterized queries to prevent SQL injection attacks succeeding. Never use string concatenation to build dynamic queries from user input data.

- **Reduce round trips.** Consider batching commands into a single database operation.
- **Consider performance and scalability objectives.** Scalability and performance objectives for the data access layer should be taken into account during design. For example, when designing an Internet-based commerce application, data layer performance is likely to be a bottleneck for the application. When data layer performance is critical, use profiling to understand and then reduce or resolve expensive data operations.

Specific Design Issues

There are several common issues that you must consider as your develop your design. These issues can be categorized into specific areas of the design. The following sections provide guidelines for the common areas where mistakes are most often made:

- Batching
- Binary Large Objects (BLOBs)
- Connections
- Data Format
- Exception Management
- Object Relational Mapping
- Queries
- Stored Procedures
- Stored Procedures vs. Dynamic SQL
- Transactions
- Validation
- XML

Batching

Batching database commands can improve the performance of your data layer. Each request to the database execution environment incurs an overhead. Batching can reduce the total overhead by increasing throughput and decreasing latency. Batching similar queries can improve performance because the database caches and can reuse a query execution plan for a similar query. Consider the following guidelines when designing batching:

- Consider using batched commands to reduce round trips to the database and minimize network traffic. However, for maximum benefit, only batch similar queries. Batching dissimilar or random queries does not provide the same level of reduction in overhead.

- Consider using batched commands and a **DataReader** to load or copy multiple sets of data. However, when loading large volumes of file-based data into the database, consider using database bulk copy utilities instead.

- Do not perform transactions on long-running batch commands that will lock database resources.

Binary Large Objects

When data is stored and retrieved as a single stream, it can be considered to be a binary large object, or BLOB. A BLOB may have structure within it, but that structure is not apparent to the database that stores it or the data layer that reads and writes it. Databases can store the BLOB data or can store pointers to them within the database. The BLOB data is usually stored in a file system if not stored directly in the database. BLOBs are typically used to store image data, but can also be used to store binary representations of objects. Consider the following guidelines when designing for BLOBs:

- Consider whether you need to store BLOB data in a database. Modern databases are much better at handling BLOB data, providing you choose an appropriate column data type, and can provide maintainability, versioning, operations, and storage of related metadata. However, consider if it is more practical to store it on disk and store just a link to the data in the database.

- Consider using BLOBs to simplify synchronization of large binary objects between servers.

- Consider whether you will need to search the BLOB data. If so, create and populate other searchable database fields instead of parsing the BLOB data.

- When retrieving the BLOB, cast it to the appropriate type for manipulation within your business or presentation layer.

Connections

Connections to data sources are a fundamental part of the data layer. All data source connections should be managed by the data layer. Creating and managing connections uses valuable resources in both the data layer and the data source. To maximize performance and security, consider the following guidelines when designing for data layer connections:

- In general, open connections as late as possible and close them as early as possible. Never hold connections open for excessive periods.

- Perform transactions through a single connection whenever possible.

- Take advantage of connection pooling by using a trusted subsystem security model, and avoiding impersonation or the use of individual identities if possible.

- For security reasons, avoid using a System or User Data Source Name (DSN) to store connection information.

- Consider if you should design retry logic to manage the situation where the connection to the data source is lost or times out. However, if the underlying cause is something like a resource contention issue, retrying the operation may exacerbate the problem leading to scaling issues. See Chapter 15, "Designing Data Components" for more information.

Data Format

Choosing the appropriate data format provides interoperability with other applications, and facilitates serialized communications across different processes and physical machines. Data format and serialization are also important in order to allow the storage and retrieval of application state by the business layer. Consider the following guidelines when designing your data format:

- Consider using XML for interoperability with other systems and platforms, or when working with data structures that can change over time.

- Consider using **DataSets** for disconnected scenarios in simple CRUD-based applications.

- If you must transfer data across physical boundaries, consider serialization and interoperability requirements. For example, consider how you will serialize custom business objects, how you will translate them into Data Transfer Objects (DTOs) where this is a requirement, and what formats the receiving layer can accept.

For more information on data formats, see Chapter 15, "Designing Data Components." For information on designing and using components in your application, see Chapter 10, "Component Guidelines."

Exception Management

Design a centralized exception management strategy so that exceptions are caught and thrown consistently in your data layer. If possible, centralize exception handling logic in components that implement crosscutting concerns in your application. Pay particular attention to exceptions that propagate through trust boundaries and to other layers or tiers. Design for unhandled exceptions so they do not result in application reliability issues or exposure of sensitive application information. Consider the following guidelines when designing your exception management strategy:

- Identify the exceptions that should be caught and handled in the data access layer. For example, deadlocks and connection issues can often be resolved within the data layer. However, some exceptions, such as and concurrency violations, should be surfaced to the user for resolution.

- Design an appropriate exception propagation strategy. For example, allow exceptions to propagate to boundary layers where they can be logged and transformed as necessary before passing them to the next layer. Consider including a context identifier so that related exceptions can be associated across layers when performing root cause analysis of errors and faults.

- Consider implementing a retry process for operations where data source errors or timeouts occur, where it is safe to do so.

- Ensure that you catch exceptions that will not be caught elsewhere (such as in a global error handler), and clean up resources and state after an exception occurs.

- Design an appropriate logging and notification strategy for critical errors and exceptions that logs sufficient detail from exceptions and does not reveal sensitive information.

Object Relational Mapping

When designing an object oriented (OO) application, consider the impedance mismatch between the OO model and the relational model, and the factors that can make it difficult to translate between them. For example, encapsulation in OO designs, where fields are hidden, may contradict the public nature of properties in a database. Other examples of impedance mismatch include differences in the data types, structural differences, transactional differences, and differences in how data is manipulated. The two common ways to handle these mismatches are design patterns for data access such as Repository, and Object/Relational Mapping (O/RM) tools. A Domain Driven Design approach, which is based on modeling entities based on objects within a domain, is often an appropriate choice. For information about Domain Driven Design, see Chapter 3, "Architectural Patterns and Styles" and Chapter 13, "Designing Business Entities."

Consider the following guidelines when designing for object relational mapping:

- Consider using a framework that provides an Object/Relational Mapping (O/RM) layer between domain entities and the database. Modern O/RM solutions are available that can significantly reduce the amount of custom code required.

- If you are working in a greenfield environment, where you have full control over the database schema, you can use an O/RM tool to generate a schema to support the defined object model, and to provide a mapping between the database and domain entities.

- If you are working in a brownfield environment, where you must work with an existing database schema, you can use an O/RM tool to help you to map between the domain model and the existing relational model.

- If you are working with a smaller application or do not have access to O/RM tools, implement a common data access pattern such as Repository. With the Repository pattern, the repository objects allow you to treat domain entities as if they were located in memory.

- When working with Web applications or services, group entities and support options that will partially load domain entities with only the required data—a process usually referred to as lazy loading. This allows applications to handle the higher user load required to support stateless operations, and limit the use of resources by avoiding holding initialized domain models for each user in memory.

Queries

Queries are the primary data manipulation operations for the data layer. They are the mechanism that translates requests from the application into CRUD actions on the database. As queries are so essential, they should be optimized to maximize database performance and throughput. Consider the following guidelines when using queries in your data layer:

- Use parameterized SQL queries and typed parameters to mitigate security issues and reduce the chance of SQL injection attacks succeeding. Do not use string concatenation to build dynamic queries from user input data.

- Consider using objects to build queries. For example, implement the Query Object pattern or use the parameterized query support provided by ADO.NET. Also consider optimizing the data schema in the database for query execution.

- When building dynamic SQL queries, avoid mixing business processing logic with logic used to generate the SQL statement. Doing so can lead to code that is very difficult to maintain and debug.

Stored Procedures

In the past, stored procedures represented a performance improvement over dynamic SQL statements. However, with modern database engines, the performance of stored procedures and dynamic SQL statements (using parameterized queries) are generally similar. When considering the use of stored procedures, the primary factors are abstraction, maintainability, and your environment. This section contains guidelines to help you design your application when using stored procedures. For guidance on choosing between using stored procedures and dynamic SQL statements, see the section that follows.

In terms of security and performance for stored procedures, the primary guidelines are to use typed parameters and avoid dynamic SQL within the stored procedure. Parameters are one of the factors that influence the use of cached query plans instead of rebuilding the query plan from scratch. When parameter types and the number of parameters change, new query execution plans are generated, which can reduce performance. Consider the following guidelines when designing stored procedures:

- Use typed parameters as input values to the procedure and output parameters to return single values. Consider using XML parameters or table-value parameters for passing lists or tabular data. Do not format data for display in stored procedures; instead, return the appropriate types and perform formatting in the presentation layer.

- Use parameter or database variables if it is necessary to generate dynamic SQL within a stored procedure. However, bear in mind that using dynamic SQL in stored procedures can affect performance, security, and maintainability.

- Avoid the creation of temporary tables while processing data. However, if temporary tables must be used, consider creating them in memory instead of on disk.

- Implement appropriate error handling designs, and return errors that the application code can handle.

Stored Procedures vs. Dynamic SQL

The choice between stored procedures and dynamic SQL focuses primarily on the use of SQL statements dynamically generated in code instead of SQL implemented within a stored procedure in the database. When choosing between stored procedures and dynamic SQL, you must consider the abstraction requirements, maintainability, and environment constraints. In addition, in many cases, the choice between stored procedures and dynamic SQL queries includes developer preference or skill set.

The main advantages of stored procedures are that they provide an abstraction layer to the database, which can minimize the impact on application code when the database schema changes. Security is also easier to implement and manage because you can restrict access to everything except the stored procedure, and take advantage of fine-grained security features supported by most databases (though be aware that this may affect your ability to take advantage of connection pooling).

The main advantages of dynamic SQL statements are that they are often considered more flexible than stored procedures, and can enable more rapid development. Many Object/Relational Mapping (O/RM) frameworks generate dynamic queries for you, considerably reducing the amount of code developers must write.

Consider the following guidelines when choosing between stored procedures and dynamic SQL:

- If you have a small application that has a single client and few business rules, dynamic SQL is often the best choice.

- If you have a larger application that has multiple clients, consider how you can achieve the required abstraction. Decide where that abstraction should exist: at the database in the form of stored procedures, or in the data layer of your application in the form of data access patterns or O/RM products.

- For data-intensive operations, stored procedures allow you to perform the operations closer to the data, which can improve performance.

- To minimize application code changes when the database schema changes, you might consider using stored procedures to provide access to the database. This can help to isolate and minimize changes to application code during schema normalization or optimization. Changes to inputs and outputs of a stored procedure can affect application code, but these changes can often be isolated in specific components that access the stored procedure. Object/Relational Mapping (O/RM) frameworks can also help you to isolate and minimize application code changes when schemas are updated.

- When considering dynamic SQL queries, you should understand the impact that changes to database schemas will have on your application. As a result, you should implement the data access layer in such a way that it decouples business components from the execution of database queries. Several patterns, such as Query Object and Repository, can be used to provide this separation. Object/Relational Mapping (O/RM) frameworks can help to achieve a clean separation between your business components and the execution of database queries.

- Consider the team you have for development of the application. If you do not have a team that is familiar with database programming, consider tools or patterns that are more familiar to your development staff.

- Consider debugging support. Dynamic SQL is easier for application developers to debug.

Transactions

A transaction is an exchange of sequential information and associated actions that are treated as an atomic unit in order to satisfy a request and ensure database integrity. A transaction is only considered complete if all information and actions are complete, and the associated database changes are made permanent. Transactions support undo (rollback) database actions following an error, which helps to preserve the integrity of data in the database.

It is important to identify the appropriate concurrency model and determine how you will manage transactions. You can choose between an optimistic model and a pessimistic model for concurrency. With *optimistic concurrency*, locks are not held on data and updates require code to check, usually against a timestamp, that the data has not changed since it was last retrieved. With *pessimistic concurrency*, data is locked and cannot be updated by another operation until the lock is released.

Consider the following guidelines when designing transactions:

- Consider transaction boundaries, so that retries and composition are possible, and enable transactions only when you need them. Simple queries may not require an explicit transaction, but you should make sure that you are aware of your database's default transaction commit and isolation level behavior. By default Microsoft SQL Server® database executes each individual SQL statement as an individual transaction (auto-commit transaction mode).

- Keep transactions as short as possible to minimize the amount of time that locks are held. Try to avoid using locks for long-running transactions, or locking during access to shared data, which may block access to data by other code. Avoid the use of exclusive locks, which can cause contention and deadlocks.

- Use the appropriate isolation level, which defines how and when changes become available to other operations. The tradeoff is data consistency versus contention. A high isolation level will offer higher data consistency at the price of overall concurrency. A lower isolation level improves performance by lowering contention at the cost of consistency.

- If you are using the **System.Transactions** namespace classes, consider using the implicit model provided by the **TransactionScope** object in the **System.Transactions** namespace. Although implicit transactions are not as fast as manual, or explicit, transactions, they are easier to develop and lead to middle tier solutions that are flexible and easy to maintain. When using manual transactions, consider implementing the transaction within a stored procedure.

- Where you cannot apply a commit or rollback, or if you use a long-running transaction, implement compensating methods to revert the data store to its previous state in case an operation within the transaction fails.

- If you must execute multiple queries against a database, consider the use of multiple active result sets (MARS), which provides support for multiple forward only, read only results sets and allows multiple queries to be executed using the same connection. MARS can be useful in transaction-heavy concurrent applications.

Validation

Designing an effective input and data validation strategy is critical for the security of your application. Determine the validation rules for data received from other layers and from third-party components, as well as from the database or data store. Understand your trust boundaries so that you can validate any data that crosses these boundaries. Consider the following guidelines when designing a validation strategy:

- Validate all data received by the data layer from all callers. Ensure that you correctly handle NULL values, and filter out invalid characters.
- Consider the purpose to which data will be put when designing validation. For example, user input used in the creation of dynamic SQL should be examined for characters or patterns that occur in SQL injection attacks.
- Return informative error messages if validation fails.

For more information on validation techniques, see Chapter 17, "Crosscutting Concerns."

XML

Extensible Markup Language (XML) is useful for interoperability and for maintaining data structure outside of the database. For performance reasons, be careful when using XML for very large volumes of data. If you must handle large volumes of data as XML, use attribute-based schemas where data values are stored as attributes, instead of element-based schemas that store the data values as the values of elements, and are consequently larger. Consider the following guidelines when designing for the use of XML:

- Consider using XML readers and writers to access XML formatted data, especially for extremely large sets of XML data. If you need to interact with a relational database, consider using objects that support this functionality, such as the ADO.NET **DataSet**. Use common settings for whitespace and comment handling on XML readers and writers.
- Consider using an XML schema to define formats and to provide validation for data stored and transmitted as XML. Consider using custom validators for complex data parameters within your XML schema. However, bear in mind that validation will impose a performance penalty.
- Store XML in typed columns in the database, if available, for maximum performance. Set up indexes (if your database supports them) if you will be regularly querying the XML data.

Technology Considerations

The following guidelines will help you to choose an appropriate implementation technology and techniques, depending on the type of application you are designing and the requirements of that application:

- If you require basic support for queries and parameters, consider using ADO.NET objects directly.

- If you require support for more complex data access scenarios, or want to simplify your data access code, consider using the Enterprise Library Data Access Application Block. For more details about Enterprise Library, see Appendix F, "patterns & practices Enterprise Library."

- If you are building a data driven Web application with pages based on the data model of the underlying database, consider using ASP.NET Dynamic Data.

- If you want to manipulate XML-formatted data, consider using the classes in the **System.Xml** namespace and its subsidiary namespaces, or Linq to XML (XLinq).

- If you are using ASP.NET to create user interfaces, consider using a **DataReader** to access data to maximize rendering performance. **DataReaders** are ideal for read-only, forward-only operations in which each row is processed quickly.

- If you are accessing SQL Server, consider using classes in the ADO.NET **SqlClient** namespace to maximize performance.

- If you are accessing SQL Server 2008, consider using a FILESTREAM for greater flexibility in the storage of and access to BLOB data.

- If you are designing an object-oriented business layer based on the Domain Model pattern, consider using an Object/Relational Mapping (O/RM) framework, such as the ADO.NET Entity Framework or the open source NHibernate framework (see Additional Resources at the end of this chapter for more information).

For guidance on choosing a data access technology, see Chapter 15, "Designing Data Components." For information about the data access technologies available on the Microsoft platform, see the Appendix C "Data Access Technology Matrix."

Performance Considerations

Performance is a function of both your data layer design and your database design. Consider both together when tuning your system for maximum data throughput. Consider the following guidelines when designing for performance:

- Use connection pooling and tune performance based on results obtained by running simulated load scenarios.

- Consider tuning isolation levels for data queries. If you are building an application with high-throughput requirements, special data operations may be performed at lower isolation levels than the rest of the transaction. Combining isolation levels can have a negative impact on data consistency, so you must carefully analyze this option on a case by case basis.

- Consider batching commands to reduce the number of round trips to the database server.

- Consider using optimistic concurrency with nonvolatile data to mitigate the cost of locking data in the database. This avoids the overhead of locking database rows, including the connection that must be kept open during a lock.

- If using a **DataReader**, use ordinal lookups for faster performance.

Security Considerations

The data layer should protect the database against attacks that try to steal or corrupt data. It should allow only as much access to the various parts of the data source as is required. The data layer should also protect the mechanisms used to gain access to the data source. Consider the following guidelines when designing for security:

- When using SQL Server, consider using Windows authentication with an implementation of the trusted subsystem model. For information on the trusted subsystem model, see Chapter 19, "Physical Tiers and Deployment."

- Encrypt connection strings in configuration files instead of using a System or User Data Source Name (DSN).

- When storing passwords, use a salted hash instead of an encrypted version of the password.

- Require that callers send identity information to the data layer for auditing purposes.

- Use parameterized SQL queries and typed parameters to mitigate security issues and reduce the chance of SQL injection attacks succeeding. Do not use string concatenation to build dynamic queries from user input data.

Deployment Considerations

When deploying the data layer, the goal of the software architect is to consider the performance and security issues in the production environment. Consider the following guidelines when deploying your data layer:

- Locate the data access layer on the same tier as the business layer to improve application performance unless scalability or security concerns prevent this.

- If you must support a remote data access layer, consider using the TCP protocol to improve performance.

- Consider locating the data access layer on a different server to the database. The physical characteristics of a database server are often optimized for that role, and will rarely match the optimum operating characteristics for the data layer. The combination of both on one physical tier is extremely likely to reduce application performance.

Design Steps for the Data Layer

A correct approach to designing the data layer will reduce development time and assist in maintenance of the data layer after the application is deployed. This section briefly outlines an effective design approach for the data layer. Perform the following key steps when designing your data layer:

1. Create an overall design for your data access layer. Identify data source constraints by determining if you are working with a greenfield or brownfield environment, and determine the associated restrictions. In addition, if any new development is required, consider how it will coexist with the data source in its current state.

   - In a **greenfield** scenario, where there is no prior work related to the data source, you have full control over the schema used by your data source. Restrictions are based on the data source itself.

   - In a **brownfield** scenario, you do not have control over data source schemas, and the data source could be anything from a database to gateway components used to interact with existing components. You must understand the complexity and constraints of the existing business. For example, you must determine if there a predefined operational data store or other restriction that will prevent you from changing the existing schema. However, you can usually add new tables or views to an existing schema. Also, determine if you are interacting with the data layer using Web services or with a legacy application using gateway components. In these cases, you will be restricted to operations defined in the Web service contract or in the interface exposed by the gateway components.

2. Choose the entity types you need. Data access components deal with entities. Entities are used to contain and manage the data used by your application, and you should consider including any data validation code you require within the entities. Choosing an appropriate data type and format for your business entities is also important as it determines how interoperability and serialization requirements are met. For guidance on choosing the type of entities to use, and the types commonly used in business and data components, see Chapter 13, "Designing Business Entities." Consider the following while choosing and implementing the appropriate data format:

- If you must support disconnected scenarios in simple CRUD-based applications, then use **DataSets** or individual **DataTables**. The most common approach is to use the ADO.NET provider. This is ideal when you are working with an existing application that already uses the ADO.NET providers. If you are developing a new application, you can use LINQ to Datasets to populate **DataSets** using LINQ queries.

- If your data access layer will be accessed by other applications and you require interoperability with other systems and platforms, use an XML format.

- If application maintainability is important, use custom business entities. This requires additional code to map the entities to database operations; however, Object/Relational Mapping (O/RM) solutions can reduce the amount of custom code required. Choose the ADO.NET Entity Framework, or another O/RM framework such as the open source NHibernate framework, if you need more flexibility.

- Implement entities by deriving them from a base class that provides basic functionality and encapsulates common tasks. However, be careful not to overload the base class with unrelated operations, which would reduce the cohesiveness of entities derived from the base class and may result in maintainability and performance issues.

- Design entities to rely on data access logic components for database interaction. Centralize implementation of all data access policies and related business logic. For example, if your business entities access SQL Server databases directly, all applications deployed to clients that use the business entities will require SQL connectivity and logon permissions.

3. Choose your data access technology. Identify the functionality required for your data access logic and choose a technology that meets these requirements. For information on the range of data access technologies available on the Microsoft platform, see Appendix C "Data Access Technology Matrix."

4. Design your data access components. Enumerate the data sources that you will access and decide on the method of access for each data source. Determine whether helper components are required or desirable to simplify development and maintenance of data access components. Finally, identify relevant design patterns. For example, consider using the Table Data Gateway, Query Object, Repository, and other patterns. For more information, see Chapter 15, "Designing Data Components."

5. Design your service agents. Use the appropriate tool to add a service reference. This will generate a proxy and the data classes that represent the data contract from the service. Then determine how the service will be used in your application. For most applications, you should access the functionality and data provided by the service agents through data access components, which will provide a consistent interface regardless of the data source. For smaller applications, the business layer—or even the presentation layer—may access the service agent directly.

Relevant Design Patterns

Key patterns are organized by categories, as detailed in the following table. Consider using these patterns when making design decisio ns for each category.

Category	Relevant patterns
General	**Active Record.** Include a data access object within a domain entity. **Data Mapper.** Implement a mapping layer between objects and the database structure that is used to move data from one structure to another while keeping them independent. **Data Transfer Object.** An object that stores the data transported between processes, reducing the number of method calls required. **Domain Model.** A set of business objects that represents the entities in a domain and the relationships between them. **Query Object.** An object that represents a database query. **Repository.** An in-memory representation of a data source that works with domain entities. **Row Data Gateway.** An object that acts as a gateway to a single record in a data source. **Table Data Gateway.** An object that acts as a gateway to a table or view in a data source and centralizes all of the select, insert, update, and delete queries. **Table Module.** A single component that handles the business logic for all rows in a database table or view.
Batching	**Parallel Processing.** Allow multiple batch jobs to run in parallel to minimize the total processing time. **Partitioning.** Partition multiple large batch jobs to run concurrently.

Category	Relevant patterns
Transactions	**Capture Transaction Details.** Create database objects, such as triggers and shadow tables, to record changes to all tables belonging to the transaction. **Coarse Grained Lock.** Lock a set of related objects with a single lock. **Implicit Lock.** Use framework code to acquire locks on behalf of code that accesses shared resources. **Optimistic Offline Lock.** Ensure that changes made by one session do not conflict with changes made by another session. **Pessimistic Offline Lock.** Prevent conflicts by forcing a transaction to obtain a lock on data before using it. **Transaction Script.** Organize the business logic for each transaction in a single procedure, making calls directly to the database or through a thin database wrapper.

For more information on the Domain Model, Table Module, Coarse-Grained Lock, Implicit Lock, Transaction Script, Active Record, Data Mapper, Data Transfer Object, Optimistic Offline Locking, Pessimistic Offline Locking, Query Object, Repository, Row Data Gateway, and Table Data Gateway patterns, see Fowler, Martin. *Patterns of Enterprise Application Architecture*. Addison-Wesley, 2002. Or at http://martinfowler.com/eaaCatalog/.

For more information on the Capture Transaction Details pattern, see *"Data Patterns"* at http://msdn.microsoft.com/en-us/library/ms998446.aspx.

Additional Resources

To more easily access Web resources on general data access guidelines and information, see the online version of the bibliography at: http://www.microsoft.com/architectureguide.

- *".NET Data Access Architecture Guide"* at http://msdn.microsoft.com/en-us/library/ms978510.aspx.
- *"Concurrency Control"* at http://msdn.microsoft.com/en-us/library/ms978457.aspx.
- *"Data Patterns"* at http://msdn.microsoft.com/en-us/library/ms998446.aspx.
- *"Designing Data Tier Components and Passing Data Through Tiers"* at http://msdn.microsoft.com/en-us/library/ms978496.aspx.
- *"Typing, storage, reading, and writing BLOBs"* at http://msdn.microsoft.com/en-us/library/ms978510.aspx#daag_handlingblobs.
- *"Using stored procedures instead of SQL statements"* at http://msdn.microsoft.com/en-us/library/ms978510.aspx.
- *"NHibernate Forge"* community site at http://nhforge.org/Default.aspx.

9

Service Layer Guidelines

Overview

When providing application functionality through services, it is important to separate the service functionality into a separate service layer. This chapter will help you to understand how the service layer fits into the application architecture, and learn the steps for designing the service layer. This includes guidance on the common issues you face when designing the service layer, and the key patterns and technology considerations for the service layer.

Within the service layer, you define and implement the service interface and the data contracts (or message types). One of the more important concepts to keep in mind is that a service should never expose details of the internal processes or the business entities used within the application. In particular, you should ensure that your business layer entities do not unduly influence your data contracts. The service layer should provide translator components that translate data formats between the business layer entities and the data contracts.

Figure 1 shows how a service layer fits into the overall design of your application.

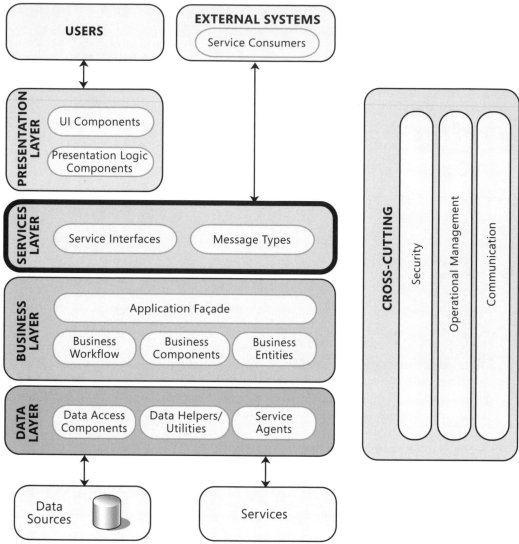

Figure 1
Overall view of a typical application showing the service layer

The services layer will usually include the following:

- **Service interfaces.** Services expose a service interface to which all inbound messages are sent. You can think of a service interface as a façade that exposes the business logic implemented in the application (typically, logic in the business layer) to potential consumers.

- **Message types.** When exchanging data across the service layer, data structures are wrapped by message structures that support different types of operations. The services layer will also usually include data types and contracts that define the data types used in messages.

For more information about the components commonly used in the services layer, see Chapter 10, "Component Guidelines." For more information about designing service interfaces, see Chapter 18, "Communication and Messaging."

Design Considerations

There are many factors that you should consider when designing the service layer. Many of these design considerations relate to proven practices concerned with layered architectures. However, with a service, you must take into account message-related factors. The main thing to consider is that a service uses message-based interaction, typically over a network, which is inherently slower than direct in-process interaction, and that interaction between the service and its consumers will typically be asynchronous. In addition, messages passed between a service and a consumer can be routed, modified, delivered in a different order to which they were sent, or even lost if a guaranteed delivery mechanism is not in use. These considerations require a design that will account for the nondeterministic behavior of messaging. Consider the following guidelines when designing the service layer:

- **Design services to be application-scoped and not component-scoped.** Service operations should be coarse grained and focused on application operations. Defining service operations that are too fine grained can result in performance or scalability problems. However, you should ensure that the service does not return very large unbounded volumes of data. For example, for a service that may return a large amount of demographic data, you should provide an operation that returns an appropriately sized subset of the data rather than returning all of the data in one call. You should ensure that the size of the subset is appropriate for your service and its consumers.

- **Design services and data contracts for extensibility and without the assumption that you know who the client is.** In other words, data contracts should be designed so that, if possible, you can extend them without affecting consumers of the service. However, to avoid excessive complexity or to manage changes that are not backwards compatible, you may have to create new versions of the service interface that operate alongside existing versions instead. You should not make assumptions about the client, or about how they plan to use the service that you provide.

- **Design only for the service contract.** The service layer should implement and provide only the functionality detailed in the service contract, and the internal implementation and details of a service should never be exposed to external consumers. Also, if you need to change the service contract to include new functionality implemented by a service, and the new operations and types are not backward compatible with the existing contracts, consider versioning your contracts. Define new operations exposed by the service in a new version of a service contract, and define and new schema types in a new version of the data contract. For information about designing message contracts, see Chapter 18, "Communication and Messaging."

- **Separate service layer concerns from infrastructure concerns.** Code to manage crosscutting concerns should not be combined with service logic code within the service layer. Doing so can lead to implementations that are difficult to extend and maintain. Generally, you should implement code to manage crosscutting concerns in separate components, and access these components from your business layer components.

- **Compose entities from standard elements.** When possible, use standard elements to compose the complex types and data transfer objects used by your service.

- **Design to assume the possibility of invalid requests.** You should never assume that all messages received by the service are valid. Implement validation logic to check all input based on value, range, and type; and reject or sanitize all invalid data. For more information about validation, see Chapter 17, "Crosscutting Concerns."

- **Ensure that the service can detect and manage repeated messages (idempotency).** When designing the service, implement well-known patterns such as Idempotent Receiver and Replay Protection to ensure that duplicate messages are not processed, or that repeated processing has no effect on the result.

- **Ensure that the service can manage messages arriving out of order (commutativity).** If it is possible that messages will arrive out of order, implement a design that will store messages and then process them in the correct order.

Specific Design Issues

You must consider several common issues as you develop your service layer design. These issues can be categorized into specific areas of the design. The following sections provide guidelines for each category where mistakes are most often made:

- Authentication
- Authorization
- Communication
- Exception Management
- Messaging Channels

- Message Construction
- Message Endpoint
- Message Protection
- Message Routing
- Message Transformation
- Service Interface
- Validation

For more information about message protocols, asynchronous communication, interoperability, performance, and technology options, see Chapter 18, "Communication and Messaging."

Authentication

Authentication is used to determine the identity of the service consumer. Designing an effective authentication strategy for your service layer is important for the security and reliability of your application. Failure to design a good authentication strategy can leave your application vulnerable to spoofing attacks, dictionary attacks, session hijacking, and other types of attacks. Consider the following guidelines when designing an authentication strategy:

- Identify a suitable mechanism for securely authenticating users, taking advantage of the features of the underlying platform where possible, and determine the trust boundaries at which authentication must be applied.
- Consider the implications of using different trust settings for executing service code.
- Ensure that secure protocols such as Secure Sockets Layer (SSL) are used when you use Basic authentication, or when credentials are passed as plain text. Consider using message-level security mechanisms supported by the WS* standards (Web Services Security, Web Services Trust, and Web Services SecureConversation) with SOAP messages.

Authorization

Authorization is used to determine which resources or actions can be accessed by an authenticated service consumer. Designing an effective authorization strategy for your service layer is important for the security and reliability of your application. Failure to design a good authorization strategy can leave your application vulnerable to information disclosure, data tampering, and elevation of privileges. Your authorization strategy should typically represent coarse grained actions or activities rather than the resources needed to carry them out. Consider the following guidelines when designing an authorization strategy:

- Set appropriate access permissions on resources for users, groups, and roles. Execute services under the most restrictive account that is appropriate.

- Avoid highly granular authorization if possible in order to maintain the effectiveness and manageability of your authorization strategy.
- Use URL authorization and/or file authorization when using Windows authentication.
- Where appropriate, restrict access to publicly accessible Web methods by using declarative principle permission demands.

Communication

When designing the communication strategy for your service, the protocol you choose should be based on the deployment scenario your service must support. Consider the following guidelines when designing a communication strategy:

- Analyze your communication requirements and determine if you need request-response or duplex communication, and if message communication must be one way or two way. Also, determine whether you need to make asynchronous calls.
- Determine how to handle unreliable or intermittent communication, perhaps by implementing a service agent or using a reliable message queuing system such as Message Queuing.
- If the service will be deployed within a closed network, consider using Transmission Control Protocol (TCP) to maximize communication efficiency. If the service will be deployed into a public facing network, consider using the Hypertext Transfer Protocol (HTTP).
- Consider using dynamic URL behavior with configured endpoints for maximum flexibility. For example, use configuration or a directory service such as Universal Discovery Description and Integration (UDDI) where practical rather than hard coding endpoint URLs.
- Validate endpoint addresses in messages, and ensure you protect sensitive data in messages.

Exception Management

Designing an effective exception management strategy for your service layer is important for the security and reliability of your application. Failure to do so can make your application vulnerable to denial of service (DoS) attacks, and can also allow it to reveal sensitive and critical information. Raising and handling exceptions is an expensive operation, so it is important for the design to take into account the potential impact on performance. A good approach is to design a centralized exception management and logging mechanism, and consider providing access points that support instrumentation and centralized monitoring in order to assist system administrators. Consider the following guidelines when designing an exception management strategy:

- Catch only exceptions that you can handle, and consider how you will manage message integrity when an exception occurs. Ensure that you correctly handle unhandled exceptions, and avoid using exceptions to control business logic.

- Use SOAP Fault elements or custom extensions to return exception details to the caller.

- Ensure that you log exceptions, and that you do not reveal sensitive information in exception messages or log files.

For more information on exception management techniques, see Chapter 17, "Crosscutting Concerns."

Messaging Channels

Communication between a service and its consumers consists of sending data through a channel. In most cases, you will use channels provided by your chosen service infrastructure, such as Windows Communication Foundation (WCF). You must understand which patterns your chosen infrastructure supports, and determine the appropriate channel for interaction with consumers of the service. Consider the following guidelines when designing message channels:

- Determine appropriate patterns for messaging channels, such as Channel Adapter, Messaging Bus, and Messaging Bridge and choose those appropriate for your scenario. Ensure that you also choose an appropriate service infrastructure compatible with requirements.

- Determine how you will intercept and inspect the data between endpoints if necessary.

- Ensure that you handle exception conditions on the channel.

- Consider how you will provide access to clients that do not support messaging.

Message Construction

When data is exchanged between a service and consumer, it must be wrapped inside a message. The format of that message is based on the types of operations you must support. For example, you may be exchanging documents, executing commands, or raising events. Consider the following guidelines when designing a message construction strategy:

- Determine the appropriate patterns for message constructions, such as Command, Document, Event, and Request-Reply and choose those appropriate for your scenario.

- Divide very large quantities of data into smaller chunks, and send them in sequence.

- When using slow message delivery channels, consider including expiration information in messages that are time sensitive. The service should ignore expired messages.

Message Endpoint

The message endpoint represents the connection that applications use to interact with your service. The implementation of your service interface represents the message endpoint. When designing the service implementation, you must consider the possibility that duplicate or invalid messages can be sent to your service. Consider the following guidelines when designing message endpoints:

- Determine relevant patterns for message endpoints, such as Gateway, Mapper, Competing Consumers, and Message Dispatcher and choose those appropriate for your scenario.

- Determine if you should accept all messages, or whether you need to implement a filter to handle specific messages.

- Design for idempotency in your message interface. Idempotency is the situation where you could receive duplicate messages from the same consumer, but should handle only one. In other words, an idempotent endpoint will guarantee that only one message will be handled, and all duplicate messages will be ignored.

- Design for commutativity in your message interface. Commutativity is related to the order in which messages are received. In some cases, you may need to store inbound messages so that they can be processed in the correct order.

- Design for disconnected scenarios. For example, you might need to support guaranteed delivery by caching or storing messages for later delivery. Ensure you do not attempt to subscribe to endpoints while disconnected.

Message Protection

When transmitting sensitive data between a service and its consumer, you should design for message protection. You can use transport layer protection (such as IPSec or SSL) or message-based protection (such as encryption and digital signatures). Consider the following guidelines when designing message protection:

- In most cases, you should consider using message-based security techniques to protect message content. Message-based security helps to protect sensitive data in messages by encrypting it, and a digital signature will help to protect against repudiation and tampering of the messages. However, keep in mind that each layer of security will affect performance.

- If interactions between the service and the consumer are not routed through intermediaries, such as other servers and routers, you can use transport layer security such as IPSec or SSL. However, if the message passes through one or more intermediaries, always use message-based security. With transport layer security, the message is decrypted and then encrypted at each intermediary through which it passes—which represents a security risk.

- For maximum security, consider using both transport layer and message-based security in your design. Transport layer security will help to protect the headers information that cannot be encrypted using message based security.

Message Routing

A message router is used to decouple a service consumer from the service implementation. There are three main types of routers that you might use: simple, composed, and pattern-based. Simple routers use a single router to determine the final destination of a message. Composed routers combine multiple simple routers to handle more complex message flows. Architectural patterns are used to describe different routing styles based on simple message routers. Consider the following guidelines when designing message routing:

- Determine relevant patterns for message routing, such as Aggregator, Content-Based Router, Dynamic Router, and Message Filter and choose those appropriate for your scenario.

- If sequential messages are sent from a consumer, the router must ensure that they are all delivered to the same endpoint in the required order (commutativity).

- A message router may inspect information in the message to determine how to route the message. As a result, you must ensure that the router can access that information. You may need to add routing information to the header. If you encrypt the message you must ensure that the unencrypted header contains the information required to route the message.

Message Transformation

When passing messages between a service and consumer, there are many cases where the message must be transformed into a format that the consumer can understand. You can use adapters to provide access to the message channel for clients that do not support messaging, and translators to convert the message data into a format that each consumer understands. Consider the following guidelines when designing message transformation:

- Determine the requirements and locations for performing transformations. Take into account the performance overhead of transformation, and try to minimize the number of transformations you execute.

- Determine relevant patterns for message transformation, such as Canonical Data Mapper, Envelope Wrapper, and Normalizer. However, use the Canonical Data Mapper model only when this is necessary.

- Use metadata to define the message format.

- Consider using an external repository to store the metadata.

Service Interface

The service interface represents the contract exposed by your service. The contract defines the operations that your service supports and their associated parameters and data transfer objects. When designing a service interface, you should consider boundaries that must be crossed and the type of consumers that will access your service. For example, service operations should be coarse grained and application scoped. One of the biggest mistakes with service interface design is to treat the service as a component with fine-grained operations. This results in a design that requires multiple calls across physical or process boundaries, which can decrease performance and increase latency. Consider the following guidelines when designing a service interface:

- Consider using a coarse-grained interface to batch requests and minimize the number of calls over the network.
- Avoid designing service interfaces in such a way that changes to the business logic will affect the interface. However, if business requirement change, there may be no other options.
- Do not implement business rules in a service interface.
- Consider using standard formats for parameters to provide maximum compatibility with different types of clients. Do not make assumptions in your interface design about the way that clients will use the service.
- Do not use object inheritance to implement versioning for the service interface.
- Disable tracing and debug-mode compilation for all services, except during development and testing.

Validation

To protect the service layer, you should validate all requests received by it. Failure to do so can leave your application vulnerable to both malicious attacks and errors caused by invalid input. There is no comprehensive definition of what constitutes a valid input or malicious input. In addition, how your application uses input influences the risk of the exploit. Consider the following guidelines when designing a validation strategy:

- Consider centralizing your validation approach to maximize testability and reuse.
- Constrain, reject, and sanitize all message content, including parameters. Validate for length, range, format, and type.
- Consider using schemas to validate messages. For information about validation using schemas, see "Message Validation" at http://msdn.microsoft.com/en-us/library/cc949065.aspx and "Input/Data Validation" at http://msdn.microsoft.com/en-us/library/cc949061.aspx.

REST and SOAP

Representational State Transfer (REST) and SOAP represent two different styles for implementing services. Technically, REST is an architectural pattern built with simple verbs that overlay well on HTTP. While REST architectural principles could be applied with protocols other than HTTP, in practice REST implementations are used in conjunction with HTTP. SOAP is an XML-based messaging protocol that can be used with any communication protocol, including HTTP.

The main difference between these two approaches is the way that the service state is maintained. Do not think of the service state as the application or session state; instead, think of it as the different states that an application passes through during its lifetime. With SOAP, movement through different states can be accomplished through interaction with a single service endpoint, which may encapsulate and provide access to many operations and message types.

With REST, a limited set of operations is allowed, and these operations are applied to resources represented and addressable by URIs (HTTP addresses). The messages capture the current or required state of the resource. REST works well with Web applications, so you can take advantage of HTTP support for non-XML MIME types or streaming content from a service request. Service consumers navigating through REST resources interact with URIs in the same way as a human user might navigate through and interact with Web pages.

While both REST and SOAP can be used with most service implementations, the REST approach is often better suited for publicly accessible services or cases where a service can be accessed by unknown consumers. SOAP is much better suited to implementing a range of procedural interactions, such as an interface between layers of an application. With SOAP, you are not restricted to HTTP. The WS-* standards, which can be utilized in SOAP, provide a standard and therefore interoperable method of dealing with common messaging issues such as security, transactions, addressing, and reliability. REST can also provide the same type of functionality, but you must often create a custom mechanism because only a few standards currently exist for these areas.

In general, you can use the same principles when designing SOAP based interactions as you do for stateless REST interactions. Both approaches exchange data (the payload) using verbs. In the case of SOAP, the set of verbs is open ended and is defined by the service endpoint. In the case of REST, the set of verbs is constrained to preset verbs that mirror the HTTP protocol. Consider the following guidelines when choosing between REST and SOAP:

- SOAP is a protocol that provides a basic messaging framework upon which abstract layers can be built, and is commonly used as an RPC framework that passes calls and responses over networks using XML-formatted messages.

- SOAP handles issues such as security and addressing through its internal protocol implementation, but requires a SOAP stack to be available.

- REST is a technique that can utilize other protocols, such as JavaScript Object Notation (JSON), the Atom publishing protocol, and custom Plain Old XML (POX) formats.

- REST exposes an application and data as a state machine, not just a service end-point. It allows standard HTTP calls such as GET and PUT to be used to query and modify the state of the system. REST is stateless by nature, meaning that each individual request sent from the client to the server must contain all of the information necessary to understand the request since the server does not store the session state data.

Design Considerations for REST

REST represents an architecture style for distributed systems, and is designed to reduce complexity by dividing a system into resources. The resources and the operations supported by a resource are represented and exposed as a set of URIs over the HTTP protocol. Consider the following guidelines when designing REST resources:

- Identify and categorize resources that will be available to clients.

- Choose an approach for resource representation. A good practice would be to use meaningful names for REST starting points and unique identifiers for specific resource instances. For example, http://www.contoso.com/employee/ represents an employee starting point. http://www.contoso.com/employee/smithah01 uses an employee ID to indicate a specific employee.

- Decide if multiple representations should be supported for different resources. For example, you can decide if the resource should support an XML, Atom, or JSON format and make it part of the resource request. A resource could be exposed as both (for example, http://www.contoso.com/example.atom and http://www.contoso.com/example.json).

- Decide if multiple views should be supported for different resources. For example, decide if the resource should support GET and POST operations, or only GET operations. Avoid overuse of POST operations if possible, and avoid putting actions in the URI.

- Do not implement the maintenance of user session state within a service, and do not attempt to use hypertext (such as hidden controls in Web pages) to manage state. For example, when users submit requests such as adding an item to a shopping cart, store the data in a persistent state store such as a database.

Design Considerations for SOAP

SOAP is a message-based protocol that is used to implement the message layer of a service. The message is composed of an envelope that contains a header and body. The header can be used to provide information that is external to the operation being performed by the service. For example, a header may contain security, transaction, or routing information. The body contains contracts, in the form of XML schemas, which are used to implement the service. Consider the following guidelines when designing SOAP messages:

- Determine how you will handle faults and errors, and how you will return appropriate error information to clients. For more information, see "*Exception Handling in Service Oriented Applications*" at http://msdn.microsoft.com/en-us/library/cc304819.aspx.

- Define the schemas for the operations that can be performed by a service, the data structures passed with a service request, and the errors or faults that can be returned from a service request.

- Choose the appropriate security model for your services. For more information, see "*Improving Web Services Security: Scenarios and Implementation Guidance for WCF*" at http://msdn.microsoft.com/en-us/library/cc949034.aspx.

- Avoid using complex types in message schemas. Try to use only simple types to maximize interoperability.

For more information about REST and SOAP, see Chapter 25, "Designing Service Applications."

Technology Considerations

The following guidelines will help you to choose an appropriate implementation technology for your service layer:

- Consider using ASP.NET Web services (ASMX) for simplicity, but only when a Web server running Microsoft Internet Information Services (IIS) is available.

- Consider using WCF services if you require advanced features such as reliable sessions and transactions, activity tracing, message logging, performance counters, and support for multiple transport protocols.

- If you decide to use ASMX for your service, and you require message-based security and binary data transfer, you may consider using Web Service Extensions (WSE). However, in general, you should consider moving to WCF if you require WSE functionality.

- If you decide to use WCF for your service:
  - Consider using HTTP transport based on SOAP specifications if you want interoperability with non-WCF or non-Windows clients.
  - Consider using the TCP protocol and binary message encoding with transport security and Windows authentication if you want to support clients within an intranet.
  - Consider using the named pipes protocol and binary message encoding if you want to support WCF clients on the same machine.
  - Consider defining service contracts that use an explicit message wrapper instead of an implicit one. This allows you to define message contracts as inputs and outputs for your operations, which means that you can extend the data contracts included in the message contract without affecting the service contract.

For more information about messaging technology options, see Chapter 18, "Communication and Messaging."

Deployment Considerations

The service layer can be deployed on the same tier as other layers of the application, or on a separate tier in cases where performance and isolation requirements demand this. However, in most cases the service layer will reside on the same physical tier as the business layer in order to minimize the performance impact when exposing business functionality. Consider the following guidelines when deploying the service layer:

- Deploy the service layer to the same tier as the business layer to improve application performance, unless performance and security issues inherent within the production environment prevent this.
- If the service is located on the same physical tier as the service consumer, consider using the named pipes or shared memory protocols.
- If the service is accessed only by other applications within a local network, consider using TCP for communications.
- If the service is publicly accessible from the Internet, use HTTP for your transport protocol.

For more information on deployment patterns, see Chapter 19, "Physical Tiers and Deployment."

Design Steps for the Service Layer

The approach used to design a service layer starts by defining the service interface, which consists of the contracts that you plan to expose from your service. This is commonly referred to as Contract First Design. Once the service interface has been defined, the next step is to design the service implementation; which is used to translate data contracts into business entities and to interact with the business layer. The following basic steps can be used when designing a service layer:

1. Define the data and message contracts that represent the schema used for messages.
2. Define the service contracts that represent operations supported by your service.
3. Define the fault contracts that return error information to consumers of the service.
4. Design transformation objects that translate between business entities and data contracts.
5. Design the abstraction approach used to interact with the business layer.

You can use design tools such as the patterns & practices Web Service Software Factory: Modeling Edition (also known as the Service Factory) to generate Web services. This is an integrated collection of resources designed to help you quickly and consistently build Web services that adhere to well-known architecture and design patterns. For more information, see *"Web Service Software Factory: Modeling Edition"* at http://msdn.microsoft.com/en-us/library/cc487895.aspx.

For information about designing message contracts and Contract-First Design, see Chapter 18, "Communication and Messaging." For information about abstraction in layered architectures, see Chapter 5, "Layered Application Guidelines."

Relevant Design Patterns

Key patterns are organized by categories as shown in the following table. Consider using these patterns when making design decisions for each category.

Category	Relevant patterns
Communication	**Duplex.** Two-way message communication where both the service and the client send messages to each other independently, irrespective of the use of the One-Way or the Request-Reply pattern. **Fire and Forget.** A one-way message communication mechanism used when no response is expected. **Reliable Sessions.** End to end reliable transfer of messages between a source and a destination, regardless of the number or type of intermediaries that separate the endpoints. **Request Response.** A two-way message communication mechanism where the client expects to receive a response for every message sent.
Messaging Channels	**Channel Adapter.** A component that can access the application's API or data and publish messages on a channel based on this data, and can receive messages and invoke functionality inside the application. **Message Bus.** Structure the connecting middleware between applications as a communication bus that enables the applications to work together using messaging. **Messaging Bridge.** A component that connects messaging systems and replicates messages between these systems. **Point-to-Point Channel.** Send a message on a Point-to-Point Channel to ensure that only one receiver will receive a particular message. **Publish-Subscribe Channel.** Create a mechanism to send messages only to the applications that are interested in receiving the messages, without knowing the identity of the receivers.
Message Construction	**Command Message.** A message structure used to support commands. **Document Message.** A structure used to transfer documents or a data structure reliably between applications. **Event Message.** A structure that provides reliable asynchronous event notification between applications. **Request-Reply.** Use separate channels to send the request and the reply.

Category	Relevant patterns
Message Endpoint	**Competing Consumer.** Set multiple consumers on a single message queue and have them compete for the right to process the messages, which allows the messaging client to process multiple messages concurrently. **Durable Subscriber.** In a disconnected scenario, messages are saved and then made accessible to the client when connecting to the message channel in order to provide guaranteed delivery. **Idempotent Receiver.** Ensure that a service will only handle a message once. **Message Dispatcher.** A component that sends messages to multiple consumers. **Messaging Gateway.** Encapsulate message-based calls into a single interface in order to separate it from the rest of the application code. **Messaging Mapper.** Transform requests into business objects for incoming messages, and reverse the process to convert business objects into response messages. **Polling Consumer.** A service consumer that checks the channel for messages at regular intervals. **Selective Consumer.** The service consumer uses filters to receive messages that match specific criteria. **Service Activator.** A service that receives asynchronous requests to invoke operations in business components. **Transactional Client.** A client that can implement transactions when interacting with a service.
Message Protection	**Data Confidentiality.** Use message-based encryption to protect sensitive data in a message. **Data Integrity.** Ensure that messages have not been tampered with in transit. **Data Origin Authentication.** Validate the origin of a message as an advanced form of data integrity. **Exception Shielding.** Prevent a service from exposing information about its internal implementation when an exception occurs. **Federation.** An integrated view of information distributed across multiple services and consumers. **Replay Protection.** Enforce message idempotency by preventing an attacker from intercepting a message and executing it multiple times. **Validation.** Check the content and values in messages to protect a service from malformed or malicious content.

(continued)

Category	Relevant patterns
Message Routing	**Aggregator.** A filter that collects and stores individual related messages, combines these messages, and publishes a single aggregated message to the output channel for further processing. **Content-Based Router.** Route each message to the correct consumer based on the contents of the message; such as existence of fields, specified field values, and so on. **Dynamic Router.** A component that dynamically routes the message to a consumer after evaluating the conditions/rules specified by the consumer. **Message Broker (Hub and Spoke).** A central component that communicates with multiple applications to receive messages from multiple sources, determines the correct destination, and route the message to the correct channel. **Message Filter.** Prevent undesired messages, based on a set of criteria, from being transmitted over a channel to a consumer. **Process Manager.** A component that enables routing of messages through multiple steps in a workflow.
Message Transformation	**Canonical Data Mapper.** Use a common data format to perform translations between two disparate data formats. **Claim Check.** Retrieve data from a persistent store when required. **Content Enricher.** Enrich messages with missing information obtained from an external data source. **Content Filter.** Remove sensitive data from a message and minimize network traffic by removing unnecessary data from a message. **Envelope Wrapper.** A wrapper for messages that contains header information used, for example, to protect, route, or authenticate a message. **Normalizer.** Convert or transform data into a common interchange format when organizations use different formats.
REST	**Behavior.** Applies to resources that carry out operations. These resources generally contain no state of their own, and only support the POST operation. **Container.** Builds on the entity pattern by providing the means to dynamically add and/or update nested resources. **Entity.** Resources that can be read with a GET operation, but can only be changed by PUT and DELETE operations. **Store.** Allows entries to be created and updated with the PUT operation. **Transaction.** Resources that support transactional operations.
Service Interface	**Façade.** Implement a unified interface to a set of operations in order to provide a simplified interface and reduce coupling between systems. **Remote Façade.** Create a high level unified interface to a set of operations or processes in a remote subsystem by providing a coarse-grained interface over fine-grained operations in order to make that subsystem easier to use, and to minimize calls across the network. **Service Interface.** A programmatic interface that other systems can use to interact with the service.
SOAP	**Data Contract.** A schema that defines data structures passed with a service request. **Fault Contracts.** A schema that defines errors or faults that can be returned from a service request. **Service Contract.** A schema that defines operations that the service can perform.

For more information on the Duplex and Request Response patterns, see "*Designing Service Contracts*" at http://msdn.microsoft.com/en-us/library/ms733070.aspx.

For more information on the Request-Reply pattern, see "*Request-Reply*" at http://www.eaipatterns.com/RequestReply.html.

For more information on the Command, Document Message, Event Message, Durable Subscriber, Idempotent Receiver, Polling Consumer, and Transactional Client patterns, see "*Messaging Patterns in Service-Oriented Architecture, Part I*" at http://msdn.microsoft.com/en-us/library/aa480027.aspx.

For more information on the Data Confidentiality and Data Origin Authentication patterns, see "*Chapter 2: Message Protection Patterns*" at http://msdn.microsoft.com/en-us/library/aa480573.aspx.

For more information on the Replay Detection, Exception Shielding, and Validation patterns, see "*Chapter 5: Service Boundary Protection Patterns*" at http://msdn.microsoft.com/en-us/library/aa480597.aspx.

For more information on the Claim Check, Content Enricher, Content Filter, and Envelope Wrapper patterns, see "*Messaging Patterns in Service Oriented Architecture, Part 2*" at http://msdn.microsoft.com/en-us/library/aa480061.aspx.

For more information on the Remote Façade pattern, see "*P of EAA: Remote Façade*" at http://martinfowler.com/eaaCatalog/remoteFacade.html.

For more information on REST patterns such as Behavior, Container, and Entity, see "*REST Patterns*" at http://wiki.developer.mindtouch.com/REST/REST_Patterns.

For more information on the Aggregator, Content-Based Router, Publish-Subscribe, Message Bus, and Point-to-Point patterns, see "*Messaging patterns in Service-Oriented Architecture, Part I*" at http://msdn.microsoft.com/en-us/library/aa480027.aspx.

Additional Resources

To more easily access Web resources, see the online version of the bibliography at: http://www.microsoft.com/architectureguide.

- "*Enterprise Solution Patterns Using Microsoft .NET*" at http://msdn.microsoft.com/en-us/library/ms998469.aspx.
- "*Web Service Security Guidance*" at http://msdn.microsoft.com/en-us/library/aa480545.aspx.
- "*Improving Web Services Security: Scenarios and Implementation Guidance for WCF*" at http://www.codeplex.com/WCFSecurityGuide.
- "*WS-* Specifications*" at http://www.ws-standards.com/ws-atomictransaction.asp.

10

Component Guidelines

Overview

Components provide a way to isolate specific sets of functionality within units that you can distribute and install separately from other functionality. This chapter contains some general guidelines for creating components, and describes the types of components commonly found in each layer of applications that are designed using the layered approach described elsewhere in this guide. However, the techniques for building components are generally applicable irrespective of the application structure.

General Guidelines for Component Design

When designing components for use in your applications, consider the following general guidelines:

- **Apply the SOLID design principles to the classes within your component.** The SOLID principles are, briefly, the following:

  - **Single responsibility principle.** A class should have only responsibility.

  - **Open/closed principle.** Classes should be extensible without requiring modification.

  - **Liskov substitution principle.** Subtypes must be substitutable for their base types.

  - **Interface segregation principle.** Class interfaces should be client specific and fine grained. Classes should expose separate interfaces for different clients where the interface requirements differ.

  - **Dependency inversion principle.** Dependencies between classes should be replaced by abstractions to allow top down design without requiring design of low level modules first. Abstractions should not depend upon details—details should depend upon abstractions.

- **Design components to be highly cohesive.** Do not overload components by adding unrelated or mixed functionality. For example, always avoid mixing data access logic and business logic within your business components. Where functionality is cohesive, you can create assemblies that contain more than one component and install components in the appropriate layers of your application—even when the layers are physically separated.

- **A component should not rely on internal details of other components.** Each component or object should call a method of another object or component, and that method should have information about how to process the request and, if appropriate, how to route it to appropriate subcomponents or other components. This helps to create an application that is more maintainable and adaptable.

- **Understand how components will communicate with each other.** This requires an understanding of the deployment scenarios your application must support. You must determine if communication across physical boundaries or process boundaries should be supported, or if all components will run within the same process.

- **Keep crosscutting code abstracted from the application-specific logic.** Crosscutting code refers to code related to security, communications, or operational management such as logging and instrumentation. Mixing the code that implements these functions with the component logic can lead to a design that is difficult to extend and maintain.

- **Apply the key principles of the component-based architectural style.** These principles are that components should be reusable, replaceable, extensible, encapsulated, independent, and not context specific. For information about the component-based architectural style, see Chapter 3, "Architectural Patterns and Styles."

Layered Component Distribution

Each layer of an application will contain a series of components that implement the functionality for that layer. These components should be cohesive and loosely coupled to simplify reuse and maintenance. Figure 1 shows the types of components commonly found in each layer.

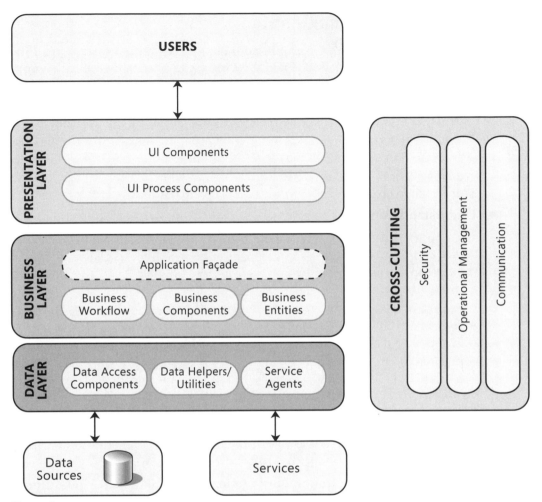

Figure 1
Types of components commonly found in each layer

The following sections describe the components shown in Figure 1.

Presentation Layer Components

Presentation layer components implement the functionality required to allow users to interact with the application. The following types of components are commonly found in the presentation layer:

- **User Interface Components.** The specific user interface for the application is encapsulated into user interface (UI) components. These are the application's visual elements used to display information to the user and accept user input. UI components designed to work in a Separated Presentation pattern implementation are sometimes called Views. In most cases, their specific role is to present the user with an interface that represents the application's underlying data and logic in the most appropriate way, and to interpret user input gestures and forward them to presentation logic components that define how the input affects the underlying data and application state. In some cases, the user interface components may contain logic that is specific to the user interface implementation. In general, however, they should contain as little application logic as possible as this can affect maintainability and reuse, and make them hard to unit test.

- **Presentation Logic Components.** Presentation logic is the application code that defines the logical behavior and structure of the application in a way that is independent of any specific user interface implementation. Presentation logic components are primarily concerned with implementing the application's use cases (or user stories), and orchestrating the user's interactions with the underlying logic and state of the application in a UI independent way. They are also responsible for organizing data from the business layer in a consumable format for the UI components; for example, they may aggregate data from multiple sources, and transform data for display more easily. Presentation logic components can be further subdivided into the following two categories:

  - **Presenter, Controller, Presentation Model, and ViewModel Components.** Used when implementing the Separated Presentation pattern, these kinds of components often encapsulate presentation logic within the presentation layer. To maximize reuse opportunities and testability, these components are not specific to any specific UI classes, elements, or controls.

  - **Presentation Entity Components.** These components encapsulate business logic and data and make it easy for the UI and presentation logic components in the presentation layer to consume; for example, by performing data type conversion or by aggregating data from several sources. In some cases, these are the business entities from the business layer consumed directly by the presentation tier. In other cases, they may represent a subset of the business entity components and be specifically designed to support the presentation layer of the application. Presentation entities help to ensure data consistency and validity in the presentation layer. In some separated presentation patterns these components are sometimes referred to as models.

For more information about designing your presentation layer, see Chapter 6, "Presentation Layer Guidelines." For more information about designing presentation components, see Chapter 11, "Designing Presentation Components."

Services Layer Components

Your application may expose a service layer to interact with clients or other systems using. Services layer components provide other clients and applications with a way to access business logic in the application, and make use of the functionality of the application by passing messages to and from it over a communication channel. The following types of components are commonly found in the services layer:

- **Service Interfaces.** Services expose a service interface to which all inbound messages are sent. The definition of the set of messages that must be exchanged with a service in order for the service to perform a specific business task constitutes a contract. You can think of a service interface as a façade that exposes the business logic implemented in the application (typically, logic in the business layer) to potential consumers.

- **Message Types.** When exchanging data across the service layer, data structures are wrapped by message structures that support different types of operations. For example, you might have a Command message, a Document message, or another type of message. These message types are the message contracts for communication between service consumers and providers. The services layer will usually also expose data types and contracts that define the data types used in messages, and isolate the internal data types from those contained in the message type. This avoids exposure of internal data types to external consumers, which would cause issues in terms of versioning the interface.

For more information about communication and messaging, see Chapter 18, "Communication and Messaging."

Business Layer Components

Business layer components implement the core functionality of the system, and encapsulate the relevant business logic. The following types of components are commonly found in the business layer:

- **Application Façade.** This optional component typically provides a simplified interface to the business logic components, often by combining multiple business operations into a single operation that makes it easier to use the business logic, and reduces dependencies because external callers do not need to know details of the business components and relationships between them.

- **Business Logic Components.** Business logic is defined as any application logic that is concerned with the retrieval, processing, transformation, and management of application data; application of business rules and policies; and ensuring data consistency and validity. To maximize reuse opportunities, business logic components should not contain any behavior or application logic that is specific to a use case or user story. Business logic components can be further subdivided into the following two categories:

  - **Business Workflow Components.** After the UI components collect input from the user and pass it to the business layer, the application can use this input to perform a business process. Many business processes involve multiple steps that must be performed in the correct order, and may interact with each other through an orchestration. Business workflow components define and coordinate long-running, multistep business processes, and can be implemented using business process management tools. Business workflow components work with business process components that instantiate and perform operations on workflow components. For more information on business workflow components, see Chapter 14, "Designing Workflow Components."

  - **Business Entity Components.** Business entities, or—more generally—business objects, encapsulate the business logic and data necessary to represent real world elements, such as Customers or Orders, within your application. They store data values and expose them through properties; contain and manage business data used by the application; and provide stateful programmatic access to the business data and related functionality. Business entities also validate the data contained within the entity and encapsulate business logic to ensure consistency and to implement business rules and behavior. For more information about business entity components, see Chapter 13, "Designing Business Entities."

There are many cases where business entities must be accessible to components and services in both the business layer and the data layer. For example, business entities can be mapped to the data source and accessed by business components. If the layers are located on the same physical tier, the business entities can be shared directly through references. However, you should still separate business logic from data access logic. You can achieve this by moving business entities into a separate assembly that can be shared by both the business services and data services assemblies. This is similar to using a dependency inversion pattern, where business entities are decoupled from the business and data layer so that both business and data layers are dependent on business entities as a shared contract.

For more information about designing your business layer, see Chapter 7, "Business Layer Guidelines." For more information about designing business components, see Chapter 12, "Designing Business Components." For more information about designing business entity components, see Chapter 13, "Designing Business Entities." For more information about designing workflow components, see Chapter 14, "Designing Workflow Components."

Data Layer Components

Data layer components provide access to data that is hosted within the boundaries of the system, and to data exposed by other networked systems. The following types of components are commonly found in the data layer:

- **Data Access Components.** These components abstract the logic required to access the underlying data stores. Most data access tasks require common logic that can be extracted and implemented in separate reusable helper components or a suitable support framework. This can reduce the complexity of the data access components and centralize the logic, which simplifies maintenance. Other tasks that are common across data layer components, and not specific to any set of components, may be implemented as separate utility components. Helper and utility components are often encapsulated in a library or framework so that they can easily be reused in other applications.

- **Service Agents.** When a business component must use functionality provided by an external service, you might need to implement code to manage the semantics of communicating with that particular service. Service agents isolate the idiosyncrasies of calling diverse services from your application, and can provide additional services such as caching, offline support, and basic mapping between the format of the data exposed by the service and the format your application requires.

For more information about designing your data layer, see Chapter 8, "Data Layer Guidelines." For more information about designing data components, see Chapter 15, "Designing Data Components."

Crosscutting Components

Many tasks carried out by the code of an application are required in more than one layer. Crosscutting components implement specific types of functionality that can be accessed from components in any layer. The following are common types of crosscutting components:

- **Components for implementing security.** These may include components that perform authentication, authorization, and validation.
- **Components for implementing operational management tasks.** These may include components that implement exception handling policies, logging, performance counters, configuration, and tracing.
- **Components for implementing communication.** These may include components that communicate with other services and applications.

For more information about managing crosscutting concerns, see Chapter 17, "Crosscutting Concerns."

Relevant Design Patterns

Key patterns for components are organized by categories as detailed in the following table. Consider using these patterns when making design decisions for each category.

Category	Relevant patterns
Business Components	**Application Façade.** Centralize and aggregate behavior to provide a uniform service layer. **Chain of Responsibility.** Avoid coupling the sender of a request to its receiver by allowing more than one object to handle the request. **Command.** Encapsulate request processing in a separate command object with a common execution interface.
Business Entities	**Domain Model.** A set of business objects that represents the entities in a domain and the relationships between them. **Entity Translator.** An object that transforms message data types to business types for requests, and reverses the transformation for responses. **Table Module.** A single component that handles the business logic for all rows in a database table or view.
Presentation Entities	**Entity Translator.** An object that transforms message data types into business types for requests, and reverses the transformation for responses.

Category	Relevant patterns
Presentation Logic	**Application Controller.** Implement a centralized point for handling screen navigation and the flow of an application. **Model-View-Controller.** Separate the UI code into three separate units: Model (data), View (interface), and Controller (processing logic), with a focus on the View. Two variations on this pattern include Passive View and Supervising Presenter, which define how the View interacts with the Model. **Model-View-ViewModel.** A variation on the presentation model pattern that uses the Command pattern to communicate from the View to the ViewModel. **Model-View-Presenter.** Separate request processing into three separate roles, with the View being responsible for handling user input and passing control to a Presenter object. **Passive View.** Reduce the view to the absolute minimum by allowing the controller to process user input and maintain the responsibility for updating the view. **Presentation Model.** Move all view logic and state out of the view, and render the view through data bind3ing and templates. **Supervising Presenter (or Supervising Controller).** A variation of the MVC pattern in which the controller handles complex logic, in particular coordinating between views, but the view is responsible for simple view-specific logic.
Service Interface	**Façade.** Implement a unified interface to a set of operations in order to provide a simplified interface and reduce coupling between systems. **Remote Façade.** Create a high level unified interface to a set of operations or processes in a remote subsystem by providing a course-grained interface over fine-grained operations in order to make that subsystem easier to use, and to minimize calls across the network. **Service Interface.** A programmatic interface that other systems can use to interact with the service.
Workflows	**Data-Driven Workflow.** A workflow that contains tasks whose sequence is determined by the values of data in the workflow or the system. **Human Workflow.** A workflow that involves tasks performed manually by humans. **Sequential Workflow.** A workflow that contains tasks that follow a sequence, where one task is initiated after completion of the preceding task. **State-Driven Workflow.** A workflow that contains tasks whose sequence is determined by the state of the system.

For more information on the Façade pattern, see Chapter 4, "Structural Patterns" in Gamma, Erich, Richard Helm, Ralph Johnson, and John Vlissides. *Design Patterns: Elements of Reusable Object-Oriented Software.* Addison Wesley Professional, 1995.

For more information on the Chain of Responsibility pattern, see *"Patterns in Practice"* at http://msdn.microsoft.com/en-us/magazine/cc546578.aspx.

For more information on the Command pattern, see 5, "Behavioral Patterns" in Gamma, Erich, Richard Helm, Ralph Johnson, and John Vlissides. *Design Patterns: Elements of Reusable Object-Oriented Software.* Addison Wesley Professional, 1995.

For more information on the Entity Translator pattern, see *"Useful Patterns for Services"* at http://msdn.microsoft.com/en-us/library/cc304800.aspx.

For more information on the Data-Driven Workflow, Human Workflow, Sequential Workflow, and State-Driven Workflow, see *"Windows Workflow Foundation Overview"* at http://msdn.microsoft.com/en-us/library/ms734631.aspx and *"Workflow Patterns"* at http://www.workflowpatterns.com/.

For more information on the Application Controller and Model-View-Controller (MVC) patterns, see Fowler, Martin. *Patterns of Enterprise Application Architecture.* Addison-Wesley, 2002. Or at http://martinfowler.com/eaaCatalog.

For more information on the Supervising Presenter and Presentation Model patterns, see *"Patterns in the Composite Application Library"* at http://msdn.microsoft.com/en-us/library/dd458924.aspx.

For more information on the Remote Façade pattern, see *"P of EAA: Remote Façade"* at http://martinfowler.com/eaaCatalog/remoteFacade.html.

patterns & practices Offerings

For more information on relevant offerings available from the Microsoft patterns & practices group, see the following resources:

- *"Composite Client Application Guidance"* at http://msdn.microsoft.com/en-us/library/cc707819.aspx.
- *"Enterprise Library"* at http://msdn.microsoft.com/en-us/library/cc467894.aspx.
- *"Smart Client Software Factory"* at http://msdn.microsoft.com/en-us/library/aa480482.aspx.
- *"Unity"* (dependency injection mechanism) at http://msdn.microsoft.com/en-us/library/dd203101.aspx.
- *"Web Client Software Factory"* at http://msdn.microsoft.com/en-us/library/bb264518.aspx.

Additional Resources

To more easily access Web resources, see the online version of the bibliography at: http://www.microsoft.com/architectureguide.

- *"Integration Patterns"* at http://msdn.microsoft.com/en-us/library/ms978729.aspx.
- Martin, Robert C. and Micah Martin. *Agile Principles, Patterns, and Practices in C#.* Prentice Hall, 2006.
- *"User Interface Control Guidelines"* at http://msdn.microsoft.com/en-us/library/bb158625.aspx.

11

Designing Presentation Components

Overview

This chapter describes the steps you should follow when designing the user interface components and presentation logic components that are part of your presentation layer. Some of the stages are related to the design of the presentation layer itself, while others focus more closely on the individual types of components you may choose to build.

You should first understand the requirements for the UI, and be able to select the appropriate technology. Then you can decide how to bind your presentation logic and data to the UI controls. You must also ensure that you understand the requirements for error handling and validation within the UI. The following sections of this chapter describe in more detail the steps for designing presentation components.

Step 1 – Understand the UI Requirements

Understanding UI requirements is the key for making decisions on the UI type, and the technology and type of controls used to implement it. Your UI requirements are driven by the functionality to be supported by the application and by user expectations.

Start by identifying the users of application, and understanding the goals and tasks these users wish to accomplish when using the application. Pay particular attention to the sequencing of tasks or operations; and determine whether the user expects a structured step-by-step user experience, or an ad-hoc unstructured experience where they can initiate multiple tasks simultaneously. As part of this process, also determine the information required by the user and the format in which it is expected. You may decide to conduct a field study to help you understand the environment in which the user will interact with the application. In addition, consider the current levels of user experience, and compare this to the user experience required for your UI to ensure that it is logical and intuitive. These factors will help you to create a user centered design.

One factor that has a large impact on your choice of technology is the functionality required in the UI. Identify if the UI must expose rich functionality or user interaction, must be highly responsive, or requires graphical or animation support. Also consider the data types, formats and presentation formatting requirements for data such as dates, times, and currency from a localization perspective. In addition, identify the personalization requirements of the application, such as allowing the user to change the layout or styles at run time.

To make the UI intuitive and easy to use, consider how you will lay out or compose the interface; and how the user will navigate through the application's UI. This will help you to choose the appropriate controls and UI technologies. Understand the physical display requirements (such as screen size and resolution) that you must support, and determine accessibility requirements (such as large text or buttons, ink input, or other specialized features). Decide how you will group related information within sections of the UI, avoid interface conflicts or ambiguity, and emphasize the important elements. Identify ways to allow users to find information quickly and easily in the application through the use of navigational controls, search functions, clearly labeled sections, site maps, and other features as appropriate.

Step 2 – Determine the UI Type Required

Based on your UI requirements, you can make a decision on the type of UI for your application. There are a number of different UI types, each with their own strengths and weaknesses. Often, you will find that your UI requirements can be fulfilled with more than one UI type. It is also possible that no single UI type completely covers all of your UI requirements. In this case, consider creating different UI types on top of a shared set of business logic. An example is creating a call center application where you want to expose some of the capabilities for customer self help on the Web and on mobile devices.

Mobile applications can be developed as thin client or rich client applications. Rich client mobile applications can support disconnected or occasionally connected scenarios. Web or thin client mobile applications support connected scenarios only. Device resources may also prove to be a constraint when designing mobile applications.

Rich client applications are usually stand-alone or networked applications with a graphical user interface that display data using a range of controls, and are deployed to a desktop or laptop computer for use by a local user. They are suitable for disconnected and occasionally connected scenarios because the application runs on the client machine. A rich client UI is a good choice when the UI must support rich functionality and rich user interaction or provide a highly dynamic and responsive user experience; or when the application must work in both connected and disconnected scenarios, take advantage of local system resources on the client machine, or integrate with other applications on that machine.

Rich Internet applications (RIAs) are usually Web applications with a rich graphical user interface that run inside a browser. RIAs are typically used for connected scenarios. A RIA is a good choice when your UI must support a dynamic and responsive user experience or use streaming media, and be widely accessible on a range of devices and platforms. They can take advantage of the processing power of the client computer, but cannot easily interact with other local system resources such as webcams, or with other client applications such as Microsoft Office.

Web applications support connected scenarios and can support many different browsers running on a range of operating systems and platforms. A Web UI is a good choice when your UI must be standards-based, accessible on the widest range of devices and platforms, and work only in a connected scenario. Web applications are also well suited to applications whose content is to searchable by Web search engines.

Console-based applications offer an alternative text only user experience, and typically run within command shells such as a Command window or Power Shell. They are most suitable for administrative or development tasks, and are unlikely to be part of a layered application design.

Step 3 – Choose the UI Technology

After you have identified the UI type for your UI components, you must choose an appropriate technology. In general, your choices depend on the UI type you have chosen. The following sections describe some appropriate technologies for each UI type:

Mobile client user interfaces can be implemented using the following presentation technologies:

- **Microsoft .NET Compact Framework.** This is a subset of the Microsoft .NET Framework designed specifically for mobile devices. Use this technology for mobile applications that must run on the device without guaranteed network connectivity.

- **ASP.NET for Mobile.** This is a subset of ASP.NET, designed specifically for mobile devices. ASP.NET for Mobile applications can be hosted on an Internet Information Services (IIS) server. Use this technology for mobile Web applications when you must support a wide range of mobile devices and browsers, and can rely on a permanent network connection.

- **Silverlight for Mobile.** This subset of the Silverlight client requires the Silverlight plug-in to be installed on the mobile device. Use this technology to port existing Silverlight applications to mobile devices, or if you want to create a richer UI than is possible using other technologies. (At the time of writing, this technology is announced but has not yet been released).

Rich client user interfaces can be implemented using the following presentation technologies:

- **Windows Presentation Foundation (WPF).** WPF applications support more advanced graphics capabilities, such as 2-D and 3-D graphics, display resolution independence, advanced document and typography support, animation with timelines, streaming audio and video, and vector-based graphics. WPF uses Extensible Application Markup Language (XAML) to define the UI, data binding, and events. WPF also includes advanced data binding and templating capabilities. WPF applications support developer/designer interaction—allowing developers to focus on the business logic, while designers focus on the look and feel—by separating the visual aspects of the UI from the underlying control logic. Use this technology when you want to create rich media-based and interactive user interfaces.

- **Windows Forms.** Windows Forms has been part of the .NET Framework since its release, and is ideally suited to line-of-business style applications. Even with the availability of Windows Presentation Foundation (WPF), Windows Forms is still a good choice for UI design if your team already has technical expertise with Windows Forms, or if the application does not have any specific rich media or interaction requirements.

- **Windows Forms with WPF User Controls.** This approach allows you to take advantage of the more powerful UI capabilities provided by WPF controls. You can add WPF to an existing Windows Forms application, perhaps as a path for gradual adaption to a fully WPF implementation. Use this approach to add rich media and interactive capabilities to existing applications, but keep in mind that WPF controls tend to work best on higher powered client machines.

- **WPF with Windows Forms User Controls.** This approach allows you to supplement WPF with Windows Forms controls that provide functionality not provided by WPF. You can use the WindowsFormsHost control provided in the WindowsFormsIntegration assembly to add Windows Forms controls to the UI. Use this approach if you must use Windows Forms controls in a WPF UI, but keep in mind that there are some restrictions and issues relating to overlapping controls, interface focus, and the rendering techniques used by the different technologies.

- **XAML Browser Application (XBAP) using WPF.** This technology hosts a sandboxed WPF application in Microsoft Internet Explorer or Mozilla Firefox on Windows. Unlike Silverlight, you can leverage the full WPF framework, but there are some limitations related to accessing system resources from the partial trust sandbox. XBAP requires Windows Vista, or both the .NET Framework 3.5 and the XBAP browser plug-in on the client desktop. XBAP is a good choice if you have an existing WPF application that you want to deploy to the Web, or you want to leverage the rich visualization and UI capabilities of WPF that are not available in Silverlight.

Rich Internet application user interfaces can be implemented using the following presentation technologies:

- **Silverlight.** This is a browser-optimized subset of WPF that works cross platform and cross browser. Compared to XBAP, Silverlight is a smaller, faster install. Due to its small footprint and cross-platform support, Silverlight is a good choice for graphical applications that do not require premium WPF graphics support, or that do not require installation of the application on the client.

- **Silverlight with AJAX.** Silverlight natively supports Asynchronous JavaScript and XML (AJAX) and exposes its object model to JavaScript located in the Web page. You can use this capability to allow interaction between your Web page components and the Silverlight application.

Web application user interfaces can be implemented using the following presentation technologies:

- **ASP.NET Web Forms.** This is the fundamental UI design and implementation technology for .NET Web applications. An ASP.NET Web Forms application needs only to be installed on the Web server, with no components required on the client desktop. Use this technology for Web applications that do not require the additional features provided by AJAX, Silverlight, MVC, or Dynamic Data described in this section.

- **ASP.NET Web Forms with AJAX.** Use AJAX with ASP.NET Web Forms to process requests between the server and client asynchronously to improve responsiveness, provide a richer user experience, and reduce the number of post backs to the server. AJAX is an integral part of ASP.NET in the .NET Framework version 3.5 and later.

- **ASP.NET Web Forms with Silverlight Controls.** If you have an existing ASP.NET application, you can use Silverlight controls to provide a user experience with rich visualization and UI capabilities, while avoiding the requirement to write a completely new Silverlight application. This is a good approach for adding Silverlight rich media content to an existing Web application. The Silverlight controls and the containing Web page can interact on the client using JavaScript.

- **ASP.NET MVC.** This technology allows you to use ASP.NET to build applications based on the Model-View-Controller (MVC) pattern. Use this technology if you need to support test-driven development, and achieve a clear separation of concerns between UI processing and UI rendering. This approach also helps you to create clean HTML and avoids mixing presentation information with logic code.

- **ASP.NET Dynamic Data.** This technology allows you to create data-driven ASP.NET applications that leverage a Language-Integrated Query (LINQ) to Entities data model. It is a good choice if you require a rapid development model for line-of-business (LOB) style data-driven applications based on simple scaffolding, while still supporting full customization.

Console-based user interfaces can be implemented using the following presentation technologies:

- **Console Applications** are text only applications that can be run from Command shells and produce output to the standard output console and error console. These applications often are built to take all input at time of invocation and run unattended.
- **Power Shell Commandlets**. Power Shell is a command-line shell and scripting environment to provide comprehensive control and automation of system and application administrative tasks. Commandlets are application-specific extensions to the Power Shell environment that provide a more deeply integrated experience into the Power Shell language.

For more information about the technologies listed in the previous sections, see Appendix B, "Presentation Technology Matrix."

Step 4 – Design the Presentation Components

After you choose the implementation technology for your UI, the next step is to design your UI components and your presentation logic components. The types of presentation components you may decide to use are the following:

- User Interface Components
- Presentation Logic Components
- Presentation Model Components

These components support a separation of concerns in the presentation layer, and are often used to implement a separated presentation pattern such as MVP (Model-View-Presenter) or MVC (Model-View-Controller) by dividing UI processing into three distinct roles: Model, View, and Controller/Presenter. Separating the concerns in the presentation layer in this way increases maintainability, testability, and opportunities for reuse. The use of abstraction patterns such as dependency injection also makes it easier to test your presentation logic.

For general component design considerations, and more information on the components commonly found in all the layers of an application, see Chapter 10, "Component Guidelines."

User Interface Components

UI components are the visual elements that display information to the user and accept user input. Within a separated presentation pattern, they are typically referred to as Views. Consider the following guidelines when designing your UI components:

- Consider dividing your pages or windows into discrete user controls in order to minimize complexity and to allow reuse of these user controls. Choose appropriate UI components, and take advantage of the data-binding features of the controls you use in the UI.

- Try to avoid inheritance hierarchies of user controls and pages to enable code reuse. Favor composition over inheritance and consider creating reusable presentation logic components instead.

- Try to avoid creating custom controls unless it is necessary for specialized display or data collection. If you find that your UI requirements cannot be achieved with the standard controls, consider buying a control toolkit before deciding to write your own custom controls. If you must create custom controls, extend existing controls if possible instead of creating a new control. Consider extending existing controls by attaching behaviors to them, rather than inheriting from them, and consider implementing designer support for custom controls to make it easier for developers to use them.

Presentation Logic Components

Presentation logic components handle the nonvisualization aspects of the user interface. This will often include validation, responding to user actions, communicating between UI components, and orchestrating user interactions. Presentation logic components are not always necessary; create them only if you will perform significant processing in the presentation layer that must be separated from the UI components, or to improve opportunities for unit testing your presentation logic. Consider the following guidelines when designing presentation logic components:

- If the UI requires complex processing or must communicate with other layers, consider using presentation logic components to decouple this processing from the UI components.

- Use presentation logic components to store state related to (but not specific to) the UI. Avoid implementing business logic and business rules, other than input and data validation, within the presentation logic components. Also, avoid implementing rendering or UI specific logic in the presentation logic components.

- Use presentation logic components to help your application recover from a failure or error by using them to make sure after recovery that the user interface is in a consistent state.

- Where the UI requires complex workflow support, consider creating separate workflow components that use a workflow system such as Windows Workflow Foundation or a custom mechanism within the application's business layer. For more information, see Chapter 14, "Designing Workflow Components."

Presentation Model Components

Presentation model components represent data from your business layer in a consumable format for your UI and presentation logic components in the presentation layer. Models typically represent data, and so they use the data access and possibly the business layer components to collect that data. If the model also encapsulates business logic, it is usually called a presentation entity. Presentation model components may, for example, aggregate data from multiple sources, transform data for the UI to display more easily, implement validation logic, and may help to represent business logic and state within the presentation layer. They are typically used to implement separated presentation patterns, such as MVP or MVC. Consider the following guidelines when designing presentation model components:

- Determine if you require presentation model components. Typically, you might use presentation layer models if the data or the format to be displayed is specific to the presentation layer, or if you are using a separated presentation pattern such as MVP or MVC.

- If you are working with data-bound controls, design or choose appropriate presentation model components that you can easily bind to UI controls. If using custom objects, collections, or data sets as your presentation model component format, ensure that they implement the correct interfaces and events to support data binding.

- If you perform data validation in the presentation layer, consider adding the code for this to your presentation model components. However, also consider how you can take advantage of centralized validation code or code libraries.

- Consider the serialization requirements for the data you will pass to your presentation model components if this data will be passed over the network or stored on disk on the client.

You must also choose a suitable data type for your presentation model components and presentation entities. This choice is driven by the application requirements, and constrained by your infrastructure and development capabilities. You must first choose a data format for your presentation layer data and decide if your components will also encapsulate business logic and state. Next, you must decide how you will present the data within the user interface. The common data formats for presentation data are the following:

- **Custom class.** Use a custom class if you want to represent your data as a complex object that maps directly to your business entities. For example, you might create a custom Order object to represent order data. You can also use a custom class to encapsulate business logic and state and to perform presentation layer validation or to implement custom properties.

- **Array and Collection.** Use an array or a collection when you must bind data to controls such as list boxes and drop-down lists that use single column values.

- **DataSet and DataTable.** Use a DataSet or a DataTable when you are working with simple table-based data with data-bound controls such as grids, list boxes, and drop-down lists.

- **Typed Dataset.** Use a Typed DataSet when you want tight coupling with your business entities to avoid discrepancies due to database changes.

- **XML.** This format is useful when working with a Web client, where the data can be embedded in a Web page or retrieved via a Web service or HTTP request. XML is a good choice when you are using controls such as a tree view or grid. XML is also easy to store, serialize, and pass over communication channels.

- **DataReader.** Use a DataReader to retrieve data when fully connected and the data is to be accessed in a read-only, forward-only manner. The DataReader provides an efficient way to process data from your database sequentially, or to retrieve large volumes of data. However, it ties your logic very closely to the schema of your database and is not generally recommended.

Presentation Entities

Presentation model components should, where possible, encapsulate both the data from your business layer, and business logic and behavior. This helps to ensure data consistency and validity in the presentation layer, and helps to improve the user's experience.

In some cases, your presentation model components may be the business entities from your business layer, directly consumed by the presentation layer. In other cases, your presentation model components may represent a subset of your business entity components, specifically designed to support the presentation layer of your application. For example, they may store the data in a format that is more easily consumable by your UI and presentation logic components. Such components are sometimes referred to as presentation entities.

When the business layer and presentation layer are both located on the client, a typical scenario for rich client applications, you will usually consume the business entities directly from the business layer. However, you may consider using presentation entities if you must store or manipulate the business data in a way that is distinct from the format or behavior of the business entities exposed by the business layer.

When the business layer is located on a separate tier from the presentation layer, you may be able to consume the business entities in the presentation tier by serializing them across the network using data transfer objects, and then resurrecting them as business entity instances on the presentation tier. Alternatively, you can resurrect the data as presentation entities if the required format and behavior differs from that of the business entities. Figure 1 shows this scenario.

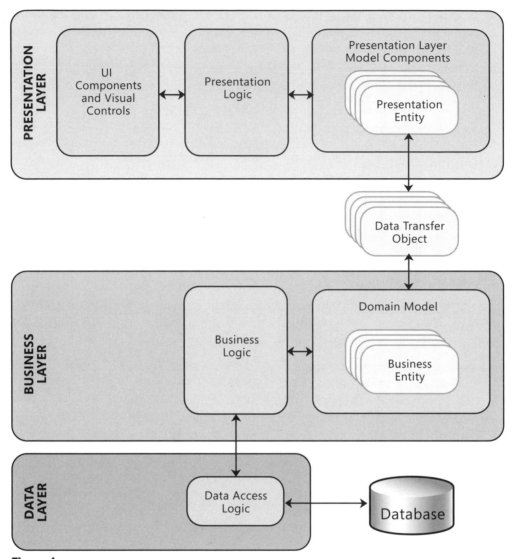

Figure 1
Presentation model components and presentation entities may be useful when the presentation layer and business layer are on separate physical tiers

Step 5 – Determine the Binding Requirements

Data binding provides a way to create a link between the controls in the user inter-face and the data or logic components in your application. Data binding allows you to display and interact with data from databases as well as data in other structures, such as arrays and collections. Data binding is the bridge between a binding target (typically a user interface control) and a binding source (typically a data structure, model, or presentation logic component).

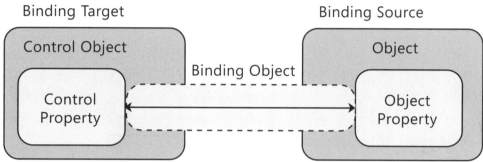

Figure 2
Objects used in data binding

As shown in Figure 2, data binding normally involves four elements that interact to update the properties of the bound control with values exposed by the binding source. Data-bound controls are controls that are bound to data sources; for example, a **DataGrid** control bound to a collection of objects. Data binding is often used with separated presentation patterns to bind the UI components (the Views) to the pre-senters or controllers (the presentation logic components) or to the presentation layer model or entity components.

Support for data binding, and its implementation, varies for each UI technology. In general, most UI technologies allow you to bind controls to objects and lists of objects. However, specific data binding technologies may require certain interfaces or events to be implemented on the data sources in order to fully support data binding, such as **INotifyPropertyChanged** in WPF or **IBindingList** in Windows Forms. If you are using a separated presentation pattern, you must ensure that your presentation logic and data components support the required interfaces or events to allow UI controls to be easily data bound to them.

There are typically two common types of binding you can use, described in the following list:

- **One-way binding.** Changes to the source property automatically update the target property, but changes to the target property are not propagated back to the source property. This type of binding is appropriate if the control being bound is implicitly read-only. An example of a one-way binding is a stock ticker. If there is no need to monitor changes to the target property, using one-way binding avoids unnecessary overhead.

- **Two-way binding.** Changes to either the source property or the target property automatically update the other. This type of binding is appropriate for editable forms or other fully interactive UI scenarios. Many editable controls in Windows Forms, ASP.NET, and WPF support two-way binding so that changes in the data source are reflected in the UI control and changes in the UI control are reflected in the data source.

Step 6 – Determine the Error Handling Strategy

UI components are the external boundary of your application, and so you should design an appropriate error handling strategy to maximize application stability and provide a positive user experience. Consider the following options when designing an error handling strategy:

- **Design a centralized exception handling strategy.** Exception and error handling is a crosscutting concern, and should be implemented using separate components that centralize the functionality and make it accessible across the layers of the application. This also eases maintenance and promotes reusability.

- **Log exceptions.** It is vital to log errors at system boundaries so that your support organization can detect and diagnose errors. This is important for presentation components, but can be challenging for code that is running on client machines. Be careful how you log Personally Identifiable Information (PII) or security sensitive information, and be aware of log size and location.

- **Display user friendly messages.** In this strategy, you display a user friendly message that shows the reason for the error and explains how the user can rectify it. For example, data validation errors should be displayed in a way that makes it clear which data is in error and why it is invalid. The message may also indicate how the user can fix the data or enter valid data.

- **Allow retry.** In this strategy, you display a user-friendly message that explains the reason for the error and asks the user to retry the operation. This strategy is useful when errors are due to a temporary exception situation such as resource unavailability or a network timeout.

- **Display generic messages.** If your application encounters an unexpected error, you should log details of the error but display only a generic message to the user.

Consider providing the user with a unique error code that they can present when contacting your support organization. This strategy is useful when dealing with unexpected exceptions. It is generally recommended that you close the application if an unhandled exception occurs in order to prevent data corruption or security risks.

For more information about exception handling techniques, see Chapter 17, "Crosscutting Concerns." For information about Enterprise Library, which provides useful features for implementing exception handling strategies, see Appendix F, "patterns & practices Enterprise Library."

Step 7 – Determine the Validation Strategy

An effective input validation strategy will help to filter unwanted and malicious data and protect your application from vulnerabilities. Typically, input validation is performed by the presentation layer, whereas business rule validation is carries out by components in the business layer. When designing a validation strategy, first identify all data inputs that must be validated. For example, inputs from a Web client in Form fields, parameters (such as GET and POST data and query strings), hidden fields, and view state should all be validated. In general, you should validate all data received from untrusted sources.

For applications that have both a client-side and a server-side component, such as RIAs or rich client applications that call services on an application server, you must perform validation on the server in addition to any validation you carry out on the client. However, you can duplicate some of the validation on the client for usability and performance reasons. Performing validation on the client is useful to give users feedback quickly if they have entered invalid data. It can save time and bandwidth, but be aware that a malicious attacker can bypass any validation you have implemented on a client.

After you have identified the data to validate, decide on your validation techniques for each item. The most common validation techniques are:

- **Accept known good** (*Allow list*, or positive validation). Accept only data that satisfies the matching criteria, and reject all other.
- **Reject known bad** (*Block list*, or negative validation). Accept data that does not contain a known set of characters or values.
- **Sanitize.** Eliminate or translate known bad characters or values in an effort to make the input safe.

In general, you should accept known good values (Allow list) rather than try to determine all the possible invalid or malicious values that must be rejected. If you are not able to define fully the list of known good values, then you can supplement the validation with a partial list of known bad values and/or sanitization as a second line of defense.

Different presentation technologies use different approaches to validating and reporting validation problems to the user. WPF, for example, uses converters and validation rule objects that are often connected using XAML, while Windows Forms provides validating and binding events.

For more information about validation techniques, see Chapter 17, "Crosscutting Concerns." For information about Enterprise Library, which provides useful features for validating objects and data both server-side and client-side, see Appendix F, "patterns & practices Enterprise Library."

patterns & practices Offerings

For more information on related offerings available from the Microsoft patterns & practices group, see the following resources:

- **Composite Client Application Guidance for WPF** for both desktop and Silverlight make it easier to create modular applications. For more information, see *"Composite Client Application Guidance"* at http://msdn.microsoft.com/en-us/library/cc707819.aspx.

- **Enterprise Library** contains a series of application blocks that address crosscutting concerns. For more information, see *"Enterprise Library"* at http://msdn.microsoft.com/en-us/library/cc467894.aspx.

- **Software Factories** speed development of specific types of application such as Smart Clients, WPF applications, and Web Services. For more information, see *"patterns & practices: by Application Type"* at http://msdn.microsoft.com/en-gb/practices/bb969054.aspx.

- **Unity Application Block** for both enterprise and Silverlight scenarios provides features for implementing dependency injection, service location, and inversion of control. For more information, see *"Unity Application Block"* at http://msdn.microsoft.com/en-us/library/dd203101.aspx.

Additional Resources

To more easily access Web resources, see the online version of the bibliography at: http://www.microsoft.com/architectureguide.

- *"Design Guidelines for Web Applications"* at http://msdn.microsoft.com/en-us/library/ms978618.aspx.

- *"Data Binding Overview"* at http://msdn.microsoft.com/en-us/library/ms752347.aspx.

- *"Design Guidelines for Exceptions"* at http://msdn.microsoft.com/en-us/library/ms229014%28VS.80%29.aspx.

12

Designing Business Components

Overview

Designing business components is an important task; if you fail to design your business components correctly, the result is likely to be code that is difficult to maintain or extend. There are several types of business components you may use when designing and implementing an application. Examples of these components include business logic components, business entities, business process or workflow components, and utility or helper components. This chapter starts with an overview of the different types of business components you will find in most application designs, with the primary focus on business logic components. It shows how different aspects of your application design, transactional requirements, and processing rules affect the design you choose. Once you have an understanding of the requirements, the final step focuses on design patterns that support those requirements.

Step 1 – Identify Business Components Your Application Will Use

Within the business layer, there are different types of components that you may need to create or use to handle business logic. The goal of this step is to understand how you identify these components, and discover which components your application requires. The following guidelines will help you to decide which types of components you require:

- Consider using **business logic components** to encapsulate the business logic and state of your application. Business logic is application logic that is concerned with the implementation of the business rules and behavior of your application, and with maintaining overall consistency through processes such as data validation. Business logic components should be designed to be easily testable and independent of the presentation and the data access layers of your application.

- Consider using **business entities** as part of a domain modeling approach to encapsulate business logic and state into components that represent the real world business entities from your business domain, such as products and orders, which your application has to work with. For more information about business entities, see Chapter 13, "Designing Business Entities."

- Consider using **business workflow components** if your application must support multistep processes executed in a specific order; uses business rules that require the interaction between multiple business logic components; or you want to change the behavior of the application by updating the workflow as the application evolves or requirements change. Also consider using business workflow components if your application must implement dynamic behavior based on business rules. In this case, consider storing the rules in a rules engine. Consider using Windows Workflow Foundation to implement your workflow components. Alternatively, consider an integration server environment such as BizTalk Server if your application must process multiple steps that depend on external resources, or has a process that must be executed as a long-running transaction. For more information about workflow components, see Chapter, 14 "Designing Workflow Components." For more information about integration services, see Appendix D, "Integration Technology Matrix."

Step 2 – Make Key Decisions for Business Components

The overall design and type of application you are creating plays a role in the business components that it will use to handle requests. For example, business components for a Web application usually deal with message-based requests, while a Windows Forms application will typically use event-based requests to interact directly with business components. In addition, there are other factors to consider when working with different application types. Some of these factors are common across types, while some are unique to an application type. Key decisions you must make with business components include:

- **Location.** Will your business components be located on the client, on an application server, or on both? Consider locating some or all business components on the client if you have a stand-alone rich client or a Rich Internet Application (RIA), if you want to improve performance, or if you are using a domain model design for business entities. Consider locating some or all business components on an application server if you must support multiple client types with common business logic, if business components require access to resources not accessible from the client, or for security reasons to protect the components within a managed and secured server environment.

- **Coupling.** How will your presentation components interact with your business components? Should you use tight coupling where the presentation components have direct knowledge of the business components, or loose coupling where an abstraction is used to hide details of the business components? For simplicity, if you have a rich client application or RIA with both sets of components located on the client, you may consider tight coupling between presentation and business components. However, loose coupling between presentation and business components will improve testability and flexibility. If you have a rich client application or RIA with business components located on an application server or Web server, design the service interface to enable their interaction to be as loosely coupled as possible.

- **Interaction.** If your business components are located on the same tier as your presentation components, consider using component-based interactions through events and methods, which maximizes performance. However, consider implementing a service interface and using message-based interactions between the presentation layer and business components if the business components are located on a separate physical tier from your Web server; if you are designing a Web application with loose coupling between the presentation and business layers; or if you have a rich client or RIA application. If you have a rich client application or RIA that is occasionally connected to an application server or Web server, you must carefully design the service interface to allow your client to resynchronize when connected.

When you use message-based interaction, consider how you will manage duplicate requests and guarantee message delivery. **Idempotency** (the ability to ignore duplicate requests) is important if you are designing a service application, a message-based application that uses a messaging system such as Microsoft Message Queuing, or a Web application where a long running process may cause the user to attempt the same action multiple times. **Guaranteed delivery** is important if you are designing a message-based application that uses a messaging system such as Microsoft Message Queuing, a service that uses message routers between the client and service, or a service that supports fire and forget operations where the client sends a message without waiting for a response. Also, consider that cached messages, which may be stored awaiting processing, can become stale.

Step 3 – Choose Appropriate Transaction Support

Business components are responsible for coordinating and managing any transactions that may be required in your business layer. However, the first step is to determine if transaction support is required. Transactions are used to ensure that a series of actions executed against one or more resource managers, such as databases or message queues, is completed as a single unit independent of other transactions. If any single action in a series fails, all other actions must be rolled back to ensure the system is left in a consistent state. For example, you might have an operation that updates three different tables using multiple business logic components. If one of those updates fails, but two succeed, the data source will be in an inconsistent state; which means that you now have invalid data on which other operations may depend. The following options are available for implementing transactions:

- **System.Transactions** uses business logic components to initiate and manage transactions. Introduced in version 2.0 of the .NET Framework along with the Lightweight Transaction Manager (LTM), it deals with nondurable resource managers or one durable resource manager. This approach requires explicit programming against the **TransactionScope** type, and can escalate the transaction scope and delegate to a Distributed Transaction Coordinator (DTC) if more than one durable resource manager is enlisted in the transaction. Consider using **System.Transactions** if you are developing a new application that requires transaction support, and you have transactions that span multiple nondurable resource managers.

- **WCF Transactions** were introduced in version 3.0 of the .NET Framework and are built on top of the **System.Transactions** functionality. They provide a declarative approach to transaction management implemented using a range of attributes and properties, such as **TransactionScopeRequired**, **TransactionAutoComplete**, and **TransactionFlow**. Consider using WCF Transactions if you must support transactions when interacting with WCF services. However, consider whether a declarative transaction definition is a requirement, rather than using code to manage transactions.

- **ADO.NET Transactions**, available since version 1.0 of the .NET Framework, require the use of business logic components to initiate and manage transactions. They use an explicit programming model where developers are required to manage nondistributed transactions in code. Consider using ADO.NET Transactions if you are extending an application that already uses ADO.NET Transactions, or if you are using ADO.NET providers for database access and the transactions are limited to a single resource. ADO.NET 2.0 and later additionally support distributed transactions using the System.Transactions features described earlier in this list.

- **Database** transactions are used for transaction management that can be incorporated into stored procedures, which may also simplify your business process design. If transactions are initiated by business logic components, the database transaction will be enlisted in the transaction created by the business component. Consider using database transactions if you are developing stored procedures that encapsulate all of the changes that must be managed by a transaction, or you have multiple applications that use the same stored procedure and transaction requirements can be encapsulated within that stored procedures.

Be aware that systems that use distributed transactions can increase coupling between sub-systems. Transactions that include remote systems are likely to affect performance due to increased network traffic. Transactions are expensive and should execute quickly, otherwise resources could be locked for excessive amounts of time which can lead to time outs, or deadlocks.

Allow only highly trusted services to participate in transactions because external services can to lock your internal resources through participation in the transaction. If you are calling services to perform business processes, avoid creating atomic transactions that span these calls unless you cannot avoid this.

Step 4 – Identify How Business Rules Are Handled

Managing business rules can be one of the more challenging aspects of application design. Generally, you should always keep business rules within the business layer. However, exactly where in the business layer should they go? You can use business logic or workflow components, a business rule engine, or use a domain model design with rules encapsulated in the model. Consider the following options for handling business rules:

- **Business Logic Components** can be used to handle simple rules or very complex rules, depending on the design pattern used to implement the business logic components. Consider using business logic components for tasks or document-oriented operations in Web applications or within services, if you are not implementing a domain model design for business entities, or you are using an external source that contains the business rules.

- **Workflow Components** are used when you want to decouple business rules from business entities, or the business entities you are using do not support the encapsulation of business rules, or when you have to encapsulate business logic that coordinates the interaction between multiple business entities.

- **Business Rules Engines** provides a way for non developers to establish and modify rules, but they also add complexity and overhead to an application and should only be used where appropriate. In other words, you would only use a rules engine if you have rules that must be adjusted based on different factors associated with the application. Consider using a business rules engine if you have volatile business rules that must be modified on a regular basis; to support customization and offer flexibility; or you want to allow business users to manage and update rules. Ensure that only the rules users should be able to modify are exposed, and that unauthorized users cannot modify rules that are critical to correct business logic behavior.

- **Domain Model Design** can be used to encapsulate business rules within business entities. However, a domain model design can be difficult to get right, and tends to focus on a specific viewpoint or context. Consider encapsulating rules in a domain model if you have a rich client application or RIA where parts of the business logic are deployed on the client and the domain model entities are initialized and persisted in memory, or you have a domain model that can be maintained within the session state associated with Web or service applications. If you locate parts of the domain model on the client, you should mirror the model on the server to apply rules and behavior, and to ensure security and maintainability.

Step 5 – Identify Patterns That Fit the Requirements

Behavioral patterns are based on observing the behavior of a system in action and looking for repeatable processes. With business components, the patterns you might use are usually behavioral design patterns. In other words, patterns that are focused on the behavior of an application at the design level. Much work has been done identifying and defining patterns that occur in different types of applications and in different layers of an application design. It is not feasible to try to learn all of the patterns that have been defined; however, you should have a good understanding of different pattern types and be able to examine your scenario to identify behavior that could be expressed as a pattern. The following table describes patterns that are commonly used with business components.

Pattern	Recommendation
Adapter	Allow classes that have incompatible interfaces to work together, allowing developers to implement sets of polymorphic classes that provide alternative implementations for an existing class.
Command	Recommended for rich client applications with menus, toolbars, and keyboard shortcut interactions that are used to execute the same commands against different components. Can also be used with the Supervising Presenter pattern to implement commands.
Chain of Responsibility	Chain request handlers together so that each handler can examine the request and either handle it or pass it on to the next handler in the chain. An alternative to "if, then, else" statements, with the ability to handle complex business rules.
Decorator	Extend the behavior of an object at run time to add or modify operations that will be performed when executing a request. Requires a common interface that will be implemented by decorator classes, which can be chained together to handle complex business rules.
Dependency Injection	Create and populate members (fields and properties) of objects using a separate class, which usually creates these dependencies at run time based on configuration files. Configuration files define containers that specify the mapping or registrations of object types. Application code can also define the mapping or registration of objects. Provides a flexible approach to modifying behavior and implementing complex business rule.
Façade	Provide coarse-grained operations that unify the results from multiple business logic components. Typically implemented as a remote façade for message-based interfaces into the business layer, and used to provide loose coupling between presentation and business layers.
Factory	Create object instances without specifying the concrete type. Requires objects that implement a common interface or extend a common base class.
Transaction Script	Recommended for basic CRUD operations with minimal business rules. Transaction script components also initiate transactions, which means all operations performed by the component should represent an atomic unit of work. With this pattern, the business logic components interact with other business components and data components to complete the operation.

Although this list represents many of the common patterns you might use with business components, there are many other patterns associated with business components. The main goal when choosing a pattern is to ensure that it fits the scenario and does not add more complexity than necessary.

Additional Resources

To more easily access Web resources, see the online version of the bibliography at: http://www.microsoft.com/architectureguide.

- For more information on business component design, see *"Application Architecture for .NET: Designing Applications and Services"* http://msdn.microsoft.com/en-us/library/ms954595.aspx.

- For more information on performance in business layers and components, see the following resources:

    - *"Architecture and Design Review of a .NET Application for Performance and Scalability"* at http://msdn.microsoft.com/en-us/library/ms998544.aspx.

    - *"Design Guidelines for Application Performance"* at http://msdn.microsoft.com/en-us/library/ms998541.aspx.

- For more information on implementing transactions in business components, see the following resources:

    - *"Introducing System.Transactions in the .NET Framework 2.0"* at http://msdn.microsoft.com/en-us/library/ms973865.aspx.

    - *"Transactions in WCF"* at http://msdn.microsoft.com/en-us/library/ms730266.aspx.

    - *"Transaction Processing in .NET 3.5"* at http://msdn.microsoft.com/en-us/library/w97s6fw4.aspx.

- For more information on implementing workflow in business components, see the following resources:

    - *"Introduction to the Windows Workflow Foundation Rules Engine"* at http://msdn.microsoft.com/en-us/library/aa480193.aspx.

    - *"Windows Workflow Foundation"* at http://msdn.microsoft.com/en-us/library/ms735967.aspx.

13

Designing Business Entities

Overview

Business entities store data values and expose them through properties; they contain and manage business data used by an application and provide stateful programmatic access to the business data and related functionality. Business entities should also validate the data contained within the entity and encapsulate business logic to ensure consistency and to implement business rules and behavior. Therefore, designing or choosing appropriate business entities is vitally important for maximizing the performance and efficiency of your business layer.

This chapter will help you to understand the design of business entity components. It starts by looking at different data formats and how data will be used in your application. Next, you will learn how the data format you choose determines the way that business rules can be implemented in your design. Finally, you will learn about design options for custom objects, and how to support serialization with different data formats.

For general component design considerations, and more information on the components commonly found in the layers of an application, see Chapter 10, "Component Guidelines."

Step 1 – Choose the Representation

In this step, you will learn about the different ways of representing business entities, and see the benefits and liabilities of each, to help you choose the correct representation for your scenario. The following list describes the most common format options:

- **Custom Business Objects.** These are common language runtime (CLR) objects that describe entities in your system. An object/relational mapping (O/RM) technology such as the ADO.NET Entity Framework (EF) or NHibernate can be used to create these objects (for more information, see Additional Resources at the end of this chapter). Alternatively, you can create them manually. Custom business objects are appropriate if you must encapsulate complex business rules or behavior along with the related data. If you need to access your custom business objects across AppDomain, process, or physical boundaries, you can implement a service layer that provides access via Data Transfer Objects (DTO) and operations that update or edit your custom business objects.

- **DataSet or DataTable.** DataSets are a form of in-memory database that usually maps closely to an actual database schema. DataSets are typically used only if you are not using an O/RM mapping mechanism and you are building a data-oriented application where the data in your application logic maps very closely to the database schema. DataSets cannot be extended to encapsulate business logic or business rules. Although DataSets can be serialized to XML, they should not be exposed across process or service boundaries.

- **XML.** This is a standards-based format that contains structured data. XML is typically used to represent business entities only if your presentation layer requires it or if your logic must work with the content based on its schema; for example, a message routing system where the logic routes messages based on some well-known nodes in the XML document. Be aware that using and manipulating XML can use large amounts of memory.

Step 2 – Choose a Design for Business Entities

If you have determined that custom objects provide the best representation for business entities, the next step is to design those objects. The design approach used for custom objects is based on the sort of object that you plan to use. For example, domain model entities require in-depth analysis of a business domain, while table module entities require an understanding of the database schema. The following is a list of common design approaches when using business objects:

- **Domain Model** is an object-oriented design pattern. The goal in a domain model design is to define business objects that represent real world entities within the business domain. When using a domain model design, the business or domain entities contain both behavior and structure. In other words, business rules and relationships are encapsulated within the domain model. The domain model design requires in-depth analysis of the business domain and typically does not map to the relational models used by most databases. Consider using the domain model design if you have complex business rules that relate to the business domain, you are designing a rich client and the domain model can be initialized and held in memory, or you are not working with a stateless business layer that requires initialization of the domain model with every request. For more information on the Domain Model and Domain-Driven Design, see the section "Domain-Driven Design" later in this chapter.

- **Table Module** is an object-oriented design pattern. The objective of a table module design is to define entities based on tables or views within a database. Operations used to access the database and populate the table module entities are usually encapsulated within the entity. However, you can also use data access components to perform database operations and populate table module entities. Consider using the table module approach if the tables or views within the database closely represent the business entities used by your application, or if your business logic and operations relate to a single table or view.

- **Custom XML objects** represent deserialized XML data that can be manipulated within your application code. The objects are instantiated from classes defined with attributes that map properties within the class to elements and attributes within the XML structure. The Microsoft .NET Framework provides components that can be used to deserialize XML data into objects and serialize objects into XML. Consider using custom XML objects if the data you are consuming is already in XML format (for example, XML files or database operations that return XML as the result set); you need to generate XML data from non-XML data sources; or you are working with read-only document-based data.

When using custom objects, your business entities are not all required to follow the same design. For example, one aspect of the application with complex rules may require a Domain Model design. However, the remainder of the application may use XML objects, a Table Module design, or domain objects as appropriate.

Step 3 – Determine Serialization Support

You must determine how you will transfer business entities across boundaries. In most cases, to pass data across physical boundaries such as **AppDomain**, process, and service interface boundaries, you must serialize the data. You may also decide to serialize the data when crossing logical boundaries; however, keep in mind the performance impact in this case. Consider the following options for transferring business entities:

- **Expose serializable business entities directly only if required.** If another layer in your application, on the same physical tier, is consuming your business entities, the most straightforward approach is to expose your business entities directly through serialization. However, the disadvantage of this approach is that you create a dependency between the consumers of your business entities and their implementation. Therefore, this approach is not generally recommended unless you can maintain direct control over the consumers of your business entities and remote access to your business entities between physical tiers is not required.

- **Convert business entities into serializable data transfer objects.** To decouple the consumers of your data from the internal implementation of your business layer, consider translating business entities into special serializable data transfer objects. Data Transfer Object (DTO) is a design pattern used to package multiple data structures into a single structure for transfer across boundaries. Data transfer objects are also useful when the consumers of your business entities have a different data representation or model, for example a presentation tier. This approach makes it possible to change the internal implementation of the business layer without affecting any consumers of the data, and allows you to version your interfaces more easily. This approach is recommended when having external clients consuming data.

- **Expose XML directly.** In some cases, you may serialize and expose your business entities as XML. The .NET Framework provides extensive serialization support for XML data. In most cases, attributes on your business entities are used to control serialization into XML.

For more information about data schemas for service interfaces, see Chapter 9, "Service Layer Guidelines." For more information about communicating between layers and tiers, see Chapter 18, "Communication and Messaging."

Domain Driven Design

Domain Driven Design (DDD) is an object-oriented approach to designing software based on the business domain, its elements and behaviors, and the relationships between them. It aims to enable software systems that are a realization of an underlying business domain by defining a domain model expressed in the language of business domain experts. The domain model can be viewed as a framework from which solutions can then be rationalized.

To apply Domain Driven Design, you must have a good understanding of the business domain you want to model, or be skilled in acquiring such business knowledge. The development team will often work with business domain experts to model the domain. Architects, developers, and subject matter experts have diverse backgrounds, and in many environments will use different languages to describe their goals, designs and requirements. However, within Domain Driven Design, the whole team agrees to only use a single language that is focused on the business domain, and which excludes any technical jargon.

As the core of the software is the domain model, which is a direct projection of this shared language, it allows the team to quickly find gaps in the software by analyzing the language around it. The creation of a common language is not merely an exercise in accepting information from the domain experts and applying it. Quite often, communication problems within development teams are due not only to misunderstanding the language of the domain, but also due to the fact that the domain's language is itself ambiguous. The Domain Driven Design process holds the goal not only of implementing the language being used, but also improving and refining the language of the domain. This in turn benefits the software being built, since the model is a direct projection of the domain language.

The domain model is expressed using entities, value objects, aggregate roots, repositories, and domain services; organized into coarse areas of responsibility known as Bounded Contexts.

Entities are objects in the domain model that have a unique identity that does not change throughout the state changes of the software. Entities encapsulate both state and behavior. An example of entity could be a Customer object that represents and maintains state about a specific customer, and implements operations that can be carried out on that customer.

Value objects are objects in the domain model that are used to describe certain aspects of a domain. They do not have a unique identity and are immutable. An example of value object could be a Transaction Amount or a Customer Address.

Aggregate Roots are entities that group logically related child entities or value objects together, control access to them, and coordinate interactions between them.

Repositories are responsible for retrieving and storing aggregate roots, typically using an Object/Relational Mapping (O/RM) framework.

Domain services represent operations, actions, or business processes; and provide functionality that refers to other objects in the domain model. At times, certain functionality or an aspect of the domain cannot be mapped to any objects with a specific lifecycle or identity; such functionality can be declared as a domain service. An example of a domain service could be catalog pricing service within the e-commerce domain.

In order to help maintain the model as a pure and helpful language construct, you must typically implement a great deal of isolation and encapsulation within the domain model. Consequently, a system based on Domain Driven Design can come at a relatively high cost. While Domain Driven Design provides many technical benefits, such as maintainability, it should be applied only to complex domains where the model and the linguistic processes provide clear benefits in the communication of complex information, and in the formulation of a common understanding of the domain.

For a summary of domain driven design techniques, see *"Domain Driven Design Quickly"* at http://www.infoq.com/minibooks/domain-driven-design-quickly. Alternatively, see *"Domain-Driven Design: Tackling Complexity in the Heart of Software"* by Eric Evans (Addison-Wesley, ISBN: 0-321-12521-5) and *"Applying Domain-Driven Design and Patterns"* by Jimmy Nilsson (Addison-Wesley, ISBN: 0-321-26820-2).

Additional Resources

To more easily access Web resources, see the online version of the bibliography at: http://www.microsoft.com/architectureguide.

- For more information on design patterns for business entities, see *"Enterprise Solution Patterns Using Microsoft .NET"* at http://msdn.microsoft.com/en-us/library/ms998469.aspx.

- For more information on designing business entities, see *"Integration Patterns"* at http://msdn.microsoft.com/en-us/library/ms978729.aspx.

- For more information on domain-driven design, see the following resources:
  - *"An Introduction To Domain-Driven Design"* at http://msdn.microsoft.com/en-us/magazine/dd419654.aspx.
  - *"Domain Driven Design and Development in Practice"* at http://www.infoq.com/articles/ddd-in-practice.

- For more information on design patterns for the business layer, see *"Service Orientation Patterns"* at http://msdn.microsoft.com/en-us/library/aa532436.aspx.

- For more information on the ADO.NET Entity Framework, see *"The ADO.NET Entity Framework Overview"* at http://msdn.microsoft.com/en-us/library/aa697427(VS.80).aspx.

- For information on business entity design with Microsoft Dynamics, see *"Business Entities"* at http://msdn.microsoft.com/en-us/library/ms940455.aspx.

- For information on business entity modeling with Microsoft Dynamics, see *"Modeling Entities"* at http://msdn.microsoft.com/en-us/library/aa475207.aspx.

- For information on using business entities with Office Business Applications (OBA), see *"Building Office Business Applications"* at http://msdn.microsoft.com/en-us/library/bb266337.aspx.

- For more information on the open source NHibernate framework, see *"NHibernate Forge"* at http://nhforge.org/Default.aspx.

14

Designing Workflow Components

Overview

There are many scenarios where a user's tasks must be completed in an ordered way based on the completion of specific steps, or to satisfy a set of underlying business rules. Workflow components can be used to encapsulate the tasks and to coordinate the steps required to complete them. Workflow components can also support tasks that are dependent on the information being processed, such as the data entered by the user or by dynamic business rules that define a business process.

This chapter examines different scenarios and provides guidance on how to design workflow components. It starts with a look at how real world scenarios map to key workflow scenarios to help you to identify the appropriate workflow style for your application. Next, it examines how requirements and rules affect the options you have for implementing workflow components. The final step provides guidance on designing workflow components to support the different options that are available.

For general component design considerations, and more information on the components commonly found in the layers of an application, see Chapter 10, "Component Guidelines."

Step 1 – Identify the Workflow Style Using Scenarios

There are three basic types of workflow style: sequential, state machine, and data driven. With sequential workflow, a task moves through a specific set of steps until it is completed. With a state machine workflow, activities are defined as a set of states and events that cause transitions from one state to another. With data driven workflow, activities are executed based on information associated with data. As a result, the first step in designing workflow components is to understand the style of workflow you must support. The following list provides guidance on when to use each of the three basic workflow styles:

- **Sequential workflow style.** In this style, the workflow controls the sequence of activities and decides which of the steps will execute next. Although a sequential workflow can include conditional branching and looping, the path it follows is predictable. Consider sequential workflows if you must execute a series of predefined steps to accomplish a certain task; or for scenarios such as systems management, business to business orchestration, and business rule processing.

- **State machine workflow style.** In this style, the workflow acquires a given state and waits for events to occur before moving into another state. Consider the state-machine style if you require workflows designed for event driven scenarios, user interface page flows such as a wizard interface, or order processing systems where the steps and processes applied depend on data within the order.

- **Data driven workflow style.** In this style, information in the document determines which activities the workflow will execute. It is appropriate for tasks such as a document approval process.

Step 2 – Choose an Authoring Mode

You can use code, markup languages, or a combination of both code and markup to author workflows. The approach you take depends on the authoring mode requirements for your solution. The authoring mode you choose will also influence how you will package and distribute the application. The choices available are the following:

- **Code-only.** Choose this option if the workflow will not change much over time, if you have complex business rules that cannot be easily expressed using markup, if your development team is more familiar with authoring managed code rather than creating markup using a visual designer, or if you want to create new workflow types that are not possible using the markup option. Code-only workflows are also easy to integrate into your source code control system.

- **Code-separation.** Choose this option if you have complex business rules that are encapsulated by business components, or you want to provide users or administrators with the ability to modify some aspects of the workflows using workflow designers.

- **Markup.** Choose this option if the workflow will change more frequently over time, if your business rules associated with the workflow can be easily expressed using markup languages, you do not need to create new workflow types, and you need the flexibility to update the workflow model without rebuilding the workflow types referenced by the model.

Step 3 – Determine How Rules Will Be Handled

At this point, you should have identified the workflow style and determined an authoring mode for creating workflows. The next step is to determine how your workflow will handle the business rules. The option you choose is based on the complexity, durability, and management requirements associated with the business rules. Consider the following factors for handling business rules in workflow components:

- **If rules are complex,** you should consider a code-only or code-separation authoring mode. Business components can be used to implement and encapsulate the rules, allowing the workflow to coordinate their execution.

- **If rules are not durable,** you should consider a markup authoring mode for simple or data-driven rules. However, if the rules are managed by an external system such as a business rules engine, consider a code-only or code-separation authoring mode.

- **If business users, administrators, or analysts will manage rules,** you should consider a solution that uses a markup authoring mode that provides a visual designer or other rule editing facility, or supports a Domain Specific Language (DSL). However, if the rules are managed by an external system such as a business rules engine, consider a code-separation authoring mode.

Step 4 – Choose a Workflow Solution

Now that you have an understanding of the workflow style, authoring mode, and rule handling requirements for your workflow, the next step is to choose a workflow solution. The choice you make is based on capabilities that each solution provides. The following technologies are available on the Microsoft platform:

- **Windows Workflow Foundation (WF).** WF provides a developer centric solution for creating sequential, state-machine, and data driven workflows. It supports code-only, code-separation, and markup authoring modes. Designer support is available through Visual Studio 2005 with extensions and directly in Visual Studio 2008 and higher. WF includes protocol facilities for secure, reliable, transacted data exchange, activity tracking, a broad choice of transport and encoding options, and provides support for long running workflows that can persist across system shutdowns and restarts.

- **Workflow Services.** Workflow Services provides integration between Windows Communication Foundation (WCF) and Windows Workflow Foundation (WF) to provide WCF-based services for workflow. Starting with Microsoft .NET Framework 3.5, WCF has been extended to provide support for workflows exposed as services and the ability to call services from within workflows. In addition, Microsoft Visual Studio 2008 includes new templates and tools that support workflow services.

- **Microsoft Office SharePoint Services (MOSS).** MOSS is a content management and collaboration platform that provides workflow support based on WF. MOSS provides a solution for human workflow and collaboration in the context of a Microsoft Office SharePoint® server. You can define approval-based workflows related to SharePoint list items using the Web interface, and define conditional and data driven workflows using the SharePoint designer or the Windows Workflow Designer in Visual Studio. For workflow customization, you can use the WF object model within Visual Studio. However, MOSS is suitable only if your business layer is confined to a single SharePoint site and does not require access to information in other sites.

- **BizTalk Server.** BizTalk supports sequential, state-machine, and data driven workflows; and code-separation, and markup authoring modes. It enables electronic document exchange relationships between companies using Electronic Data Interchange (EDI) and/or XML formats; and contains powerful orchestration capabilities for designing and executing long running, loosely coupled business processes and workflows with reliable store and forward messaging capabilities. BizTalk integrates with heterogeneous applications and systems through adapters, and provides a business rules engine and Business Activity Monitoring. If you must interact with non-Microsoft systems, perform EDI operations, or implement Enterprise Service Bus (ESB) patterns, consider using the ESB Toolkit for BizTalk Server.

Step 5 – Design Business Components to Support Workflow

In general, you should implement workflows that involve a multistep or long running process within separate components, and ensure that you handle all fault conditions within the workflows by exposing suitable exceptions. When designing business workflows, you must consider method invocations that require no reply, or have long response times. If the component must execute a specified set of steps sequentially and synchronously, consider using the pipeline pattern. Alternatively, if the process steps can be executed asynchronously in any order, consider using the event pattern.

Use the following sections to understand how you design workflows using the technologies available on the Microsoft platform.

Windows Workflow Foundation

The business components you might design to use Windows Workflow Foundation (WF) include custom workflow, activity, and state objects; as well as custom services. The components you require depend on the workflow style and authoring mode. The following list describes the process for creating the three basic types of workflows, custom services, and workflow markup using WF:

- When designing **sequential workflows**, you define or use existing **Activity** classes (code-only and code-separation), define custom workflow classes (code-only), and define business process components that interact with workflow components (code-only).

- When designing **state machine workflows**, you define state classes used to represent different states of the process (code-only and code-separation), define or use existing events that trigger state changes (code-only and code-separation), define or use existing Activity classes that manage state transitions (code-only and code-separation), define custom workflow classes (code-only), and define business process components that interact with workflow components (code-only).

- When designing **data driven workflows**, you define or use existing Activity classes (code-only and code-separation), define or use existing **Condition** classes to interact with data providers (code-only and code-separation), define custom workflow classes (code-only), and define business process components that interact with workflow components (code-only).

- When designing **custom services**, you define or use existing Activity classes to interact with the service, define a service interface that supports the required operations, design the service using proven practices, and choose the appropriate host for your service (IIS, Workflow Appliance Software (WAS), or **WorkflowServiceHost**).

- When designing **workflow markup**, you can use the Visual Studio designer (available as an extension to Visual Studio 2005 and included in Visual Studio 2008 and higher) or the SharePoint Designer to build workflows based on SharePoint lists. Alternatively, you can use a third party designer to create markup associated with the third party product, or hand-code the markup using appropriate XAML syntax.

BizTalk Server

BizTalk can support either a code-separation or a markup authoring mode. With BizTalk, you may need to design workflow components that are used within a BizTalk orchestration. Examples of workflow components include adapters and connectors. You may also need to create services that provide operations required by the workflow, or design business components that handle requests from BizTalk workflows.

You can also use BizTalk without writing custom components, which represents a markup authoring mode. In other words, if only simple operations are required, you can take advantage of the message transformation and function definition features of BizTalk Server. The following list describes the process for creating workflows using BizTalk:

- When designing workflow components for BizTalk, you define a class that implements the appropriate interface and then register the class with COM.

- When designing business components for BizTalk, you define classes that support the required operations. You can initiate atomic transactions within business components that are called by an orchestration if required, and you should design the business layer to support the required operations using proven practices.

- When designing custom services, you define or use existing BizTalk classes to interact with the service, define a service interface that supports required operations, design the service using proven practices, and choose the appropriate host for your service (IIS or WAS).

Figure 1 shows how all of these components can work together to support a BizTalk workflow.

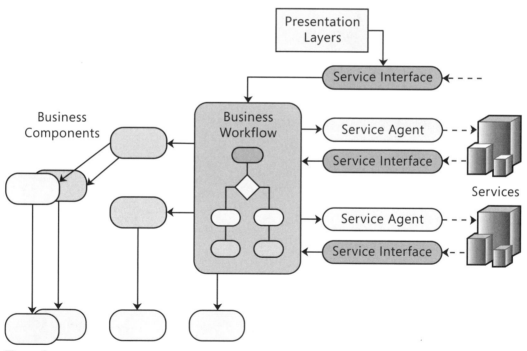

Figure 1
Components working together to support a BizTalk workflow

BizTalk with ESB

The Microsoft Enterprise Service Bus (ESB) Toolkit extends BizTalk with capabilities focused on building connected, service oriented applications. The ESB Toolkit consists of components that support and implement a messaging environment, making it easier to build message-based enterprise applications. Components provided by the toolkit include:

- **ESB Web Services.** These provide key Microsoft ESB Toolkit capabilities. The services provided include the following:
  - Itinerary on-ramp Web services that accept external messages and submits them for processing.
  - Resolver Web service that allows external applications to call the Resolver Framework to look up ESB endpoints based on resolution mechanisms supported by the Resolver Framework, such as business rules policies, UDDI registrations, static invocation, **WS-MetadataExchange** interface, and the content of the message.
  - Transformation Web service that provides features to transform message content and fulfill business requirements. Transformations can take place directly on an incoming message or on messages retrieved from the BizTalk **MessageBox** database.
  - Exception Handling Web service that accepts exception messages from external sources and publishes them to the ESB Exception Management Framework. From there, the fault processor pipeline will normalize, track, and publish the exception message to the ESB Management Portal.
  - UDDI Web service that allows applications and users to look up endpoints based on the service name, business provider, or business category; it also allows applications and users to manipulate the business providers, services, and categories stored in a UDDI repository.
  - BizTalk Operations Web service that exposes information about BizTalk hosts, orchestration, applications, and status.
- **ESB Management Portal.** This provides features such as exception and fault tracking, message resubmission, alerts and notifications, UDDI integration, reporting and analytics, and configuration capabilities.
- **ESB Pipeline Interop Components.** These include Java Messaging Service (JMS) and namespace components for use in BizTalk pipelines.
- **Exception Management Framework.** This can capture exceptions from both BizTalk messaging and orchestration subsystems and generate fault messages.
- **ESB Resolver and Adapter Provider Framework.** This implements a pluggable and configurable architecture for dynamically resolving endpoints and transform requirements, and for routing messages.

- **Itinerary Processing.** This mechanism provides a lightweight capability for dynamically describing, submitting, and executing multiple service invocations or routing/transformation requests.

- **ESB Sample Applications.** These demonstrate usage of the Microsoft ESB Toolkit, demonstrating how you can take advantage of the features it provides in your own SOA and ESB applications.

Using Windows Workflow Foundation and BizTalk Together

There are many cases where Windows Workflow Foundation (WF) or BizTalk may not individually provide full support for the workflows you must implement. When faced with this situation you can often take advantage of the appropriate features from both workflow solutions within the same application. Consider using WF and BizTalk together when you want to implement business rule workflow using WF components in a code-only authoring mode that interacts with the BizTalk rules engine, when you have existing WF workflows that must be invoked from a BizTalk orchestration, when you are writing a SharePoint workflow that must execute a BizTalk orchestration, or when a WF workflow must integrate with heterogeneous or legacy systems.

Additional Resources

To more easily access Web resources on workflow technologies, see the online version of the bibliography at: http://www.microsoft.com/architectureguide.

- *"Introduction to Programming Windows Workflow Foundation"* at http://msdn.microsoft.com/en-us/library/ms734696.aspx.

- *"Microsoft BizTalk ESB Toolkit"* at http://msdn.microsoft.com/en-us/library/dd897973.aspx.

15

Designing Data Components

Overview

Data layer components provide access to data that is hosted within the boundaries of the system, and data exposed by other networked systems. It contains components such as data access components that provide functionality for accessing the data hosted within the system boundaries, and service agent components that provide functionality for accessing data exposed by other back-end systems through Web services. Additionally it may also contain components that provide helper functions and utilities.

This chapter will help you to understand the basic steps for designing your data components. The first step is to identify the constraints associated with the data to be accessed, which will help you to choose an appropriate data access technology. The next step is to choose a mapping strategy and then determine your data access approach, which includes identifying the business entities to be used and the format of entities. Then you can determine how the data access components will connect to the data source. Finally, you determine the error handling strategy to manage the data source exceptions.

Step 1 – Choose a Data Access Technology

The choice of an appropriate data access technology must take into account the type of data you are dealing with and how you want to manipulate that data within the application. Certain technologies are better suited to specific scenarios. Use the following guidelines to map your application scenarios to the available data access technology solutions:

- **ADO.NET Entity Framework.** Consider using the ADO.NET Entity Framework (EF) if you want to create a data model and map it to a relational database; map a single class to multiple tables using inheritance; or query relational stores other than the Microsoft SQL Server family of products. EF is appropriate when you have an object model that you must map to a relational model using a flexible schema, and you need the flexibility of separating the mapping schema from the object model. If you use EF, also consider using:

  - **LINQ to Entities.** Consider using LINQ to Entities if you must execute queries over strongly typed entities, or must execute queries against relational data using LINQ syntax.

- **ADO.NET Data Services Framework.** ADO.NET Data Services is built on top of EF and allows you to expose parts of your Entity Model through a REST interface. Consider using the ADO.NET Data Services Framework if you are developing a RIA or an *n*-tier rich client application, and you want to access data through a resource-centric service interface.

- **ADO.NET Core.** Consider using ADO.NET Core if you need to use a low level API for full control over data access your application, you want to leverage the existing investment made into ADO.NET providers, or you are using traditional data access logic against the database. ADO.NET Core is appropriate if do not need the additional functionality offered by the other data access technologies, or you are building an application that must support a disconnected data access experience.

- **ADO.NET Sync Services.** Consider using ADO.NET Sync Services if you are designing an application that must support occasionally connected scenarios, or requires collaboration between databases.

- **LINQ to XML.** Consider using LINQ to XML if you are using XML data in your application, and you want to execute queries using the LINQ syntax.

For more information on data access technologies on the Microsoft platform, see Appendix C, "Data Access Technology Matrix."

Step 2 – Choose How to Retrieve and Persist Business Objects from the Data Store

After you have identified your data source requirements, the next step is to choose a strategy for populating your business objects or business entities from the data store and for persisting them back to the data store. An impedance mismatch typically exists between an object-oriented data model and the relational data store that sometimes makes it difficult to translate between them. There are a number of approaches to handling this mismatch, but these approaches differ in terms of the data types, structure, transactional techniques, and in how the data is manipulated. The most common approaches use Object/Relational Mapping (O/RM) tools and frameworks. The type of entity you use in your application is the main factor in deciding how to map those entities to data source structures. Use the following guidelines to help you choose how to retrieve and persist business objects from the data store:

- Consider using an O/RM framework that translates between domain entities and the database. If you are working in a greenfield environment, where you have full control over the database schema, you can use an O/RM tool to generate a schema to support the object model and provide a mapping between the database and domain entities. If you are working in a brownfield environment, where you must work with an existing database schema, you can use an O/RM tool to help you to map between the domain model and relational model.

- A common pattern associated with OO design is domain model, which is based on modeling entities on objects within a domain. See the Chapter 13, "Designing Business Entities" later in this chapter for information on domain driven design techniques.

- Ensure you group your entities correctly to achieve a high level of cohesion. This may mean that you require additional objects within your domain model, and that related entities are grouped into aggregate roots.

- When working with Web applications or services, group entities and provide options for partially loading domain entities with only the required data. This minimizes the use of resources by avoiding holding initialized domain models for each user in memory, and allows applications to handle higher user load.

Step 3 – Determine How to Connect to the Data Source

Now that you know how the data access components map to the data source, you should identify how to connect to the data source, protect user credentials, and perform transactions. Use the guidelines in the following sections to help you choose an appropriate approach:

- Connections
- Connection Pooling
- Transactions and Concurrency

Connections

Connections to data sources are a fundamental part of the data layer. The data layer should coordinate all data source connections, making use of the data access infrastructure. Creating and managing connections uses valuable resources in both the data layer and the data source. Use the following guidelines to ensure that you design an appropriate technique for connecting to data sources:

- Ensure that you open connections to the data source as late as possible and close them as early as possible. This will ensure that the resources are locked for as short a duration as possible, and are more freely available to other processes. If you have nonvolatile data, use optimistic concurrency to mitigate the cost of locking data in the database. This avoids the overhead of locking database rows, including the connection that must be kept open during a lock.

- Perform transactions through a single connection where possible. This allows you to use the transaction features of ADO.NET without requiring the services of a distributed transaction coordinator.

- Use connection pooling and tune performance based on results obtained by running simulated load scenarios. Consider tuning connection isolation levels for data queries. If you are building an application with high-throughput requirements, special data operations may be performed at lower isolation levels than the rest of the transaction. Combining isolation levels can have a negative impact on data consistency, so you must carefully analyze this option on a case by case basis.

- For security reasons, avoid using a System or User Data Source Name (DSN) to store connection information.

- Design retry logic to manage the situation where the connection to the data source is lost or times out.

- Batch commands and execute them against the database where possible to reduce round trips to the database server.

Another important aspect that you must consider is the security requirements associated with accessing your data source. In other words, how will data access components authenticate with a data source, and what are the authorization requirements? Use the following guidelines to ensure that you design a secure approach for connecting to data sources:

- Prefer Windows authentication to SQL Server authentication. If you are using Microsoft SQL Server, consider using Windows authentication with a trusted subsystem.

- If you do use SQL authentication, ensure that you use custom accounts with strong passwords, limit the permissions of each account within SQL Server using database roles, add ACLs to any files used to store connection strings, and encrypt connection strings in configuration files.

- Use accounts with least privilege in the database, and require callers to send identity information to the data layer for auditing purposes.

- Do not store passwords for user validation in a database; either plaintext or encrypted. Instead, store password hashes that use a salt value (random bits used as one of the inputs to the hashing function).

- If you are using SQL statements to access the data source, understand your trust boundaries and use the parameterized approach to create queries instead of string concatenation to protect against SQL injection attacks.

- Protect sensitive data sent over the network to and from SQL Server. Be aware that Windows authentication protects credentials, but not application data. Use IPSec or SSL to protect the data in the channel.

Connection Pooling

Connection pooling allows applications to reuse a connection from the pool, or create new connection and add it to the pool if no suitable connection is available. When applications close a connection, it is released back into the pool and the underlying connection remains open. This means that ADO.NET is not required to create a new connection and open it against the data source every time. Although pooling open connections does consume resources, it reduces data access delays and makes applications run more efficiently when suitable pooled connections are available. Other issues that affect connection pooling are the following:

- To maximize the effectiveness of connection pooling, consider using a trusted subsystem security model and avoid impersonation if possible. By using the minimum number of credential sets, you increase the likelihood that an existing pooled connection can be reused and reduce the change of a connection pool overflow. If every call uses different credentials, ADO.NET must create a new connection every time.

- Connections that remain open for long periods can hold on to resources on the server. A typical cause is opening connections early and closing them late (for example, by not explicitly closing and disposing a connection until it goes out of scope).

- Connections can be held open for long periods when using **DataReader** objects, which are only valid while the connection is open.

Transactions and Concurrency

If you have business critical operations in your application, consider wrapping them in transactions. Transactions allow you to execute associated actions on a database as an atomic unit, and ensure database integrity. A transaction is only considered complete if all information and actions are complete, and the associated database changes are made permanent. Transactions support undo (rollback) database actions following an error, which helps to preserve the integrity of data in the database. Use the following guidance to help you design transactions:

- If you are accessing a single data source, use connection-based transactions whenever possible. If you are using manual or explicit transactions, consider implementing the transaction within a stored procedure. If you cannot use transactions, implement compensating methods to revert the data store to its previous state.

- If you are using long-running atomic transactions, avoid holding locks for long periods. In such scenarios, use compensating locks instead. If transactions take a long time to complete, consider using asynchronous transactions that call back to the client when complete. Also, consider the use of multiple active result sets in transaction-heavy concurrent applications to avoid potential deadlock issues.

- If the chance of a data conflict from concurrent users is low (for example, when users are generally adding data or editing different rows), consider using optimistic locking during data access so that the last update applied is valid. If the chance of a data conflict from concurrent users is high (for example, when users are likely to be editing the same rows), consider using pessimistic locking during data access so that updates can only be applied to the latest version. Also consider concurrency issues when accessing static data within the application or when using threads to perform asynchronous operations. Static data is not inherently thread safe, which means that changes made in one thread will affect other threads using the same data.

- Keep transactions as short as possible to minimize lock durations and improve concurrency. However, consider that short and simple transactions may result in a *chatty* interface if it requires multiple calls to achieve one operation.

- Use the appropriate isolation level. The tradeoff is data consistency versus contention. A high isolation level will offer higher data consistency at the price of overall concurrency. A lower isolation level improves performance by lowering contention at the cost of consistency.

In general, you can choose from three types of transaction support, as described in the following list:

- **System.Transactions** namespace classes provides as part of the.NET Framework for both implicit and explicit transaction support. Consider using System.Transactions if you are developing a new application that requires transaction support, or if you have transactions that span multiple nondurable resource managers. For most transactions, the recommended approach is to use the implicit model provided by the TransactionScope object in the System.Transactions namespace. Although implicit transactions are not as fast as manual, or explicit, transactions, they are easier to develop and lead to middle tier solutions that are flexible and easy to maintain. If you do not want to use the implicit model for transactions, you can implement manual transactions using the Transaction class in System.Transactions.

- **ADO.NET Transactions** based on a single database connection. This is the most efficient approach for client controlled transactions on a single data store. Consider using ADO.NET Transactions if you are extending an application that already uses ADO.NET Transactions, you are using ADO.NET providers for database access and the transactions are limited to a single database, or you are deploying your application into an environment that does not support version 2.0 of the .NET Framework. You use ADO.NET commands to begin, commit, and roll back the operations performed within the transaction.

- **T-SQL (Database) Transactions** controlled by commands executed in the database. These are most efficient for server controlled transactions on a single data store, where the database manages all aspects of the transaction. Consider using database transactions if you are developing stored procedures that encapsulate all of the changes that must be managed by a transaction, or you have multiple applications that use the same stored procedure and transaction requirements can be encapsulated within that stored procedures.

Step 4 – Determine Strategies for Handling Data Source Errors

In this step, you should design an overall strategy to handle data source errors. All exceptions associated with data sources should be caught by the data access layer. Exceptions concerning the data itself, and data source access and timeout errors, should be handled in this layer and passed to other layers only if the failures affect application responsiveness or functionality. Use the guidelines in the following sections to help you choose an appropriate approach:

- Exceptions
- Retry Logic
- Timeouts

Exceptions

A centralized exception management strategy will enable consistent handling of exceptions. Exception handling is a crosscutting concern, so consider implementing the logic in separate components that you can share across layers. Pay particular attention to exceptions that propagate through trust boundaries and to other layers or tiers, and design for unhandled exceptions so they do not result in application reliability issues or exposure of sensitive application information. The following approach will help you in designing the exception management strategy:

- Determine exceptions that should be caught and handled in the data access layer. Deadlocks, connection issues, and optimistic concurrency checks can often be resolved within the data layer.

- Consider implementing a retry process for operations where data source errors or timeouts occur, but only where it is safe to do so.

- Design an appropriate exception propagation strategy. For example, allow exceptions to bubble up to boundary layers where they can be logged and transformed as necessary before passing them to the next layer.

- Design an appropriate logging and notification strategy for critical errors and exceptions that does not reveal sensitive information.

- Consider using existing frameworks such as the patterns & practices Enterprise Library to implement a consistent exception handling and management strategy.

Retry Logic

Design retry logic to handle errors, such as those that may occur during server or database failover. Retry logic should catch any errors that occur while connecting to the database or executing commands (queries or transactions) against the database. There may be multiple causes for the error. When an error occurs, the data component should reestablish connectivity by closing any existing connections and attempting to make a new connection, and then re-execute failed commands if necessary. It should retry the process only a certain number of times, and then finally give up and return a failure exception. Ensure that queries and requests, and any subsequent retries, are executed asynchronously so that they do not render the application unresponsive.

Timeouts

Identifying the appropriate value for connection and command timeouts is very important. Setting a connection or command timeout value that is higher than the client timeout (for example, in the case of a Web application, the browser or Web server request timeout) can result in the client request timing out before the database connection is opened. Setting a low value will cause the error handler to invoke the retry logic. If a timeout occurs while executing a transaction, database resources may remain locked after the connection is closed when connection pooling is enabled. In such cases, when the connection is closed, it should be discarded so that is not returned to the pool. This results in the transaction being rolled back, freeing the database resources.

Step 5 – Design Service Agent Objects (Optional)

Service agents are objects that manage the semantics of communicating with external services, isolate your application from the idiosyncrasies of calling diverse services, and provide additional services such as basic mapping between the format of the data exposed by the service and the format your application requires. They may also implement caching, and offline or intermittent connection support. Follow the steps below to design the service agent objects:

1. Use the appropriate tool to add a service reference. This will generate a proxy and the data classes that represent the data contract from the service.

2. Determine how the service will be used in your application. For most applications, the service agent acts as an abstraction layer between your business layer and the remote service, and can provide a consistent interface regardless of the data format. In smaller applications, the presentation layer, may access the service agent directly.

Additional Resources

To more easily access Web resources on general data access guidelines, see the online version of the bibliography at: http://www.microsoft.com/architectureguide.

- *".NET Data Access Architecture Guide"* at http://msdn.microsoft.com/en-us/library/ms978510.aspx.
- *"Data Patterns"* at http://msdn.microsoft.com/en-us/library/ms998446.aspx.
- *"Designing Data Tier Components and Passing Data Through Tiers"* at http://msdn.microsoft.com/en-us/library/ms978496.aspx.

16

Quality Attributes

Overview

Quality attributes are the overall factors that affect run-time behavior, system design, and user experience. They represent areas of concern that have the potential for application wide impact across layers and tiers. Some of these attributes are related to the overall system design, while others are specific to run time, design time, or user centric issues. The extent to which the application possesses a desired combination of quality attributes such as usability, performance, reliability, and security indicates the success of the design and the overall quality of the software application.

When designing applications to meet any of the quality attributes requirements, it is necessary to consider the potential impact on other requirements. You must analyze the tradeoffs between multiple quality attributes. The importance or priority of each quality attribute differs from system to system; for example, interoperability will often be less important in a single use packaged retail application than in a line of business (LOB) system.

This chapter lists and describes the quality attributes that you should consider when designing your application. To get the most out of this chapter, use the table on the following pages to gain an understanding of how quality attributes map to system and application quality factors, and read the description of each of the quality attributes. Then use the sections containing key guidelines for each of the quality attributes to understand how that attribute has an impact on your design, and to determine the decisions you must make to addresses these issues. Keep in mind that the list of quality attributes in this chapter is not exhaustive, but provides a good starting point for asking appropriate questions about your architecture.

Common Quality Attributes

The following table describes the quality attributes covered in this chapter. It categorizes the attributes in four specific areas linked to design, runtime, system, and user qualities. Use this table to understand what each of the quality attributes means in terms of your application design.

Category	Quality attribute	Description
Design Qualities	*Conceptual Integrity*	Conceptual integrity defines the consistency and coherence of the overall design. This includes the way that components or modules are designed, as well as factors such as coding style and variable naming.
	Maintainability	Maintainability is the ability of the system to undergo changes with a degree of ease. These changes could impact components, services, features, and interfaces when adding or changing the functionality, fixing errors, and meeting new business requirements.
	Reusability	Reusability defines the capability for components and subsystems to be suitable for use in other applications and in other scenarios. Reusability minimizes the duplication of components and also the implementation time.

Category	Quality attribute	Description
Run-time Qualities	Availability	Availability defines the proportion of time that the system is functional and working. It can be measured as a percentage of the total system downtime over a predefined period. Availability will be affected by system errors, infrastructure problems, malicious attacks, and system load.
	Interoperability	Interoperability is the ability of a system or different systems to operate successfully by communicating and exchanging information with other external systems written and run by external parties. An interoperable system makes it easier to exchange and reuse information internally as well as externally.
	Manageability	Manageability defines how easy it is for system administrators to manage the application, usually through sufficient and useful instrumentation exposed for use in monitoring systems and for debugging and performance tuning.
	Performance	Performance is an indication of the responsiveness of a system to execute any action within a given time interval. It can be measured in terms of latency or throughput. Latency is the time taken to respond to any event. Throughput is the number of events that take place within a given amount of time.
	Reliability	Reliability is the ability of a system to remain operational over time. Reliability is measured as the probability that a system will not fail to perform its intended functions over a specified time interval.
	Scalability	Scalability is ability of a system to either handle increases in load without impact on the performance of the system, or the ability to be readily enlarged.
	Security	Security is the capability of a system to prevent malicious or accidental actions outside of the designed usage, and to prevent disclosure or loss of information. A secure system aims to protect assets and prevent unauthorized modification of information.
System Qualities	Supportability	Supportability is the ability of the system to provide information helpful for identifying and resolving issues when it fails to work correctly.
	Testability	Testability is a measure of how easy it is to create test criteria for the system and its components, and to execute these tests in order to determine if the criteria are met. Good testability makes it more likely that faults in a system can be isolated in a timely and effective manner.
User Qualities	Usability	Usability defines how well the application meets the requirements of the user and consumer by being intuitive, easy to localize and globalize, providing good access for disabled users, and resulting in a good overall user experience.

The following sections describe each of the quality attributes in more detail, and provide guidance on the key issues and the decisions you must make for each one:

- Availability
- Conceptual Integrity
- Interoperability
- Maintainability
- Manageability
- Performance
- Reliability
- Reusability
- Scalability
- Security
- Supportability
- Testability
- User Experience / Usability

Availability

Availability defines the proportion of time that the system is functional and working. It can be measured as a percentage of the total system downtime over a predefined period. Availability will be affected by system errors, infrastructure problems, malicious attacks, and system load. The key issues for availability are:

- A physical tier such as the database server or application server can fail or become unresponsive, causing the entire system to fail. Consider how to design failover support for the tiers in the system. For example, use Network Load Balancing for Web servers to distribute the load and prevent requests being directed to a server that is down. Also, consider using a RAID mechanism to mitigate system failure in the event of a disk failure. Consider if there is a need for a geographically separate redundant site to failover to in case of natural disasters such as earthquakes or tornados.

- Denial of Service (DoS) attacks, which prevent authorized users from accessing the system, can interrupt operations if the system cannot handle massive loads in a timely manner, often due to the processing time required, or network configuration and congestion. To minimize interruption from DoS attacks, reduce the attack surface area, identify malicious behavior, use application instrumentation to expose unintended behavior, and implement comprehensive data validation. Consider using the Circuit Breaker or Bulkhead patterns to increase system resiliency.

- Inappropriate use of resources can reduce availability. For example, resources acquired too early and held for too long cause resource starvation and an inability to handle additional concurrent user requests.

- Bugs or faults in the application can cause a system wide failure. Design for proper exception handling in order to reduce application failures from which it is difficult to recover.

- Frequent updates, such as security patches and user application upgrades, can reduce the availability of the system. Identify how you will design for run-time upgrades.

- A network fault can cause the application to be unavailable. Consider how you will handle unreliable network connections; for example, by designing clients with occasionally-connected capabilities.

- Consider the trust boundaries within your application and ensure that subsystems employ some form of access control or firewall, as well as extensive data validation, to increase resiliency and availability.

Conceptual Integrity

Conceptual integrity defines the consistency and coherence of the overall design. This includes the way that components or modules are designed, as well as factors such as coding style and variable naming. A coherent system is easier to maintain because you will know what is consistent with the overall design. Conversely, a system without conceptual integrity will constantly be affected by changing interfaces, frequently deprecating modules, and lack of consistency in how tasks are performed. The key issues for conceptual integrity are:

- Mixing different areas of concern within your design. Consider identifying areas of concern and grouping them into logical presentation, business, data, and service layers as appropriate.

- Inconsistent or poorly managed development processes. Consider performing an Application Lifecycle Management (ALM) assessment, and make use of tried and tested development tools and methodologies.

- Lack of collaboration and communication between different groups involved in the application lifecycle. Consider establishing a development process integrated with tools to facilitate process workflow, communication, and collaboration.

- Lack of design and coding standards. Consider establishing published guidelines for design and coding standards, and incorporating code reviews into your development process to ensure guidelines are followed.

- Existing (legacy) system demands can prevent both refactoring and progression toward a new platform or paradigm. Consider how you can create a migration path away from legacy technologies, and how to isolate applications from external dependencies. For example, implement the Gateway design pattern for integration with legacy systems.

Interoperability

Interoperability is the ability of a system or different systems to operate successfully by communicating and exchanging information with other external systems written and run by external parties. An interoperable system makes it easier to exchange and reuse information internally as well as externally. Communication protocols, interfaces, and data formats are the key considerations for interoperability. Standardization is also an important aspect to be considered when designing an interoperable system. The key issues for interoperability are:

- Interaction with external or legacy systems that use different data formats. Consider how you can enable systems to interoperate, while evolving separately or even being replaced. For example, use orchestration with adaptors to connect with external or legacy systems and translate data between systems; or use a canonical data model to handle interaction with a large number of different data formats.

- Boundary blurring, which allows artifacts from one system to defuse into another. Consider how you can isolate systems by using service interfaces and/or mapping layers. For example, expose services using interfaces based on XML or standard types in order to support interoperability with other systems. Design components to be cohesive and have low coupling in order to maximize flexibility and facilitate replacement and reusability.

- Lack of adherence to standards. Be aware of the formal and de facto standards for the domain you are working within, and consider using one of them rather than creating something new and proprietary.

Maintainability

Maintainability is the ability of the system to undergo changes with a degree of ease. These changes could impact components, services, features, and interfaces when adding or changing the application's functionality in order to fix errors, or to meet new business requirements. Maintainability can also affect the time it takes to restore the system to its operational status following a failure or removal from operation for an upgrade. Improving system maintainability can increase availability and reduce the effects of run-time defects. An application's maintainability is often a function of its overall quality attributes but there a number of key issues that can directly affect maintainability:

- Excessive dependencies between components and layers, and inappropriate coupling to concrete classes, prevents easy replacement, updates, and changes; and can cause changes to concrete classes to ripple through the entire system. Consider designing systems as well-defined layers, or areas of concern, that clearly delineate the system's UI, business processes, and data access functionality. Consider implementing cross-layer dependencies by using abstractions (such as abstract classes or interfaces) rather than concrete classes, and minimize dependencies between components and layers.

- The use of direct communication prevents changes to the physical deployment of components and layers. Choose an appropriate communication model, format, and protocol. Consider designing a pluggable architecture that allows easy upgrades and maintenance, and improves testing opportunities, by designing interfaces that allow the use of plug-in modules or adapters to maximize flexibility and extensibility.

- Reliance on custom implementations of features such as authentication and authorization prevents reuse and hampers maintenance. To avoid this, use the built-in platform functions and features wherever possible.

- The logic code of components and segments is not cohesive, which makes them difficult to maintain and replace, and causes unnecessary dependencies on other components. Design components to be cohesive and have low coupling in order to maximize flexibility and facilitate replacement and reusability.

- The code base is large, unmanageable, fragile, or over complex; and refactoring is burdensome due to regression requirements. Consider designing systems as well defined layers, or areas of concern, that clearly delineate the system's UI, business processes, and data access functionality. Consider how you will manage changes to business processes and dynamic business rules, perhaps by using a business workflow engine if the business process tends to change. Consider using business components to implement the rules if only the business rule values tend to change; or an external source such as a business rules engine if the business decision rules do tend to change.

- The existing code does not have an automated regression test suite. Invest in test automation as you build the system. This will pay off as a validation of the system's functionality, and as documentation on what the various parts of the system do and how they work together.

- Lack of documentation may hinder usage, management, and future upgrades. Ensure that you provide documentation that, at minimum, explains the overall structure of the application.

Manageability

Manageability defines how easy it is for system administrators to manage the application, usually through sufficient and useful instrumentation exposed for use in monitoring systems and for debugging and performance tuning. Design your application to be easy to manage, by exposing sufficient and useful instrumentation for use in monitoring systems and for debugging and performance tuning. The key issues for manageability are:

- Lack of health monitoring, tracing, and diagnostic information. Consider creating a health model that defines the significant state changes that can affect application performance, and use this model to specify management instrumentation requirements. Implement instrumentation, such as events and performance counters, that detects state changes, and expose these changes through standard systems such as

Event Logs, Trace files, or Windows Management Instrumentation (WMI). Capture and report sufficient information about errors and state changes in order to enable accurate monitoring, debugging, and management. Also, consider creating management packs that administrators can use in their monitoring environments to manage the application.

- Lack of runtime configurability. Consider how you can enable the system behavior to change based on operational environment requirements, such as infrastructure or deployment changes.

- Lack of troubleshooting tools. Consider including code to create a snapshot of the system's state to use for troubleshooting, and including custom instrumentation that can be enabled to provide detailed operational and functional reports. Consider logging and auditing information that may be useful for maintenance and debugging, such as request details or module outputs and calls to other systems and services.

Performance

Performance is an indication of the responsiveness of a system to execute specific actions in a given time interval. It can be measured in terms of latency or throughput. Latency is the time taken to respond to any event. Throughput is the number of events that take place in a given amount of time. An application's performance can directly affect its scalability, and lack of scalability can affect performance. Improving an application's performance often improves its scalability by reducing the likelihood of contention for shared resources. Factors affecting system performance include the demand for a specific action and the system's response to the demand. The key issues for performance are:

- Increased client response time, reduced throughput, and server resource over utilization. Ensure that you structure the application in an appropriate way and deploy it onto a system or systems that provide sufficient resources. When communication must cross process or tier boundaries, consider using coarse-grained interfaces that require the minimum number of calls (preferably just one) to execute a specific task, and consider using asynchronous communication.

- Increased memory consumption, resulting in reduced performance, excessive cache misses (the inability to find the required data in the cache), and increased data store access. Ensure that you design an efficient and appropriate caching strategy.

- Increased database server processing, resulting in reduced throughput. Ensure that you choose effective types of transactions, locks, threading, and queuing approaches. Use efficient queries to minimize performance impact, and avoid fetching all of the data when only a portion is displayed. Failure to design for efficient database processing may incur unnecessary load on the database server, failure to meet performance objectives, and costs in excess of budget allocations.

- Increased network bandwidth consumption, resulting in delayed response times and increased load for client and server systems. Design high performance communication between tiers using the appropriate remote communication mechanism. Try to reduce the number of transitions across boundaries, and minimize the amount of data sent over the network. Batch work to reduce calls over the network.

Reliability

Reliability is the ability of a system to continue operating in the expected way over time. Reliability is measured as the probability that a system will not fail and that it will perform its intended function for a specified time interval. The key issues for reliability are:

- The system crashes or becomes unresponsive. Identify ways to detect failures and automatically initiate a failover, or redirect load to a spare or backup system. Also, consider implementing code that uses alternative systems when it detects a specific number of failed requests to an existing system.

- Output is inconsistent. Implement instrumentation, such as events and performance counters, that detects poor performance or failures of requests sent to external systems, and expose information through standard systems such as Event Logs, Trace files, or WMI. Log performance and auditing information about calls made to other systems and services.

- The system fails due to unavailability of other externalities such as systems, networks, and databases. Identify ways to handle unreliable external systems, failed communications, and failed transactions. Consider how you can take the system offline but still queue pending requests. Implement store and forward or cached message-based communication systems that allow requests to be stored when the target system is unavailable, and replayed when it is online. Consider using Windows Message Queuing or BizTalk Server to provide a reliable once-only delivery mechanism for asynchronous requests.

Reusability

Reusability is the probability that a component will be used in other components or scenarios to add new functionality with little or no change. Reusability minimizes the duplication of components and the implementation time. Identifying the common attributes between various components is the first step in building small reusable components for use in a larger system. The key issues for reusability are:

- The use of different code or components to achieve the same result in different places; for example, duplication of similar logic in multiple components, and duplication of similar logic in multiple layers or subsystems. Examine the application design to identify common functionality, and implement this functionality in separate components that you can reuse. Examine the application design to identify cross-cutting concerns such as validation, logging, and authentication, and implement these functions as separate components.

- The use of multiple similar methods to implement tasks that have only slight variation. Instead, use parameters to vary the behavior of a single method.

- Using several systems to implement the same feature or function instead of sharing or reusing functionality in another system, across multiple systems, or across different subsystems within an application. Consider exposing functionality from components, layers, and subsystems through service interfaces that other layers and systems can use. Use platform agnostic data types and structures that can be accessed and understood on different platforms.

Scalability

Scalability is ability of a system to either handle increases in load without impact on the performance of the system, or the ability to be readily enlarged. There are two methods for improving scalability: scaling vertically (scale up), and scaling horizontally (scale out). To scale vertically, you add more resources such as CPU, memory, and disk to a single system. To scale horizontally, you add more machines to a farm that runs the application and shares the load. The key issues for scalability are:

- Applications cannot handle increasing load. Consider how you can design layers and tiers for scalability, and how this affects the capability to scale up or scale out the application and the database when required. You may decide to locate logical layers on the same physical tier to reduce the number of servers required while maximizing load sharing and failover capabilities. Consider partitioning data across more than one database server to maximize scale-up opportunities and allow flexible location of data subsets. Avoid stateful components and subsystems where possible to reduce server affinity.

- Users incur delays in response and longer completion times. Consider how you will handle spikes in traffic and load. Consider implementing code that uses additional or alternative systems when it detects a predefined service load or a number of pending requests to an existing system.

- The system cannot queue excess work and process it during periods of reduced load. Implement store-and-forward or cached message-based communication systems that allow requests to be stored when the target system is unavailable, and replayed when it is online.

Security

Security is the capability of a system to reduce the chance of malicious or accidental actions outside of the designed usage affecting the system, and prevent disclosure or loss of information. Improving security can also increase the reliability of the system by reducing the chances of an attack succeeding and impairing system operation. Securing a system should protect assets and prevent unauthorized access to or modification of information. The factors affecting system security are confidentiality, integrity, and availability. The features used to secure systems are authentication, encryption, auditing, and logging. The key issues for security are:

- Spoofing of user identity. Use authentication and authorization to prevent spoofing of user identity. Identify trust boundaries, and authenticate and authorize users crossing a trust boundary.

- Damage caused by malicious input such as SQL injection and cross-site scripting. Protect against such damage by ensuring that you validate all input for length, range, format, and type using the constrain, reject, and sanitize principles. Encode all output you display to users.

- Data tampering. Partition the site into anonymous, identified, and authenticated users and use application instrumentation to log and expose behavior that can be monitored. Also use secured transport channels, and encrypt and sign sensitive data sent across the network

- Repudiation of user actions. Use instrumentation to audit and log all user interaction for application critical operations.

- Information disclosure and loss of sensitive data. Design all aspects of the application to prevent access to or exposure of sensitive system and application information.

- Interruption of service due to Denial of service (DoS) attacks. Consider reducing session timeouts and implementing code or hardware to detect and mitigate such attacks.

Supportability

Supportability is the ability of the system to provide information helpful for identifying and resolving issues when it fails to work correctly. The key issues for supportability are:

- Lack of diagnostic information. Identify how you will monitor system activity and performance. Consider a system monitoring application, such as Microsoft System Center.

- Lack of troubleshooting tools. Consider including code to create a snapshot of the system's state to use for troubleshooting, and including custom instrumentation that can be enabled to provide detailed operational and functional reports. Consider logging and auditing information that may be useful for maintenance and debugging, such as request details or module outputs and calls to other systems and services.

- Lack of tracing ability. Use common components to provide tracing support in code, perhaps though Aspect Oriented Programming (AOP) techniques or dependency injection. Enable tracing in Web applications in order to troubleshoot errors.

- Lack of health monitoring. Consider creating a health model that defines the significant state changes that can affect application performance, and use this model to specify management instrumentation requirements. Implement instrumentation, such as events and performance counters, that detects state changes, and expose these changes through standard systems such as Event Logs, Trace files, or Windows Management Instrumentation (WMI). Capture and report sufficient information about errors and state changes in order to enable accurate monitoring, debugging, and management. Also, consider creating management packs that administrators can use in their monitoring environments to manage the application.

Testability

Testability is a measure of how well system or components allow you to create test criteria and execute tests to determine if the criteria are met. Testability allows faults in a system to be isolated in a timely and effective manner. The key issues for testability are:

- Complex applications with many processing permutations are not tested consistently, perhaps because automated or granular testing cannot be performed if the application has a monolithic design. Design systems to be modular to support testing. Provide instrumentation or implement probes for testing, mechanisms to debug output, and ways to specify inputs easily. Design components that have high cohesion and low coupling to allow testability of components in isolation from the rest of the system.

- Lack of test planning. Start testing early during the development life cycle. Use mock objects during testing, and construct simple, structured test solutions.

- Poor test coverage, for both manual and automated tests. Consider how you can automate user interaction tests, and how you can maximize test and code coverage.

- Input and output inconsistencies; for the same input, the output is not the same and the output does not fully cover the output domain even when all known variations of input are provided. Consider how to make it easy to specify and understand system inputs and outputs to facilitate the construction of test cases.

User Experience / Usability

The application interfaces must be designed with the user and consumer in mind so that they are intuitive to use, can be localized and globalized, provide access for disabled users, and provide a good overall user experience. The key issues for user experience and usability are:

- Too much interaction (an excessive number of clicks) required for a task. Ensure you design the screen and input flows and user interaction patterns to maximize ease of use.

- Incorrect flow of steps in multistep interfaces. Consider incorporating workflows where appropriate to simplify multistep operations.

- Data elements and controls are poorly grouped. Choose appropriate control types (such as option groups and check boxes) and lay out controls and content using the accepted UI design patterns.

- Feedback to the user is poor, especially for errors and exceptions, and the application is unresponsive. Consider implementing technologies and techniques that provide maximum user interactivity, such as Asynchronous JavaScript and XML (AJAX) in Web pages and client-side input validation. Use asynchronous techniques for background tasks, and tasks such as populating controls or performing long-running tasks.

Additional Resources

To more easily access Web resources on implementing and auditing quality attributes, see the online version of the bibliography at: http://www.microsoft.com/architectureguide.

- *"Implementing System-Quality Attributes"* at http://msdn.microsoft.com/en-us/library/bb402962.aspx.

- *"Software Architecture in the New Economy"* at http://msdn.microsoft.com/en-us/library/cc168642.aspx.

- *"Quality-Attribute Auditing: The What, Why, and How"* at http://msdn.microsoft.com/en-us/library/bb508961.aspx.

- Feathers, Michael. *Working Effectively With Legacy Code.* Prentice Hall, 2004.

- Baley, Kyle and Donald Belcham. *Brownfield Application Development in .NET.* Manning Publications Co, 2008.

- Nygard, Michael. *Release It!: Design and Deploy Production-Ready Software.* Pragmatic Bookshelf, 2007.

17
Crosscutting Concerns

Overview

The majority of applications you design will contain common functionality that spans layers and tiers. This functionality typically supports operations such as authentication, authorization, caching, communication, exception management, logging and instrumentation, and validation. Such functionality is generally described as *crosscutting concerns* because it affects the entire application, and should be centralized in one location in the code where possible. For example, if code that generates log entries and writes to the application logs is scattered throughout your layers and tiers, and the requirements related to these concerns change (such as logging to a different location), you may have to update the relevant code throughout the entire system. Instead, if you centralize the logging code, you can change the behavior by changing the code in just one location.

This chapter will help you to understand the role that crosscutting concerns play in applications, identify the areas where they occur in your applications, and learn about the common issues faced when designing for crosscutting concerns. There are several different approaches to handling this functionality, from common libraries such as the patterns & practices Enterprise Library, to Aspect Oriented Programming (AOP) methods where metadata is used to insert crosscutting code directly into the compiled output or during run time execution.

General Design Considerations

The following guidelines will help you to understand the main factors for managing crosscutting concerns:

- Examine the functions required in each layer, and look for cases where you can abstract that functionality into common components, perhaps even general purpose components that you configure depending on the specific requirements of each layer of the application. It is likely that these kinds of components will be reusable in other applications.

- Depending how you physically distribute the components and layers of your application, you may need to install the crosscutting components on more than one physical tier. However, you still benefit from reusability and reduced development time and cost.

- Consider using the Dependency Injection pattern to inject instances of crosscutting components into your application based on configuration information. This allows you to change the crosscutting components that each section uses easily, without requiring recompilation and redeployment of your application. The patterns & practices Unity library provides comprehensive support for the Dependency Injection pattern. Other popular Dependency Injection libraries include StructureMap, Ninject, and Castle Windsor (see Additional Resources at the end of this chapter for more information).

- Consider using a third-party library of components that are highly configurable and can reduce development time. An example is the patterns & practices Enterprise Library, which contains application blocks designed to help you implement caching, exception handling, authentication and authorization, logging, exception handling, validation, and cryptography functions. It also contains mechanisms that implement policy injection and a dependency injection container that make it easier to implement solutions for a range of crosscutting concerns. For more information about Enterprise Library, see Appendix F, "patterns & practices Enterprise Library." Another common library is provided by the Castle Project (see Additional Resources at the end of this chapter for more information).

- Consider using Aspect Oriented Programming (AOP) techniques to weave the crosscutting concerns into your application, rather than having explicit calls in the code. The patterns & practices Unity mechanism and the Enterprise Library Policy Injection Application Block support this approach. Other examples include Castle Windsor and PostSharp (see Additional Resources at the end of this chapter for more information).

Specific Design Issues

The following sections list the key areas to consider as you develop your architecture, and contain guidelines to help you avoid the common issues in each area:

- Authentication
- Authorization
- Caching
- Communication
- Configuration Management
- Exception Management
- Logging and Instrumentation
- State Management
- Validation

Authentication

Designing a good authentication strategy is important for the security and reliability of your application. Failure to design and implement a good authentication strategy can leave your application vulnerable to spoofing attacks, dictionary attacks, session hijacking, and other types of attacks. Consider the following guidelines when designing an authentication strategy:

- Identify your trust boundaries and authenticate users and calls across the trust boundaries. Consider that calls might need to be authenticated from the client as well as from the server (mutual authentication).
- Enforce the use of strong passwords or password phrases.
- If you have multiple systems within the application or users must be able to access multiple applications with the same credentials, consider a single sign-on strategy.
- Do not transmit passwords over the wire in plain text, and do not store passwords in a database or data store as plain text. Instead, store a hash of the password.

For more information about designing an authentication strategy, and techniques for implementing it, see "Additional Resources" at the end of this chapter.

Authorization

Designing a good authorization strategy is important for the security and reliability of your application. Failure to design and implement a good authorization strategy can make your application vulnerable to information disclosure, data tampering, and elevation of privileges. Consider the following guidelines when designing an authorization strategy:

- Identify your trust boundaries and authorize users and callers across the trust boundary.

- Protect resources by applying authorization to callers based on their identity, groups, or roles. Minimize granularity by limiting the number of roles you use where possible.

- Consider using role-based authorization for business decisions. Role-based authorization is used to subdivide users into groups (roles) and then set permissions on each role rather than on individual users. This eases management by allowing you to administer a smaller set of roles rather than a larger set of users.

- Consider using resource-based authorization for system auditing. Resource-based authorization sets permissions on the resource itself; for example, an access control list (ACL) on a Windows resource uses the identity of the original caller to determine access rights to the resource. If you use resource-based authorization in WCF, you must to impersonate the original caller through the client or presentation layer, through the WCF service layer, and to the business logic code that accesses the resource.

- Consider using claims-based authorization when you must support federated authorization based on a mixture of information such as identity, role, permissions, rights, and other factors. Claims-based authorization provides additional layers of abstraction that make it easier to separate authorization rules from the authorization and authentication mechanism. For example, you can authenticate a user with a certificate or with username/password credentials and then pass that claim-set to the service to determine access to resources.

For more information about designing an authorization strategy, and techniques for implementing it, see "Additional Resources" at the end of this chapter.

Caching

Caching can improve the performance and responsiveness of your application. However, a poorly designed caching strategy can degrade performance and responsiveness. You should use caching to optimize reference data lookups, avoid network round trips, and avoid unnecessary and duplicate processing. When you implement caching, you must decide when to load the cache data and how and when to remove expired cached data. Try to preload frequently used data into the cache asynchronously or by using a batch process to avoid client delays. Consider the following guidelines when designing a caching strategy:

- Choose an appropriate location for the cache. If your application is deployed in Web farm, avoid using local caches that must be synchronized; instead consider using a transactional resource manager such as Microsoft® SQL Server® or a product that supports distributed caching, such as "Memcached" from Danga Interactive or the Microsoft project code named "Velocity" (see Additional Resources at the end of this chapter for more information).

- Consider caching data in a ready-to-use format when working with an in-memory cache. For example, use a specific object instead of caching raw database data. Consider using Microsoft Velocity to implement in-memory caching.

- Do not cache volatile data, and do not cache sensitive data unless you encrypt it.

- Do not depend on data still being in your cache; it may have been removed. Implement a mechanism to handle cache failures, perhaps by reloading the item from the source.

- Be especially careful when accessing the cache from multiple threads. If you are using multiple threads, ensure that all access to the cache is thread-safe to maintain consistency.

For more information about designing a caching strategy, see "Design Steps for Caching" later in this chapter.

Communication

Communication is concerned with the interaction between components across layers and tiers. The mechanism you choose depends on the deployment scenarios your application must support. Consider the following guidelines when designing communication mechanisms:

- Consider using message-based communication when crossing physical or process boundaries; and object-based communication when in process (when crossing only logical boundaries). To reduce round trips and improve communication performance across physical and process boundaries, design coarse-grained (chunky) interfaces that communicate less often but with more information in each communication. However, where appropriate, consider exposing a fine-grained (chatty) interface for use by in process calls and wrapping these calls in a coarse-grained façade for use by processes that access it across physical or process boundaries.

- If your messages do not need to be received in a specific order and do not have dependencies on each other, consider using asynchronous communication to avoid blocking processing or UI threads.

- Consider using Microsoft Message Queuing to queue messages for later delivery in case of system or network interruption or failure. Message Queuing can perform transacted message delivery and supports reliable once-only delivery.

- Choose an appropriate transport protocol, such as HTTP for Internet communication and TCP for intranet communication. Consider how you will determine the appropriate message exchange patterns, connection based or connectionless communication, reliability guarantees (such as service level agreements), and authentication mechanism.

- Ensure that you protect messages and sensitive data during communication by using encryption, digital certificates, and channel security features.

For more information about designing a communication strategy, see Chapter 18, "Communication and Messaging."

Configuration Management

Designing a good configuration management mechanism is important for the security and flexibility of your application. Failure to do so can make your application vulnerable to a variety of attacks, and also leads to an administrative overhead for your application. Consider the following guidelines when designing for configuration management:

- Carefully consider which settings must be externally configurable. Verify that there is an actual business need for each configurable setting, and provide the minimal configuration options necessary to meet these requirements. Excessive configurability can result in systems that are more complicated, and may leave the system vulnerable to security breaches and malfunctions due to incorrect configuration.

- Decide if you will store configuration information centrally and have it down-loaded or applied to users at startup (for example, though Active Directory Group Policy). Consider how you will restrict access to your configuration information. Consider using least privileged process and service accounts, and encrypt sensitive information in your configuration store.

- Categorize the configuration items into logical sections based on whether they apply to users, application settings, or environmental settings. This makes it easier to divide configuration when you must support different settings for different sets of users, or multiple environments.

- Categorize the configuration items into logical sections if your application has multiple tiers. If your server application runs in a Web farm, decide which parts of the configuration are shared and which parts are specific to the machine on which the application is running. Then choose an appropriate configuration store for each section.

- Provide a separate administrative UI for editing configuration information.

Exception Management

Designing a good exception management strategy is important for the security and reliability of your application. Failure to do so can make it very difficult to diagnose and solve problems with your application. It can also leave your application vulnerable to Denial of Service (DoS) attacks, and it may reveal sensitive and critical information. Raising and handling exceptions is an expensive process, so it is important that the design also takes into account performance issues. A good approach is to design a centralized exception management mechanism for your application, and to consider providing access points within your exception management system (such as WMI events) to support enterprise level monitoring systems such as Microsoft System Center. Consider the following guidelines when designing an exception management strategy:

- Design an appropriate exception propagation strategy that wraps or replaces exceptions, or adds extra information as required. For example, allow exceptions to bubble up to boundary layers where they can be logged and transformed as necessary before passing them to the next layer. Consider including a context identifier so that related exceptions can be associated across layers to assist in performing root cause analysis of errors and faults. Also ensure that the design deals with unhandled exceptions. Do not catch internal exceptions unless you can handle them or you must add more information, and do not use exceptions to control application flow.

- Ensure that a failure does not leave the application in an unstable state, and that exceptions do not allow the application to reveal sensitive information or process details. If you cannot guarantee correct recovery, allow the application to halt with an unhandled exception in preference to leaving it running in an unknown and possibly corrupted state.

- Design an appropriate logging and notification strategy for critical errors and exceptions that stores sufficient details about the exception to allow support staff to recreate the scenario, but does not reveal sensitive information in exception messages and log files.

For more information about designing an exception management strategy, see "Design Steps for Exception Management" later in this chapter.

Logging and Instrumentation

Designing a good logging and instrumentation strategy is important for the security and reliability of your application. Failure to do so can make your application vulnerable to repudiation threats, where users deny their actions, and log files may be required for legal proceedings to prove wrongdoing. You should audit and log activity across the layers of your application, which can help to detect suspicious activity and provide early indication of a serious attack. Auditing is usually considered most authoritative if the audits are generated at the precise time of resource access, and by the same routines that access the resource. Instrumentation can be implemented by using performance counters and events to give administrators information about the state, performance, and health of an application. Consider the following guidelines when designing a logging and instrumentation strategy:

- Design a centralized logging and instrumentation mechanism that captures system- and business-critical events. Avoid logging and instrumentation that is too fine grained, but consider additional logging and instrumentation that is configurable at run time for obtaining extra information and to aid debugging.

- Create secure log file management policies. Do not store sensitive information in the log files, and protect log files from unauthorized access. Consider how you will access and pass auditing and logging data securely across application layers, and ensure that you suppress but correctly handle logging failures.

- Consider allowing your log sinks, or trace listeners, to be configurable so that they can be modified at run time to meet deployment environment requirements. Libraries such as the patterns & practices Enterprise Library are useful for implementing logging and instrumentation in your applications. Other popular libraries include NLog and log4net (see Additional Resources at the end of this chapter for more information).

For more information about logging and instrumentation, see "Design Steps for Exception Management" later in this chapter.

State Management

State management concerns the persistence of data that represents the state of a component, operation, or step in a process. State data can be persisted using different formats and stores. The design of a state management mechanism can affect the performance of your application; maintaining even small volumes of state information can adversely affect performance and the ability to scale out your application. You should only persist data that is required, and you must understand the options that are available for managing state. Consider the following guidelines when designing a state management mechanism:

- Keep your state management as lean as possible; persist the minimum amount of data required to maintain state.
- Make sure that your state data is serializable if it must be persisted or shared across process and network boundaries.
- Choose an appropriate state store. Storing state in process and in memory is the technique that can offer the best performance, but only if your state does not have to survive process or system restarts. Persist your state to a local disk or local SQL Server if you want it available after a process or system restart. Consider storing state in a central location such as a central SQL Server if state is critical for your application, or if you want to share state between several machines.

Validation

Designing an effective validation mechanism is important for the usability and reliability of your application. Failure to do so can leave your application open to data inconsistencies, business rule violations, and a poor user experience. In addition, failing to adequately validate input may leave your application vulnerable to security issues such as cross-site scripting attacks, SQL injection attacks, buffer overflows, and other types of input attacks. Unfortunately there is no standard definition that can differentiate valid input from malicious input. In addition, how your application actually uses the input influences the risks associated with exploitation of the vulnerability. Consider the following guidelines when designing a validation mechanism:

- Whenever possible, design your validation system to use allow lists that define specifically what is acceptable input, rather than trying to define what comprises invalid input. It is much easier to widen the scope of an allow list later than it is to narrow a block list.
- Do not rely on only client-side validation for security checks. Instead, use client-side validation to give the user feedback and improve the user experience. Always use server-side validation to check for incorrect or malicious input because client-side validation can be easily bypassed.

- Centralize your validation approach in separate components if it can be reused, or consider using a third-party library such as the patterns & practices Enterprise Library Validation Block. Doing so will allow you to apply a consistent validation mechanism across the layers and tiers of your application.

- Be sure to constrain, reject, and sanitize user input. In other words, assume that all user input is malicious. Identify your trust boundaries and validate all input data for length, format, type, and range as it crosses trust boundaries.

For more information about designing a validation strategy, see "Design Steps for Validating Input and Data" later in this chapter.

Design Steps for Caching

Caching can play a vital role in maximizing performance. However, it is important to design an appropriate strategy for caching, as you can reduce performance by applying inappropriate techniques. The following steps will help you to design an appropriate caching strategy for your application.

Step 1 – Determine the Data to Cache

It is important to determine, as part of your application design, the data that is suitable for caching. Create a list of the data to cache in each layer of your application. Consider caching the following types of data:

- **Application-wide data.** Consider caching relatively static data that applies to all users of the application. Examples are product lists and product information.

- **Relatively static data.** Consider caching data that is fully static, or which does not change frequently. Examples are constants and fixed values read from configuration or a database.

- **Relatively static Web pages.** Consider caching the output of Web pages or sections of Web pages that do not change frequently.

- **Stored procedure parameters and query results.** Consider caching frequently used query parameters and query results.

Step 2 – Determine Where to Cache Data

When deciding on where to cache data, there are typically two things you must consider: the physical location of the cache, and the logical location of the cache.

The **physical location** will either be in-memory, or disk-based using files or a database. In-memory caching may be performed using the ASP.NET cache mechanism, Enterprise Library Caching Application Block, or a distributed in-memory caching mechanism such as Microsoft project code named "Velocity" or the Danga Interactive

"Memcached" technology. An in-memory cache is a good choice when the data is used frequently by the application, the cached data is relatively volatile and must be frequently reacquired, and the volume of cached data is relatively small. A file system-based or database cache is a good choice when accessing data from the cache store is more efficient when compared to acquiring the data from the original store, the cached data is relatively less volatile, and the services for reacquiring the data are not always available. The disk-based approach is also ideal when the volume of cached data is relatively large, or the cached data must survive process and machine restarts.

The **logical location** of the cache describes the location within the application logic. It is important to cache the data as close as possible to the location where it will be used to minimize processing and network round trips, and to maximize the performance and responsiveness of the application. Consider the following guidelines when deciding on the logical location of the cache data:

- Consider caching on the **client** when the data is page specific or user specific, does not contain sensitive information, and is lightweight.

- Consider caching on a **proxy server** or **Web server** (for Web applications) when you have relatively static pages that are requested frequently by clients, your pages are updated with a known frequency, or the results are returned from Web services. Also, consider this approach where you have pages that can generate different output based on HTTP parameters, and those parameters do not often change. This is particularly useful when the range of outputs is small.

- Consider caching data in the **presentation layer** when you have relatively static page outputs, you have small volumes of data related to user preferences for a small set of users, or you have UI controls that are expensive to create. Also consider this approach when you have data that must be displayed to the user and is expensive to create; for example, product lists and product information.

- Consider caching data in the **business layer** when you must maintain state for a service, business process, or workflow; or when relatively static data is required to process requests from the presentation layer and this data is expensive to create.

- Consider caching data in the **data layer** when you have input parameters for a frequently called stored procedure in a collection, or you have small volumes of raw data that are returned from frequently executed queries. Consider caching schemas for typed datasets in the data layer.

- Consider caching in a separate table inside the **database** any data that requires considerable query processing to obtain the result set. This may also be appropriate when you have very large volumes of data to cache, where you implement a paging mechanism to read sections of the data for display in order to improve performance.

Step 3 – Determine the Format of Your Data to Cache

After you have determined the data that you must cache and decided where to cache it, the next important task is to identify the format for the cached data. When you are caching data, store it in a format optimized for the intended use so that it does not require additional or repeated processing or transformation. This type of cached data is a good choice when you must cache data using an in-memory cache, you do not need to share the cache across processes or computers, you do not need to transport cached data between memory locations, and you must cache raw data such as **DataSets**, **DataTables**, and Web pages.

If you must store or transport the cached data, consider serialization requirements. Serializing the cached data is a good choice when you will cache data in a disk-based cache, or you will store session state on a separate server or in a SQL Server database. It is also a good approach when you must share the cache across process or computers, transport the cached data between memory locations, or cache custom objects. You can choose to serialize your data using an XML serializer or a binary serializer. An XML serializer is a good choice when interoperability is your key concern. If performance is your key concern, consider using a binary serializer.

Step 4 – Determine a Suitable Cache Management Strategy

You must determine an appropriate cache expiration and cache flushing policy. Expiration and flushing relate to the removal of cached data from the cache store. The difference is that flushing might remove valid cache items to make space for more frequently used items, whereas expiration removes invalid and expired items. Check the capabilities of your underlying cache system; not all of these options are available in all cache implementations.

Design a **cache expiration** strategy that will maintain the validity of the data and items in the cache. When deciding on the cache expiration policy, consider both time-based expiration and notification-based expiration as follows:

- In a **time-based** expiration policy, the cached data is expired or invalidated based on relative or absolute time intervals. This is a good choice when the cache data is volatile, the cached data is regularly updated, or the cached data is valid for only a specific time or interval. When choosing a time-based expiration policy, you can choose an absolute time expiration policy or a sliding time expiration policy. An absolute time expiration policy allows you to define the lifetime of cached data by specifying the time at which it will expire. A sliding time expiration policy allows you to define the lifetime of cached data by specifying the interval between the last access and the time at which it will expire.

- In a **notification-based** expiration policy, the cached data is expired or invalidated based on notifications from internal or external sources. This is a good choice when you are working with nonvolatile cache data, the cached data is updated at irregular intervals, or the data is valid unless changed by external or internal systems. Common sources of notifications are disk file writes, WMI events, SQL dependency notifications, and business logic operations. A notification will expire or invalidate the dependent cache item(s).

Design a **cache flushing** strategy so that storage, memory, and other resources are used efficiently. When deciding on the cache flushing strategy, you can choose explicit flushing or scavenging as follows:

- **Explicit flushing** requires you to determine when an item should be flushed and then remove it. This is good choice when you must support the scenario of removing damaged or obsolete cached data, you are working with custom stores that do not support scavenging, or you are working with a disk-based cache.

- **Scavenging** requires you to determine the conditions and heuristics in which an item should be scavenged. This is good choice when you want to activate scavenging automatically when system resources become scarce, you want to remove seldom used or unimportant items from the cache automatically, or you are working with a memory-based cache.

Common scavenging heuristics include the following:

- The **Least Recently Used** algorithm scavenges the items that have not been used for the longest period of time.

- The **Least Frequently Used** algorithm scavenges the items that have been used least frequently since they were loaded.

- The **Priority** algorithm instructs the cache to assign a priority to cached items and attempt to preserve those with highest priority when it scavenges the cache.

Step 5 – Determine How to Load the Cache Data

Choosing the appropriate option for loading your cache helps to maximize the performance and responsiveness of your application. When determining how to populate the cache, consider how much of the data you want to be available when the application starts or when you initially load the cache, and the implications on application startup time and performance. For example, you may decide to pre-load data into the cache when the application initializes, or to acquire and cache data only when it is requested. Loading data into the cache at application startup can increase an application's responsiveness, but also increases its startup time. On the other hand, loading data into the cache only when it is first accessed decreases startup time but can also reduce initial responsiveness.

You can use either proactive or reactive loading when designing your cache population strategy, as follows:

- Choose **proactive loading** to retrieve all of the data for the application when it starts and then cache it for the lifetime of the application. Proactive loading is a good choice if your cached data is relatively static or has a known update frequency, a known lifetime, and a known size. If you do not know the size of the data, you might exhaust system resources loading it all. It is also a good choice if the source for your cached data is a slow database; or data is retrieved across a slow network or from an unreliable Web service.

- Choose **reactive loading** to retrieve data as it is requested by the application and cache it for future requests. Reactive loading is a good choice if your cached data is relatively volatile, you are not sure of your cache data lifetime, your cached data volume is large, and your cache data source is reliable and responsive.

Design Steps for Exception Management

A robust and well designed exception management strategy can simplify application design, and improve security and manageability. It can also make it easier for developers to create the application, and reduces development time and cost. The following steps will help you to design an appropriate exception management strategy for your application.

Step 1 – Identify Exceptions That You Want to Handle

When designing exception management for your application, it is important to identify the exceptions that you want to handle. You should handle system or application exceptions such as those raised by users accessing system resources for which they do not have permission; and system failures due to disk, CPU, or memory issues. You must also identify the business exceptions that you want to handle. These are exceptions caused by actions such as violations of business rules.

Step 2 – Determine Your Exception Detection Strategy

Your design should mandate that structured exception handling is used consistently throughout the entire application. This creates a more robust application that is less likely to be left in an inconsistent state. Structured exception handling provides a way to manage exceptions using try, catch, and finally blocks to detect errors occurring within your code, and react to them appropriately.

The key considerations when detecting exceptions are to only catch the exception when you must gather exception details for logging, add relevant extra information to the exception, clean up any resources used in the code block, or retry the operation to recover from the exception. Do not catch an exception and then allow it to propagate up the call stack if you do not need to carry out any of these tasks.

Step 3 – Determine Your Exception Propagation Strategy

Consider the following exception propagation strategies. Your application can (and should) use a mixture of any or all of these strategies depending on the requirements of each context:

- **Allow exceptions to propagate.** This strategy is useful in that you do not need to gather exception details for logging, add relevant extra information to the exception, clean up any resources used in the code block, or retry the operation to recover from the exception. You simply allow the exception to propagate up through the code stack.

- **Catch and rethrow exceptions.** In this strategy, you catch the exception, carry out some other processing, and then rethrow it. Usually, in this approach, the exception information remains unaltered. This strategy is useful when you have to clean up resources, log exception information, or if you need to attempt to recover from the error.

- **Catch, wrap, and throw exceptions.** In this strategy, you catch generic exceptions and react to them by cleaning up resources or performing any other relevant processing. If you cannot recover from the error, you wrap the exception within another exception that is more relevant to the caller and then throw the new exception so that it can be handled by code higher in the code stack. This strategy is useful when you want to keep the exception relevancy and/or provide additional information to the code that will handle the exception.

- **Catch and discard exceptions.** This is not the recommended strategy, but might be suitable in some specific scenarios. You catch the exception and proceed with normal application execution. If required, you can log the exception and perform resource cleanup. This strategy may be useful for system exceptions that do not affect user operations, such as an exception raised when a log is full.

Step 4 – Determine Your Custom Exception Strategy

Consider if you need to design custom exceptions or if you can use just the standard .NET Framework exception types. Do not use a custom exception if a suitable exception is already available in your exception hierarchy or within the .NET Framework. However, use a custom exceptions if your application must identify and handle a specific exception in order to avoid using conditional logic or if it must include additional information to suit a specific requirement.

If you do need to create custom exception classes, ensure that the class name ends with "Exception," and implement the standard constructors for your custom exception class—including the serialization constructor. This is important in order to integrate with the standard exception mechanism. Implement a custom exception by deriving from a suitable more general exception in order to specialize it to meet your requirements.

In general, when designing your exception management strategy, you should create an exception hierarchy and organize your custom exceptions within it. This helps users to quickly analyze and trace problems. Your custom exceptions should indicate the layer in which the exception occurred, the component in which the exception might have occurred, and the type of exception that occurred (such as a security, system, or business exception).

Consider storing your application's exception hierarchy in a single assembly that can be referenced throughout your application code. This helps to centralize the management and deployment of your exception classes. Also, consider how you will marshal exceptions across boundaries. The .NET Framework Exception classes support serialization. When you are designing custom exception classes, ensure that they also support serialization.

Step 5 – Determine Appropriate Information to Gather

When handling exceptions, one of the most important aspects is a sound strategy for gathering exception information. The information captured should accurately represent the exception condition. It should also be relevant and informative to the audience. Audiences usually fall into one of the three categories: end users, application developers, and operators. Analyze the audience you are addressing by looking into the scenario and individual context.

End users require a meaningful and well presented description. When gathering exception information for end users, consider providing user friendly message that indicates the nature of the error, and information on how to recover from the error if this is appropriate. Application developers require more detailed information in order to assist with problem diagnosis.

When gathering exception information for application developers, make sure you provide the precise location in the code where the exception occurred; and exception details such as the exception type and state of the system when the exception occurred. Operators require relevant information that allows them to react appropriately and take the necessary recovery steps. When gathering exception information for operators, consider providing exception details and knowledge that will assist operators to locate the people to notify and the information they will require to solve the problem.

Irrespective of the audience that will receive the exception information, it is useful to provide rich exception information. Store the information in a log file for later examination, and analysis of exception frequency and details. By default, you should capture at least the date and time, machine name, exception source and type, exception message, stack and call traces, application domain name, assembly name and version, thread ID, and user details.

Step 6 – Determine Your Exception Logging Strategy

There is a range of options available for logging exception information. The following key considerations will help you to choose a logging option:

- Choose **Windows Event Log** or **Windows Eventing 6.0** when your application is deployed on a single machine, you need to leverage existing tools to view the log, or reliability is a prime concern.

- Choose a **SQL Database** when your application is deployed in a farm or cluster, you need to centralize your logging, or you need flexibility as to how the exception information is structured and logged.

- Choose a **custom log file** when your application is deployed on single machine, you need complete flexibility for choosing the log format, or you want a simple and easy to implement log store. Ensure that you limit the size of the log file by trimming or consolidating the log periodically to prevent it becoming too large.

- Choose **Message Queuing** as a delivery mechanism to pass exception messages to their final destination when reliability is your prime concern, your applications are deployed in farm or cluster, or you must centralize logging.

For any application, you can choose a mix of these options depending upon your scenario and exception policy. For example, security exceptions may be logged to the Security Event Log and business exceptions may be logged to a database.

Step 7 – Determine Your Exception Notification Strategy

As part of your exception management design, you must also decide on your notification strategy. Exception management and logging are often not sufficient in enterprise applications. You should consider complementing them with notifications to ensure that administrators and operators are made aware of exceptions. You can use technologies such as WMI events, SMTP e-mail, SMS text messages, or other custom notification systems.

Consider using external notification mechanisms such as log monitoring systems or a third-party environment that detects the error conditions in the log data and raises appropriate notifications. This is a good choice when you want to decouple your monitoring and notification system from your application code and have just logging code inside your applications. Alternatively, consider adding custom notification mechanisms inside your application when you want to generate immediate notifications without relying on external monitoring systems.

Step 8 – Determine How to Handle Unhandled Exceptions

When an exception is not handled until the last point or boundary, and there is no way to recover from the exception before returning control to the user, your application must handle this unhandled exception. For unhandled exceptions, you should gather the required information, write it to a log or audit file, send any notifications required for the exception, perform any cleanup required, and finally communicate the error information to the user.

Do not expose all of the exception details. Instead, provide a user friendly generic error message. In the case of clients that have no user interface, such as Web services, you might choose to throw a generic exception in place of detailed exception. This prevents system details from being exposed to the end-user.

Consider using the patterns & practices Exception Handling Application Block and the patterns & practices Logging Application Block to implement a consistent exception management, logging, and notification strategy for your applications. The Exception Handling Application Block supports a range of exception handling options, and the Logging Application Block can receive, format, and send log messages and notifications to a wide range of logs and other destinations. For more information, see Appendix F, "patterns & practices Enterprise Library."

Design Steps for Validating Input and Data

The following steps will help you to design an appropriate validation strategy for your application. When designing input and data validation for your application, the first task is to identify the trust boundaries and key scenarios when data should be validated. Next, identify the data to be validated and the location where it should be validated. You should also determine how to implement a reusable validation strategy. Finally, determine the validation strategy appropriate for your application.

Step 1 – Identify your Trust Boundaries

Trust boundaries define the separation between trusted and untrusted data. Data on one side of the trust boundary is trusted and, on the other side, it is not trusted. You should first identify data that is crossing trust boundaries to determine what you must validate. Consider the use of input validation and data validation at every trust boundary to mitigate security threats such as cross-site scripting and code injection. Examples of trust boundaries are a perimeter firewall, the boundary between the Web server and database server, and the boundary between your application and a third-party service.

Identify the systems and subsystems that your application communicates with, and the outer system boundaries that are crossed when writing to files on a server, making calls to the database server, or calling a Web service. Identify the entry points at the trust boundaries and the exit points where you write data from client input or from un-trusted sources such as shared databases.

Step 2 – Identify Key Scenarios

After you identify the trust boundaries within your application, you should define the key scenarios where you must validate data. All user entered data should be considered malicious until validated. For example, in a Web application, data in the presentation layer that should be validated includes values in form fields, query strings, and hidden fields; parameters sent in GET and POST requests; uploaded data (malicious users can intercept HTTP requests and modify the contents); and cookies (which reside on the client machine and could be modified).

In the business layer, business rules impose a constraint on the data. Any violation of these rules is assumed to be a validation error, and the business layer should raise an error to represent the violation. If you use a rules engine or workflow, ensure that it validates the results for each rule based upon the information required for that rule and the conclusions made from the evaluation of previous rules.

Step 3 – Determine Where to Validate

In this step, you determine where to perform validation—on the client, or on both the server and the client. Never depend on client-side validation alone. Use client-side validation to provide a more interactive UI, but always implement server-side validation to validate the data securely within your trust boundary. Data and business rules validation on the client can reduce round trips to the server and improve user experience. In a Web application, the client browser should support DHTML and JavaScript, ideally implemented in a separate .js file to provide reusability and to allow the browser to cache it. The simplest approach in a Web application is to use the ASP.NET validation controls. This is a set of server controls that can validate data client side, and will automatically validate server side as well.

Server-side data and business rules validation can be implemented using ASP.NET validation controls in a Web application. Alternatively, for both Web and other types of applications, consider using the patterns & practices Validation Application Block to create validation logic that can be reused across layers. The Validation Application Block can be used in Windows Forms, ASP.NET, and WPF applications. For more information about the Validation Application Block, see Appendix F, "patterns & practices Enterprise Library."

Step 4 – Identify Validation Strategies

The common strategies for data validation are:

- **Accept known good** (allow list or positive validation): Accept only data that satisfies specific criteria, and reject all other. Use this strategy where possible, as it is the most secure approach.

- **Reject known bad** (block list or negative validation): Accept data that does not meet specific criteria (such as containing a specified set of characters). Use this strategy cautiously and as a secondary line of defense as it is very difficult to create a complete list of criteria for all known invalid input.

- **Sanitize:** Eliminate or translate characters in an effort to make the input safe. As with the block list (negative validation) approach, use this strategy cautiously and as a secondary line of defense as it is very difficult to create a complete list of criteria for all known invalid input.

Relevant Design Patterns

Key patterns connected with crosscutting concerns can be organized into categories, as shown in the following table. Consider using these patterns when making design decisions for each category.

Category	Relevant patterns
Caching	**Cache Dependency.** Use external information to determine the state of data stored in a cache. **Page Cache.** Improve the response time for dynamic Web pages that are accessed frequently, but that change less often and consume a large amount of system resources to construct.
Communication	**Intercepting Filter.** A chain of composable filters (independent modules) that implement common pre-processing and post-processing tasks during a Web page request. **Pipes and Filters.** Route messages through pipes and filters that can modify or examine the message as it passes through the pipe. **Service Interface.** A programmatic interface that other systems can use to interact with the service.

For more information on the Page Cache, Intercepting Filter, and Service Interface patterns, see *"Enterprise Solution Patterns Using Microsoft .NET"* at http://msdn.microsoft.com/en-us/library/ms998469.aspx.

For more information on the Pipes and Filters pattern, see *"Integration Patterns"* at http://msdn.microsoft.com/en-us/library/ms978729.aspx.

patterns & practices Solution Assets

For more information on related solution assets available from the Microsoft patterns & practices group, see the following resources:

- **Enterprise Library** provides a series of application blocks that simplify common tasks such as caching, exception handling, validation, logging, cryptography, credential management, and facilities for implementing design patterns such as Inversion of Control and Dependency Injection. For more information, see the *"Microsoft Enterprise Library"* at http://msdn2.microsoft.com/en-us/library/cc467894.aspx.

- **Unity Application Block** is a lightweight, extensible dependency injection container that helps you to build loosely coupled applications. For more information, see *"Unity Application Block"* at http://msdn.microsoft.com/en-us/library/cc468366.aspx.

Additional Resources

To more easily access Web resources, see the online version of the bibliography at: http://www.microsoft.com/architectureguide.

For more information on authentication and authorization, see the following articles:

- *"Authorization"* at http://msdn.microsoft.com/en-us/library/cc949059.aspx.
- *"Authorization In WCF-Based Services"* at http://msdn.microsoft.com/en-us/magazine/cc948343.aspx.
- *"Designing Application-Managed Authorization"* at http://msdn.microsoft.com/en-us/library/ms954586.aspx.
- *"Enterprise Authorization Strategy"* at http://msdn.microsoft.com/en-us/library/bb417064.aspx.
- *"Federated Identity: Scenarios, Architecture, and Implementation"* at http://msdn.microsoft.com/en-us/library/aa479079.aspx.
- *"Guidance on Patterns & Practices: Security"* at http://msdn.microsoft.com/en-us/library/ms954624.aspx.
- *"Trusted Subsystem Design"* at http://msdn.microsoft.com/en-us/library/aa905320.aspx.

For more information on the remaining topics covered in this chapter, see the following articles:

- *"Caching Architecture Guide for .NET Framework Applications"* at http://msdn.microsoft.com/en-us/library/ms978498.aspx.
- *"Cohesion and Coupling"* at http://msdn.microsoft.com/en-us/magazine/cc947917.aspx.
- Duffy, Joe. Concurrent Programming on Windows. Addison-Wesley 2009.
- *"Enterprise Solution Patterns Using Microsoft .NET"* at http://msdn.microsoft.com/en-us/library/ms998469.aspx.
- *"Exception Management Architecture Guide"* at http://msdn.microsoft.com/en-us/library/ms954599.aspx.
- *"Integration Patterns"* at http://msdn.microsoft.com/en-us/library/ms978729.aspx.
- *"Microsoft Project Code Named Velocity"* at http://msdn.microsoft.com/en-us/data/cc655792.aspx.

For information on some of the popular third party libraries and frameworks that you might find useful for managing crosscutting concerns, see the following resources:

- Castle Project at http://www.castleproject.org/index.html.
- Ninject at http://ninject.org/.
- PostSharp at http://www.postsharp.org/.
- StructureMap at http://structuremap.sourceforge.net/Default.htm.
- memcached at http://www.danga.com/memcached/.
- NLog at http://www.nlog-project.org/.
- log4net at http://logging.apache.org/log4net/.

18

Communication and Messaging

Overview

One of the key factors that affect the design of an application—particularly a distributed application—is the way that you design the communication infrastructure for each part of the application. Components must communicate with each other; for example, to send user input to the business layer, and then to update the data store through the data layer. When components are located on the same physical tier, you can often rely on direct communication between these components. However, if you deploy components and layers on physically separate servers and client machines—as is likely in most scenarios—you must consider how the components in these layers will communicate with each other efficiently and reliably.

In general, you must choose between direct communication (such as method calls between components) and message-based communication. There are many advantages to using message-based communication, such as the ability to decouple your components from each other. Decoupling components not only improves maintainability but can also provide flexibility that makes it easier to change your deployment strategy in the future. However, message-based communication raises issues that you must consider, such as performance, reliability, and security.

This chapter presents design guidelines that will help you to choose the appropriate communication approach, understand how to get the best results from your chosen approach, and anticipate security and reliability issues that might arise. However, the bulk of this chapter focuses on designing a suitable message-based communication mechanism, together with guidelines for asynchronous and synchronous communication, data format, performance, security, interoperability, and choice of implementation technology.

General Design Guidelines

When designing a communication strategy for your application, consider the performance impact of communicating between layers, as well as between tiers. Because each communication across a logical or a physical boundary increases processing overhead, design for efficient communication by reducing round trips and minimizing the amount of data sent over the network. Consider the following guidelines when deciding on a communication strategy:

- **Consider communication strategies when crossing boundaries.** Understand each of your boundaries and how they affect communication performance. For example, the computer process, machine, and managed-to-unmanaged code transition all represent boundaries that that may be crossed when communicating with components of the application or external services and applications.

- **Consider using message-based communication when crossing process boundaries.** Use Windows Communication Foundation (WCF) with either the TCP or named pipes protocol for maximum performance.

- **Consider using message-based communication when crossing physical boundaries.** Consider using WCF to communicate with remote machines across physical boundaries. Consider using Microsoft Message Queuing for once only reliable delivery of messages.

- **Maximize performance and responsiveness when accessing remote layers.** When communicating with remote layers, reduce communication requirements by using coarse-grained message-based communication methods and use asynchronous communication if possible to avoid blocking or freezing the UI.

- **Consider the serialization capabilities of the data formats passed across boundaries.** If you require interoperability with other systems, consider XML serialization. Keep in mind that XML serialization imposes increased overhead. If performance is critical, consider binary serialization because it is faster and the resulting serialized data is smaller than the XML equivalent.

- **Ensure that you protect messages and sensitive data during communication.** Consider using encryption, digital certificates, and channel security features.

- **Implement mechanisms to enforce idempotency and commutativity.** Ensure that your application code can detect and manage messages that arrive more than once (idempotency) and multiple messages that arrive out of order (commutativity).

Message-Based Communication Guidelines

Message-based communication allows you to expose a service to your callers by defining a service interface that clients call by passing XML-based messages over a transport channel. Message-based calls are generally made from remote clients, but message-based service interfaces can support local callers as well. A message-based communication style is well suited to the following scenarios:

- You are implementing a business system that represents a medium to long term investment; for example, when building a service that will be exposed to and used by partners for a considerable time.

- You are implementing large scale systems that must offer high-availability, or must operate over unreliable networks. In this case, a message store and forward mechanism can provide improved reliability.

- You are building a service that you want to isolate from other services it uses, and from services that consume it. The use of message-based service interfaces that advertise interface details to clients makes it easy for any clients to use the service without requiring specific implementations for individual clients.

- You are dealing with real world business processes that use the asynchronous model.

Consider the following guidelines when using message-based communication:

- Be aware that a connection will not always be present, and that messages may need to be stored and then sent when a connection becomes available.

- Consider how to handle the case when a message response is not received. To manage the conversation state, your business logic can log the sent messages for later processing in case a response is not received.

- Consider using acknowledgements to force the correct sequencing of messages.

- Use standard protocols, such as HTTP for Internet communication and TCP for intranet communication. Do not implement a custom communication channel unless there is no default combination of endpoint, protocol, and format that suits your needs.

- If message response timing is critical for your communication, consider a synchronous programming model in which your client waits for each response message. Alternatively, where clients can continue to execute while waiting for a response, consider an asynchronous model.

When designing your message-based communication strategy, you should also consider specific topics that can affect the stability, reusability, performance, and overall success of your design. The following sections describe these issues in more detail:

- Asynchronous vs. Synchronous Communication
- Coupling and Cohesion
- Data Formats
- Interoperability
- Performance
- State Management

Asynchronous vs. Synchronous Communication

Consider the key tradeoffs when choosing between synchronous and asynchronous communication styles. Synchronous communication is best suited to scenarios in which you must guarantee the order in which calls are received, or when you must wait for the call to return. Asynchronous communication is best suited to scenarios in which responsiveness is important or you cannot guarantee that the target will be available. Consider the following guidelines when deciding whether to use synchronous or asynchronous communication:

- For maximum performance, loose coupling, and minimized system overhead, consider using an asynchronous communication model. If some clients can only make synchronous calls, consider wrapping existing asynchronous service methods in a component that performs synchronous communication with the client.

- In cases where you must guarantee the order in which operations take place, or where you use operations that depend on the outcome of previous operations, consider a synchronous model.

- For asynchronous in-process calls, use the platform features (such as **Begin** and **End** versions of methods and callbacks) to implement asynchronous method calls. For asynchronous out of process calls, such as calls across physical tiers and boundaries, consider using messaging or asynchronous service requests.

If you choose asynchronous communication and cannot guarantee network connectivity or the availability of the target, consider using a store and forward message delivery mechanism to avoid losing messages. When choosing a store and forward design strategy, consider using local caches to store messages for later delivery in case of system or network interruption. Alternatively, consider using Message Queuing to queue messages for later delivery in case of system or network interruption or failure. Message Queuing can perform transacted message delivery and supports reliable once only delivery. If you need to interoperate with other systems and platforms at the enterprise level, or perform electronic data interchange, consider using BizTalk Server provide a robust delivery mechanism.

Coupling and Cohesion

Communication methods that impose interdependencies between the distributed parts of the application will result in a tightly coupled application. A loosely coupled application uses methods that impose a minimum set of requirements for communication to occur. Consider the following guidelines when designing for coupling and cohesion:

- For loose coupling, consider using a message-based technology such as ASP.NET Web services (ASMX) or WCF, and self describing data and ubiquitous protocols such as HTTP, REST, and SOAP.
- To maintain cohesion, ensure that interfaces contain only methods that are closely related in purpose and functional area.

Data Formats

The most common data formats for passing data across tiers are scalar values, XML, DataSets, and custom objects. Use the following table to understand the key considerations for choosing a data type.

Type	Considerations
Scalar values	You want built-in support for serialization. You can handle the likelihood of schema changes. Scalar values produce tight coupling that will require method signatures to be modified, thereby affecting the calling code.
XML	You need loose coupling, where the caller must know about only the data that defines the business entity and the schema that provides metadata for the business entity. You must support different types of callers, including third-party clients. You need built-in support for serialization.
DataSet	You need support for complex data structures. You must handle sets and complex relationships. You must track changes to data within the **DataSet**. You want built-in support for serialization.
Custom objects	You need support for complex data structures. You are communicating with components that know about the object type. You want to support binary serialization for performance.

Consider the following guidelines when selecting a data format for a communication channel:

- If your application works mainly with instance data, consider using simple values for better performance. Simple value types will reduce your initial development costs; however, they produce tight coupling that can increase maintenance costs if the types must change in the future.
- XML may require additional upfront schema definition but will result in loose coupling that can reduce future maintenance costs and increase interoperability (for example, if you want to expose your interface to additional XML-compliant callers).

- **DataSets** work well for complex data types, especially if they are populated directly from a database. However, it is important to understand that **DataSets** also contain schema and state information that increases the overall volume of data passed across the network, and their special format may restrict interoperability with other systems. Consider using **DataSets** if your application works mainly with sets of data and needs functionality such as sorting, searching, and data binding.

- Custom objects work best when none of the other options meet your requirements, or when you are communicating with components that expect a custom object. They tend to impose a lower overhead than **DataSets** and support both binary and XML serialization. Usually the custom objects you use to transmit data across the communication channel will be data transfer objects (DTOs) that contain data extracted from your business entities.

- Ensure that type information is not lost during the communication process. Binary serialization preserves type fidelity, which is useful when passing objects between client and server. However, this approach means that you must implement a more rigorous versioning system for interfaces. Default XML serialization serializes only public properties and fields and does not preserve type fidelity.

Interoperability

The main factors that influence interoperability of applications and components are the availability of suitable communication channels, and the formats and protocols that the participants can understand. Consider the following guidelines for maximizing interoperability:

- To enable communication with wide variety of platforms and devices, consider using standard protocols and data formats such as HTTP and XML. Keep in mind that your protocol decisions may affect the availability of clients you are targeting. For example, target systems might be protected by firewalls that block some protocols.

- Consider versioning issues for interfaces and contracts. Changes to a service may be required due to changing business needs, information technology requirements, or other issues. Where these changes result in an incompatible interface, message contract, or data contract, consider creating a new version that clients can use while allowing existing clients to use the previous version where they do not need to access the functionality exposed by the new interface. For more information, see *"Service Versioning"* at http://msdn.microsoft.com/en-us/library/ms731060.aspx.

- The data format you choose may affect interoperability. For example, target systems might not understand platform specific types, or might have different ways of handling and serializing types.

- Your security encryption and decryption decisions may affect interoperability. For example, some message encryption/decryption techniques might not be available on all systems.

Performance

The design of your communication interfaces and the data formats you use will also have a considerable impact on the performance of your application, especially when crossing process or machine boundaries. While other considerations, such as inter-operability, may require specific interfaces and data formats, there are techniques you can use to improve performance related to communication between different layers or tiers of your application. Consider the following guidelines for performance:

- Do not pass unnecessary data to remote methods where possible, and minimize the volume of data sent across the network. This reduces serialization overhead and network latency. However, avoid fine-grained (chatty) interfaces for cross-process and cross-machine communication. These require the client to make multiple method calls to perform a single logical unit of work. Consider using the Façade pattern to provide a coarse-grained wrapper for existing chatty interfaces.

- Consider using DTOs to pass data as a single unit instead of passing individual data types one at a time.

- If serialization performance is critical for your application, consider using custom classes with binary serialization.

- If XML is required for interoperability, consider using attribute-based structures for large amounts of data instead of element-based structures.

State Management

It may be necessary for the communicating parties in an application to maintain state across multiple requests. Consider the following guidelines when deciding how to implement state management:

- Only maintain state between calls if it is absolutely necessary. Maintaining state consumes resources, can affect the performance of your application, and can limit your deployment options.

- If you are using a stateful programming model within a component or service, consider using a durable data store such as a database to store state information, and use a token to access the information.

- If you are designing an ASMX service, consider using the **ApplicationContext** class to preserve state because it provides access to the default state stores for application scope and session scope.

- If you are designing a WCF service, consider using the extensible objects provided by the platform for state management. These extensible objects allow state to be stored in various scopes such as service host, service instance context, and operation context. Note that all of these states are held in memory and are not durable. If you require durable state, you can use the durable storage (introduced in the .NET Framework 3.5) or implement your own custom solution.

Contract First Design

Traditionally, developers have built services using a *code first* approach where they design the service based on requirements, and expose an interface suited to the code and the requirements. However, the *contract first* approach is becoming more popular as it can reduce the incompatibilities that may occur between disparate systems and a wide range of clients.

Contract first design is the process of designing the service contract in terms of the data, messages, and interface it will expose, and then generating the service interface code from the contract. From there, you can implement the code behind the service interface that performs the processing required. This allows you to concentrate on the format of the messages and the data types they use at the beginning of the process to maximize interoperability and compatibility.

You can use modeling tools to help you design the interface, such as the patterns & practices Web Service Software Factory: Modeling Edition (see http://msdn.microsoft.com/servicefactory/). Alternatively, you can design the interface using XML, XSD, and schemas; and then use tools such as WSDL.exe with the **/server** switch to generate the interface definition. Message bus technologies such as Microsoft BizTalk Server encourage the use of contract first design principles.

Principles to bear in mind when applying contract first design are the following:

- Working with XML schemas and data types means that you do not and cannot think in terms of platform-specific data types. This can make it more difficult to define the interface, but ensures maximum interoperability and compatibility. Where you require complex data structures, compose them from simple and standard XML types that all clients can use.

- Consider the platforms, clients, and systems that may interact with the service. Plan for any limitations in data types or formats that this may impose.

- Consider using tools to help you design the service contracts. This can considerably simplify and speed up the process.

- Collaborate with interested parties during the contract design process if possible. Others may have specific requirements or requests that would make the contract easier to use, more widely acceptable, and maximize reusability.

For more information about contract first design, see *"Contract-First Service Development"* at http://msdn.microsoft.com/en-us/magazine/cc163800.aspx.

Security Considerations

A secure communication strategy will protect sensitive data from being read when passed over the network; protect sensitive data from being tampered with; and, if necessary, guarantee the identity of the caller. There are two fundamental areas of concern for securing communications: transport security and message security. For maximum protection, consider combining transport and message security techniques.

Transport Security

Transport security is used to provide point-to-point security between the two end-points, and the transport layer passes user credentials and claims to the recipient. Protecting the channel prevents attackers from accessing all messages on the channel. Common approaches to transport security are Secure Sockets Layer (SSL) encryption and Internet Protocol Security (IPSec). Consider the following when deciding whether to use transport security:

- Transport security uses common industry standards that provide good interoperability, and is usually faster for encryption and signing since it is accomplished at lower layers—sometimes even in the network hardware. However, it supports a limited set of credentials and claims compared to message security.

- If interactions between the service and the consumer are not routed through intermediaries, you can use transport security. If the message passes through one or more intermediaries, use message security instead. With transport security, the message is decrypted and then reencrypted at each intermediary it passes through, which represents a security risk.

- Transport security is a good choice for securing communication between a client and a service located on a private network such as an intranet.

Message Security

Message security can be used with any transport protocol. You should protect the content of individual messages passing over the channel whenever they pass outside your own secure network, and even within your network for highly sensitive content. Common approaches to message security are encryption and digital signatures. Consider the following guidelines when deciding whether to use message security:

- Consider implementing message security for sensitive messages that pass out of your secure network, such as services exposed over the Internet. However, keep in mind that message security generally has a higher impact on communication performance than transport security. You can use partial or selective message encryption and signing to improve overall performance.

- If there are intermediaries between the client and the service, use message security for sensitive messages because it guarantees end-to-end security. Intermediate servers will terminate the SSL or IPSec connection when they receive the message, and then create a new SSL or IPSec connection to pass it to the next server. Therefore, there is a risk that messages that do not use message security will be accessible on the intermediate server.

Technology Options

On the Microsoft platform, you can choose between two messaging technologies: Windows Communication Foundation (WCF) and ASP.NET Web Services (ASMX). The following sections will help you to understand the capabilities of each, and choose the one most appropriate for your scenarios.

WCF Technology Options

WCF provides a comprehensive mechanism for implementing services in a range of situations, and allows you to exert fine control over the configuration and content of the services. The following guidelines will help you to understand how you can use WCF:

- Consider using WCF in the following situations:
  - Communicating with Web services where you require interoperability with other platforms that also support SOAP, such as the J2EE-based application servers.
  - Communicating with Web services using messages not based on SOAP, such as applications that use formats such as Really Simple Syndication (RSS).
  - Communicating using SOAP messages and binary encoding for data structures when both the server and the client use WCF.
  - Building REST Singleton and Collection Services, ATOM Feed and Publishing Protocol Services, and HTTP Plain XML Services.
- Consider using WS-MetadataExchange in SOAP requests to obtain descriptive information about a service, such as its Web Services Description Language (WSDL) definition and policies.
- Consider using WS-Security to implement authentication, data integrity, data privacy, and other security features.
- Consider using WS-Reliable Messaging to implement reliable end-to-end communication, even when one or more Web services intermediaries must be traversed.
- Consider using WS-Coordination to coordinate two-phase commit transactions in the context of Web services conversations.

WCF supports several different protocols for communication:

- For services accessed from the Internet, consider using the HTTP protocol.
- For services accessed from within a private network, consider using the TCP protocol.
- For services accessed from the same machine, consider using the named pipes protocol, which supports a shared buffer or streams for passing data.

ASMX Technology Options

ASMX provide a simpler solution for building Web services based on ASP.NET and exposed through an Internet Information Services (IIS) Web server. ASMX has the following characteristics:

- Can be accessed over the Internet using only the HTTP protocol. Uses port 80 by default, but this can be easily reconfigured.
- Has no support for Distributed Transaction Coordinator (DTC) transaction flow. You must program long-running transactions using custom implementations.
- Supports IIS authentication, Roles stored as Windows groups for authorization, IIS and ASP.NET impersonation, and SSL transport security.
- Supports the endpoint technology implemented in IIS.
- Provides cross-platform interoperability.

Additional Resources

To more easily access Web resources, see the online version of the bibliography at: http://www.microsoft.com/architectureguide.

- *"Data Transfer and Serialization"* at http://msdn.microsoft.com/en-us/library/ms730035.aspx.
- *"Endpoints: Addresses, Bindings, and Contracts"* at http://msdn.microsoft.com/en-us/library/ms733107.aspx.
- *"Messaging Patterns in Service-Oriented Architecture"* at http://msdn.microsoft.com/en-us/library/aa480027.aspx.
- *"Principles of Service Design: Service Versioning"* at http://msdn.microsoft.com/en-us/library/ms954726.aspx.
- *"Web Service Messaging with Web Services Enhancements 2.0"* at http://msdn.microsoft.com/en-us/library/ms996948.aspx.
- *"Web Services Protocols Interoperability Guide"* at http://msdn.microsoft.com/en-us/library/ms734776.aspx.
- *"Windows Communication Foundation Security"* at http://msdn.microsoft.com/en-us/library/ms732362.aspx.
- *"XML Web Services Using ASP.NET"* at http://msdn.microsoft.com/en-us/library/ba0z6a33.aspx.

Application Archetypes

This section of the guide contains a series of topics that will help you to understand the capabilities, features, benefits, and liabilities of each of the common application types that you may decide to create. The first topic contains an overview of the basic application types such as Web, mobile, rich client, services, and RIA. The remaining chapters describe each of these types in detail, as well as more specialist types of applications such as hosted and cloud-based services, and applications that take advantage of SharePoint and Microsoft Office. For more information, see the following chapters:

- Chapter 20, "Choosing an Application Type"
- Chapter 21, "Designing Web Applications"
- Chapter 22, "Designing Rich Client Applications"
- Chapter 23, "Designing Rich Internet Applications"
- Chapter 24, "Designing Mobile Applications"
- Chapter 25, "Designing Service Applications"
- Chapter 26, "Designing Hosted and Cloud Services"
- Chapter 27, "Designing Office Business Applications"
- Chapter 28, "Designing SharePoint LOB Applications"

19

Physical Tiers and Deployment

Overview

Application architecture designs exist as models, documents, and scenarios. However, applications must be deployed into a physical environment where infrastructure limitations may negate some of the architectural decisions. Therefore, you must consider the proposed deployment scenario and the infrastructure as part of your application design process. This chapter describes the options available for deployment of different types of applications, including distributed and nondistributed styles; ways to scale the application; and guidance and patterns for performance, reliability, and security issues. By considering the possible deployment scenarios for your application as part of the design process, you prevent a situation where the application cannot be deployed successfully, or fails to perform to its design requirements because of technical infrastructure limitations.

Choosing a deployment strategy requires design tradeoffs. For example, there might be protocol or port restrictions, or specific deployment topologies not supported in your target environment. Identify your deployment constraints early in the design phase to avoid surprises later; involve members of your network and infrastructure teams to help with this process. When choosing a deployment strategy:

- Understand the target physical environment for deployment.
- Understand the architectural and design constraints based on the deployment environment.
- Understand the security and performance impacts of your deployment environment.

Distributed and Nondistributed Deployment

When creating your deployment strategy, first determine if you will use a distributed or a nondistributed deployment model. If you are building a simple intranet application for your organization, which will be accessed by finite set of users, consider nondistributed deployment. If you are building a more complex application, which you must optimize for scalability and maintainability, consider a distributed deployment.

Nondistributed Deployment

In a nondistributed deployment, all of the functionality and layers reside on a single server except for data storage functionality, as shown in the example in Figure 1.

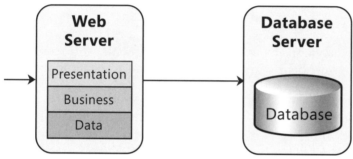

Figure 1
Nondistributed deployment

This approach has the advantage of simplicity and minimizes the number of physical servers required. It also minimizes the performance impact inherent when communication between layers must cross physical boundaries between servers or server clusters. Keep in mind that by using a single server, even though you minimize communication performance overhead, you can hamper performance in other ways. Because all of your layers share resources, one layer can negatively affect all of the other layers when it is under heavy utilization. In addition, the servers must be generically configured and designed around the strictest of operational requirements, and must support the peak usage of the largest consumers of system resources. The use of a single tier reduces your overall scalability and maintainability because all the layers share the same physical hardware.

Distributed Deployment

In a distributed deployment, the layers of the application reside on separate physical tiers. Tiered distribution organizes the system infrastructure into a set of physical tiers to provide specific server environments optimized for specific operational requirements and system resource usage. It allows you to separate the layers of an application on different physical tiers, as shown in the example in Figure 2.

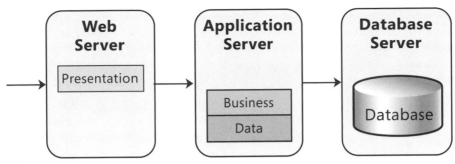

Figure 2
Distributed deployment

A distributed approach allows you to configure the application servers that host the various layers in order to best meet the requirements of each layer. However, because the primary driver for optimizing component deployment is to match a component's resource consumption profile to an appropriate server, this implies that a direct mapping of layers to tiers is often not the ideal distribution strategy.

Multiple tiers enable multiple environments. You can optimize each environment for a specific set of operational requirements and system resource usage. You can then deploy components onto the tier that most closely matches their resource needs to maximize operational performance and behavior. The more tiers you use, the more deployment options you have for each component. Distributed deployment provides a more flexible environment where you can more easily scale out or scale up each physical tier as performance limitations arise, and when processing demands increase. However, keep in mind that adding more tiers adds complexity, deployment effort, and cost.

Another reason for adding tiers is to apply specific security policies. Distributed deployment allows you to apply more stringent security to the application servers; for example, by adding a firewall between the Web server and the application servers, and by using different authentication and authorization options.

Performance and Design Considerations for Distributed Environments

Distributing components across tiers can reduce performance because of the cost of remote calls across physical boundaries. However, distributing components can improve scalability opportunities, improve manageability, and reduce costs over time. Consider the following guidelines when designing an application that will run on a physically distributed infrastructure:

- Choose communication paths and protocols between tiers to ensure that components can securely interact with minimum performance degradation. Take advantage of asynchronous calls, one-way calls, or message queuing to minimize blocking when making calls across physical boundaries.

- Consider using services and operating system features such as distributed transaction support and authentication that can simplify your design and improve interoperability.

- Reduce the complexity of your component interfaces. Highly granular interfaces (chatty interfaces) that require many calls to perform a task work best when located on the same physical machine. Interfaces that make only one call to accomplish each task (chunky interfaces) provide the best performance when the components are distributed across separate physical machines. However, where you must support in-process calls as well as calls from other physical tiers, you may consider implementing a highly granular interface for in-process calls and a façade for use from other physical tiers that wraps the calls to provide a chunky interface.

- Consider separating long-running critical processes from other processes that might fail by using a separate physical cluster, and determine your failover strategy. For example, Web servers typically provide plenty of memory and processing power, but may not have robust storage capabilities (such as RAID mirroring) that can be replaced rapidly in the event of a hardware failure.

- Determine how best to plan for the addition of extra servers or resources that will increase performance and availability.

- When layers communicate across physical boundaries, you must consider how you will manage state across tiers, as this will affect scalability and performance. Choices for state management typically include:

  - **Stateless.** All the state required will be provided when calling into a tier. This tends to be more scalable, but often requires the client to supply state information.

  - **Stateful.** State will be stored or recovered for each client request. This tends to require more resources and is therefore a less scalable solution, but it is often convenient because it does not require the client to track and provide state information.

Recommendations for Locating Components within a Distributed Deployment

When designing a distributed deployment, you must determine which logical layers and components you will put into each physical tier. In most cases, you will place the presentation layer on the client or on the Web server; the service, business, and data layers on the application server; and the database on its own server. In some cases, you may want to modify this pattern. Consider the following guidelines when determining where to locate components in a distributed environment:

- Only distribute components where necessary. Common reasons for implementing distributed deployment include security policies, physical constraints, shared business logic, and scalability.

- If the business components are used synchronously by the presentation components, deploy the business components on the same physical tier as the presentation components in order to maximize performance and ease operational management.
- Do not locate presentation and business components on the same tier if there are security implications that require a trust boundary between them. For example, you might want to separate business and presentation components in a rich client application by placing the presentation components on the client and the business components on the server.
- Deploy service agent components on the same tier as the code that calls the components, unless there are security implications that require a trust boundary between them.
- Deploy business components that are called asynchronously together with workflow components on a separate physical tier from the other layers where possible.
- Deploy business entities on the same physical tier as the components that use them.

Distributed Deployment Patterns

Several common patterns represent application deployment structures found in most solutions. When it comes to determining the best deployment solution for your application, it helps to first identify the common patterns. Once you have a good understanding of the different patterns, you then consider scenarios, requirements, and security constraints to choose the most appropriate pattern.

Client-Server Deployment

This pattern represents a basic structure with two main components: a client and a server. In this scenario, the client and server will usually be located on two separate tiers. Figure 3 represents a common Web application scenario where the client interacts with a Web server.

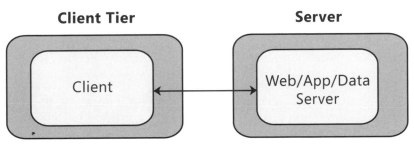

Figure 3
A common Web application scenario

Consider the client/server pattern if you are developing a client that will access an application server, or a stand-alone client that will access a separate database server.

n-Tier Deployment

The *n*-tier pattern represents a general distribution pattern where components of the application are separated across one or more servers. Commonly, you will choose a 2-tier, 3-tier, or 4-tier pattern as described in the following sections. While you will often locate all of the components of a layer on the same tier, this is not always the case. Layers do not have to be confined to a single tier—you can partition workloads across multiple servers if required. For example, you may decide to have side-by-side tiers that contain different aspects of your business logic.

2-Tier Deployment

Effectively this is the same physical layout as the client/server pattern. It differs mainly on the ways that the components on the tiers communicate. In some cases, as shown in Figure 4, all of the application code is located on the client, and the database is located on a separate server. The client makes use of stored procedures or minimal data access functionality on the database server.

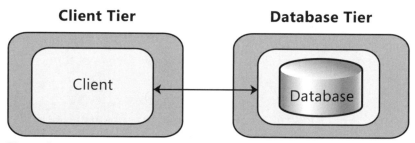

Figure 4
2-tier deployment with all the application code located on the client

Consider the 2-tier pattern if you are developing a client that will access an application server, or a stand-alone client that will access a separate database server.

3-Tier Deployment

In a 3-tier design, the client interacts with application software deployed on a separate server, and the application server interacts with a database that is located on another server, as shown in Figure 5. This is a very common pattern for most Web applications and Web services, and sufficient for most general scenarios. You might implement a firewall between the client and the Web/App tier, and another firewall between the Web/App tier and the database tier.

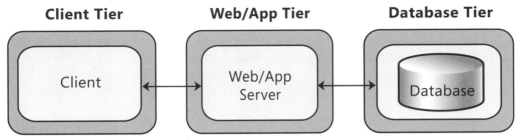

Figure 5
3-tier deployment with the application code on a separate tier

Consider the 3-tier pattern if you are developing an Intranet-based application where all servers are located within the private network or an Internet based application and security requirements do not prevent you from implementing business logic on the public facing Web or application server.

4-Tier Deployment

In this scenario, shown in Figure 6, the Web server is physically separated from the application server. This is often done for security reasons, where the Web server is deployed into a perimeter network and accesses the application server located on a different subnet. In this scenario, you might implement a firewall between the client and the Web tier, and another firewall between the Web tier and the application or business logic tier.

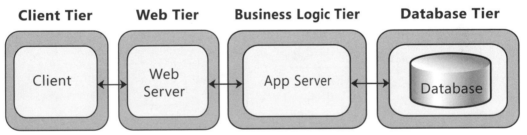

Figure 6
4-tier deployment with the Web code and the business logic on separate tiers

Consider the 4-tier pattern if security requirements dictate that business logic cannot be deployed to the perimeter network, or you have application code that makes heavy use of resources on the server and you want to offload that functionality to another server.

Web Application Deployment

Consider using distributed deployment for your Web applications if security concerns prohibit you from deploying your business logic on your front-end Web server. Use a message-based interface for your business layer, and consider using the TCP protocol with binary encoding to communicate with the business layer for best performance. You should also consider using load balancing to distribute requests so that they are handled by different Web servers, avoid server affinity when designing scalable Web applications, and design stateless components for your Web application. See the section "Performance Patterns" later in this chapter for more details.

Rich Internet Application Deployment

A distributed architecture is the most likely scenario for deployment because rich Internet application (RIA) implementations move presentation logic to the client. If your business logic is shared by other applications, consider using distributed deployment. Also, consider using a message-based interface for your business logic.

Rich Client Application Deployment

In an *n*-tier deployment, you can locate presentation and business logic on the client, or locate only the presentation logic on the client. Figure 7 illustrates the case where the presentation and business logic are deployed on the client.

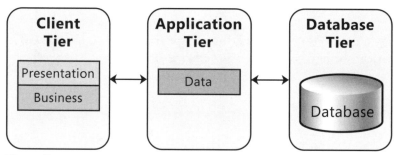

Figure 7
Rich client with the business layer on the client tier

Figure 8 illustrates the case where the business and data access logic are deployed on an application server.

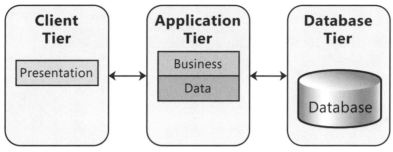

Figure 8
Rich client with the business layer on the application tier

Performance Patterns

Performance deployment patterns represent proven design solutions to common performance problems. When considering a high performance deployment, you can scale up or scale out. Scaling up entails improvements to the hardware on which you are already running. Scaling out entails distributing your application across multiple physical servers to distribute the load. When planning to use a scale out strategy, you will generally make use of a load balancing strategy. This is usually referred to as a load-balanced cluster or, in the case of Web servers, a Web farm. The following sections describe these patterns. For more information about choosing when and how to scale up or scale out, see the section "Scale Up and Scale Out" later in this chapter.

Load-balanced Cluster

You can install your service or application onto multiple servers that are configured to share the workload, as shown in Figure 9. This type of configuration is known as a load-balanced cluster.

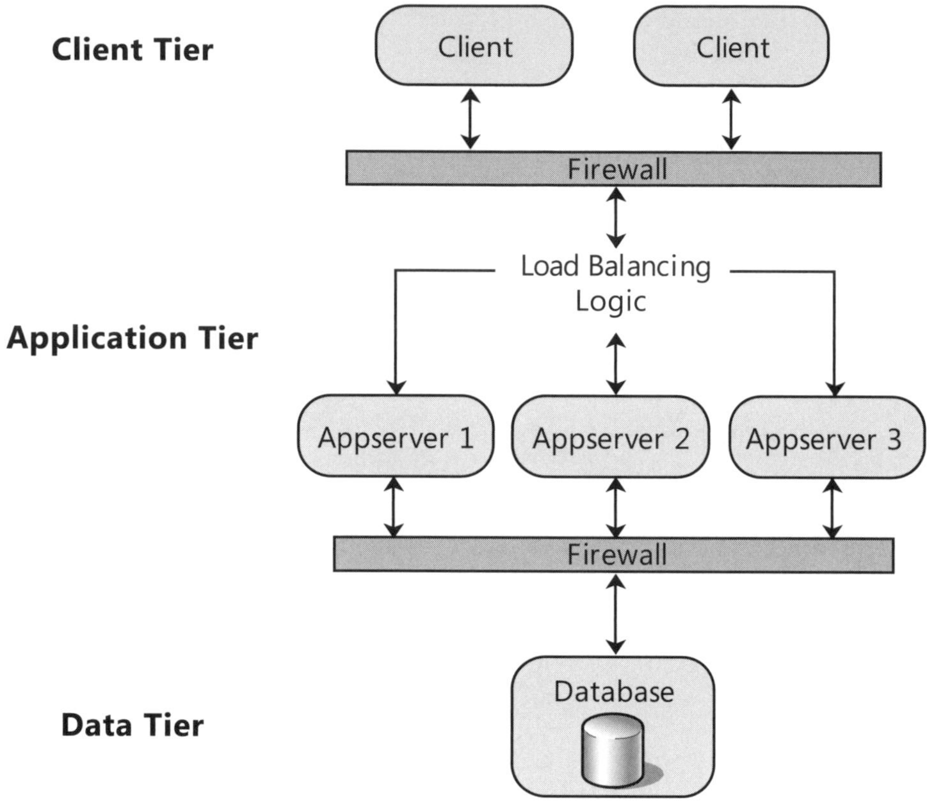

Figure 9
A load-balanced cluster

Load balancing scales the performance of server-based programs, such as a Web server, by distributing client requests across multiple servers. Load-balancing technologies, commonly referred to as load balancers, receive incoming requests and redirect them to a specific host if necessary. The load-balanced hosts concurrently respond to different client requests, even multiple requests from the same client. For example, a Web browser might obtain the multiple images within a single Web page from different hosts in the cluster. This distributes the load, speeds up processing, and reduces the response time.

Depending on the routing technology used, it may detect failed servers and remove them from the routing list to minimize the impact of a failure. In simple scenarios, the routing may be on a *round robin* basis where a DNS server hands out the addresses of individual servers in rotation. Figure 10 illustrates a simple Web farm (a load-balanced cluster of Web servers) where each server hosts all of the layers of the application except for the data store.

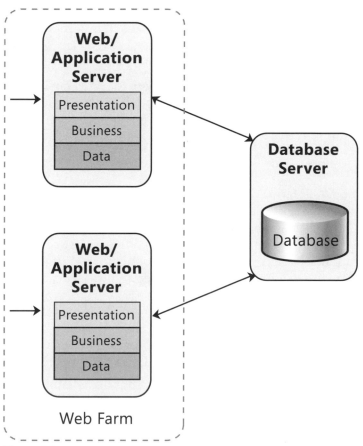

Figure 10
A simple Web farm

Load-balanced clusters are most scalable and efficient if they do not have to track and store information between each client request; in other words, if they are stateless. If they must track state, then you may need to use affinity and session techniques.

Affinity and User Sessions

Applications may rely on the maintenance of session state between requests from the same client. A Web server, for example, may need to keep track of user information between requests. A Web farm can be configured to route all requests from the same user to the same server—a process known as affinity—in order to maintain state where this is stored in memory on the Web server. However, for increased availability and reliability, you should use a separate session state store with a Web farm to remove the requirement for affinity. During development, if you are using Internet Information Services (IIS) 6.0 or later, you can configure IIS to operate in Web Garden mode to help ensure correct session state handling within your application as you develop it.

In ASP.NET, you must also configure all of the Web servers to use a consistent encryption key and method for ViewState encryption where you do not implement affinity. You should also enable affinity for sessions that use Secure Sockets Layer (SSL) encryption where the system supports this feature, or use a separate cluster for SSL requests.

Application Farms

As with Web servers and Web farms, you can also scale out your business and data layers if they reside on different physical tiers from the presentation layer by using an application farm. Requests from the presentation tier are distributed to each server in the farm so that each has approximately the same load. You may decide to separate the business layer components and the data layer components on different application farms, depending on the requirements of each layer and the expected loading and number of users.

Reliability Patterns

Reliability deployment patterns represent proven design solutions to common reliability problems. The most common approach to improving the reliability of your deployment is to use a failover cluster to ensure the availability of your application, even if a server fails.

Failover Cluster

A failover cluster is a set of servers that are configured in such a way that if one server becomes unavailable, another server automatically takes over for the failed server and continues processing. Figure 11 shows a failover cluster.

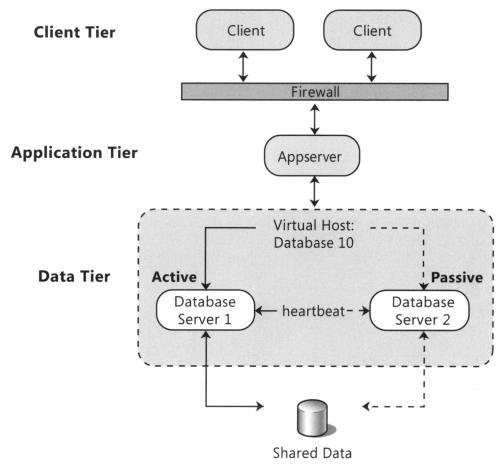

Figure 11
A failover cluster

Install your application or service on multiple servers that are configured to take over for one another when a failure occurs. The process of one server taking over for a failed server is commonly known as failover. Each server in the cluster has at least one other server in the cluster identified as its standby server.

Security Patterns

Security patterns represent proven design solutions to common security problems. The impersonation/delegation approach is a good solution when you must flow the context of the original caller to downstream layers or components in your application. The trusted subsystem approach is a good solution when you want to handle authentication and authorization in upstream components and access a downstream resource with a single trusted identity.

Impersonation/Delegation

In the impersonation/delegation authorization model, resources and the types of operations (such as read, write, and delete) permitted for each one are secured using Windows Access Control Lists (ACLs) or the equivalent security features of the targeted resource (such as tables and procedures in SQL Server). Users access the resources using their original identity through impersonation, as illustrated in Figure 12. Bear in mind that this approach may result in the requirement for a domain account, which makes it unattractive in some scenarios.

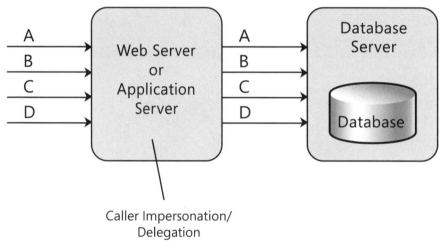

Figure 12
The impersonation/delegation authorization model

Trusted Subsystem

In the trusted subsystem (or trusted server) model, users are partitioned into application defined, logical roles. Members of a particular role share the same privileges within the application. Access to operations (typically expressed by method calls) is authorized based on the role membership of the caller. With this role-based (or operations-based) approach to security, access to operations (not networked resources) is authorized based on the role membership of the caller. Roles, analyzed and defined at application design time, are used as logical containers that group together users who share the same security privileges or capabilities within the application. The middle-tier service uses a fixed identity to access downstream services and resources, as illustrated in Figure 13.

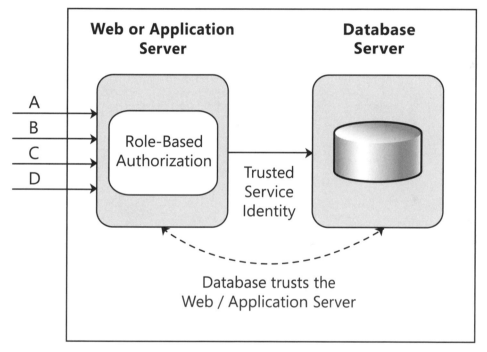

Figure 13
The trusted subsystem (or trusted server) model

Multiple Trusted Service Identities

In some situations, you might require more than one trusted identity. For example, you might have two groups of users, one who should be authorized to perform read/write operations and the other read-only operations. The use of multiple trusted service identities provides the ability to exert more granular control over resource access and auditing, without having a large impact on scalability. Figure 14 illustrates the multiple trusted service identities model.

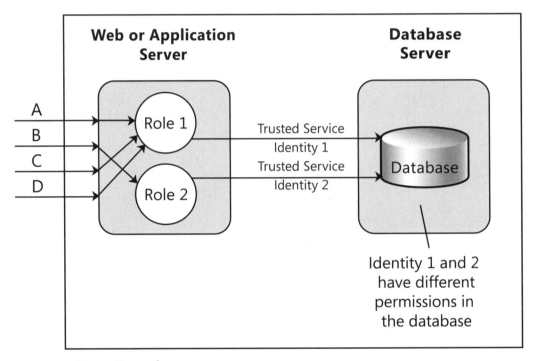

Figure 14
The multiple trusted service identities model

Scale Up and Scale Out

Your approach to scaling is a critical design consideration. Whether you plan to scale out your solution through a load-balanced cluster or a partitioned database, you must ensure that your design supports the option you choose. In general cases, when you scale your application, you can choose from and combine two basic choices: **scale up** (get a bigger box) and **scale out** (get more boxes).

With the **scale up** approach, you add hardware such as processors, RAM, and network interface cards (NICs) to your existing servers to support increased capacity. This is a simple option and can be cost-effective up to a certain level because it does not introduce additional maintenance and support costs. However, any single points of failure remain, which is a risk. In addition, beyond a certain threshold, adding more hardware to the existing servers may not produce the desired results, and getting the last 10% of theoretical performance from a single machine though upgrades can be very expensive.

For an application to scale up effectively, the underlying framework, runtime, and computer architecture must scale up as well. When scaling up, consider which resources are limiting application performance. For example, if it is memory bound or network bound, adding CPU resources will not help.

With the **scale out** approach, you add more servers and use load balancing and clustering solutions. In addition to handling additional load, the scale out scenario also mitigates hardware failures. If one server fails, there are additional servers in the cluster that can take over the load. For example, you might have multiple load-balanced Web servers in a Web farm that host the presentation and business layers. Alternatively, you might physically partition your application's business logic, and use a separate load-balanced middle tier for that logic while hosting the presentation layer on a load-balanced front tier. If your application is I/O constrained and you must support an extremely large database, you might partition your database across multiple database servers. In general, the ability of an application to scale out depends more on its architecture than on the underlying infrastructure.

Considerations for Scaling Up

Scaling up with additional processor power and increased memory can be a cost-effective solution. This approach also avoids introducing the additional management cost associated with scaling out and using Web farms and clustering technology. You should look at scale up options first and conduct performance tests to see whether scaling up your solution meets your defined scalability criteria and supports the necessary number of concurrent users at an acceptable performance level. You should have a scaling plan for your system that tracks its observed growth.

Designing to Support Scale Out

If scaling up your solution does not provide adequate scalability because you reach CPU, I/O, or memory thresholds, you must scale out and introduce additional servers. Consider the following practices in your design to ensure that your application can be scaled out successfully:

- **Identity and scale out bottlenecks.** Shared resources that cannot be further scaled up often represent a bottleneck. For example, you might have a single SQL Server instance that is accessed from multiple application servers. In this case, partitioning the data so that it can served by multiple SQL Server instances will allow your solution to scale out. If you anticipate that your database server may become a bottleneck, an initial design that includes data partitioning can save a significant amount of effort later.

- **Define a loosely coupled and layered design.** A loosely coupled layered design with clean remotable interfaces are easier to scale out than a design that uses tightly coupled layers with chatty interactions. A layered design will have natural clutch points, making it ideal for scaling out at the layer boundaries. The trick is to find the right boundaries. For example, business logic may be relocated more easily to a load-balanced middle-tier application server farm.

Design Implications and Tradeoffs

You should consider aspects of scalability that may vary by application layer, tier, or type of data. Identify tradeoffs required so that you are aware of where you have flexibility and where you do not. In some cases, scaling up and then out with Web or application servers might not be the best approach. For example, even though you could use an 8-processor server, economics would probably drive you to use a set of smaller servers instead of a one large one.

On the other hand, scaling up and then out might be the right approach for your database servers, depending on the role of the data and how the data is used. There are limitations on the number of servers that you can load balance or failover, and additional issues such as how you partition the database will affect the process. In addition, apart from technical and performance considerations, you must also take into account operational and management implications, and the related total cost of ownership).

Typically, you optimize the price and performance within the boundaries of any other constraints. For example, using four 2-processor Web or application servers may be optimal when you evaluate price and performance compared with using two 4-processor servers. However, you must also consider other constraints, such as the maximum number of servers you can locate behind a particular load-balancing infrastructure, and power consumption or space constraints within the data center.

Also consider using virtualized servers to implement server farms and for hosting services. This approach can help you to balance performance and cost while obtaining maximum resource usage and return on investment.

Stateless Components

The use of stateless components, such as those you may implement in a Web front end with no in-process state, means that you can produce a design that better supports both scaling up and scaling out. To achieve a stateless design, it is likely that a number of design tradeoffs will be required in your application, but the benefits in terms of scalability generally outweigh the disadvantages.

Data and Database Partitioning

If your application uses a very large database and you anticipate an I/O bottleneck, ensure that you design for database partitioning up front. Moving to a partitioned database later usually results in a significant amount of costly rework, and often requires a complete redesign of the database. Partitioning provides several benefits, including the ability to restrict queries to a single partition (thereby limiting the resource usage to only a fraction of the data), and the ability to engage multiple partitions (thereby achieving greater parallelism and superior performance because you can have more disks working to retrieve the data).

However, in some situations, multiple partitions may not be appropriate and could have a negative impact. For example, some operations that use multiple disks might be performed more efficiently with concentrated data.

When considering the impact of partitioning data storage on your deployment scenarios, the decisions depend largely on the type of data. The following list summarizes the relevant factors:

- **Static, reference, and read-only data.** For this type of data, you can easily maintain many replicas in the appropriate locations if this improves performance and scalability. It has minimal impact on design and can usually be driven by optimization considerations. Consolidating several logically separate and independent databases on one database server may or may not be appropriate, even if you have the disk capacity, and distributing replicas closer to the consumers of that data may be an equally valid approach. However, be aware that whenever you replicate, you have a loosely synchronized system that requires mechanisms to maintain the appropriate synchronization.

- **Dynamic (often transient) data that is easily partitioned.** This is data relevant to a particular user or session, such as a shopping cart, and the data for user A is not related in any way to the data for user B. This data is slightly more complicated to handle than static, read-only data, but you can still optimize and distribute it quite easily because this type of data can be partitioned. There are no dependencies between the groups, right down to the individual user level. The important aspect of this data is that you do not query across partitions. For example, you query for the contents of user A's shopping cart but do not query all carts that contain a particular item. Note that, if subsequent requests can come to different Web or application server, all these servers must be able to access the relevant partition.

- **Core data.** This is the main case where the scale up, then out approach usually applies. Generally, you do not want to hold this type of data in many places because of the complexity of keeping it synchronized. This is the classic case in which you would typically want to scale up as far as you can (ideally, remaining as a single logical instance with suitable clustering), and only consider partitioning and distributing the data when scaling out is the only option. Advances in database technology, such as distributed partitioned views, have made partitioning much easier; although you should do so only when it is necessary. The decision is rarely prompted by the database growing to too large a size, but is more often driven by other considerations such as who owns the data, the geographic usage distribution, proximity to the consumer, and availability.

- **Delay-synchronized data.** Some data used in applications does not have to be synchronized immediately, or even at all. A good example of this is retail store data such as "Users who bought X also bought Y and Z." This data is mined from the core data, but need not be updated in real time. Designing strategies that move data from core to partitionable (dynamic), and then to static, is a key factor in building highly scalable applications.

For information on patterns for moving and replicating data, see "*Data Movement Patterns*" at http://msdn.microsoft.com/en-us/library/ms998449.aspx.

Network Infrastructure Security Considerations

Make sure that you understand the network structure provided by your target environment, and understand the baseline security requirements of the network in terms of filtering rules, port restrictions, supported protocols, and so on. Recommendations for maximizing network security include:

- Identify how firewalls and firewall policies are likely to affect your application's design and deployment. Firewalls should be used to separate Internet-facing applications from the internal network, and to protect the database servers. Firewalls only allow communication through specifically configured ports and, therefore, can block some protocols and prevent the use of some communication options. This includes authentication, such as Windows authentication, between the Web server and an application or database server behind the firewall.

- Consider which protocols, ports, and services can access internal resources from the Web servers in the perimeter network or from rich client applications. Identify the protocols and ports that the application design requires, and analyze the potential threats that occur from opening additional ports or using nonstandard protocols.

- Communicate and record any assumptions made about network and application layer security, and the security functions each component will handle. This ensures that security controls and policies are not overlooked when both the development and the network team assume that the other team is addressing the issue.

- Pay attention to the security defenses such as firewalls, packet filters, and hardware systems that your application relies upon the network to provide, and ensure that these defenses are in place.

- Consider the implications of a change in network configuration, and how this will affect security.

Manageability Considerations

The choices you make when deploying an application affect the capabilities for managing and monitoring the application. You should take into account the following recommendations:

- Deploy components of the application that are used by multiple consumers in a single central location, such as a server or application farm that is available to all applications, to avoid duplication.

- Ensure that data is stored in a location where backup and restore facilities can access it.

- Components that rely on existing software or hardware (such as a proprietary network that can only be established from a particular computer) must be physically located on the same computer.

- Some libraries and adaptors cannot be deployed freely without incurring extra cost, or may be charged on a per CPU basis; therefore, you may want to centralize these features to minimize costs.

- Groups within an organization may own a particular service, component, or application that they must manage locally.

- Monitoring tools such as System Center Operations Manager require access to physical machines to obtain management information, and this may impact deployment options.

Relevant Design Patterns

Key patterns are organized into categories such as Deployment, Manageability, Performance and Reliability, and Security; as shown in the following table. Consider using these patterns when making design decisions for each category.

Category	Relevant patterns
Deployment	**Layered Application.** An architectural pattern where a system is organized into layers. **Three-Layered Services Application.** An architectural pattern where the layers are designed to maximize performance while exposing services that other applications can use. **Tiered Distribution.** An architectural pattern where the layers of a design can be distributed across physical boundaries. **Three-Tiered Distribution.** An architectural pattern where the layers of a design are distributed across three physical tiers. **Deployment Plan.** Describes the processes for mapping logical layers onto physical tiers, taking into account constraints imposed by the infrastructure.
Manageability	**Adapter.** An object that supports a common interface and translates operations between the common interface and other objects that implement similar functionality with different interfaces. **Provider.** A component that exposes an API that is different from the client API, in order to allow any custom implementation to be seamlessly plugged in. Many applications that provide instrumentation expose providers that can be used to capture information about the state and health of your application and the system hosting the application.
Performance & Reliability	**Server Clustering.** A distribution pattern where multiple servers are configured to share the workload and appear to clients as a single machine or resource. **Load-balanced Cluster.** A distribution pattern where multiple servers are configured to share the workload. Load balancing provides both improvements in performance by spreading the work across multiple servers, and reliability where one server can fail and the others will continue to handle the workload. **Failover Cluster.** A distribution pattern that provides a highly available infrastructure tier to protect against loss of service due to the failure of a single server or the software that it hosts.
Security	**Brokered Authentication.** Authenticate against a broker, which provides a token to use for authentication when accessing services or systems. **Direct Authentication.** Authenticate directly against the service or system that is being accessed. **Impersonation and Delegation.** The process of assuming a different identity on a temporary basis so that a different security context or set of credentials can be used to access a resource, and where a service account is allowed to access a remote resource on behalf of another user. **Trusted Subsystem.** The application acts as a trusted subsystem to access additional resources. It uses its own credentials instead of the user's credentials to access the resource.

For more information on the Layered Application, Three-Layered Services Application, Tiered Distribution, Three-Tiered Distribution, and Deployment Plan patterns, see *"Deployment Patterns"* at http://msdn.microsoft.com/en-us/library/ms998478.aspx.

For more information on the Adapter pattern, see Chapter 4, "Structural Patterns" in Gamma, Erich, Richard Helm, Ralph Johnson, and John Vlissides. *Design Patterns: Elements of Reusable Object-Oriented Software.* Addison Wesley Professional, 1995.

For more information on the Provider pattern, see *"Provider Model Design Pattern and Specification, Part 1"* at http://msdn.microsoft.com/en-us/library/ms972319.aspx.

For more information on the Server Clustering, Load-Balanced Cluster, and Failover Cluster patterns, see *"Performance and Reliability Patterns"* at http://msdn.microsoft.com/en-us/library/ms998503.aspx.

For more information on the Brokered Authentication, Direct Authentication, Impersonation and Delegation, and Trusted Subsystem patterns, see *"Web Service Security"* at http://msdn.microsoft.com/en-us/library/aa480545.aspx.

Additional Resources

To more easily access Web resources that may be useful when designing a deployment strategy, see the online version of the bibliography at: http://www.microsoft.com/architectureguide.

- For more information on authorization techniques, see *"Designing Application-Managed Authorization"* at http://msdn.microsoft.com/en-us/library/ms954586.aspx.

- For more information on deployment scenarios and considerations, see *"Deploying .NET Framework-based Applications"* at http://msdn.microsoft.com/en-us/library/ms954585.aspx.

- For more information on design patterns, see *"Enterprise Solution Patterns Using Microsoft .NET"* at http://msdn.microsoft.com/en-us/library/ms998469.aspx.

20

Choosing an Application Type

Overview

This chapter will help you to understand the application types covered in this guide, the tradeoffs necessary, and the design impact for choosing an application type. After reading this chapter, you will be able to determine the appropriate application type for your scenario and requirements. The chapter provides brief details of each of the five basic application archetypes, and links to more detail information in other chapters.

The requirements, technology constraints, and type of user experience you plan to deliver will determine the application type you choose. For example, you must decide whether the clients you intend to serve will have a permanent network connection available, whether you must deliver rich media content to anonymous users for viewing in a Web browser, or whether you will predominantly service a small number of users on a corporate intranet.

Use the following application archetypes summary to review each application type, its description, and common scenarios. Use the table in this section to help you make an informed choice of application type, based on the benefits and considerations for each type.

Application Archetypes Summary

The following are the common basic types of applications that you may decide to build:

- **Mobile applications.** Applications of this type can be developed as thin client or rich client applications. Rich client mobile applications can support disconnected or occasionally connected scenarios. Web or thin client applications support connected scenarios only. Device resources may prove to be a constraint when designing mobile applications.

- **Rich client applications.** Applications of this type are usually developed as stand-alone applications with a graphical user interface that displays data using a range of controls. Rich client applications can be designed for disconnected and occasionally connected scenarios if they need to access remote data or functionality.

- **Rich Internet applications.** Applications of this type can be developed to support multiple platforms and multiple browsers, displaying rich media or graphical content. Rich Internet applications run in a browser sandbox that restricts access to some features of the client.

- **Service applications.** Services expose shared business functionality and allow clients to access them from a local or a remote system. Service operations are called using messages, based on XML schemas, passed over a transport channel. The goal of this type of application is to achieve loose coupling between the client and the server.

- **Web applications.** Applications of this type typically support connected scenarios and can support different browsers running on a range of operating systems and platforms.

There are many other more specific types of application that you can design and build. In general, these types are specializations or combinations of the basic types described in this list.

Application Type Considerations

The following table indicates the benefits and considerations for the common application archetypes.

Application type	Benefits	Considerations
Mobile applications	Support for handheld devices. Availability and ease of use for out of office users. Support for offline and occasionally-connected scenarios.	Input and navigation limitations. Limited screen display area.

Application type	Benefits	Considerations
Rich client applications	Ability to leverage client resources. Better responsiveness, rich UI functionality, and improved user experience. Highly dynamic and responsive interaction. Support for offline and occasionally connected scenarios.	Deployment complexity; however, a range of installation options such as ClickOnce, Windows Installer, and XCOPY are available. Challenging to version over time. Platform specific.
Rich Internet applications (RIA)	The same rich user interface capability as rich clients. Support for rich and streaming media and graphical display. Simple deployment with the same distribution capabilities (reach) as Web clients. Simple upgrade and version updating. Cross-platform and cross-browser support.	Larger application footprint on the client compared to a Web application. Restrictions on leveraging client resources compared to a rich client application. Requires deployment of a suitable runtime framework on the client.
Service applications	Loosely coupled interactions between client and server. Can be consumed by different and unrelated applications. Support for interoperability.	No UI support. Dependent on network connectivity.
Web applications	Broad reach and a standards-based UI across multiple platforms. Ease of deployment and change management.	Dependent on continual network connectivity. Difficult to provide a rich user interface.

Each application type can be implemented using one or more technologies. Scenarios and technology constraints, as well as the capabilities and experience of your development team, will drive your choice of technology.

The following sections describe each of the application types in more detail:

- Mobile Application Archetype
- Rich Client Application Archetype
- Rich Internet Application Archetype
- Service Archetype
- Web Application Archetype

This guide also contains details of some of the more specialized application types. For more information, see the following:

- Chapter 26 "Designing Hosted and Cloud Services"
- Chapter 27 "Designing Office Business Applications"
- Chapter 28 "Designing SharePoint LOB Applications"

Mobile Application Archetype

A mobile application will normally be structured as a multilayered application consisting of user experience (presentation), business, and data layers, as shown in Figure 1.

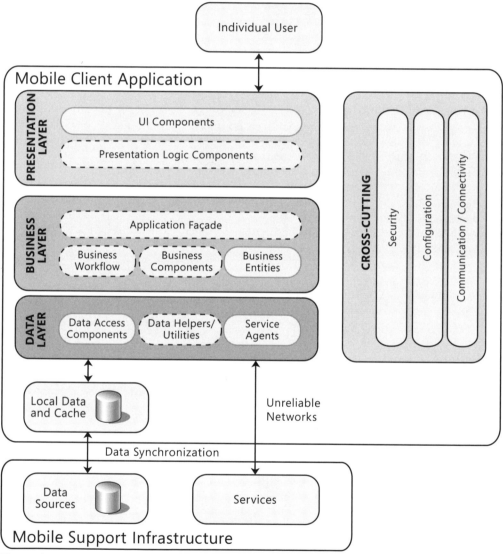

Figure 1
The typical structure of a mobile application

When developing a mobile application, you may choose to develop a thin Web-based client or a rich client. If you are building a rich client, the business and data layers are likely to be on the device itself. If you are building a thin client, the business and data layers will be on the server. Mobile applications commonly make use of locally cached data to support offline or disconnected operation, and synchronize this data when connected. They may also consume services exposed by other applications, including S+S hosted services and Web services. Data source synchronization and other services are often exposed in a controlled way to a mobile client application through a specific server-based infrastructure.

Consider using mobile applications if:

- Your users depend on handheld devices.
- Your application supports a simple UI that is suitable for use on small screens.
- Your application must support offline or occasionally connected scenarios. In this case, a mobile rich client application is usually the most appropriate.
- Your application must be device independent and can depend on network connectivity. In this case, a mobile Web application is usually the most appropriate.

To learn how to design a mobile application, see Chapter 24, "Designing Mobile Applications."

Rich Client Application Archetype

Rich client user interfaces can provide a highly responsive, interactive, and rich user experience for applications that must operate in stand-alone, connected, occasionally connected, and disconnected scenarios. A rich client application will normally be structured as a multilayered application consisting of user experience (presentation), business, and data layers, as shown in the Figure 2.

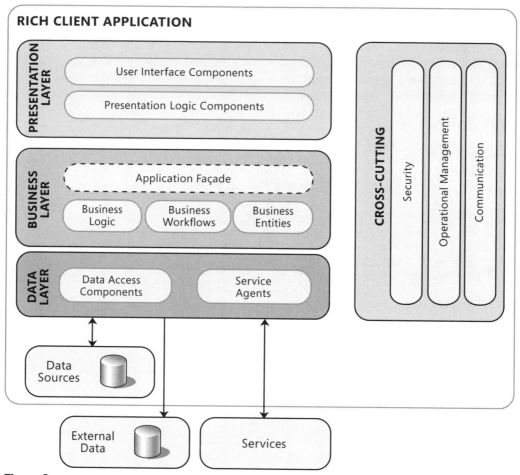

Figure 2
The typical structure of a rich client application

A rich client application may use data stored on a remote server, data stored locally, or a combination of both. It may also consume services exposed by other applications, including S+S hosted services and Web services.

Consider using rich client applications if:

- Your application must support disconnected or occasionally connected scenarios.
- Your application will be deployed on client PCs.
- Your application must be highly interactive and responsive.
- Your application UI must provide rich functionality and user interaction but does not require the advanced graphics or media capabilities of a RIA.
- Your application must utilize the resources of the client PC.

To learn how to design a rich client application, see Chapter 22, "Designing Rich Client Applications."

Rich Internet Application Archetype

A rich Internet application (RIA) runs in the browser in a sandbox. The benefits of a RIA over traditional Web applications include richer user experience, improved user responsiveness, and improved network efficiency. A RIA will normally be structured as a multilayered application consisting of user experience (presentation), service, business, and data layers, as shown in Figure 3.

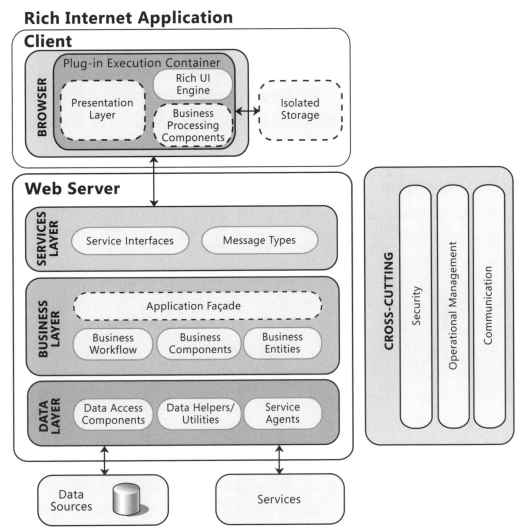

Figure 3
The typical structure of a rich Internet application

RIAs generally depend on a client-side plug-in or hosted execution environment (such as a XAML runtime or Silverlight). This plug-in communicates with remote Web server hosts that generate the code and data consumed by the client plug-in or execution environment.

Consider using rich Internet applications if:

- Your application must support rich media and provide a highly graphical display.
- Your application must provide a rich, interactive, and responsive UI compared to Web applications.
- Your application will leverage client-side processing in a restricted manner.
- Your application will utilize client-side resources in a restricted manner.
- You want the simplicity of a Web-based deployment model.

To learn how to design a rich Internet application, see Chapter 23, "Designing Rich Internet Applications."

Service Archetype

In the context of this guide, a *service* is a public interface that provides access to a unit of functionality. Services literally provide some programmatic *service* to the caller that consumes the service. A service application that exposes such services will normally be structured as a multilayered application consisting of service, business, and data layers, as shown in Figure 4.

SERVICES

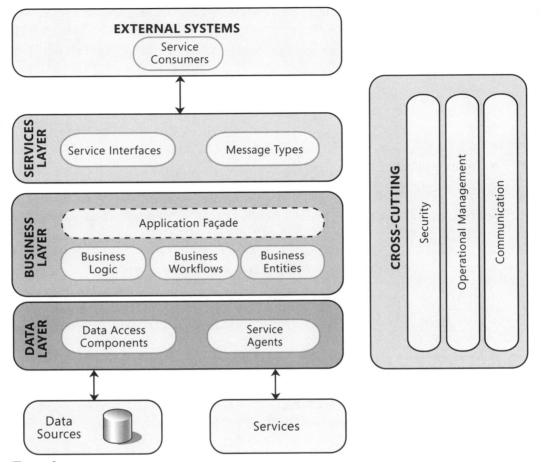

Figure 4
The typical structure of a service application

Services are loosely coupled, and can be combined to provide functionality that is more complex. Services are distributable, and can be accessed from a remote machine as well as from the machine on which the service is running. Services are also message oriented. This means that the interfaces are defined by a Web Services Description Language (WSDL) document and operations are called using messages based on XML schemas, which are passed over a transport channel. In addition, services support a heterogeneous environment by focusing inter-operability on the message/interface definition. If components can understand the message and interface definition, they can use the service regardless of their base technology.

Consider using service applications if:

- Your application will expose functionality that does not require a UI.
- Your application must be loosely coupled with its clients.
- Your application must be shared with or consumed by other external applications.
- Your application must expose functionality that will be consumed by applications over the Internet, an intranet, or on the local machine.

To learn how to design services and service applications, see Chapter 25, "Designing Service Applications."

Web Application Archetype

The core of a Web application is its server-side logic. This logic may be comprised of many distinct layers. A typical example is a three-layered architecture comprising presentation, business, and data layers, as shown in Figure 5.

Web Application

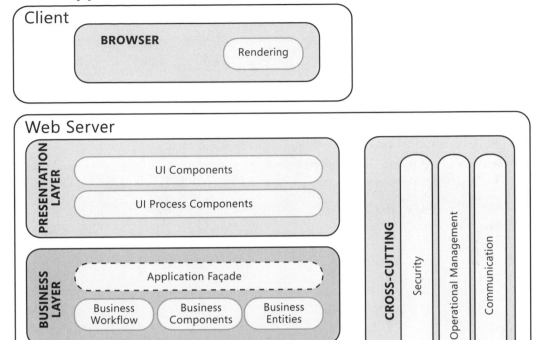

Figure 5
The typical structure of a Web application

A Web application will normally access data stored on a remote database server. It may also consume services exposed by other applications, including S+S hosted services and Web services.

Consider using Web applications if:

- Your application does not require the rich UI and media support offered by a rich Internet application.
- You want the simplicity of a Web-based deployment model.
- Your user interface must be platform independent.
- Your application must be available over the Internet.
- You want to minimize client-side dependencies and resource consumption, such as disk or processor usage.

To learn how to design a Web application, see Chapter 21, "Designing Web Applications."

21 Designing Web Applications

Overview

In this chapter, you will learn the general design considerations and key attributes for a Web application. This includes the guidelines for a layered structure; guidelines for performance, security, and deployment; and the key patterns and technology considerations.

A Web application is an application that can be accessed by the users through a Web browser or a specialized user agent. The browser creates HTTP requests for specific URLs that map to resources on a Web server. The server renders and returns HTML pages to the client, which the browser can display. The core of a Web application is its server-side logic. The application can contain several distinct layers. The typical example is a three-layered architecture comprised of presentation, business, and data layers. Figure 1 illustrates a typical Web application architecture with common components grouped by different areas of concern.

Web Application

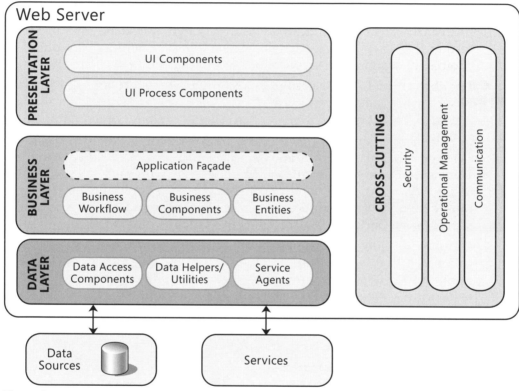

Figure 1
The typical structure of a Web application

The presentation layer usually includes UI and presentation logic components; the business layer usually includes business logic, business workflow and business entities components, and optionally a façade; and the data layer usually includes data access and service agent components. For more information about layered design, see Chapter 5, "Layered Application Guidelines." For more information about the components used in each layer, see Chapter 10, "Component Guidelines."

General Design Considerations

When designing a Web application, the goal of the software architect is to minimize the complexity by separating tasks into different areas of concern while designing a secure, high performance application. Follow these guidelines to ensure that your application meets your requirements, and performs efficiently in scenarios common to Web applications:

- **Partition your application logically.** Use layering to partition your application logically into presentation, business, and data access layers. This helps you to create maintainable code and allows you to monitor and optimize the performance of each layer separately. A clear logical separation also offers more choices for scaling your application.

- **Use abstraction to implement loose coupling between layers.** This can be accomplished by defining interface components, such as a façade with well known inputs and outputs that translates requests into a format understood by components within the layer. In addition, you can also use Interface types or abstract base classes to define a shared abstraction that interface components must implement.

- **Understand how components will communicate with each other.** This requires an understanding of the deployment scenarios your application must support. You must determine if communication across physical boundaries or process boundaries should be supported, or if all components will run within the same process.

- **Consider caching to minimize server round trips.** When designing a Web application, consider using techniques such as caching and output buffering to reduce round trips between the browser and the Web server, and between the Web server and downstream servers. A well designed caching strategy is probably the single most important performance related design consideration. ASP.NET caching features include output caching, partial page caching, and the Cache API. Design your application to take advantage of these features.

- **Consider logging and instrumentation.** You should audit and log activities across the layers and tiers of your application. These logs can be used to detect suspicious activity, which frequently provides early indications of an attack on the system. Keep in mind that it can be difficult to log problems that occur with script code running in the browser.

- **Consider authenticating users across trust boundaries.** You should design your application to authenticate users whenever they cross a trust boundary; for example, when accessing a remote business layer from the presentation layer.

- **Do not pass sensitive data in plaintext across the network.** Whenever you must pass sensitive data such as a password or authentication cookie across the network, consider encrypting and signing the data or using Secure Sockets Layer (SSL) encryption.

- **Design your Web application to run using a least-privileged account.** If an attacker manages to take control of a process, the process identity should have restricted access to the file system and other system resources in order to limit the possible damage.

For more information on general design considerations, see Chapter 17, "Crosscutting Concerns."

Specific Design Issues

You must consider several common issues as you develop your design. These issues can be categorized into specific areas of the design. The following sections provide guidelines to help you avoid the common issues in each area:

- Application Request Processing
- Authentication
- Authorization
- Caching
- Exception Management
- Logging and Instrumentation
- Navigation
- Page Layout
- Page Rendering
- Session Management
- Validation

Application Request Processing

At a high level, a Web application can perform request processing in two ways. With the post back approach, the browser primarily communicates with the server using Web Forms post backs. A popular alternative approach is to use RESTful service calls between the browser and the server. These two approaches each have advantages and disadvantages, and your choice may impact how you address the design issues described below.

When choosing a request processing strategy, you should consider how much control you require over the UI in your application, your development and testing approach, and your performance and scaling requirements.

The post back approach typically allows a forms-based development experience, and uses rich server-side controls that render the corresponding HTML, associated view state, and interaction logic to the browser. Consider this approach if you developing a forms-based Web application and require a rapid application development (RAD) experience.

The REST-full approach typically allows finer-grained control over the UI of your application, and provides more flexibility in terms of navigation, testability, and separation of concerns. Consider using this approach if your application requires flexible navigation, fine control over its UI, may use alternate UI rendering technologies, or if you are using a test-driven development approach.

Regardless of the request processing strategy you choose, you should ensure separation of concerns by implementing the request processing logic and application logic separately from the UI. Several patterns help achieve this. In general, the Model-View-Presenter (MVP) or similar patterns can be used in a Web Forms post back approach to help provide a clean separation of concerns. The Model-View-Controller (MVC) pattern is typically used in a REST-full request processing approach.

Also consider the following guidelines when designing a request processing strategy:

- Consider centralizing the common preprocessing and post processing steps of Web page requests to promote logic reuse across pages. For example, consider creating an HTTP module, or a base class derived from the ASP.NET Page class, to contain your common preprocessing and post processing logic.

- Choose an appropriate approach or pattern for your UI processing. Consider dividing UI processing into three distinct roles—model, view, and controller/presenter—by using MVC, MVP, or similar patterns. Avoid mixing processing and rendering logic in your components.

- If you are designing views for handling large amounts of data, consider giving the view access to the model by using the Supervising Presenter (or Supervising Controller) pattern, which is a form of the MVP pattern. If your application does not have a dependency on view state and you have a limited number of control events, consider using the MVC pattern.

- Consider using the Intercepting Filter pattern to implement the processing steps as pluggable filters when appropriate.

- Ensure that you protect all sensitive data sent over the network, especially over the Internet. Use secure channel protocols such as SSL, and consider encrypting and digitally signing all highly sensitive data sent over both internal and external networks.

Authentication

Designing an effective authentication strategy is important for the security and reliability of your application. Improper or weak authentication can leave your application vulnerable to spoofing attacks, dictionary attacks, session hijacking, and other types of attack. Consider the following guidelines when designing an authentication strategy:

- Identify trust boundaries within Web application layers. This will help you to determine where to authenticate users.

- Enforce secure account management practices such as account lockouts and password expirations, and strong password policies that specify the minimum password length and complexity.

- Use a platform- supported authentication mechanism such as Windows Authentication when possible. Where you decide to use Forms Authentication, take advantage of the built-in support in ASP.NET instead of designing a custom authentication mechanism. Consider using a federated service or single sign on (SSO) if you want to allow users to log on to several sites with a single set of credentials.

- When you must store passwords in a database, do not store them as plaintext; instead, store a hash (or salted hash) of the password.

Authorization

Authorization determines the tasks that an authenticated identity can perform, and identifies the resources that can be accessed. Designing an effective authorization strategy is important for the security and reliability of your application. Improper or weak authorization leads to information disclosure, data tampering, and elevation of privileges. Defense in depth is the key security principle to apply to your application's authorization strategy. Consider the following guidelines when designing an authorization strategy:

- Authorize users as they cross all trust boundaries. Use URL authorization for page and directory access control. Access downstream resources using a trusted identity based on the trusted subsystem model as described in Chapter 19, "Physical Tiers and Deployment."

- Consider the granularity of your authorization settings. Building your authorization with too much granularity will increase your management overhead; however, using less granularity may reduce flexibility.

- Use impersonation and delegation to take advantage of the user-specific auditing and granular access controls of the platform, but consider the effect on performance and scalability.

Caching

Caching improves the performance and responsiveness of your application. However, incorrect caching choices and poor caching design can degrade performance and responsiveness. You should use caching to optimize reference data lookups, avoid network round trips, and avoid unnecessary and duplicate processing. To implement caching, you must first decide when to load data into the cache. Try to load cache data asynchronously or by using a batch process to avoid client delays. Consider the following guidelines when designing caching:

- Cache data in a ready to use format when possible, and avoid caching volatile data that changes regularly. Avoid caching sensitive information unless it is encrypted.

- Use output caching to cache pages that are relatively static. This dramatically improves performance, while still supporting variation based on submitted values. If only parts of the page are relatively static, consider using partial page caching with user controls.

- Pool shared resources that are expensive, such as network connections, instead of caching them.

For more information on caching, see Chapter 17, "Crosscutting Concerns."

Exception Management

Designing an effective exception management strategy is important for the security and reliability of your application. Correct exception handling in your Web pages prevents sensitive exception details from being revealed to the user, improves application robustness, and helps to avoid leaving your application in an inconsistent state in the event of an error. Consider the following guidelines when designing an exception management strategy:

- Provide user friendly error messages to notify users of errors in the application, but ensure that you avoid exposing sensitive data in error pages, error messages, log files, and audit files.

- Ensure that you catch unhandled exceptions, and clean up resources and state when an exception occurs. Design a global exception handler that displays a global error page or an error message for all unhandled exceptions. Avoid the use of custom exceptions when not necessary.

- Do not catch exceptions unless you must handle them; for example, to remove sensitive information or add additional information to the exception. Do not use exceptions to control application logic flow.

For more information on exception management, see Chapter 17, "Crosscutting Concerns."

Logging and Instrumentation

Designing an effective logging and instrumentation strategy is important for the security and reliability of your application. You should audit and log activity across the tiers of your application. These logs can be used to detect suspicious activity, which frequently provides early indications of an attack on the system, and can help to address repudiation threats where users deny their actions. Log and audit files may be required in legal proceedings to prove the wrongdoing of individuals. Auditing is generally considered to be most authoritative if the audit is generated at the precise time of resource access, and by the routine that accesses the resource. Consider the following guidelines when designing a logging and instrumentation strategy:

- Consider auditing in all layers of the application for user management events, system critical events, business critical operations, and unusual activities.
- Create secure log file management policies such as restricting access to log files, and allowing only write access to users. Ensure that your logging and instrumentation mechanisms are configurable during deployment and when in production.
- Do not store sensitive information in log or audit files.

Navigation

Design your navigation strategy in a way that separates it from the processing logic. Your strategy should allow users to navigate easily through your screens or pages. Designing a consistent navigation structure for your application will help to minimize user confusion as well as reduce the apparent complexity of the application. Consider the following guidelines when designing your navigation strategy:

- If you are using a Web Forms post back approach, consider using design patterns such as MVP to decouple UI processing from output rendering. Avoid mixing navigation logic with your user interface components by handling navigation in the Presenter.
- If you are using a REST-full approach, consider using a MVC pattern to decouple application logic, data, and navigation into separate components. Typical MVC application implementation provide flexible navigation support by directing requests to a controller component that then coordinates the application's UI and data.
- Consider encapsulating navigation in a master page so that it is consistent throughout the application. However, avoid hard coding navigation paths in your application. Also, ensure that users can only navigate to views for which they are authorized.

- Consider using a site map to help users find pages on the site, and to allow search engines to crawl the site if appropriate. Consider using visual elements such as embedded links, navigation menus, and breadcrumb navigation in the UI to help users understand where they are, what is available on the site, and how to navigate the site quickly. Consider using wizards to implement navigation between forms in a predictable way.

Page Layout

Design your application so that the page layout can be separated from the specific UI components and UI processing. When choosing a layout strategy, consider whether designers or developers will be building the layout. If designers will be building the layout, choose a layout approach that does not require coding or the use of development-focused tools. Consider the following guidelines when designing your layout strategy:

- Use Cascading Style Sheets (CSS) for layout whenever possible, rather than table-based layout. However, use table-based layout when you must support a grid layout or where the data is represented as a table. Bear in mind that table-based layout can be slow to render, and there may be issues with complex layout.

- Use a common layout for pages where possible to maximize accessibility and ease of use. Avoid designing and developing large pages that accomplish multiple tasks, particularly where only a few tasks are usually executed with each request. Minimize page size where possible to maximize performance and reduce bandwidth requirements.

- Use master pages in ASP.NET applications to provide a common appearance and behavior for all of the pages, and to allow updates to the site with minimum effort. Consider extracting common sections of pages into separate user controls to reduce the overall complexity and allow reuse of these controls.

- Consider using the ASP.NET AJAX server controls and the ASP.NET AJAX client-side library to make client script more easily portable between different browsers. Also, avoid mixing client-side script with HTML code. Doing so makes the page more complex and harder to maintain. Place client side script in separate script files so they can be cached by the browser.

- When migrating an existing Web application, consider using Silverlight controls in ASP.NET pages to provide a rich user experience and minimize application reengineering.

Page Rendering

When designing for page rendering, you must ensure that you render the pages efficiently and maximize interface usability. Consider the following guidelines when designing a page-rendering strategy:

- Consider using client-side script or ASP.NET AJAX for an improved user experience and better responsiveness by reducing the number of post backs required. Using custom client-side script can make applications harder to test because script support varies between different browsers and versions. Instead, consider using ASP.NET AJAX, which supports most common browsers. Remember that the use of client-side code of any type (including script emitted by the built-in ASP.NET controls) can affect accessibility. Ensure that you provide appropriate accessibility support for specialist user agents and disabled users.

- Consider data-binding options. For example, you can bind collections, **DataReader** objects, **DataSet** tables, and custom objects to many ASP.NET controls. Use data-paging techniques to minimize scalability issues associated with large amounts of data, and to improve performance and response times.

- Consider designing to support localization in UI components.

- Abstract the user process components from data rendering and acquisition functions.

Session Management

When designing a Web application, an efficient and secure session management strategy is important for performance and reliability. You must consider session management factors such as what to store, where to store it, and how long information will be kept. Consider the following guidelines when designing a session management strategy:

- Consider if you actually do need to store session state. Using session state adds overhead to each page request.

- Ensure that you persist session data when required, but consider using read-only sessions or disabling session state altogether to improve performance where this is appropriate.

- If you have a single Web server, require optimum session state performance, and have a relatively limited number of concurrent sessions, use the in-process state store. However, if your session data is expensive to recreate, and you require durability in the event of an ASP.NET restart, use the session state service running on the local Web server. For multiple server (Web farm) scenarios, where you must centralize session data storage across servers, consider using the SQL Server state store.

- If you are storing state on a separate server, protect your session state communication channel using techniques such as SSL or IPSec.

- Prefer basic types for session data to reduce serialization costs.

Validation

Designing an effective validation solution is important for the security and reliability of your application. Improper or weak validation can leave your application vulnerable to cross-site scripting attacks, SQL injection attacks, buffer overflows, and other types of input attack. Consider the following guidelines when designing a validation strategy:

- Validate all data crossing the trust boundaries of your application. Assume that all client controlled data is malicious and must be validated.
- Design your validation strategy to constrain, reject, and sanitize malicious input; and validate all input data based on length, range, format, and type.
- Use client-side validation for optimum user experience and reduced network round trips, but always validate on the server for security reasons.
- Investigate third-party solutions, design patterns, and libraries that can help you to centrally manage and reuse validation rules and code.

For more information on validation techniques, see Chapter 17, "Crosscutting Concerns."

Design Considerations for Layers

If you have chosen to use a layered design for your application, consider the specific issues for each layer described in the following sections.

Presentation Layer

The presentation layer of your Web application displays the UI and facilitates user interaction. The design should focus on separation of concerns, where the user interaction logic is decoupled from the UI components. You should consider using separate UI components and presentation logic components in complex interfaces, and base your UI components on standard Web controls where possible. You can compile the controls into an assembly for reuse across applications, or if you need to add additional features to existing server controls.

For Web applications, the presentation layer consists of a server-side component (which renders the HTML) and a client-side component (the browser or user agent that executes scripts and displays the HTML). Usually, all presentation logic exists in the server components, and the client components only display the HTML. With client-side techniques such as AJAX, it is possible to execute logic on the client, usually to improve the user experience. Doing so requires extra development effort and testing. If you decide to do any validation on the client, ensure that you repeat the validation on the server, as any client side validation can easily be circumvented.

Business Layer

When designing the business layer for your Web application, consider how to implement the business logic and long-running workflows. Using a separate business layer that implements the business logic and workflows can improve the maintainability and testability of your application, and allow you to centralize and reuse common business logic functions. Consider designing business entities that represent the real world data, and use these to pass data between components.

Design your business layer to be stateless, which helps to reduce resource contention and increase performance, and consider using a message-based interface. This works well with a stateless Web application business layer. If you perform business critical operations in your business layer, design to use transactions to maintain integrity and prevent data loss.

Data Layer

Consider designing a data layer for your Web application that abstracts the logic necessary to access the database. Using a separate data layer makes the application easier to configure and maintain, and hides the details of the database from other layers of the application. Design entity objects that the data layer can populate or use to update the data source, and use data transfer objects (DTOs) when interacting with other layers and to pass the data between layers.

Design the data layer to take advantage of connection pooling to minimize the number of open connections, and consider using batch operations to reduce round trips to the database. The data layer may also need to access external services using service agents. Also, ensure that you design an exception handling strategy to handle data access errors, and to propagate exceptions to the business layer.

Service Layer

Consider designing a separate service layer if you plan to deploy your business layer on a remote tier, or if you plan to expose your business logic using a Web service. Design the services to achieve maximum reusability by not assuming the specific details of clients that will use them, and avoid changes over time that might break the service interface for existing clients. Instead, implement versions of the interface to allow clients to connect to the appropriate version.

If your business layer resides on a remote tier, design coarse-grained service methods in order to minimize the number of round trips, and to provide loose coupling. Also, design the services to be idempotent (so that they can manage the situation where the same request message arrives more than once) and commutative (so that they can manage the situation where messages that perform a specific set of task steps arrive in the wrong order). Ensure that you do not implement business rules in a service interface, which can make is more difficult to keep the interface stable and may generate unnecessary dependencies across components and clients.

Finally, consider interoperability requirements by choosing appropriate protocols and transport mechanisms. For example, use ASMX for broad reach and WCF for more fine control over configuration. Decide whether the interface will expose SOAP, REST, or both methods. For more information about exposing services, see Chapter 9, "Service Layer Guidelines" and Chapter 18, "Communication and Messaging."

Testing and Testability Considerations

Testability is a measure of how well your system or components allow you to create test criteria and execute tests to determine if the criteria are met. You should consider testability when designing your architecture because it makes it easier to diagnose problems earlier and reduces maintenance cost. Consider the following guidelines for testability:

- Clearly define the inputs and outputs of the application's layers and components during the design phase.

- Consider separated presentation patterns, such as MVC or MVP in the presentation layer. This allows the presentation logic to be unit tested.

- Design a separate business layer to implement the business logic and workflows, which improves the testability of your application.

- Design loosely coupled components that can be tested individually.

- Design an effective logging and tracing strategy, which allows you to detect or troubleshoot errors that might otherwise be difficult to find. Provide logging and tracing information that can be consumed by monitoring or management tools. This will help you to locate and focus on the faulty code when errors occur. Log files should contain information that can be used to replicate the issue.

Technology Considerations

On the Microsoft platform, from an ASP.NET standpoint, you can combine the ASP. NET Web Forms model with a range of other technologies, including ASP.NET AJAX, ASP.NET MVC, Silverlight, and ASP.NET Dynamic Data. Consider the following guidelines:

- If you want to build applications that are accessed through a Web browser or specialized user agent, consider using ASP.NET.

- If you want to build applications that provide increased interactivity and background processing, with fewer page reloads, consider using ASP.NET with AJAX.

- If you want to build applications that include rich media content and interactivity, consider using ASP.NET with Silverlight controls.

- If you are using ASP.NET, consider using master pages to implement a consistent UI across all pages.

- If you are building a data driven Web application with pages based on the data model of the underlying database, consider using ASP.NET Dynamic Data.

- If you are using a test-driven development approach, or need fine-grained control over your UI, consider using the MVC pattern and ASP.NET MVC to cleanly separate application and navigation logic from your application's UI.

Deployment Considerations

When deploying a Web application, you should take into account how layer and component location will affect the performance, scalability, and security of the application. You might also need to consider design tradeoffs. Use either a distributed or a nondistributed deployment approach, depending on the business requirements and infrastructure constraints. Nondistributed deployment will generally maximize performance by reducing the number of calls that must cross physical boundaries. However, distributed deployment will allow you to achieve better scalability and allows each layer to be secured separately.

Nondistributed Deployment

In a nondistributed deployment scenario, all the logically separate layers of the Web application are physically located on the same Web server, except for the database. You must consider how the application will handle multiple concurrent users, and how to secure the layers that reside on the same server. Figure 2 shows this scenario.

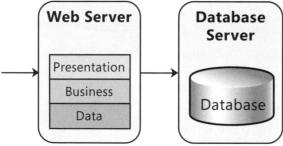

Figure 2
Nondistributed deployment of a Web application

Consider the following guidelines when choosing a nondistributed deployment:

- Use nondistributed deployment if your Web application is performance sensitive, because the local calls to other layers reduce the impact on performance that would be caused by remote calls across tiers.
- If you do not need to share the business logic with other applications, and only the presentation layer will access it, design a component-based interface for your business layer.
- If your business logic and presentation logic run in the same process, avoid authentication at the business layer.
- Use a trusted identity (through the trusted subsystem model) to access the database. This improves the performance and scalability of your application.
- Decide how you will protect sensitive data passed between the Web server and the database server.

Distributed Deployment

In a distributed deployment scenario, the presentation and business layers of the Web application reside on separate physical tiers, and communicate remotely. You will typically locate your business and data access layers on the same sever. Figure 3 shows this scenario.

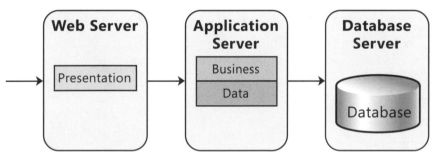

Figure 3
Distributed deployment of a Web application

Consider the following guidelines when choosing a distributed deployment:

- Do not deploy your business layer on separate tier unless it is necessary; for example, to maximize scalability, or when security concerns prohibit you from deploying your business logic on your front-end Web server.
- Consider using a message-based interface for your business layer.
- Consider using the TCP protocol with binary encoding to communicate with the business layer for best performance.
- Consider protecting sensitive data passed between different physical tiers.

Load Balancing

When you deploy your Web application on multiple servers, you can use load balancing to distribute requests so that they are handled by different Web servers. This helps to maximize response times, resource utilization, and throughput. Figure 4 shows this scenario.

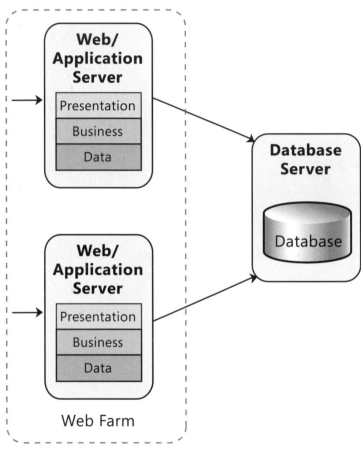

Figure 4
Load balancing a Web application

Consider the following guidelines when designing your Web application to use load balancing:

- Avoid server affinity when designing Web applications if possible because this can negatively affect the application's ability to scale out. Server affinity occurs when all requests from a particular client must be handled by the same server. It usually occurs when you use locally updatable caches, or in-process or local session state stores. If you must support server affinity, configure the cluster to route all requests from the same user to the same server.

- Consider designing stateless components for your Web application; for example, a Web front end that has no in-process state and no stateful business components. If you must store state for users, avoid the use of in-process session management in a Web farm unless you can configure affinity and guarantee that requests from the same user will be routed to the same server. Instead, use of an out-of-process state server service or a database server.

- Consider using Windows Network Load Balancing (NLB) as a software solution to implement redirection of requests to the servers in an application farm.

- Consider using clustering to minimize the impact of hardware failures.

- Consider partitioning your database across multiple database servers if your application has high input/output requirements.

For more information on deployment patterns, see Chapter 19, "Physical Tiers and Deployment."

Relevant Design Patterns

Key patterns are organized into categories such as Caching, Exception Management, Logging and Instrumentation, Page Layout, Presentation, Request Processing, and Service Interface Layer; as shown in the following table. Consider using these patterns when making design decisi ons for each category.

Category	Relevant patterns
Caching	**Cache Dependency.** Use external information to determine the state of data stored in a cache. **Page Cache.** Improve the response time for dynamic Web pages that are accessed frequently but change less often and consume a large amount of system resources to construct.
Exception Management	**Exception Shielding.** Filter exception data that should not be exposed to external systems or users.
Logging and Instrumentation	**Provider.** Implement a component that exposes an API that is different from the client API, to allow any custom implementation to be seamlessly plugged in.
Page Layout (UI)	**Composite View.** Combine individual views into a composite representation. **Template View.** Implement a common template view, and derive or construct views using this template view. **Transform View.** Transform the data passed to the presentation tier into HTML to be displayed on the UI. **Two-Step View.** Transform the model data into a logical presentation without any specific formatting, and then convert that logical presentation into the actual formatting required.
Presentation	**Model-View-Controller.** Separate the data in the domain, the presentation, and the actions based on user input into three separate classes. The Model manages the behavior and data of the application domain, responds to requests for information about its state (usually from the View), and responds to instructions to change state (usually from the Controller). The View manages the display of information. The Controller interprets the mouse and keyboard inputs from the user, informing the model and/or the view to change as appropriate. **Model-View-Presenter.** Separate request processing into three roles, with the View being responsible for handling user input, the Model responsible for application data and business logic, and the Presenter responsible for presentation logic andfor coordinating the interaction between the View and the Model. **Passive View.** A variant of the MVC pattern. Reduce the view to the absolute minimum by allowing the controller to process user input and maintain the responsibility for updating the view. **Supervising Presenter (or Supervising Controller).** A variation of the MVC pattern in which the controller handles complex logic, in particular coordinating between views, but where the view is responsible for simple view specific logic.

Category	Relevant patterns
Request Processing	**Intercepting Filter.** Create a chain of composable filters (independent modules) to implement common preprocessing and post processing tasks during a Web page request. **Page Controller.** Accept input from the request and handle it for a specific page or action on a Web site. **Front Controller.** Consolidate request handling by channeling all requests through a single handler object, which can be modified at run time with decorators.
Service Interface Layer	**Façade.** Implement a unified interface to a set of operations to provide a simplified, reduced coupling between systems. **Service Interface.** A programmatic interface that other systems can use to interact with the service.

For more information on the Page Cache pattern, see *"Enterprise Solution Patterns Using Microsoft .NET"* at http://msdn.microsoft.com/en-us/library/ms998469.aspx.

For more information on the Model-View-Controller (MVC), Page Controller, Front Controller, Template View, Transform View, and Two-Step View patterns, see Fowler, Martin. *Patterns of Enterprise Application Architecture.* Addison-Wesley, 2002. Or at http://martinfowler.com/eaaCatalog.

For more information on the Composite View, Supervising Presenter, and Presentation Model patterns, see *"Patterns in the Composite Application Library"* at http://msdn.microsoft.com/en-us/library/cc707841.aspx.

For more information on the Exception Shielding pattern, see *"Useful Patterns for Services"* at http://msdn.microsoft.com/en-us/library/cc304800.aspx.

For more information on the Service Interface pattern, see *"Service Interface"* at http://msdn.microsoft.com/en-us/library/ms998421.aspx.

For more information on the Provider pattern, see *"Provider Model Design Pattern and Specification, Part I"* at http://msdn.microsoft.com/en-us/library/ms998421.aspx.

Additional Resources

To more easily access Web resources, see the online version of the bibliography at: http://www.microsoft.com/architectureguide.

- For more information on designing and implementing Web client applications, see *"Design and Implementation Guidelines for Web Clients"* at http://msdn.microsoft.com/en-us/library/ms978605.aspx.

- For more information on designing distributed Web applications, see *"Designing Distributed Applications"* at http://msdn.microsoft.com/en-us/library/aa292470(VS.71).aspx.

- For more information on Web application performance issues, see *"Improving .NET Application Performance and Scalability"* at http://msdn.microsoft.com/en-us/library/ms998530.aspx.

- For more information on Web application security, see *"Improving Web Application Security: Threats and Countermeasures"* at http://msdn.microsoft.com/en-us/library/ms994921.aspx.

22

Designing Rich Client Applications

Overview

In this chapter, you will learn about the key scenarios for using rich client applications, the components found in a rich client application, and the important design considerations for rich client applications. You will also learn about deployment scenarios for rich client applications, and the key patterns and technology considerations for designing rich client applications.

Rich client UIs can provide high performance, interactive, and rich user experiences for applications that must operate in stand-alone, connected, occasionally connected, and disconnected scenarios. Windows Forms, Windows Presentation Foundation (WPF), and Microsoft Office Business Application (OBA) development environments and tools are available that allow developers to quickly and easily build rich client applications.

While these technologies can be used to create stand-alone applications, they can also be used to create applications that run on the client machine but communicate with services exposed by other layers (both logical and physical) and other applications that expose operations the client requires. These operations may include data access, information retrieval, searching, sending information to other systems, back up, and related activities. Figure 1 shows an overall view of typical rich client architecture, and identifies the components usually found in each layer.

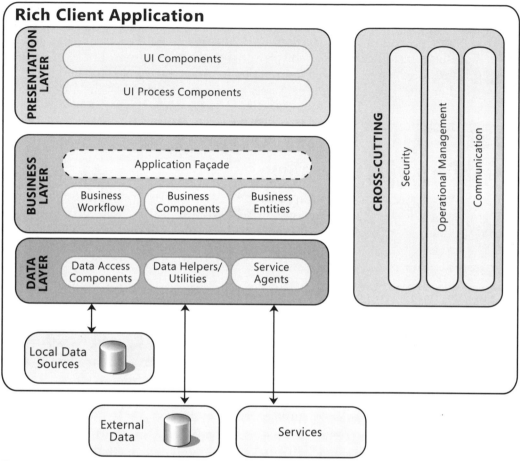

Figure 1
Overall view of typical rich client architecture

A typical rich client application is decomposed into three layers: the presentation layer, business layer and data layer. The presentation layer usually contains UI and presentation logic components; the business layer usually contains business logic, business workflow and business entity components; and the data layer usually contains data access and service agent components. For more information about layered design, see Chapter 5, "Layered Application Guidelines." For more information about the components appropriate for each layer, see Chapter 10, "Component Guidelines."

Rich client applications may be fairly thin applications consisting of mainly a presentation layer, which access a remote business layer hosted on server machines through services. An example of this is a data entry application that sends all of the data to the server for processing and storage.

At the other end of the scale, they may be complex applications that perform most of the processing themselves and only communicate with other services and data stores to consume or send back information. An example of this is an application such as Microsoft Excel® spreadsheet software that performs complex local tasks, stores state and data locally and only communicates with remote servers to fetch and update linked data. These types of rich clients may contain their own business layers and data access layers. The guidelines for the business and data layers in such applications are the same as those discussed generally for all applications.

General Design Considerations

When designing a rich client application, the goal of the software architect is to choose an appropriate technology and design a structure that minimizes complexity by separating tasks into different areas of concern. The design should meet the requirements for the application in terms of performance, security, reusability, and ease of maintenance.

Consider the following guidelines when designing rich client applications:

- **Choose an appropriate technology based on application requirements.** Suitable technologies include Windows Forms, WPF, XAML Browser Applications (XBAP), and OBA.

- **Separate presentation logic from interface implementation.** Consider design patterns such as Presentation Model and Supervising Presenter (or Supervising Controller) that separate UI rendering from UI logic; which eases maintenance, promotes reusability, and improves testability. The use of separate components within the application can reduce dependencies, make maintenance and testing easier, and promote reusability.

- **Identify the presentation tasks and presentation flows.** This will help you to design each screen and each step in a multi screen or Wizard process.

- **Design to provide a suitable and usable interface.** Take into account features such as layout, navigation, choice of controls, and localization to maximize accessibility and usability.

- **Apply separation of concerns across all layers.** For example, extract business rules and other tasks not related to presentation and locate these in a separate business layer. Separate data access code into separate components located in a data layer.

- **Reuse common presentation logic.** Libraries that contain templates, generalized client-side validation functions, and helper classes may be reusable in several applications.

- **Loosely couple your client from any remote services it uses.** Use a message-based interface to communicate with services located on separate physical tiers.

- **Avoid tight coupling to objects in other layers.** Use the abstraction provided by common interface definitions, abstract base classes, or messaging when communicating with other layers of the application. For example, implementing the Dependency Injection and Inversion of Control patterns can provide a shared abstraction between layers.

- **Reduce round trips when accessing remote layers.** Use coarse-grained methods and execute them asynchronously if possible to avoid blocking or freezing the UI.

For more information about designing the business layer, see Chapter 7, "Business Layer Guidelines." For more information about designing the data layer, see Chapter 8, "Data Layer Guidelines."

Specific Design Issues

There are several common issues that you must consider as your develop your design. These issues can be categorized into specific areas of the design. The following sections contain guidelines to help you resolve the common issues in each area:

- Business Layer
- Communication
- Composition
- Configuration Management
- Data Access
- Exception Management
- Maintainability
- Presentation Layer
- State Management
- Workflow

Business Layer

A typical thin rich client acts as the interface to a business system, and the business layer is part of that business system and is usually exposed as a service. However, in a typical thick rich client, the business layer is located on the client itself. Consider the following guidelines when designing the business layer for a rich client:

- Identify the business layers and service interfaces that the application will use. If the application will access remote services, import the interface definitions and write code that accesses these service functions using the interfaces. This helps to minimize coupling between the client and a remote business layer or services that it uses.

- If your business logic does not contain sensitive information, consider locating some of the business rules on the client to improve performance of the UI and the client application. If your business logic *does* contain sensitive information, you should locate the business layer on a separate tier.

- Consider how the client will obtain information required to operate business rules and other client-side processing, update this information automatically as it changes, and how users or administrators will update the business rules as requirements change. You may decide to have the client obtain business rule information from a remote server when it starts up.

For more information about designing the business layer, see Chapter 7, "Business Layer Guidelines."

Communication

If the business and data layers of a rich client application are located on a remote tier and exposed as services, or if a rich client uses other remote services, it can communicate with these services using a variety of protocols and methods. These may include HTTP requests, Simple SMTP e-mail messages, SOAP Web service messages, DCOM for remote components, remote database access protocols, or other TCP/IP-based standard or custom communication protocols. If the business layer and data layer are located on the client, the presentation layer can use object-based methods to interact with them. Consider the following guidelines when designing a communication strategy:

- When communicating with services on a remote physical tier, use a message-based protocol when possible. This gives you a more natural way to make asynchronous calls to avoid blocking the presentation layer, and to support load balanced and failover server configurations. Use coarse-grained interfaces to minimize network traffic and maximize performance.

- Where required, enable offline processing for the application. Detect and monitor the connection state. When disconnected, cache information locally and then resynchronize when communication is re-enabled. Consider holding application state and data locally in a persistent cache to allow disconnected start up and a shutdown/restart cycles without information loss.

- To protect sensitive information and communication channels, consider using IPSec and SSL to secure the channel, encryption to protect data, and digital signatures to detect data tampering.

- If the application must consume or send large sets or amounts of data, consider the potential performance and network impact. Choose more efficient communication protocols such as TCP, using compression mechanisms to minimize the data payload size for message-based protocols such as SMTP and SOAP, or custom binary formats when the application does not need to support open communication standards.

For more information about communication between clients and layers of the application, see Chapter 18, "Communication and Messaging."

Composition

To maximize extensibility and maintainability of the application—particularly where it exposes a complex UI as is common in many business scenarios—consider implementing the interface using the Composition design pattern, where the UI consists of separate modules or forms loaded dynamically at run time. This approach is useful when users may open several forms to perform specific tasks, and work with data in a range of different ways. Users can open and close forms as required, and the application can maximize performance and reduce start up delays by loading these forms only when required. Also consider how you can support personalization for users, so that they can modify the layout and content to suit their own requirements. Consider the following guidelines when designing a composition strategy:

- Based on functional specifications and requirements, identify the appropriate types of interface components you require. For example, possible components include Windows Forms, WPF forms, Office-style documents, user controls, or custom modules.

- Identify an appropriate composition mechanism, where composition is appropriate, and consider composing views from reusable modular parts. For example, use the Composite View pattern to build a view from modular, atomic component parts. You may alternatively decide to use a composition framework such as the patterns & practices Composite Client Application Guidance, or built-in features of your development environment such as user controls or document panels. However, be careful with dependencies between components, and use abstraction patterns when possible to avoid issues with maintainability. Implement, where possible, features for managing auto update and versioning of composable components.

- If you must support communication between different forms and presentation components that make up a composite interface, consider implementing decoupled communication techniques such as the Publish/Subscribe or Command pattern. This will minimize the coupling between these components and improve testability.

- Take advantage of appropriate templates and data binding techniques available in your chosen implementation technology to simplify and minimize the code required for each form that you use within a composable interface.

- Consider implementing personalization so that users can customize the layout of composable components within the interface.

Configuration Management

Rich client applications will usually require configuration information loaded at start-up, and sometimes during execution. This information may be network or connection information, user settings, UI business rules, or general display and layout settings. You may decide to store some or all of this information locally, or download it from a remote server when the application starts. You may also need to persist changes to the information as the application runs or when it ends; for example, storing user preferences, layout settings, and other UI data in the user's local profile. Consider the following guidelines when designing a configuration management strategy:

- Determine what configurable data may change during the life of your application; for example, file locations, developer versus production settings, logging, assembly references, and contact information for notifications. If necessary, design the application to detect and dynamically apply the configuration changes.

- Choose local or centralized storage locations. User managed data (including profile information or personalization settings) should generally be stored locally, though you may consider storing it centrally to enable roaming. Global application settings should be stored in a central location, and perhaps downloaded locally for performance reasons.

- Identify sensitive configuration information and implement a suitable mechanism for protecting it during transit over the network, when persisted locally, and even when stored in memory.

- Take into account any global security policies and Group Policy overrides that might affect or override local configurations.

Data Access

Rich client applications will usually access data stored on a remote server, as well as data stored on the local machine. Data access often has a significant impact on performance, and is the most obvious factor in the user's perception of an application and its usability and responsiveness. You should aim to maximize performance of data access routines and data transmission across tiers. You must also design the application with regard to the types of data it will use. If the client application cannot handle the data in the exposed format, you must implement a translation mechanism that converts it. However, this will have an impact on performance. Consider the following guidelines when designing a data access strategy:

- Whenever possible, load data asynchronously so that the UI is still responsive while the data is loading. However, you must also be aware of conflicts that might occur if the user attempts to interact with the data before loading is complete, and design the interface to protect against errors arising from this.

- If the client will consume very large amounts of data, consider chunking these and loading them asynchronously into a local cache to improve performance. You must plan how you will handle inconsistencies between the local copy and the original data, perhaps by using methods such as time stamps or events.

- In occasionally connected scenarios, monitor connectivity and implement a service dispatcher mechanism to support batch processing so that users can perform multiple updates to data.

- Determine how you will detect and manage concurrency conflicts that arise when multiple users attempt to update the central data store. Explore optimistic and pessimistic concurrency models.

For more information about data access and handling data in rich client applications, see "Data Handling Considerations" later in this chapter.

Exception Management

All applications and services are subject to the occurrence of errors and exceptions, and you must implement a suitable strategy for detecting and managing these errors and exceptions. A robust and well designed exception management strategy can simplify application design, and improve security and manageability. It can also make it easier for developers to create the application, and reduces development time and cost. In a rich client application, you will usually need to notify the user. In addition, for anything other than trivial UI errors such as validation messages, you should consider logging errors and exceptions for use by operations staff and monitoring systems. The main challenge here is usually collating log information or designing a centralized server-based logging sink that can be accessed by all clients. Consider the following guidelines when designing an exception management strategy:

- Identify the errors and exceptions that are likely to arise within the application, and identify which of these require only user notification. Errors such as validation failures are usually only notified locally to the user. However, errors such as repeated invalid logon attempts or detection of malicious data should be logged and administrators notified. All execution exceptions and application failures should be logged and, optionally, administrators notified.

- Identify an overall strategy for handling exceptions. This may involve actions such as wrapping exceptions with other application specific or custom exceptions that contain additional data to assist in resolving failures, or replacing exceptions to prevent exposure of sensitive information. Also, implement a mechanism for detecting and logging unhandled exceptions. A framework for managing exceptions, such as the patterns & practices Enterprise Library, may be useful for these tasks.

- Determine how you will store exception information, how you will pass it to other layers of the application if required, and how you will notify administrators. Consider using a monitoring tool or environment that can read events from the local machine and present a view of the application state to administrators.

- Ensure that you sanitize exception information that is exposed to users in order to prevent sensitive information from being displayed or stored in log and audit files. If necessary, encrypt information and use secure channels to communicate exceptions and errors to other physical tiers of the application.

- Only catch exceptions that you can handle. For example, catch data conversion exceptions that can occur when trying to convert null values. Do not use exceptions to control business logic.

For more information about exception handling, see Chapter 17, "Crosscutting Concerns."

Maintainability

It is vital to minimize maintenance cost and effort for all applications and components. You should implement mechanisms that reduce maintenance liabilities; for example, by using design patterns that provide good separation of concerns and loose coupling between components. Rich client applications are usually located on remote client machines, and are subsequently more difficult to operate than server installed applications. Other issues to consider, therefore, include deployment, updates, patches, and versioning. Consider the following guidelines when designing a maintainability strategy:

- Implement a suitable mechanism for manual and/or automatic updates to the application and its components. You must take into account versioning issues to ensure that the application has consistent and interoperable versions of all the components it uses.

- Choose an appropriate deployment approach based on the environment in which your application will be used. For example, you might require an installation program for applications that are publically available, or you may be able to use system tools such as Microsoft System Center to deploy applications within a closed environment.

- Design the application so that components are loosely coupled and interchangeable where possible. This allows you to change individual components depending on requirements, run-time scenarios, and individual user requirements or preferences. Also, design to minimize dependencies between components and layers so that the application or the individual layers and components can be used in different scenarios where appropriate.

- Implement logging and auditing as appropriate for the application to assist administrators and developers when debugging the application and solving run-time problems.

For more information about maintainability, see Chapter 16, "Quality Attributes."

Presentation Layer

The presentation layer is the part of the application that the user sees and interacts with, and it must therefore satisfy many requirements. These requirements encompass general factors such as usability, performance, design, and interactivity. A poor user experience can result in a severely negative impact on an application that performs well in all other respects. It is important to design your application to support a compelling and intuitive user experience from the outset, as the user experience is influenced by many different aspects of your application's architecture. Consider the following guidelines when designing the presentation features of your application:

- Investigate how you can separate the logic for managing user interaction from the UI, and from the data with which the user works—perhaps by applying a Separated Presentation style. This makes it easier to update parts of the application, allows developers and designers to work separately on the components, and improves testability.

- Implement command and navigation strategies and mechanisms that are flexible and can be updated easily. Consider implementing well-known design patterns such as Command, Publish/Subscribe, and Observer to decouple commands and navigation from the components in the application and to improve testability.

- Take advantage of data binding capabilities to display data whenever possible, especially for tabular and multirow data presentation. This reduces the code required, simplifies development, and reduces coding errors. It can also automatically synchronize data in different views or forms. Use two-way binding where the user must be able to update the data.

- Consider how you will display documents in an Office document–style interface, or when displaying document content or HTML in other UI elements. Ensure that the user is protected from invalid and malicious content that might reside in documents.

- Ensure that the application UI can be internationalized and then localized to all geographical and cultural scenarios where it may be used. This includes changing the language, text direction, and content layout based on configuration or auto detection of the user's culture. Also, ensure that you provide appropriate support for accessibility and navigation.

For more information about presentation layer design considerations, see Chapter 6, "Presentation Layer Guidelines."

State Management

State management concerns the persistence of data that represents the state of a component, operation, or step in a process. State data may include user settings, configuration information, workflow information, business rule values, and data that the UI displays. The application must be able to save this data, access it as required, and handle conflicts, restarts, and connection status changes. Consider the following guidelines when designing a state-management strategy:

- Determine the state information that the application must store, including estimates of the size, the frequency of changes, and the processing or overhead cost of re-creating or refetching the data; and ensure that your chosen state management mechanism can provide appropriate support.

- If you have large volumes of state data, consider using a local disk-based mechanism to store it. If the application requires data to be available when it starts up, use a persistent mechanism such as isolated storage or a disk file.

- When storing sensitive data, ensure that you implement the appropriate level of protection by using encryption and/or digital signatures.

- Consider at what granularity you must maintain state information. For example, determine the state information that applies to all users of an application and the information that applies only to specific users or roles.

Workflow

Some rich client applications require view flow or workflow support to enable multi-step operations or Wizard-style UI elements. You can implement these features using separate components or custom solutions, or you can take advantage of a framework such as Windows Workflow Foundation (WF). Consider the following guidelines when designing a workflow strategy:

- Use workflow within business components for operations that involve multistep or long-running processes. Consider creating separate components to implement your workflow and view flow tasks. This reduces dependencies and makes it easier to interchange components as requirements change.

- For simple workflow and view flow requirements, it is usually sufficient to use custom code based on well-known patterns such as Use Case Controller and ViewFlow. For workflow and view flow requirements that are more complex, consider using a workflow engine such as WF.

- Consider how you will capture, manage, and display errors in workflows. Also, identify how you will handle partially completed tasks, and whether it is possible to recover from a failure and continue the task or whether you must restart the process.

For more information about workflow components, see Chapter 14, "Designing Workflow Components."

Security Considerations

Security encompasses a range of factors and is vital in all types of applications. Rich client applications must be designed and implemented with security in mind, and—where they act as the presentation layer for business applications—must play their part in protecting and securing the other layers of the application. Security issues involve a range of concerns, including protecting sensitive data, user authentication and authorization, guarding against attack from malicious code and users, and auditing and logging events and user activity. Consider the following guidelines when designing a security strategy:

- Determine the appropriate technology and approach for authenticating users, including support for multiple users of the same rich client application instance. You should consider how and when to log on users, whether you must support different types of users (different roles) with differing permissions (such as administrators and standard users), and how you will record successful and failed logons. Take into account the requirements for disconnected or offline authentication where this is relevant.

- Consider using Windows Integrated Authentication or a federated authentication solution if users must be able to access multiple applications with the same credentials or identity. If you cannot use Windows Integrated Authentication, you may be able to use an external agency that offers federated authentication support. If you cannot use an external agency, consider using a certificate-based system, or create a custom solution for your organization.

- Consider the requirement to validate inputs, both from the user and from sources such as services and other application interfaces. You might need to create custom validation mechanisms, or you might be able to take advantage of the validation features of the technology you are working with. The Microsoft Visual Studio® Windows Forms development environment contains validation controls. Alternatively, consider a third party validation framework such as the Enterprise Library Validation Application Block, which provides comprehensive features for validation in the UI and in the business layer. Irrespective of your validation choice, remember that you must always validate data when it crosses trust boundaries.

- Consider how you will protect data stored in the application and in resources such as files, caches, and documents used by the application. Encrypt sensitive data where it might be exposed, and consider using a digital signature to prevent tampering. In maximum security applications, consider encrypting volatile information stored in memory. Also, remember to protect sensitive information that is sent from the application over a network or communication channel.

- Consider how you will implement auditing and logging for the application, and what information to include in these logs. Remember to protect sensitive information in the logs using encryption, and optionally use digital signatures for the most sensitive information that is vulnerable to tampering.

Data Handling Considerations

Application data can be made available from server-side applications through a Web service. Cache this data on client to improve performance and enable offline usage. Rich client applications can also use local data. Data use by rich client applications falls into two categories:

- **Read-only reference data.** This is data that does not change often and is used by the client for reference purposes, such as a product catalog. Store reference data on the client to reduce the amount of data interchange between the client and the server in order to improve the performance of your application, enable offline capabilities, provide early data validation, and generally improve the usability of your application.

- **Transient data.** This is data that can be changed on the client as well as on the server. One of the most challenging aspects of dealing with transient data in rich client applications is dealing with concurrency issues where the same data can be modified by multiple clients at the same time. You must keep track of any client-side changes made to transient data on the client and manage updates on the server that may contain conflicting changes.

Caching Data

Rich clients often must cache data locally, whether it is read-only reference data or transient data. Caching data can improve performance in your application and provide the data necessary to work offline. To enable data caching, rich client applications should implement some form of caching infrastructure that can handle the data caching details transparently. The common types of caching are:

- **Short term data caching.** Data is not persistent, so the application cannot run offline.

- **Long term data caching.** Caching data in a persistent medium, such as isolated storage or the local file system, allows the application to work when there is no connectivity to the server. Rich client applications should differentiate between data that has been successfully synchronized with the server and data that is still tentative.

Data Concurrency

When serving multiple clients simultaneously, changes to the data held on the server can occur before a specific client's changes can be synchronized with the server. This can lead to data corruption or inconsistencies. You must, therefore, implement a mechanism to ensure that any data conflicts are handled appropriately when the data is synchronized, and that the resulting data is consistent and correct. Common approaches for handling data concurrency are:

- **Pessimistic concurrency.** Pessimistic concurrency assumes that the risk of a data conflicts is high. To prevent data conflicts, it allows one client to maintain a lock over the data, thereby preventing any other clients from accessing or modifying the data until the client's own changes are completed and committed. This pattern is also known as the pessimistic offline lock pattern.

- **Optimistic concurrency.** Optimistic concurrency assumes that the risk of data conflicts is low. With optimistic concurrency, the data is not locked by a client while it is being updated. To detect data conflicts, the original data and the changed data are both sent to the server. The original data is checked against the current data to see if it has been updated since it was last retrieved. If not, the changes are applied; otherwise a data conflict exception is raised. This pattern is also known as the optimistic offline lock pattern.

The ADO.NET **DataSet** helps clients to work with data while offline. **DataSets** can keep track of local changes made to the data, which makes it easier to synchronize the data with the server and reconcile data conflicts. **DataSets** can also be used to merge data from different sources.

Data Binding

Windows Forms, WPF, and Silverlight data binding supports bidirectional binding that allows you to bind a data structure to a UI component, display the current data values to the user, allow the user to edit the data, and then automatically update the underlying data using the values entered by the user. Data binding can be used to display read-only data to users, allow users to update data within the UI, provide master\detail views of data, allow users to explore complex related data items, and provide lookup table functionality that allows the UI to display user friendly names for data items instead of data row key values.

For more information about designing the data layer, see Chapter 8, "Data Layer Guidelines." For more information about designing data components for rich client applications, see Chapter 15, "Designing Data Components."

Offline/Occasionally Connected Considerations

An application is occasionally connected if, during unspecified periods, it cannot interact with services or data over a network in a timely manner. Occasionally connected rich client applications are capable of performing work when not connected to a networked resource, and can update the networked resources in the background when a connection is available.

When designing occasionally connected applications, aim to favor asynchronous communication when interacting with data and services over a network and minimize or eliminate complex interactions with network located data and services. This makes it easier to implement a synchronization mechanism for use when a connection is available.

In order to work when disconnected, your application should implement data caching capabilities that provide all of the data necessary on the client for the user to continue working when offline. You must also determine how to prevent the application using stale data. In general, you should consider designing a store and forward mechanism where messages are created, stored while disconnected, and eventually forwarded to their respective destinations when a connection becomes available. The most common implementation of store and forward is a message queue.

Consider the following two approaches when designing for an occasionally connected scenario:

- **Data centric.** Applications that use the data centric strategy have a relational database management system (RDBMS) installed locally on the client, and use the built-in capabilities of the database system to propagate local data changes back to the server, handle the synchronization process, and detect and resolve any data conflicts.

- **Service oriented.** Applications that use the service-oriented approach store information in messages, and arrange these messages in queues while the client is offline. After the connection is reestablished, the queued messages are sent to the server for processing.

Technology Considerations

There are several different technologies available that you can use to implement a rich client application. The following guidelines will help you to choose an appropriate implementation technology, and provide guidance on the use of appropriate patterns and system functions for configuration and monitoring:

- **Choose a suitable development technology:**
    - Consider WFP for applications that will fully support rich media and graphics.
    - Consider using Windows Forms if you have existing Windows Forms investments, or if you are building LOB applications that do not require rich visualization and should execute with minimal hardware requirements.
    - Consider XBAP for applications that are downloaded from a Web server and then execute in the browser.
    - Consider OBA for applications that are predominantly document-based, or are used for reporting.
- **Explore patterns & practices assets that can help you to design and implement the application:**
    - Consider using the Smart Client Software Factory if you decide to use Windows Forms and you are designing composite interfaces.
    - Consider using the Composite Client Application Guidance if you decide to use WPF and/or Silverlight, and you wish to develop modular applications that typically feature multiple screens, rich, flexible user interaction and data visualization, and role-determined behavior.
    - Consider Enterprise Library to help you implement solutions for cross-cutting concerns such as exception handling, caching, and validation.
- **If you decide to use WPF:**
    - Consider implementing the Presentation Model or View Model pattern to make the UI logic unit testable and to make it easier to re-skin your application.
    - WPF allows you to attach additional behaviors to existing control implementations. Use this approach instead of attempting to subclass a control.
- **If you want to support remote administration and monitoring:**
    - Consider implementing Group Policy overrides for your application configuration. This is required to meet Certified for Windows logo requirements.
    - Consider using technologies such as SNMP and WMI to expose exceptions and health state.

Deployment Considerations

There are several options for the deployment of rich client applications. You might have a stand-alone application where all of the application logic, including data, is deployed on the client machine. Another option is client/server, where the application logic is deployed on the client and the data is deployed on a database tier. Finally, there are several n-tier options where one or more application servers host part of the application logic.

Stand-alone Deployment

Figure 2 illustrates a stand-alone deployment where all of the application logic and data is deployed on the client.

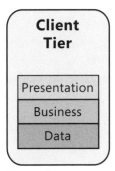

Figure 2
Stand-alone deployment for a rich client application

Client/Server Deployment

In a client/server deployment, all of the application logic is deployed on the client and the data is deployed on a database server, as shown in Figure 3.

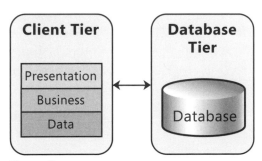

Figure 3
Client/server deployment for a rich client application

N-Tier Deployment

In an *n*-tier deployment, you can place presentation and business logic on the client, or only the presentation logic on the client. Figure 4 illustrates the case where the presentation and business logic are deployed on the client.

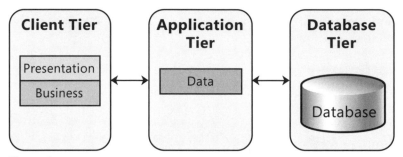

Figure 4
N-tier deployment with the business layer located on the client tier

Figure 5 illustrates the case where the business and data access logic are deployed on an application server.

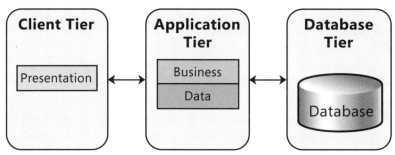

Figure 5
N-tier deployment with the business layer located on the application tier

For more information on deployment strategies, see Chapter 19, "Physical Tiers and Deployment."

Deployment Technologies

Several options exist for deploying a rich client application to a physical machine. Each has specific advantages and liabilities, and you should research the options to ensure that the one you choose is suitable for the target environments in which your application will execute. The options are the following:

- **Click Once deployment.** This approach requires little user interaction, provides automated updates, and requires little effort for the developer. However, it can only be used to deploy a single solution that is not part of a larger solution; it cannot deploy additional files or registry keys; it cannot interact with the user to configure the installation; and it cannot provide a branded installation.

- **XCOPY deployment.** If no registry settings or component registration are required, the executable can be copied directly to the client machine hard disk.

- **Windows Installer (.MSI) package.** This is a comprehensive setup program that can install components, resources, registry settings, and other artifacts required by the application. Users require administrator privileges to install MSI packages themselves. There are solutions available, such as Microsoft System Center Configuration Manager, for distributing applications in a corporate environment.

- **XBAP package.** The application is downloaded through the browser and runs in a constrained security environment on the machine. Updates can be pushed to the client automatically.

Relevant Design Patterns

Key patterns are organized into categories such as Communication, Composition, Configuration Management, Exception Management, Presentation, State Management, and Workflow; as shown in the following table. Consider using these patterns when making design decisions for each category.

Category	Relevant patterns
Communication	**Asynchronous Callback.** Execute long-running tasks on a separate thread that executes in the background, and provide a function for the thread to call back into when the task is complete. **Gateway.** Provide access to an external system through a common abstract interface so that consumers are not required to understand the external system interface. **Service Locator.** Centralize distributed service object lookups, provide a centralized point of control, and act as a cache that eliminates redundant lookups. **Service Agent and Proxy.** Implement a component that the consuming application can use without knowing that it is not accessing the actual target component or service. The component passes calls to the remote component or service, and returns the result to the consuming application. The proxy abstracts the details of communication with other remote components, typically when using ASMX or WCF services. **Service Interface.** A programmatic interface that other systems can use to interact with the service.
Composition	**Composite View.** Combine individual views into a composite view. **Template View.** Implement a common template view, and derive or construct views using the template view. **Two-Step View.** Transform the model data into a logical presentation without any specific formatting, and then convert that logical presentation into the actual formatting required. **View Helper.** Delegate business data processing responsibilities to helper classes.
Configuration Management	**Provider.** Implement a component that exposes an API that is different from the client API in order to allow any custom implementation to be seamlessly plugged in.
Exception Management	**Exception Shielding.** Prevent a service from exposing information about its internal implementation when an exception occurs.
Presentation	**Application Controller.** An object that contains all of the flow logic and is used by other Controllers that work with a Model and display the appropriate View. **Model-View-Presenter.** Separate request processing into three roles, with the View being responsible for handling user input, the Model responsible for application data and business logic, and the Presenter responsible for presentation logic andfor coordinating the interaction between the View and the Model. **Model-View-ViewModel.** A variation of Model-View-Controller (MVC) that is tailored for modern UI development platforms where the View is the responsibility of a designer rather than a classic developer. **Presentation Model.** Separate the responsibilities for the visual display of the user interface and the presentation state and behavior into different classes named, respectively, the view and the presentation model. The view class manages the user interface controls and encapsulates any visual state or behavior that is specific to the UI. The presentation model class encapsulates presentation behavior and state and acts as a façade onto the underlying model.
State Management	**Context Object.** An object used to manage the current execution context.

Category	Relevant patterns
Workflow	**View Flow.** Manage navigation from one view to another based on state in the application or environment, and the conditions and limitations required for correct operation of the application. **Work Flow.** Manage the flow of control in a complex process-oriented application in a predefined manner while allowing dynamic route modification through decision and branching structures that can modify the routing of requests.

For more information on the Template View, Transform View, and Two-Step View patterns, see Fowler, Martin. *Patterns of Enterprise Application Architecture*. Addison-Wesley, 2002. Or at http://martinfowler.com/eaaCatalog.

For more information on the Provider pattern, see *"Provider Model Design Pattern and Specification, Part I"* at http://msdn.microsoft.com/en-us/library/ms998421.aspx.

For more information on the Asynchronous Callback pattern, see *"Creating a Simplified Asynchronous Call Pattern for Windows Forms Applications"* at http://msdn.microsoft.com/en-us/library/ms996483.aspx.

For more information on the Service Interface pattern, see *"Service Interface"* at http://msdn.microsoft.com/en-us/library/ms998421.aspx.

For more information on the Exception Shielding pattern, see *"Useful Patterns for Services"* at http://msdn.microsoft.com/en-us/library/cc304800.aspx.

For more information on the Composite View pattern, see *"Patterns in the Composite Application Library"* at http://msdn.microsoft.com/en-us/library/dd458924.aspx.

For more information on the Presentation Model pattern, see *"Presentation Model"* at http://msdn.microsoft.com/en-us/library/dd458863.aspx.

Additional Resources

To more easily access Web resources, see the online version of the bibliography at: http://www.microsoft.com/architectureguide.

- For more information on building composite applications, see *"Composite Client Application Guidance"* at http://msdn.microsoft.com/en-us/library/cc707819.aspx.

- For more information on designing rich client and smart client applications, see the *"Smart Client Architecture and Design Guide"* at http://msdn.microsoft.com/en-us/library/ms998506.aspx.

- For more information on caching architectures, see the *"Caching Architecture Guide for .NET Framework Applications"* at http://msdn.microsoft.com/en-us/library/ms978498.aspx.

- For more information on deployment scenarios and considerations, see *"Deploying .NET Framework-based Applications"* at http://msdn.microsoft.com/en-us/library/ms954585.aspx.

23

Designing Rich Internet Applications

Overview

In this chapter, you will learn about the key scenarios for Rich Internet Applications (RIAs), understand the components found in a RIA, and learn about the key design considerations for RIAs. This includes the guidelines for performance, security, and deployment; in addition to key patterns and technology considerations for designing RIAs.

RIAs support rich graphics and streaming media scenarios, while providing most of the deployment and maintainability benefits of a Web application. RIAs may run inside a browser plug-in, such as Microsoft® Silverlight®, as opposed to extensions that utilize browser code, such as Asynchronous JavaScript and XML (AJAX). A typical RIA implementation utilizes a Web infrastructure combined with a client-side application that handles the presentation. The plug-in provides library routines for rich graphics support as well as a container that limits access to local resources for security purposes. RIAs have the ability to run more extensive and complex client-side code than possible in a normal Web application, thus providing the opportunity to reduce the load on the Web server. Figure 1 shows the typical structure of a RIA implementation.

Rich Internet Application

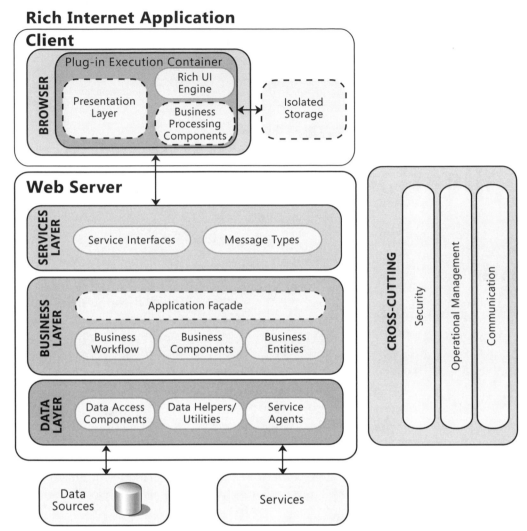

Figure 1
Architecture of a typical RIA implementation. Broken lines indicate optional components.

A typical Rich Internet Application is decomposed into three layers: the presentation layer, business layer, and data layer. The presentation layer usually contains UI and presentation logic components; the business layer usually contains business logic, business workflow and business entities components; the data layer usually contains data access and service agent components.

Note: It is common in RIAs to move some of business processing and even the data access code to the client. Therefore, the client may in fact contain some or all of the functionality of the business and data layers, depending on the application scenario. Figure 1 shows how some business processing is usually implemented on the client.

RIAs can range from thin interfaces that overlay back end business services, to complex applications that perform most of the processes themselves and only communicate with back end services to consume or send back information. Therefore, the design and implementation varies. However, in terms of the presentation layer and the way that it communicates with back end services, there are some common approaches to good architectural design. Most of these are based on well-known design patterns that encourage the use of separate components within the application to reduce dependencies, make maintenance and testing easier, and promote reusability.

For more information about layered design, see Chapter 5, "Layered Application Guidelines." For more information about the components appropriate for each layer, see Chapter 10, "Component Guidelines."

General Design Considerations

The following guidelines provide information about several aspects you should consider when designing a RIA, and will help to ensure that your application meets your requirements and performs efficiently in scenarios common to RIAs:

- **Choose a RIA based on audience, rich interface, and ease of deployment.** Consider designing a RIA when your vital audience is using a browser that supports RIAs. If part of your vital audience is on a non-RIA supported browser, consider whether limiting browser choice to a supported version is a possibility. If you cannot influence the browser choice, consider if the loss of audience is significant enough to require choice of an alternative type of application, such as a Web application using AJAX. With a RIA, the ease of deployment and maintenance is similar to that of a Web application, assuming that your clients have a reliable network connection. RIA implementations are well suited to Web-based scenarios where you need visualization beyond that provided by basic HTML. They are likely to have more consistent behavior and require less testing across the range of supported browsers when compared to Web applications that utilize advanced functions and code customizations. RIA implementations are also perfect for streaming-media applications. They are less suited to extremely complex multi-page UIs.

- **Design to use a Web infrastructure utilizing services.** RIA implementations require an infrastructure similar to Web applications. Typically, a RIA will perform processing on the client, but also communicate with other networked services; for example, to persist data in a database.

- **Design to take advantage of client processing power.** RIAs run on the client computer and can take advantage of all the processing power available there. Consider moving as much functionality as possible onto the client to improve user experience. Sensitive business rules should still be executed on the server, because the client logic can be circumvented.

- **Design for execution within the browser sandbox.** RIA implementations have higher security by default and therefore may not have access to all resources on a machine, such as cameras and hardware video acceleration. Access to the local file system is limited. Local storage is available, but there is a maximum limit.

- **Determine the complexity of your UI requirements.** Consider the complexity of your UI. RIA implementations work best when using a single screen for all operations. They can be extended to multiple screens, but this requires extra code and screen flow consideration. Users should be able to easily navigate or pause, and return to the appropriate point in a screen flow, without restarting the whole process. For multi-page UIs, use deep linking methods. Also, manipulate the Uniform Resource Locator (URL), the history list, and the browser's back and forward buttons to avoid confusion as users navigate between screens.

- **Use scenarios to increase application performance or responsiveness.** List and examine the common application scenarios to decide how to divide and load components of your application, as well as how to cache data or move business logic to the client. To reduce the download and startup time for the application, segregate functionality into separate downloadable components.

- **Design for scenarios where the plug-in is not installed.** Because RIA implementations require a browser plug-in, you should design for non-interruptive plug-in installation. Consider whether your clients have access to, have permission to, and will want to install the plug-in. Consider what control you have over the installation process. Plan for the scenario where users cannot install the plug-in by displaying an informative error message, or by providing an alternative Web UI.

In addition to the guidelines above that are especially applicable to RIA implementations, consider the more general guidelines for rich client applications in general (including mobile rich clients). These guidelines include separating presentation logic from interface implementation, identifying presentation tasks and presentation flows, separating business rules and other tasks not related to the interface, reusing common presentation logic, loosely coupling your client to any remote services it uses, avoiding tight coupling to objects in other layers, and reducing round trips when accessing remote layers. For more information, see Chapter 22, "Designing Rich Client Applications."

Specific Design Issues

There are several common issues that you must consider as your develop your design. These issues can be categorized into specific areas of the design. The following sections contain guidelines to help you resolve the common issues in each area:

- Business Layer
- Caching
- Communication
- Composition
- Data Access
- Exception Management
- Logging
- Media and Graphics
- Mobile
- Portability
- Presentation
- State Management
- Validation

Business Layer

In most scenarios, RIAs will access data or information located outside the application. While the nature of the information will vary, it is likely to be extracted from a business system. To maximize performance and usability, you might consider locating some of the business processing tasks on the client. Consider the following guidelines when designing interaction with business and service layers:

- Identify the business layers and service interfaces that the application will use. The business layer on the client should access the service interfaces using a service agent. Service agents can typically be implemented by generating a service proxy using the service definition.

- If your business logic does not contain sensitive information, consider locating some of the business rules on the client to improve performance and responsiveness of the application. If your business logic does contain sensitive information, you should locate it on the application server.

- Consider how the client will obtain information required to operate business rules and other client-side processing, and how it will update the business rules automatically as requirements change. You might want to have the client obtain business rule information from the business layer when it starts up.

- If your RIA implementation allows creation of an instance without a UI, consider using it to implement business processes using more structured, powerful, or familiar programming languages (such as C#) instead of using less flexible browser-supported languages.

- If your business logic is duplicated on the client and the server, use the same code language on the client and server if your RIA implementation allows it. This will reduce any differences in language implementations and make it easier to be consistent in how rules are processed. Domain models that can exist on both the server and client side should be as similar as possible.

- For security reasons, do not put sensitive unencrypted business logic on the client. The code in downloaded XAP files can easily be decompiled. Implement sensitive business logic on the server and access it using Web services.

For more information about implementing the business layer, see Chapter 7, "Business Layer Guidelines."

Caching

RIA implementations generally use the normal browser caching mechanism. Caching resources intelligently will improve application performance. Consider the following guidelines when designing a caching strategy:

- By dividing large client applications into smaller separately downloadable components, you can cache these components to improve performance and minimize network round trips. Avoid downloading and instantiating the entire application at start up if possible. Use installation, updates, and user scenarios to derive ways to divide and load application modules. For example, load stubs at start up and then dynamically load additional functionality in the background. Consider using events to intelligently preload modules just before they may be required.

- Allow the browser to cache objects that are not likely to change during a session. Utilize specific RIA local storage for information that changes during a session, or which should persist between sessions.

- To avoid unintended exceptions, check that isolated storage is large enough to contain the data you will write to it. Storage space does not increase automatically; you must ask the user to increase it.

For more information about designing a caching strategy, see Chapter 17, "Crosscutting Concerns."

Communication

RIA implementations should use the asynchronous call model for services to avoid blocking browser processes. Cross domain, protocol, and service efficiency issues should be considered as part of your design. If your RIA implementation allows it, consider using a different thread for background operations. Consider the following guidelines when designing a communication strategy:

- If you have long-running operations, consider using a background thread or asynchronous execution to avoid blocking the UI thread.

- Ensure that the RIA and the services it calls use compatible bindings that include security information. If you are authenticating through services, design your services to use a binding that your RIA implementation supports.

- To protect sensitive information and communication channels, consider using Internet Protocol Security (IPSec) and Secure Sockets Layer (SSL) to secure the channel, encryption to protect data, and digital signatures to detect data tampering.

- If your RIA client must access a server other than the one from which it was downloaded, ensure that you use a cross-domain configuration mechanism to permit access to the other servers/domains.

- Consider using a duplex mechanism with Windows Communication Foundation (WCF) to push data to the client if client polling causes heavy server load, or to push information to the server when this is significantly more efficient than using services; for example, real time multiplayer gaming scenarios utilizing a central server. However, be aware that firewalls and routers may block some ports and protocols. See "Additional Resources" at the end of this chapter for more information.

For more information about designing services, see Chapter 25, "Designing Service Applications." For more information about communication protocols and techniques, see Chapter 18, "Communication and Messaging."

Composition

Composition lets you build applications that can be maintained or extended more easily without reimplementation or redeployment of the entire application. You can implement your application from a number of modules, and have the components within those modules be loosely coupled. This can allow the application to be extended by deploying a new module or a new version of a module; or allow the application to be more easily customized or personalized by the user, or tailored to the user's role or task. Consider the following guidelines when designing a composition strategy:

- Evaluate whether composition is appropriate for your scenario; and, if so, which composition model patterns are most suitable. Composition can help you to design applications that can be reused in different scenarios with minimal or no changes. However, avoid designs that introduce dependencies that will require frequent application redeployment.

- Composition is well suited to mash-up applications that integrate information and functionality from disparate sources, or in situations where the application user extensible or customizable.

Data Access

RIA implementations request data from the Web server through services in the same way as an AJAX client. After data reaches the client, it can be cached to maximize performance. Consider the following guidelines when designing a data-access strategy:

- Use client-side caching to minimize the number of round trips to the server, and to provide a more responsive UI.
- Filter data at the server rather than at the client to reduce the amount of data that must be sent over the network.

For more information about designing a data layer, see Chapter 8, "Data Layer Guidelines."

Exception Management

A robust and well designed exception management strategy can simplify application design, and improve security and manageability. It can also make it easier for developers to create the application, and reduces development time and cost. In a RIA, you will usually need to notify the user when an error occurs. In addition, for anything other than trivial UI errors such as validation messages, you should consider logging errors and exceptions on the server for use by operations staff and monitoring systems. You must also consider managing asynchronous exceptions, as well as exception coordination between the client and server code. Consider the following guidelines when designing an exception management mechanism:

- Design for both synchronous and asynchronous exceptions. Use try/catch blocks to trap exceptions in synchronous code. Put exception handling for asynchronous service calls in a separate handler designed specifically for such exceptions; for example, in Silverlight, this is the **OnError** handler.
- Design an approach for catching and handling unhandled exceptions. Unhandled exceptions in RIAs are passed to the browser. They will allow execution to continue after the user dismisses a browser error message. Provide a friendly error message for the user if possible. Stop program execution if continued execution would be harmful to the data integrity of the application or could mislead the user into thinking the application is still in a stable state.
- Only catch internal exceptions that you can handle. For example, catch data conversion exceptions that can occur when trying to convert null values. Do not use exceptions to control business logic.
- Design an appropriate exception propagation strategy. For example, allow exceptions to bubble up to boundary layers where they can be logged and transformed as necessary before passing them to the next layer.
- Design an appropriate logging and notification strategy for critical errors and exceptions that does not reveal sensitive information.

For more information about designing an exception management strategy, see Chapter 17, "Crosscutting Concerns."

Logging

Logging for the purpose of debugging or auditing can be challenging in a RIA implementation. For example, access to the client file system is not available in Silverlight applications, and execution of the client and the server proceed asynchronously. Log files from a client user must be combined with server log files to gain a full picture of program execution. Consider the following guidelines when designing a logging strategy:

- Consider the limitations of the logging component in the RIA implementation. Some RIA implementations log each user's information in a separate file, perhaps in different locations on the disk.

- Determine a strategy to transfer client logs to the server for processing. Recombination of different users' logs from the same machine may be necessary if troubleshooting a client machine–specific issue. Avoid segregating logs by machine instead of by user, as there could be several users for each client machine.

- If using isolated storage for logging, consider the maximum size limit and the need to ask the user to increase storage capacity when required.

- Ensure that you log critical errors, and consider enabling logging and transferring logs to the server when exceptions are encountered.

Media and Graphics

RIA implementations provide a much richer experience and better performance than ordinary Web applications. Research and utilize the built-in media capabilities of your RIA platform. Keep in mind the features that may not be available on the RIA platform compared to a stand-alone media player. Consider the following guidelines when designing for multimedia and graphics:

- Design to utilize streaming media and video in the browser instead of invoking a separate player utility. In general, you should always use adaptive streaming in conjunction with RIA clients to gracefully and seamlessly handle varying bandwidth issues.

- To increase performance, position media objects on whole pixels and present them in their native size, and utilize the native vector graphics engine for the best drawing performance.

- If programming an extremely graphics-intensive application, investigate if your RIA implementation provides hardware acceleration. If it does not, create a baseline for what is acceptable drawing performance. Consider a plan to reduce load on the graphics engine if it falls below acceptable limits.

- Be aware of the size of your drawing areas. Only redraw parts of an area that are actually changing. Reduce overlapping regions when not necessary to reduce blending. Use profiling and debugging methods—for example, the "**EnableRedrawRegions** = true" setting in Silverlight—to discover which areas are being redrawn. Note that certain effects, such as blurring, can cause every pixel in an area to be redrawn. Windowless and transparent controls can also cause unintended redrawing and blending.

Mobile

RIA implementations provide a much richer experience than an ordinary mobile application. Utilize the built-in media capabilities of the RIA platform you are using. Consider the following guidelines when designing for mobile device multimedia and graphics:

- When a RIA must be distributed to a mobile client, research whether a RIA plug-in implementation is available for the device you want to support. Find out if the RIA plug-in has reduced functionality compared to non-mobile platforms.

- Attempt to use a single or similar codebase. Then, if required, branch code for specific devices.

- Ensure that your UI layout and implementation is suitable for the smaller screen size of mobile devices. RIAs work on mobile devices, but consider using different layout code on each type of device to reduce the impact of different screen sizes when designing for Windows Mobile.

For more information about implementing a mobile application, see Chapter 24, "Designing Mobile Applications."

Portability

One of the main benefits of RIAs is the portability of compiled code between different browsers, operating systems, and platforms. Similarly, using a single source codebase, or similar codebases, reduces the time and cost of development and maintenance while still providing platform flexibility. Consider the following guidelines when designing for portability:

- Make full use of the native RIA code libraries and design for the goal of "write once, run everywhere," but be willing to fork code in cases where overall project complexity or feature tradeoffs dictate that you must do so.

- When deciding whether to design a RIA or a Web application, consider that the differences between browsers will require Web applications to undergo extensive testing of ASP.NET and JavaScript code. With a RIA application, the plug-in creator, and not the developer, is responsible for consistency across different platforms. This considerably reduces the cost of testing for each platform and browser combination.

- If your audience will be running the RIA on multiple platforms, do not use features available only on one platform; for example, Windows Integrated Authentication. Design a solution based on portable RIA routines and features that are available in a range of clients.

- If you are targeting rich client and RIA applications, consider languages and development environments such as the patterns & practices Composite Client Application Guidance that can target both platforms. For more information, see *"Composite Client Application Guidance"* at http://msdn.microsoft.com/en-us/library/cc707819.aspx.

Presentation

Because RIA applications are normally constrained to the browser, they tend to work best when designed as one central interface. Applications with multiple pages require that you consider how you will link between pages. Consider the following guidelines when designing for presentation:

- Use Separated Presentation patterns to separate the visual representation of your application from the presentation logic of your application.

- Take advantage of data binding capabilities to display data whenever possible, especially for tabular and multirow data presentation. This reduces the code required, simplifies development, and reduces coding errors. It can also automatically synchronize data in different views or forms. Use two-way binding where the user must be able to update the data.

- For multipage UIs, use deep-linking methods to allow unique identification of and navigation to individual application pages.

- Trap the browser forward and back button events to avoid unintentional navigation away from your page. Also, consider the ability to manipulate the browser's address text box content, and history list in order to implement normal Web page-like navigation.

For more information about implementing presentation layers, see Chapter 6, "Presentation Layer Guidelines."

State Management

You can store application state on the client using isolated storage, which is useful for maintaining or caching state locally between user sessions. Isolated storage is not managed in the same way as the browser cache.Applications that write data to isolated storage must either delete it directly, or explicitly instruct the user to remove the data.Consider the following guidelines when designing for state management:

- Determine the state information that the application must store, including estimates of the size, the frequency of changes, and the processing or overhead cost of re-creating or refetching the data.

- Store state on the client in isolated storage to persist it during and between sessions. State that is required for the application to function should always be stored on the server. This also allows users to access saved state when logging on from a different computer.

- Design for multiple concurrent sessions because you cannot prevent multiple RIA instances from initializing. Design either for concurrency in your state management, or to detect and prevent multiple sessions from corrupting application state.

Validation

Validation must be performed using code on the client or through services located on the server. If you require more than trivial validation on the client, isolate validation logic in a separate downloadable assembly. This makes the rules easy to maintain. Consider the following guidelines when designing for validation:

- Use client-side validation to maximize the user experience, but always use server-side validation as well for security. In general, assume that all client-controlled data is malicious. The server should revalidate all data sent to it. Design to validate input from all sources, such as the query string, cookies, and HTML controls.

- Design your validation mechanisms to constrain, reject, and sanitize data. Validate input for length, range, format, and type. Identify trust boundaries on the server and validate data that passes across them.

- Consider using isolated storage to hold client-specific validation rules. For rules that require access to server resources, evaluate whether it is more efficient to use a single service call that performs validation on the server.

- If you have a large volume of client-side validation code that may change, consider locating it in a separate downloadable module so it can be easily replaced without downloading the entire RIA application again.

For more information about validation techniques, see Chapter 17, "Crosscutting Concerns."

Security Considerations

Security encompasses a range of factors and is vital in all types of applications. Rich Internet applications must be designed and implemented with security in mind, and—where they act as the presentation layer for business applications—must play their part in protecting and securing the other layers of the application. Security issues involve a range of concerns, including protecting sensitive data, user authentication and authorization, guarding against attack from malicious code and users, and auditing and logging events and user activity.

Consider the following guidelines when designing a security strategy:

- Determine the appropriate technology and approach for authenticating users. You should consider how and when to log on users, whether you need to support different types of users (different roles) with differing permissions (such as administrators and standard users), and how you will record successful and failed logons.

- Consider using Windows Integrated Authentication, a single sign-on (SSO) mechanism, or a federated authentication solution if users must be able to access multiple applications with the same credentials or identity. If you cannot use Windows Integrated Authentication, you may be able to use an external agency that offers federated authentication support. If you cannot use an external agency, consider using a certificate-based system, or create a custom solution for your organization.

- Consider the need to validate inputs, both from the user and from sources such as services and other application interfaces. You might need to create custom validation mechanisms, or you might be able to take advantage of the validation features of the UI Technology you are working with.

- Consider how you will implement auditing and logging for the application, and what information to include in these logs. Remember to protect sensitive information in the logs using encryption, and optionally use digital signatures for the most sensitive information that is vulnerable to tampering.

Data Handling Considerations

Application data is typically accessed through networked services. Cache this data on the client to improve performance and enable offline usage. Application data falls typically into two categories:

- **Read-only reference data.** This is data that does not change often and is used by the client for reference purposes, such as a product catalog. Store reference data on the client to reduce the amount of data interchange between the client and the server in order to improve the performance of your application, enable offline capabilities, provide early data validation, and generally improve the usability of your application.

- **Transient data.** This is data that can be changed on the client as well as on the server. One of the most challenging aspects of dealing with transient data in rich Internet applications is dealing with concurrency issues where the same data can be modified by multiple clients at the same time. You must keep track of any client-side changes made to transient data on the client and manage updates on the server that may contain conflicting changes.

Technology Considerations

The following guidelines discuss Silverlight and Microsoft Windows Communication Foundation (WCF) and provide specific guidance for these technologies. At the time of writing, the latest versions are WCF 3.5 and Silverlight 3.0. Use the guidelines to help you to choose and implement an appropriate technology.

Versions and Target Platforms

- At the time of the release of this guide, Silverlight for Mobile was an announced product and in development, but not released.

- Silverlight currently supports the Safari, Firefox, and Microsoft Internet Explorer browsers using a plug-in. Through these browsers, Silverlight currently supports Mac and Windows. Support for Windows Mobile was also announced in 2008. An open source implementation of Silverlight, called Moonlight, provides support for Linux and Unix/X11 systems.

- Silverlight supports the C#, Iron Python, Iron Ruby, and Visual Basic® .NET development languages. Most XAML code will also run in both WPF and Silverlight hosts.

- In Silverlight 2.0, you must implement custom code for input and data validation. Silverlight 3.0 provides support for exception-based data validation through data binding. Check the documentation to verify if this is true for later versions.

Security

- The .NET cryptography APIs are available in Silverlight and should be utilized when storing sensitive data and communicating it to the server if it is not already encrypted using another mechanism.

- Silverlight logs to an individual file in the user store for a specific logged in user. It cannot log to one file for the whole machine.

- Silverlight does not obfuscate downloaded modules, which can be decompiled and the programming logic extracted.

Communication

- Silverlight supports only asynchronous calls to Web services.

- Silverlight supports only Basic HTTP binding. WCF in .NET 3.5 supports Basic HTTP binding, but security is not turned on by default. Be sure to turn on at least transport security to secure your service communications.

- Silverlight supports two file formats to deal with calling services in a different domain to the source of the current page. You can use either a ClientAccessPolicy.xml file specific to Silverlight, or a CrossDomain.xml file compatible with Adobe Flash. Place the file in the root of the server(s) to which your Silverlight client needs access.

- Consider using ADO.NET Data Services in a Silverlight application if you must transfer large volumes of data from the server.

- Silverlight does not currently support SOAP faults exposed by services due to the browser security model. Services must return exceptions to the client through a different mechanism.

Controls

- Silverlight contains controls specifically designed for it. Third parties are likely to have additional control packages available.

- Use Silverlight windowless controls if you want to overlay viewable HTML content and controls on top of a Silverlight application.

- Silverlight allows you to attach additional behaviors to existing control implementations. Use this approach instead of attempting to subclass a control.

- Silverlight performs antialiasing for all UI components, so consider the recommendations regarding snapping UI elements to whole pixels.

Storage

- The local storage mechanism for Silverlight is the client machine's Isolated Storage cache. The initial maximum size is 1 megabyte (MB). The maximum storage size is unlimited; however, Silverlight requires that your application request the user to increase the storage size.

See also *"Contrasting Silverlight and WPF"* at
http://msdn.microsoft.com/en-us/library/dd458872.aspx.

Deployment Considerations

RIA implementations provide many of the same benefits as Web applications in terms of deployment and maintainability. Design your RIA as separate modules that can be downloaded individually and cached to allow replacement of one module instead of the whole application. Version your application and components so that you can detect the versions that clients are running. Consider the following guidelines when designing for deployment and maintainability:

- Consider how you will manage the scenario where the RIA browser plug-in is not installed.
- Consider how you will redeploy modules when the application instance is still running on a client.
- Divide the application into logical modules that can be cached separately, and that can be replaced easily without requiring the user to download the entire application again.
- Version your components.

Installation of the RIA Plug-In

Consider how you will manage installation of the RIA browser plug-in when it is not already installed:

- **Intranet.** If available, use application distribution software or the Group Policy feature of the Microsoft Active Directory® directory service to preinstall the plug-in on each computer in the organization. Alternatively, consider using Windows Update, where Silverlight is an optional component. Finally, consider manual installation through the browser, which requires the user to have Administrator privileges on the client machine.
- **Internet.** Users must install the plug-in manually, so you should provide a link to the appropriate location to download the latest plug in. For Windows users, Windows Update provides the plug-in as an optional component.
- **Plug-in updates.** In general, updates to the plug-in take into account backward compatibility. You may target a particular plug-in version, but consider implementing a plan to verify your application's functionality on new versions of the browser plug-in as they become available. For intranet scenarios, distribute a new plug-in after testing your application. In Internet scenarios, assume that automatic plug-in updates will occur. Test your application using the plug-in beta to ensure a smooth user transition when the plug-in is released.

Distributed Deployment

Because RIA implementations copy or move presentation logic to the client, a distributed architecture is the most likely scenario for deployment. In a distributed RIA deployment, the presentation logic is on the client; the business layer can be on the client, on the server, or shared across the client and server; and the data layer resides on the Web server or application server. Typically, you will move some of your business logic (and even, perhaps, some of the data access logic) to the client to maximize performance. In this case, your business and data access layers will tend to extend across the client and the application server, as shown in Figure 2.

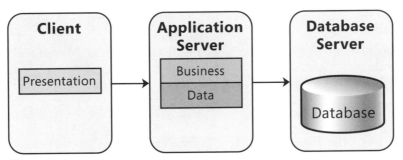

Figure 2
Distributed deployment for a RIA

Consider the following guidelines for deploying a RIA:

- If your applications are large, factor in the processing requirements for downloading the RIA components to clients.
- If your business logic is shared by other applications, consider exposing it as a service on the server so that all applications can access it.
- If you use sockets or WCF in your application and you are not using port 80, consider how firewalls that commonly block other ports will affect your application.
- Ensure that you use a crossdomain.xml file so that RIA clients can access other domains when required.

Load Balancing

When you deploy your application on multiple servers, you can use load balancing to distribute RIA client requests to different servers. This improves response times, increases resource utilization, and maximizes throughput. Figure 3 shows a load-balanced scenario.

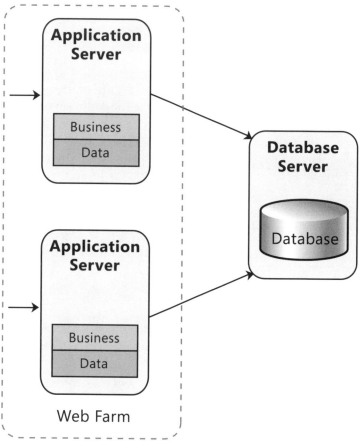

Figure 3
Load balancing a RIA deployment

Consider the following guidelines when designing your application to use load balancing:

- Avoid server affinity. *Server affinity* occurs when all requests from a particular client must be handled by the same server. It is most often introduced by using locally updatable caches or in-process or local session state stores.
- Consider storing all state on the client and designing stateless business components.
- Consider using network load balancing software to implement redirection of requests to the servers in an application farm.

Web Farm Considerations

If your RIA application has significant business logic, data access or data processing requirements on the application server, consider using a Web farm that distributes requests from RIA clients to multiple servers. A Web farm allows you to scale out your application, and reduces the impact of hardware failures. You can use either load balancing or clustering solutions to add more servers for your application. Consider the following guidelines:

- Consider using clustering to reduce the impact of hardware failures, and partitioning your database across multiple database servers if your application has high I/O requirements.

- If you must support server affinity, user-specific cached data or state, configure the Web farm to route all requests for the same user to the same server.

- Do not use in-process session management in a Web farm unless you implement server affinity, because requests from the same user cannot be guaranteed to be routed to the same server otherwise. Use the out-of-process session service or a database server for this scenario.

For more information on deployment patterns and scenarios, see Chapter 19, "Physical Tiers and Deployment."

Relevant Design Patterns

Key patterns are organized into categories such as Layers, Communication, Composition, and Presentation; as shown in the following table. Consider using these patterns when making design decisions for each category.

Category	Relevant patterns
Layers	**Service Layer.** An architectural design pattern where the service interface and implementation is grouped into a single layer.
Communication	**Asynchronous Callback.** Execute long-running tasks on a separate thread that executes in the background, and provide a function for the thread to call back into when the task is complete. **Command.** Encapsulate request processing in a separate command object that exposes a common execution interface.
Composition	**Composite View.** Combine individual views into a composite view. **Inversion of Control.** Populate any dependencies of objects on other objects or components that must be fulfilled before the object can be used by the application.

(continued)

Category	Relevant patterns
Presentation	**Application Controller.** An object that contains all of the flow logic and is used by other Controllers that work with a Model and display the appropriate View. **Supervising Presenter.** Separate presentation design into three separate roles, with the View being responsible for handling user input and being data bound against a Model component that encapsulate business data. A Presenter object implements presentation logic and coordinates interactions between the View and Model. **Presentation Model.** A variation of Model-View-Presenter (MVP) pattern that is tailored for modern UI development platforms where the View is the responsibility of a designer rather than a developer.

For more information on the Composite View pattern, see *"Patterns in the Composite Application Library"* at http://msdn.microsoft.com/en-us/library/dd458924.aspx.

For more information on the Model-View-Controller (MVC) and Application Controller patterns, see Fowler, Martin. *Patterns of Enterprise Application Architecture.* Addison-Wesley, 2002. Or at http://martinfowler.com/eaaCatalog.

For more information on the Command pattern, see Chapter 5, "Behavioral Patterns" in Gamma, Erich, Richard Helm, Ralph Johnson, and John Vlissides. *Design Patterns: Elements of Reusable Object-Oriented Software.* Addison Wesley Professional, 1995.

For more information on the Asynchronous Callback pattern, see *"Creating a Simplified Asynchronous Call Pattern for Windows Forms Applications"* at http://msdn.microsoft.com/en-us/library/ms996483.aspx.

For more information on the Service Layer pattern, see *"P of EAA: Service Layer"* at http://www.martinfowler.com/eaaCatalog/serviceLayer.html.

Additional Resources

To more easily access Web resources, see the online version of the bibliography at: http://www.microsoft.com/architectureguide.

- For information on Silverlight, see the official Silverlight Web site at http://silverlight.net/default.aspx.

- For information on using WCF with Silverlight, see *"How to: Build a Duplex Service"* at http://msdn.microsoft.com/en-us/library/cc645027(VS.95).aspx and *"How to: Access a Duplex Service with the Channel Model"* at http://msdn.microsoft.com/en-us/library/cc645028(VS.95).aspx.

- For Silverlight blogs, see Brad Abrams's blog at http://blogs.msdn.com/brada/ and Scott Guthrie's blog at http://weblogs.asp.net/Scottgu/.

24
Designing Mobile Applications

Overview

This chapter will help you to understand when and how mobile applications are an appropriate solution, and the key design considerations for mobile applications. This includes learning about the components found in a mobile application; specific issues for mobile applications such as deployment, power usage, and synchronization; and the key patterns and technology considerations.

A mobile application will normally be structured as a multilayered application consisting of presentation, business, and data layers. When developing a mobile application, you may choose to develop a thin Web-based client or a rich client. If you are building a rich client, the business and data services layers are likely to be located on the device itself. If you are building a thin client, all of the layers will be located on the server. Figure 1 illustrates common rich client mobile application architecture with components grouped by areas of concern.

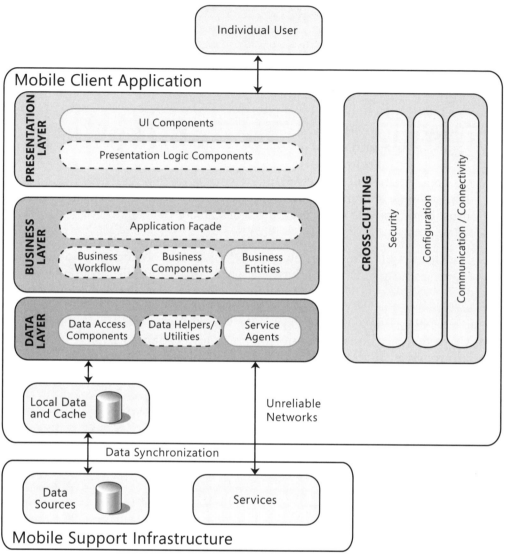

Figure 1
The typical structure of a mobile application

A mobile application generally contains user interface components in the presentation layer, and perhaps may include presentation logic components. The business layer, if it exists, will usually contain business logic components, any business workflow and business entity components that are required by the application, and, optionally, a façade. The data layer will usually include data access and service agent components. In order to minimize the footprint on the device, mobile applications generally use less rigid layering approaches and fewer discrete components. For more information about layered design, see Chapter 5, "Layered Application Guidelines." For more information about the components appropriate for each layer, see Chapter 10, "Component Guidelines."

General Design Considerations

The following design guidelines provide information about different aspects that you should consider when designing a mobile application. Follow these guidelines to ensure that your application meets your requirements and performs efficiently in scenarios common to mobile applications:

- **Decide if you will build a rich client, a thin Web client, or rich Internet application (RIA).** If your application requires local processing and must work in an occasionally connected scenario, consider designing a rich client. A rich client application will be more complex to install and maintain. If your application can depend on server processing and will always be fully connected, consider designing a thin client. If your application requires a rich UI, only limited access to local resources, and must be portable to other platforms, design an RIA client.

- **Determine the device types you will support.** When choosing which device types to support, consider screen size and resolution, CPU performance characteristics, memory and storage space, and development tool environment availability. In addition, factor in user requirements and organizational constraints. You may require specific hardware such as a global positioning system (GPS) or a camera, which may impact not only your application type, but also your device choice.

- **Consider occasionally connected and limited-bandwidth scenarios when appropriate.** If your mobile device is a stand-alone device, you will not need to account for connection issues. When network connectivity is required, mobile applications should handle cases when a network connection is intermittent or not available. It is vital in this case to design your caching, state management, and data access mechanisms with intermittent network connectivity in mind; batch communications for delivery when connectivity is available. Choose hardware and software protocols based on speed, power consumption, and granularity, and not just on ease of programming.

- **Design a UI appropriate for mobile devices, taking into account platform constraints.** Mobile devices require a simpler architecture, simpler UI, and other specific design decisions in order to work within the constraints imposed by the device hardware. Keep these constraints in mind and design specifically for the device instead of trying to reuse the architecture or UI from a desktop or Web application. The main constraints are memory, battery life, ability to adapt to difference screen sizes and orientations, security, and network bandwidth.

- **Design a layered architecture appropriate for mobile devices that improves reuse and maintainability.** Depending on the application type, multiple layers may be located on the device itself. Use the concept of layers to maximize separation of concerns, and to improve reuse and maintainability for your mobile application. However, aim to achieve the smallest footprint on the device by simplifying your design compared to a desktop or Web application.

- **Consider device resource constraints such as battery life, memory size, and processor speed.** Every design decision should take into account the limited CPU, memory, storage capacity, and battery life of mobile devices. Battery life is usually the most limiting factor in mobile devices. Backlighting, reading and writing to memory, wireless connections, specialized hardware, and processor speed all have an impact on the overall power usage. When the amount of memory available is low, the Windows Mobile operating system may ask your application to shut down or sacrifice cached data, slowing program execution. Optimize your application to minimize its power and memory footprint while considering performance during this process.

Specific Design Issues

There are several common issues that you must consider as your develop your design. These issues can be categorized into specific areas of the design. The following sections contain guidelines to help you resolve the common issues in each area:

- Authentication and Authorization
- Caching
- Communication
- Configuration Management
- Data Access
- Device Specifics
- Exception Management
- Logging
- Porting Applications
- Power Management
- Synchronization
- Testing
- User Interface
- Validation

Authentication and Authorization

Designing an effective authentication and authorization strategy is important for the security and reliability of your application. Weak authentication can leave your application vulnerable to unauthorized use. Mobile devices are usually designed to be single user devices and normally lack basic user profile and security tracking beyond just a simple password. Other common desktop mechanisms are also likely to be missing. The discoverability of mobile devices over protocols such as Bluetooth can present users with unexpected risks. Mobile application design can also be especially challenging due to connectivity interruptions. Consider all possible connectivity scenarios, whether over the air or hard wired. Consider the following guidelines when designing authentication and authorization:

- Design authentication and authorization for both fully connected and occasionally connected scenarios; including synchronization over the air, cradled (PC) synchronization, Bluetooth discovery, synchronization over a Virtual Private Network (VPN), and local SD memory card synchronization.

- Consider that different devices might have variations in their programming security models, which can affect authorization for resource access.

- Do not assume that security mechanisms available on larger platforms will be available on a mobile platform, even if you are using the same tools. For example, access control lists (ACLs) are not available in Windows Mobile, and consequently there is no operating system–level file security.

- Identify trust boundaries within your mobile application layers; for example, between the client and the server or the server and the database. This will help you to determine where and how to authenticate.

Caching

Use caching to improve the performance and responsiveness of your application, and to support operation when there is no network connection. Caching can optimize reference data lookups, avoid network round trips, and prevent unnecessarily duplicated processing. When deciding what data to cache, consider the limited resources of the device; you will have less storage space available than on a desktop computer. Consider the following guidelines when designing caching:

- Identify your performance objectives. For example, determine your minimum response time and battery life. Test the performance of the specific devices you will be using. Most mobile devices use only flash memory, which is likely to be slower than the memory used in desktop computers.

- Design for minimum memory footprint. Cache only data that is absolutely necessary for the application to function, or expensive to transform into a ready to use format. If designing a memory-intensive application, detect low memory scenarios and design a mechanism for prioritizing the data to discard as available memory decreases. However, consider caching any data, including volatile data, that the application will need in an occasionally connected or offline scenario. Also, ensure that the application can survive the situation where cached data is not available in offline or occasionally connected scenarios.

- Choose the appropriate cache location, such as on the device, at the mobile gateway, or in the database server. Consider using SQL Server Compact edition for caching instead of device memory because memory consumed by the application may be cleared in low-memory situations.

- Ensure that sensitive data is encrypted when caching, especially when caching data in removable memory media, but also consider encryption when caching data in device memory.

For more information about designing a caching strategy, see Chapter 17, "Crosscutting Concerns."

Communication

Device communication includes wireless communication (over the air) and wired communication with a host computer, as well as more specialized communication such as Bluetooth or Infrared Data Association (IrDA). When communicating over the air, consider data security to protect sensitive data from theft or tampering. If you are communicating through Web service interfaces, use mechanisms such as the WS-Secure standards to secure the data. Keep in mind that wireless device communication is more likely to be interrupted than communication from a computer, and that your application might be required to operate for long periods in a disconnected state. Consider the following guidelines when designing your communication strategy:

- Design asynchronous, threaded communication to improve performance and usability in occasionally connected scenarios. Limited bandwidth connections common on mobile devices can reduce performance and affect usability, especially if they block the user interface. Use appropriate communication protocols, and consider how the application will behave when multiple connection types are available. Consider allowing users to choose the connection to use, and to switch off communication to preserve battery life when appropriate.

- If you are designing an application that will run on a mobile phone, consider the effects of receiving a phone call during communication or program execution. Design the application to allow it to suspend and resume, or even exit the application.

- Protect communication over untrusted connections, such as Web services and other over the air methods. Consider using encryption and digital signatures for sensitive data, and ensure that data passed over a VPN is protected. However, consider the effects of communication security on performance and battery life.

- If you must access data from multiple sources, interoperate with other applications, or work while disconnected, consider using Web services for communication. Ensure you manage connections efficiently, especially in limited bandwidth communication scenarios.

- If you are using WCF for communication and must implement message queuing, consider using WCF store and forward.

For more information about communication protocols and techniques, see Chapter 18, "Communication and Messaging."

Configuration Management

When designing device configuration management, consider how to handle device resets, as well as whether you want to allow configuration of your application over the air or from a host computer. Consider the following guidelines when designing your configuration management strategy:

- Choose an appropriate format for configuration information. Consider a binary format over XML to minimize memory use. Consider using compression library routines to reduce the memory requirements for storing configuration and state information. Ensure that you encrypt sensitive data stored in configuration files.

- Ensure that your design supports restoration of configuration after a device reset. Consider how you will synchronize configuration information over the air and with a host computer when cradled, and ensure that you are familiar with the techniques used by different manufacturers for loading configuration settings.

- If you have your enterprise data in Microsoft SQL Server 2005 or 2008 and require an accelerated time to market, consider using merge replication with a "buy and configure" application from a third party. Merge replication can synchronize data in a single operation regardless of network bandwidth or data size.

- If you have an Active Directory infrastructure, consider using the System Center Mobile Device Manager interface to manage group configuration, authentication, and authorization of devices. See "Technology Considerations" for the requirements of Mobile Device Manager.

Data Access

Data access on a mobile device is constrained by unreliable network connections and the hardware constraints of the device itself. When designing data access, consider how low bandwidth, high latency, and intermittent connectivity will affect your design. Consider the following guidelines when designing data access:

- Consider using a local device database that provides synchronization services, such as SQL Server Compact Edition. Only design a custom mechanism to synchronize data if the standard data synchronization features cannot meet your requirements.

- Program for data integrity. Files that remain open during device suspend and power failures may cause data integrity issues, especially when data is stored on a removable storage device. Include exception handling and retry logic to ensure that file operations succeed. To ensure data integrity in cases where the device loses power or connectivity, consider using transactions with SQL Server Mobile.

- Do not assume that removable storage will always be available, as a user can remove it at any time. Check for the existence of a removable storage device before writing to it or using **FlushFileBuffers**.

- If you use XML to store or transfer data, consider its overall size and impact on performance. XML increases both bandwidth and local storage requirements. Use compression algorithms or a non-XML transfer method.

- Minimize performance impact by designing for efficient database access and data processing. Consider the use of typed objects instead of **DataSets** to reduce memory overhead and improve performance. If you are only reading and not writing data, utilize **DataReaders**. Avoid process intensive operation such as navigating through large data sets.

For more information about designing a data layer, see Chapter 8, "Data Layer Guidelines."

Device Specifics

Mobile device design and development is unique due to the constrained and differing nature of device hardware. You may be targeting multiple devices with very different hardware parameters. Keep the heterogeneous device environment in mind when designing your mobile application. Factors include variations in screen size and orientation, limitations in memory and storage space, and network bandwidth and connectivity. Your choice of a mobile operating system will generally depend on the target device type. Consider the following guidelines when determining your device strategy:

- Optimize the application for the device by considering factors such as screen size and orientation, network bandwidth, memory storage space, processor performance, and other hardware capabilities.

- Consider device-specific capabilities that you can use to enhance your application functionality such as accelerometers, graphics processing units, GPS, haptic (touch, force, and vibration) feedback, compass, camera, and fingerprint readers.

- If you are developing for more than one device, design first for the subset of functionality that exists on all of the devices and then customize the code to detect and use device-specific features when they are available.

- Consider limited memory resources and optimize your application to use the minimum amount of memory. When memory is low, the system may release cached intermediate language (IL) code to reduce its own memory footprint, return to interpreted mode, and thus slow overall execution.

- Create modular code to allow easy module removal from executables. This covers cases where separate smaller executable files are required due to constraints in device memory size.

- Consider using programming shortcuts as opposed to following pure programming practices that can inflate code size and memory consumption. For example, examine the cost of using pure object-oriented practices such as abstract base classes and repeated object encapsulation. Consider using lazy initialization so that objects are instantiated only when required.

Exception Management

Designing an effective exception management strategy is important for the security and reliability of your application. Good exception handling in your mobile application prevents sensitive exception details from being revealed to the user, improves application robustness, and helps keep your application from remaining in an inconsistent state when an error occurs. Consider the following guidelines when designing for exception management:

- Design your application to recover to a known good state after an exception occurs without revealing sensitive information to the end user.
- Catch exceptions only if you can handle them, and do not use exceptions to control logic flow. Ensure that you design a global error handler to catch unhandled exceptions.
- Design an appropriate logging and notification strategy that stores sufficient details about exceptions, but bear in mind memory and storage limitations of mobile devices. Ensure that user friendly exception messages are displayed, and that they do not reveal sensitive information for critical errors and exceptions.

For more information about designing an exception management strategy, see Chapter 17, "Crosscutting Concerns."

Logging

Because of the limited memory available on mobile devices, logging and instrumentation should be limited to only the most necessary cases; for example, attempted intrusion into the device. When devices are designed to be a part of a larger infrastructure, choose to track most device activity at the infrastructure level. Generally, auditing is considered most authoritative if the audits are generated at the precise time of resource access, and by the same routines that access the resource. Consider the fact that some of the logs might have to be generated on the device and must be synchronized with the server during periods of network connectivity. Consider the following guidelines when designing logging:

- There is no Event Log mechanism in Windows Mobile. Consider using a third-party logging mechanism that supports the .NET Compact Framework, such as OpenNetCF, NLog, or log4Net (see Additional Resources at the end of this chapter for more details). Also, consider how you will access logs stored on the device.

- If you carry out extensive logging on the device, consider logging in an abbreviated or compressed format to minimize memory and storage impact. Alternatively, consider remote logging instead of logging on the device.

- Consider using platform features such as health monitoring on the server, and mobile device services on the device, to log and audit events. Explore adding remote health monitoring capabilities using the Open Mobile Alliance Device Management (OMA DM) standard.

- Synchronize between the mobile database logs and the server database logs to maintain audit capabilities on the server. If you have an Active Directory infrastructure, consider using the System Center Mobile Device Manager to extract logs from mobile devices. See "Technology Considerations" for the requirements of Mobile Device Manager.

- Do not store sensitive information in log and audit files unless absolutely necessary, and ensure that any sensitive information is protected through encryption.

- Decide what constitutes unusual or suspicious activity on a device, and log information based on these scenarios.

Porting Applications

Developers often want to port part or all of an existing application to a mobile device. Certain types of applications will be easier to port than others, and it is unlikely that you will be able to port the code directly without modification. Consider the following guidelines when designing to port your existing application to a mobile device:

- If you are porting a rich client application from the desktop, rewrite the application in its entirety. Rich clients are rarely designed to suit a small screen size and limited memory and disk resources.

- If you are porting a Web application to a mobile device, consider rewriting the UI for the smaller screen size. Also, consider communication limitations and interface chattiness as these can translate into increased power usage and connection costs for the user.

- If you are porting a RIA client, carry out research to discover which code will port without modification. Consult the "Technology Considerations" section of this chapter for specific advice.

- Research and utilize tools to assist in porting. For example, Java-to-C++ convertors are available. When converting from Smartphone to Pocket PC code, Visual Studio allows you to change the target platform and provides warnings when you are using Smartphone-specific functionality. You can also link Visual Studio Desktop and Mobile projects to discover what is portable between the two projects.

- Do not assume that you can port custom controls to a mobile application without modification. Supported APIs, memory footprint, and UI behavior are different on a mobile device. Test the controls as early as possible so that you can plan to rewrite them or find an alternative if required.

Power Management

Power is the major limiting design factor for mobile devices. All design decisions should take into account how much power the device consumes, and their effect on overall battery life. If you have a choice, consider devices that can draw power from Universal Serial Bus (USB) or other types of data connections. Research communication protocols and investigate their relative power consumption. Consider the following guidelines when designing for power consumption:

- Implement power profiles to increase performance when the device is plugged into external power and not charging its battery. Allow the user to turn off features of the device when not in use or when not required. Common examples are screen backlighting, hard drives, GPS functions, speakers, and wireless communications.

- To conserve battery life, do not update the UI while the application is running in the background.

- Choose protocols, design service interfaces, and batch communications in such a way as to transfer the smallest number of bytes possible over the air. Consider both power usage as well as network speed when choosing communication methods, and consider deferring nonessential wireless communications until the device is using external power.

- If you are considering using the 3G hardware communications protocol, consider that while it is significantly faster, it also currently uses much more power than its predecessors, such as the Edge protocol. When you are using 3G, be sure to communicate in batched bursts and to shut down communication at times when it is not required.

Synchronization

Consider whether you want to support over the air synchronization, cradled synchronization, or both. Because synchronization will often involve sensitive data, consider how to secure your synchronization data, especially when synchronizing over the air. Design your synchronization to handle connection interruptions gracefully, either by canceling the operation or by allowing it to resume when a connection becomes available. Merge replication allows both upload-only and bidirectional synchronization and is a good choice for infrastructures utilizing newer versions of SQL Server. Consider the Microsoft Sync Framework, which can provide robust synchronization services in a wide variety of situations. Consider the following guidelines when designing synchronization:

- If your users will be synchronizing with a host computer, consider including cradled synchronization in your design. If your users must synchronize data when away from the office, consider including over the air synchronization in your design.

- Ensure that the application can recover when synchronization is reset or when synchronization is interrupted, and decide how you will manage synchronization conflicts.

- Ensure that synchronization communication is protected, perhaps using encryption and digital certificates, and use secure channels. Be especially sure to apply appropriate authentication and authorization when using Bluetooth synchronization.

- If you must support bidirectional synchronization to SQL Server, consider using merge replication synchronization. Remember that merge synchronization will synchronize all of the data in the merge set, which may require additional network bandwidth and can adversely affect performance.

- Consider store and forward synchronization using WCF rather than e-mail or SMS (text message), as WCF guarantees delivery and works well in occasionally connected scenarios.

Testing

Mobile application debugging can be much more costly than debugging a similar application on a computer. Consider this debugging cost when deciding which devices, and how many devices, your application will support. Also keep in mind that it can be harder to get debug information from the device, and that device emulators do not always perfectly simulate the device hardware environment. Consider the following guidelines when designing your debugging strategy:

- Understand your debugging costs when choosing which devices to support. Factor in tools support, the cost of initial (and perhaps replacement) test devices, and the cost of software-based device emulators.

- If you have access to the physical device you are targeting, debug your code on the actual device rather than using an emulator. If the device is not available, use an emulator for initial testing and debugging. Consider that an emulator might run code more slowly than the actual device.

- As soon as you obtain the physical device, switch to running code on the device connected to a normal computer. Test scenarios where your device is fully disconnected from any network or connection, including being disconnected from a computer debugging session, and perform final testing on your device when not connected to a computer. Add temporary or permanent mechanisms to debug problems in this scenario. Consider the needs of people who will support the device.

- If you are an OEM and your device has not yet been created, note that it is possible to debug a mobile program on a dedicated x86-based Windows CE computer. Consider this option until your device is available.

User Interface

When designing the UI for a mobile application, do not try to adapt or reuse the UI from a desktop application. Design your device UI so that it is as simple as possible and tailored specifically for pen-based input and limited data entry capabilities where appropriate. Consider the fact that your mobile application will run in full screen mode and will only be able to display a single window at a time; and, therefore, blocking operations will prevent the user from interacting with the application. Consider the following guidelines when designing the UI for your mobile application:

- Design for a single window, full screen UI. If your device will be a single user device running only the main application, consider using kiosk mode. Keep in mind that Windows Mobile does not support a kiosk mode, so you will need to use Windows CE.

- Take into account the various screen sizes and orientations of your target devices when designing your application UI. Also, consider the limitations imposed by the small screen size, limited API, and reduced range of UI controls compared to desktop environments.

- Design for usability by supporting touchscreen or stylus-driven UI. Place menu bars and other controls at the bottom of the screen (expanding upwards when required) to prevent the user's hands from obscuring the display. Support touchscreen input by making buttons large enough, and lay out controls so that the UI is usable using a finger or stylus for input.

- Give the user visual indication of blocking operations; for example, an hourglass cursor.

Validation

Use validation to protect the device and your application, and to improve usability. Validating input values before submitting them to a remote server can reduce communication roundtrips and improve the performance and usability of the application, especially in occasionally connected or disconnected scenarios. When designing validation, consider the following guidelines:

- Validate data input by the user where possible to prevent unnecessary communication and server roundtrips. This also makes the application more responsive when the user enters invalid values.

- Validate all data received during communication with a host computer and during over the air communication.

- Ensure that you protect hardware resources, such as the camera and initiation of phone calls, by validating code and actions that automatically initiate these features.

- Consider the limited resources and performance of the device by designing efficient validation mechanisms that have the minimum memory footprint.

For more information about validation techniques, see Chapter 17, "Crosscutting Concerns."

Technology Considerations

The following guidelines contain suggestions and advice for common scenarios for mobile applications and technologies.

Microsoft Silverlight for Mobile

At the time of release of this guidance, Silverlight for Mobile was an announced product under development but not released. Consider the following guidelines if you are using Silverlight for Mobile:

- If you want to build applications that support rich media and interactivity and have the ability to run on both a mobile device and desktop, consider using Silverlight for Mobile. Silverlight 2.0 code created to run on the desktop in the Silverlight 2.0 plug-in will run in the Windows Mobile Silverlight plug-in in the latest version of Microsoft Internet Explorer® for Mobile browser. Consider that while it is possible to use the same Silverlight code on both mobile device and desktop, you should take into account the differing screen size and resource constraints of a mobile device. Consider optimizing the code for Windows Mobile.

- If you want to develop Web pages for both desktop and mobile platforms, consider Silverlight for Mobile or normal ASP.NET/HMTL instead of using ASP.NET for Mobile, unless you know that your device cannot support either alternative. As device browsers have become more powerful, they are able to process the same native HTML and ASP.NET targeted at the desktop, thus making ASP.NET mobile-specific development less important. ASP.NET for Mobile currently supports a variety of mobile devices through specific markup adapters and device profiles. While ASP.NET for Mobile automatically renders content to match device capabilities at run time, there is overhead associated with testing and maintaining the device profiles. Development support for these controls is included in Microsoft Visual Studio 2003 and 2005, but is not included in Visual Studio 2008. Run-time support is currently still available but may be discontinued in the future. For more information, see "Additional Resources" at the end of this chapter.

.NET Compact Framework

Consider the following guidelines if you are using the Microsoft .NET Compact Framework:

- If you are familiar with the Microsoft .NET Framework and are developing for both the desktop and mobile platforms concurrently, consider that the .NET Compact Framework is a subset of the .NET Framework class library. It also contains some classes exclusively designed for Windows Mobile. The .NET Compact Framework supports only the Microsoft Visual Basic® and Microsoft Visual C#® development systems.

- If you have issues tracing into a subset of Windows Mobile code with the Visual Studio debugger, consider that you might require multiple debug sessions. For example, if you have both native and managed code in the same debug session, Visual Studio might not follow the session across the boundary. In this case, you will require two instances of Visual Studio running and you must track the context between them manually.

Windows Mobile

Consider the following general guidelines for Windows Mobile applications:

- If you are targeting an application for both Windows Mobile Professional and Windows Mobile Standard editions, consider that the Windows Mobile security model varies on the different versions of Windows Mobile. Code that works on one platform might not work on the other because of the differing security models for APIs. Check the Windows Mobile documentation for your device and version. Also see the "Additional Resources" section at the end of this chapter.

- If you will have to manage your application in the future or are upgrading an existing application, be sure that you understand the Windows Mobile operating system derivation, product naming, and versioning tree. There are slight differences between each version that could potentially impact your application.

  - Windows Mobile is derived from releases of the Windows CE operating system.

  - Both Windows Mobile version 5.x and 6.x are based on Windows CE version 5.x.

  - Windows Mobile Pocket PC was renamed Windows Mobile Professional starting with Windows Mobile 6.0.

  - Windows Mobile Smartphone was renamed Windows Mobile Standard starting with Windows Mobile 6.0.

  - Windows Mobile Professional and Windows Mobile Standard have slight differences in their APIs. For example, the Windows Mobile Standard (Smartphone) lacks a Button class in its Compact Framework implementation because softkeys are used for data entry instead.

- Always use the Windows Mobile APIs to access memory and file structures. Do not access them directly after you have obtained a handle to either structure. Windows CE version 6.x (and thus the next release of Windows Mobile) uses a virtualized memory model and a different process execution model than previous versions. This means that structures such as file handles and pointers may no longer be actual physical pointers to memory. Windows Mobile programs that relied on this implementation detail in versions 6.x and before will fail when moved to the next version of Windows Mobile.

- The Mobile Device Manager (MDM) is a possible solution for authorizing, tracking, and collecting logs from mobile devices, assuming that you have an Active Directory infrastructure. As well as Windows Mobile 6.1 on the managed devices, MDM also requires a number of other products to be installed on the server in order to function fully, including:
  - Windows Server Update Service (WSUS) 3.0
  - Windows Mobile Device Management Server
  - Enrollment Server
  - Gateway Server
  - Active Directory as part of Windows Server
  - SQL Server 2005 or above
  - Microsoft Certificate Authority
  - Internet Information Server (IIS) 6.0
  - .NET Framework 2.0 or above

Windows Embedded

Consider the following guidelines if you are choosing a Windows Embedded technology:

- If you are designing for a set top box or other larger footprint device, consider using Windows Embedded Standard.
- If you are designing for a point of service device such as an automated teller machine (ATMs, customer-facing kiosks, or self checkout systems), consider using Windows Embedded for Point of Service.
- If you are designing for a GPS-enabled device or a device with navigation capabilities, consider using Microsoft Windows Embedded NavReady™ software. Note that Windows Embedded NavReady 2009 is built on Windows Mobile 5.0, while Windows Mobile version 6.1 is used in the latest versions for Windows Mobile Standard and Professional. If you are targeting a common codebase for NavReady and other Windows Mobile devices, be sure to verify that you are using APIs available on both platforms.

Deployment Considerations

Mobile applications can be deployed using many different methods. Consider the requirements of your users, as well as how you will manage the application, when designing for deployment. Ensure that you design to allow for the appropriate management, administration, and security for application deployment. Deployment scenarios for Windows Mobile device applications, with the more common ones listed first, are:

- Microsoft Exchange ActiveSync® technology using a Windows Installer file (MSI).
- Over the air, using HTTP, SMS, or CAB files to provide install and run functionality.
- Mobile Device Manager–based, using Active Directory to load from a CAB or MSI file.
- Post load and autorun, which loads a company-specific package as part of the operating system.
- Site loading, manually using an SD card.

Consider the following guidelines when designing your deployment strategy:

- If your users must be able to install and update applications while away from the office, consider designing for over the air deployment.
- If you are using CAB file distribution for multiple devices, include multiple device executables in the CAB file. Have the device detect which executable to install, and discard the rest.
- If your application relies heavily on a host computer, consider using ActiveSync to deploy your application.
- If you are deploying a baseline experience running on top of Windows Mobile, considering using the post-load mechanism to automatically load your application immediately after the Windows Mobile operating system starts up.
- If your application will be run only at a specific site, and you want to manually control distribution, consider deployment using an SD memory card.

For more information on deployment patterns and scenarios, see Chapter 19, "Physical Tiers and Deployment."

Relevant Design Patterns

Key patterns are organized into categories such as Caching, Communication, Data Access, Synchronization, and UI; as shown in the following table. Consider using these patterns when making design decisions for each category.

Category	Relevant patterns
Caching	**Lazy Acquisition.** Defer the acquisition of resources as long as possible to optimize device resource use.
Communication	**Active Object.** Support asynchronous processing by encapsulating the service request and service completion response. **Communicator.** Encapsulate the internal details of communication in a separate component that can communicate through different channels. **Entity Translator.** An object that transforms message data types into business types for requests, and reverses the transformation for responses. **Reliable Sessions.** End to end reliable transfer of messages between a source and a destination, regardless of the number or type of intermediaries that separate the endpoints.
Data Access	**Active Record.** Include a data access object within a domain entity. Data Transfer Object (DTO). An object that stores the data transported between processes, reducing the number of method calls required. **Domain Model.** A set of business objects that represents the entities in a domain and the relationships between them. **Transaction Script.** Organize the business logic for each transaction in a single procedure, making calls directly to the database or through a thin database wrapper.
Synchronization	**Synchronization.** A component installed on a device tracks changes to data and exchanges information with a component on the server when a connection is available.
UI	**Application Controller.** An object that contains all of the flow logic, and is used by other Controllers that work with a Model and display the appropriate View. **Model-View-Controller.** Separate the data in the domain, the presentation, and the actions based on user input into three separate classes. The Model manages the behavior and data of the application domain, responds to requests for information about its state (usually from the View), and responds to instructions to change state (usually from the Controller). The View manages the display of information. The Controller interprets the mouse and keyboard inputs from the user, informing the model and/or the view to change as appropriate. **Model-View-Presenter.** Separate request processing into three roles, with the View being responsible for handling user input, the Model responsible for application data and business logic, and the Presenter responsible for presentation logic and for coordinating the interaction between the View and the Model. **Pagination.** Separate large amounts of content into individual pages to optimize system resources and minimize use of screen space.

Additional Resources

To more easily access Web resources, see the online version of the bibliography at:
http://www.microsoft.com/architectureguide.

- For more information on the Windows Embedded technology options, see the *"Windows Embedded Developer Center"* at http://msdn.microsoft.com/en-us/embedded/default.aspx.

- For more information on software factories dedicated to mobile devices, see *"patterns & practices Mobile Client Software Factory"* at http://msdn.microsoft.com/en-us/library/aa480471.aspx.

- For information on the Microsoft Sync Framework, see the *"Microsoft Sync Framework Developer Center"* at http://msdn.microsoft.com/en-us/sync/default.aspx.

- For more information on the OpenNETCF.Diagnostics.EventLog in the Smart Device Framework, see *"Instrumentation for .NET Compact Framework Applications"* at http://msdn.microsoft.com/en-us/library/aa446519.aspx.

- For more information on ASP.NET Mobile, see "Roadmap for ASP.NET Mobile Development" at http://www.asp.net/mobile/road-map/.

- For more information on adding ASP.NET Mobile source code support into Visual Studio 2008, see *"Tip/Trick: ASP.NET Mobile Development with Visual Studio 2008"* at http://blogs.msdn.com/webdevtools/archive/2007/09/17/tip-trick-asp-net-mobile-development-with-visual-studio-2008.aspx.

- For more information on security model permissions in Windows Mobile 6.x, see *"Security Model for Windows Mobile 5.0 and Windows Mobile 6"* at http://blogs.msdn.com/jasonlan/archive/2007/03/13/new-whitepaper-security-model-for-windows-mobile-5-0-and-windows-mobile-6.aspx.

- For more information on Apache Logging Services "log4Net," see http://logging.apache.org/log4net/index.html.

- For more information on Jarosław Kowalski's "NLog," see http://www.nlog-project.org/introduction.html.

- For more information on the OpenNetCF Community, see http://community.opennetcf.com/.

25

Designing Service Applications

Overview

In this chapter, you will learn about the nature and use of services, the general guidelines for different service scenarios, and the key attributes of services. You will also see guidelines for the layers within a services application, and key factors you must consider in terms of performance, security, deployment, patterns, and technology considerations.

A *service* is a public interface that provides access to a unit of functionality. Services literally provide some programmatic service to the caller, who consumes the service. Services are loosely coupled and can be combined within a client, or combined within other services, to provide functionality that is more complex. Services are distributable and can be accessed from a remote machine as well as from the machine on which they are running. Services are message-oriented, meaning that service interfaces are defined by a Web Services Description Language (WSDL) file, and operations are called using Extensible Markup Language (XML)-based message schemas that are passed over a transport channel. Services support a heterogeneous environment by focusing interoperability at the message/interface definition. If components can understand the message and interface definition, they can use the service regardless of their base technology. Figure 1 shows an overall view of a typical services application architecture.

Services

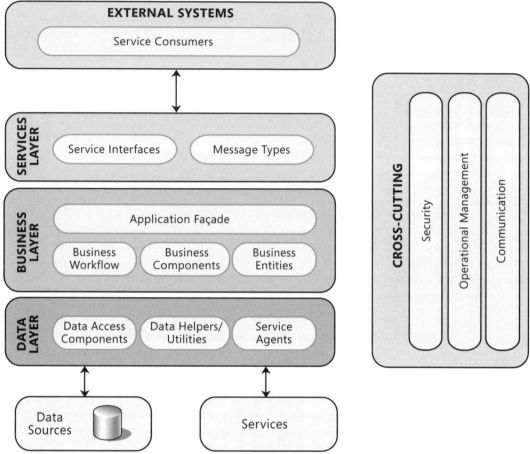

Figure 1
A common services application architecture

A typical services application is composed of three layers: the service layer, business layer, and data layer. The service layer may include service interfaces, message types, and data types components; the business layer may include business logic, business workflow, and business entity components; and the data layer may include data access and service agent components. For more information about layered design, see Chapter 5, "Layered Application Guidelines." For more information about the components appropriate for each layer, see Chapter 10, "Component Guidelines."

Services are flexible by nature and can be used in a wide variety of scenarios and combinations. The following are typical scenarios:

- **Service exposed over the Internet.** This scenario describes a service that is consumed by a range of clients over the Internet. This scenario includes business-to-business as well as consumer-focused services. A stockbroker Web site that consumes Web services from stock exchanges and provides stock quotes would be an example of this scenario. Decisions on authentication and authorization must be based on Internet trust boundaries and credentials options. For example, user name and password authentication or the use of certificates is more likely in the Internet scenario than the intranet scenario.

- **Service exposed over an intranet.** This scenario describes a service that is consumed over an intranet by a (usually restricted) set of internal or corporate clients. An enterprise-level document management application would be an example of this scenario. Decisions on authentication and authorization must be based on intranet trust boundaries and credentials options. For example, Windows authentication using Active Directory is more likely to be the chosen user store in the intranet scenario than in the Internet scenario.

- **Service exposed on the local machine.** This scenario describes a service that is consumed by an application on the local machine. Transport and message protection decisions must be based on local machine trust boundaries and users.

- **Mixed scenario.** This scenario describes a service that is consumed by multiple applications over the Internet, an intranet, and/or the local machine. A line-of-business (LOB) service application that is consumed internally by a rich client application and over the Internet by a Web application would be an example of this scenario.

General Design Considerations

When designing service-based applications, you should follow the general guidelines that apply to all services such as designing for coarse-grained operations, honoring the service contract, and anticipating invalid requests or requests that arrive in the wrong order. In addition to the general guidelines, there are specific guidelines that you should follow for different types of services. For example, with a Service-Oriented Architecture (SOA), you should ensure that the operations are application-scoped and that the service is autonomous. Alternatively, you might have an application that provides workflow services, or you might be designing an operational data store that provides a service-based interface. Consider the following guidelines when designing service applications:

- **Consider using a layered approach to designing service applications and avoid tight coupling across layers.** Separate the business rules and data access functions into distinct components where appropriate. Use abstraction to provide an interface into the business layer. This abstraction can be implemented by using public object interfaces, common interface definitions, abstract base classes, or messaging. For more information about abstraction in layered architecture, see Chapter 5, "Layered Application Guidelines."

- **Design coarse-grained operations.** Avoid chatty calls to the service interface, which can lead to very poor performance. Service operations should be coarse-grained and focused on application operations. Consider using the Façade pattern to package smaller fine-grained operations into single coarse-grained operations. For example, with demographics data, you should provide an operation that returns all of the data in one call instead of requiring multiple calls that return subsets of the data.

- **Design data contracts for extensibility and reuse.** Data contracts should be designed so that you can extend them without affecting consumers of the service. When possible, compose the complex types used by your service from standard elements. The service layer should have knowledge of business entities used by the business layer. Typically, this is achieved by creating a separate assembly that contains business entities, which is shared between the service layer and business layer.

- **Design only for the service contract.** The service layer should implement and provide only the functionality detailed in the service contract, and the internal implementation and details of a service should never be exposed to external consumers. Also, if you need to change the service contract to include new functionality implemented by a service, and the new operations and types are not backward compatible with the existing contracts, consider versioning your contracts. Define new operations exposed by the service in a new version of a service contract, and define new schema types in a new version of the data contract. For information about designing message contracts, see Chapter 18, "Communication and Messaging."

- **Design services to be autonomous.** Services should not require anything from consumers of the service, and should not assume who the consumer is or how they plan to use the service you provide.

- **Design to assume the possibility of invalid requests.** Never assume that all messages received by the service are valid. Implement validation logic to check all messages against the appropriate schemas; and reject or sanitize all invalid messages. For more information about validation, see Chapter 17, "Crosscutting Concerns." Ensure that the service can detect and manage repeated messages (idempotency) by implementing well-known patterns, or by taking advantage of infrastructure services, to ensure that duplicate messages are not processed. In addition, ensure that the service can manage messages arriving out of order (commutativity), perhaps by implementing a design that will store messages and then process them in the correct order.

- **Design services based on policy and with explicit boundaries.** A services application should be self contained, with strict boundaries. Access to the service should only be allowed through the service interface layer. The service should publish a policy that describes how consumers can interact with the service. This is particularly important for public services, where consumers can examine the policy to determine interaction requirements.

- **Separate service concerns from infrastructure operational concerns.** Crosscutting logic should never be combined with application logic. Doing so can lead to implementations that are difficult to extend and maintain.

- **Use separate assemblies for major components in the service layer.** For example, the interface, implementation, data contracts, service contracts, fault contracts, and translators should all be separated into their own assemblies.

- **Avoid using data services to expose individual tables in a database.** This will lead to chatty service calls and interdependencies between service operations, which can lead to dependency issues for consumers of the service. In addition, try to avoid implementing business rules within services because different consumers of the data will have unique viewpoints and rules, and this will impose restrictions on the use of the data.

- **Design workflow services to use interfaces supported by your workflow engine.** Attempting to create custom interfaces can restrict the types of operations supported, and will increase the effort required to extend and maintain the services. Instead of adding workflow services to an existing service application, consider designing an autonomous service that supports only workflow requirements.

Specific Design Issues

The following sections contain guidelines to help you resolve the common issues that arise as you develop a services architecture:

- Authentication
- Authorization
- Business Layer
- Communication
- Data Layer
- Exception Management
- Message Construction
- Message Endpoint
- Message Protection
- Message Transformation
- Message Exchange Patterns
- Representational State Transfer
- Service Layer
- SOAP
- Validation

Authentication

The design of an effective authentication strategy for your service depends on the type of service host you are using. For example, if the service is hosted in Internet Information Services (IIS), you can take advantage of the authentication support provided by IIS. If the service is hosted by using a Windows Service, you must use message-based or transport-based authentication. Consider the following guidelines when designing an authentication strategy:

- Identify a suitable mechanism for securely authenticating users, and apply authentication across all trust boundaries. Consider federated services and single sign on (SSO) mechanisms where appropriate.
- Consider the implications of using different trust settings for executing service code.
- Ensure that secure protocols such as Secure Sockets Layer (SSL) are used with Basic authentication, or when credentials are passed as plain text. Use secure mechanisms such as Web Services Security (WS-Security) with SOAP messages.

Authorization

Designing an effective authorization strategy is important for the security and reliability of your service application. Failure to design a good authorization strategy can leave your application vulnerable to information disclosure, data tampering, and elevation of privileges. Consider the following guidelines when designing an authorization strategy:

- Set appropriate access permissions on resources for users, groups, and roles; and apply granular level authorization across all trust boundaries. Execute services under the most restrictive account that is appropriate.
- Consider using Uniform Resource Locator (URL) authorization and/or file authorization when protecting URL- and file-based resources.
- Where appropriate, restrict access to publicly accessible service methods using declarative principle permission demands.

Business Layer

The business layer in a services application uses a façade to translate service operations into business operations. The primary goal when designing a service interface is to use coarse-grained operations, which can internally translate into multiple business operations. The business layer façade is responsible for interacting with the appropriate business process components. Consider the following guidelines when designing your business layer:

- Components in the business layer should have no knowledge of the service layer. The business layer and any business logic code should not have dependencies on code in the service layer, and should never execute code in the service layer.

- When supporting services, use a façade in the business layer. The façade represents the main entry point into the business layer. Its responsibility is to accept coarse-grained operations and break them down into multiple business operations. However, if your service may be accessed from the local machine or from a client that will not access the service across physical boundaries, you may consider exposing the fine-grained operations as well where this is useful to the client.

- Design the business layer to be stateless. Service operations should contain all of the information, including state information, which the business layer uses to process a request. Because a service can handle a large number of consumer interactions, attempting to maintain state in the business layer would consume considerable resources in order to maintain state for each unique consumer. This would restrict the number of requests that a service could handle at any one time.

- Implement all business entities within a separate assembly. This assembly represents a shared component that can be used by both the business layer and the data access layer. Note, however, that business entities should not be exposed across a service boundary; instead use data transfer objects (DTOs) to transfer data between services.

For more information about implementing the business layer, see Chapter 7, "Business Layer Guidelines." For information about business entities, see Chapter 13, "Designing Business Entities."

Communication

When designing the communication strategy for your service application, the protocol you choose should be based on the deployment scenario for your service. Consider the following guidelines when designing a communication strategy:

- If the service will be deployed within a closed network, you can use Transmission Control Protocol (TCP) for communication that is more efficient. If the service will be deployed on a public-facing network, you should choose Hypertext Transfer Protocol (HTTP).

- Determine how to handle unreliable or intermittent communication reliably, perhaps by caching messages and sending them when a connection is available, and how to handle asynchronous calls. Decide if message communication must be one way or two way, and whether you need to use the Duplex, Request Response, and Request-Reply patterns.

- Use dynamic URL behavior with configured endpoints for maximum flexibility, and determine how you will validate endpoint addresses in messages.

- Choose appropriate communication protocols, and ensure that you protect data sent across communication channels using encryption and/or digital signatures.

For more information about communication protocols and techniques, see Chapter 18, "Communication and Messaging."

Data Layer

The data layer in a services application includes the data access functionality that interacts with external data sources. These data sources could be databases, other services, the file system, SharePoint lists, or any other applications that manage data. Data consistency is critical to the stability and integrity of your service implementation, and failure to validate the consistency of data received by the service can lead to invalid data inserted into the data store, unexpected exceptions, and security breaches. As a result, you should always include data consistency checks when implementing a service. Consider the following guidelines when designing your data layer:

- The data layer should be deployed to the same tier as the business layer where possible. Deploying the data layer on a separate physical tier will require serialization of objects as they cross physical boundaries.

- Always use abstraction when implementing an interface to the data layer. This is normally achieved by using the Data Access or Table Data Gateway patterns, which use well-known types for inputs and outputs.

- For simple Create, Read, Update, and Delete (CRUD) operations, consider creating a class for each table or view in the database. This represents the Table Module pattern, where each table has a corresponding class with operations that interact with the table. Plan how you will handle transactions.

- Avoid using impersonation or delegation to access the database. Instead, use a common entity to access the database, while providing user identity information so that log and audit processes can associate users with the actions they perform.

For more information about implementing the data layer, see Chapter 8, "Data Layer Guidelines."

Exception Management

Designing an effective exception-management strategy is important for the security and reliability of your service application. Failure to do so can leave your application vulnerable to Denial of Service (DoS) attacks, and may also allow it to reveal sensitive and critical information. Raising and handling exceptions is an expensive operation, so it is important that the design take into account the potential impact on performance. A good approach is to design a centralized exception management and logging mechanism, and to consider providing access points that support instrumentation and centralized monitoring in order to assist system administrators. Consider the following guidelines when designing an exception management strategy:

- Ensure that you catch unhandled exceptions, and clean up resources after an exception occurs. Avoid exposing sensitive data in service exceptions, log files, and audit files.

- Do not catch exceptions unless you can handle them; for example, to remove sensitive information or add additional information to the exception. Do not use exceptions to control application logic flow. Avoid the use of custom exceptions when not necessary.

- Use SOAP Fault elements or custom extensions to return exception details to the caller.

For more information about designing an exception management strategy, see Chapter 17, "Crosscutting Concerns."

Message Construction

When data is exchanged between a service and a consumer, it must be wrapped inside a message. The format of that message is based on the types of operations you must support. For example, you might be exchanging documents, executing commands, or raising events. When using slow message delivery channels, you should also consider including expiration information in the message. Consider the following guidelines when designing a message construction strategy:

- Determine the appropriate patterns for message construction (such as Command, Document, Event, and Request-Response).

- Divide very large quantities of data into relatively small chunks, and send them in sequence.

- Include expiration information in messages that are time sensitive. The service should ignore expired messages.

Message Endpoint

The message endpoint represents the connection that applications use to interact with your service. The implementation of your service interface provides the message endpoint. When designing the service implementation, you must consider the type of message that you are consuming. In addition, you should design for a range of scenarios related to handling messages. Consider the following guidelines when designing message endpoints:

- Determine relevant patterns for message endpoints (such as Gateway, Mapper, Competing Consumers, and Message Dispatcher).

- Design for disconnected scenarios. For example, you may need to support guaranteed delivery by caching or storing messages for later delivery. Ensure you do not attempt to subscribe to endpoints while disconnected.

- Determine if you should accept all messages, or implement a filter to handle specific messages.

- Design for idempotency in your service interface. Idempotency is the situation where you could receive duplicate messages from the same consumer, but should only handle one. In other words, an idempotent endpoint will guarantee that only one message will be handled, and that all duplicate messages will be ignored.

- Design for commutativity. Commutativity is the situation where the messages could arrive out of order. In other words, a commutative endpoint will guarantee that messages arriving out of order will be stored and then processed in the correct order.

Message Protection

When transmitting sensitive data between a service and its consumer, you should design for message protection. You can use transport layer protection (such as IPSec or SSL) or message-based protection (such as encryption and digital signatures). Consider the following guidelines when designing message protection:

- Use message-based security when you require end to end security and it is possible that intermediaries such as servers and routers will exist between the service and the caller. Message-based security helps to protect sensitive data in messages by encrypting it, and a digital signature will help to protect against repudiation and tampering of the messages. However, keep in mind that applying security will affect performance.

- If interactions between the service and the consumer are not routed through intermediaries, such as other servers and routers, you can use transport layer security such as IPSec or SSL. However, if the message passes through one or more intermediaries, always use message-based security. With transport layer security, the message is decrypted and then encrypted at each intermediary through which it passes—which represents a security risk.

- For maximum security, consider using both transport layer and message-based security in your design. Transport layer security will help to protect the headers information that cannot be encrypted using message based security.

- When designing extranet or business-to-business services, consider using message-based brokered authentication with X.509 certificates. In the business-to-business scenario, the certificate should be issued by a commercial certificate authority. For extranet services, you can use certificates issued through an organization-based certificate service.

Message Transformation

When passing messages between a service and consumer, there are many cases where the message must be transformed into a format that the consumer can understand. This normally occurs in cases where consumers that cannot use messaging must process data retrieved from a message-based system. You can use adapters to provide access to the message channel for such consumers, and translators to convert the message data into a format that each consumer understands. Consider the following guidelines when designing for message transformation:

- Determine if you must perform transformation; and, if so, identify relevant patterns for message transformation. For example, the Normalizer pattern can be used to translate semantically equivalent messages into a common format. Avoid using a canonical model when not necessary.

- Ensure you perform transformations at the appropriate location to avoid repeated processing and unnecessary overheads.

- Use metadata to define the message format, and consider using an external repository to store this metadata.

- Consider using mechanisms such as BizTalk Server that can perform message transformations between a range of formats and client types.

Message Exchange Patterns

A Message Exchange Pattern defines a conversation between a service and the service consumer. This conversation represents a contract between the service and the consumer. The W3C standards group defines two patterns for SOAP messages: Request-Response and SOAP Response. Another standards group named OASIS has defined a Business Process Execution Language (BPEL) for services. BPEL defines a process for exchanging business process messages. In addition, other organizations have defined specific message exchange patterns for exchanging business process messages. Consider the following guidelines when designing message exchange patterns:

- Choose patterns that match your requirements without adding unnecessary complexity. For example, avoid using a complex business process exchange pattern if the Request-Response pattern is sufficient. For one-way messages, consider the Fire and Forget pattern.

- When using business process modeling techniques, be careful not to design exchange patterns based on process steps. Instead, the patterns should support operations that combine process steps.

- Use existing standards for message exchange patterns instead of inventing your own. This promotes a standards-based interface that will be understood by many consumers. In other words, consumers will be more inclined to interact with standards-based contracts instead of having to discover and adapt to non-standard contracts.

Representational State Transfer

Representational State Transfer (REST) is an architectural style that is based on HTTP and works very much like a Web application. However, instead of a user interacting with and navigating through Web pages, applications interact with and navigate through REST resources using the same semantics as a Web application. In REST, a resource is identified by a Uniform Resource Identifier (URI), and the actions that can be performed against a resource are defined by using HTTP verbs such as GET, POST, PUT, and DELETE. Interaction with a REST service is accomplished by performing HTTP operations against a URI, which is typically in the form of an HTTP-based URL. The result of an operation provides a representation of the current state for that resource. In addition, the result can contain links to other resources that you can move to from the current resource.

The most common misconception about REST is that it is only useful for CRUD operations against a resource. REST can be used with any service that can be represented as a state machine. In other words, as long as you can break a service down into distinguishable states, such as retrieved and updated, you can convert those states into actions and demonstrate how each state can lead to one or more states. Consider how the UI of a Web application represents a state machine. When you access a page, the information displayed represents the current state of that information. You might have the ability to change that state by POSTing form fields, or by moving to another page using links that are included in the current page. A RESTful service works the same way, in that an application can perform a GET operation on a resource to get the current state of that resource, change the state of the resource by performing a PUT operation, or move to a different resource using links provided by the current resource.

Both application state and resource state exist in RESTful services. The client stores all application state, while the server stores only the resource state. Each individual request sent from the client to the server must contain all of the information necessary for the server to fully understand that request. In other words, the client must transfer any relevant application state in its request. The client can then make decisions on how to modify the resource state, based upon the server responses. Passing the application state each time allows the application design to scale, as you can now add multiple identical Web servers and load balance in such a way that the client needs no affinity to one particular server or any shared application state.

A REST style service has the qualities of safety and idempotency. Safety refers to the ability to repeat a request many times and get back the same answer without side effects. Idempotency refers to behavior where making a single call has the same consequences as making the same call several times. The presence of these qualities adds robustness and reliability because, even if HTTP is unreliable, you can safely reissue a request when the server is nonresponsive or returns a failure.

Consider the following guidelines when designing REST resources:

- Consider using a state diagram to model and define resources that will be supported by your REST service. Do not use session state within a REST service.

- Choose an approach for resource identification. A good practice would be to use meaningful names for REST starting points and unique identifiers, as part of their overall path, for specific resource instances. Avoid putting actions into the URI with QueryString values.

- Decide if multiple representations should be supported for different resources. For example, decide if the resource should support an XML, Atom, or JavaScript Object Notation (JSON) format and make it part of the resource request. A resource could be exposed as both (for example) http://www.contoso.com/example.atom and http://www.contoso.com/example.json (note: links are to placeholder sites). Do not use QueryString values to define actions on a URI. Instead, all actions are based on the HTTP operation performed against a URI.

- Do not overuse the POST operation. A good practice is to use specific HTTP operations such as PUT or DELETE as appropriate to reinforce the resource-based design and the use of a uniform interface.

- Take advantage of the HTTP application protocol to use common Web infrastructure (caching, authentication, common data representation types, and so on).

- Ensure that your GET requests are safe, meaning that they always return the same result when called. Consider making your PUT and DELETE requests idempotent, meaning that repeated identical requests should have the same effect as a single request.

Service Layer

The service layer contains components that define and implement services for your application. Specifically, this layer contains the service interface (which is composed of contracts), the service implementation, and translators that convert internal business entities to and from external data contracts. Consider the following guidelines when designing your service layer:

- Do not implement business rules in the service layer. The service layer should only be responsible for managing service requests and for translating data contracts into entities for use by the business layer.

- Access to the service layer should be defined by policies. Policies provide a way for consumers of the service to determine the connection and security requirements, as well as other details related to interacting with the service.

- Use separate assemblies for major components in the service layer. For example, the interface, implementation, data contracts, service contracts, fault contracts, and translators should all be separated into their own assemblies.

- Interaction with the business layer should only be through a well-known public interface. The service layer should never call the underlying business logic components.
- The service layer should have knowledge of business entities used by the business layer. This is typically achieved by creating a separate assembly that contains business entities shared between the service layer and business layer.

SOAP

SOAP is a message-based protocol in which the message is composed of an XML envelope that contains a header and body. The header can provide information that is external to the operation performed by the service. For example, a header may contain security, transaction, or routing information. The body contains contracts, in the form of XML schemas, which define the service and the actions it can perform. Compared to REST, SOAP gives more protocol flexibility, and so you can utilize higher-performance protocols such as TCP. SOAP supports the WS-* standards including security, transactions, and reliability. Message security and reliability ensure that the messages not only reach their destination, but also that those messages have not been read or modified during transit. Transactions provide the ability to group operations and provide roll back ability in the case of a failure.

SOAP is useful when performing RPC-type interactions between services or decoupled layers of an application. It excels at providing an interface between new and legacy systems on an internal network. A service layer can be placed on top of an older system, allowing API-type interaction with the system without having to redesign the system to expose a REST resource model. SOAP is also useful where information is actively routed to one or more systems that may change communication protocols frequently over their lifetimes. It is also helpful when you want to encapsulate information or objects in an opaque manner and then store or relay that information to another system.

If you want your application to be scalable by using Web farms or load balancing, avoid storing session state on the server. Storing sessions on the server means that a particular server must service the client throughout the duration of the session or, in the case of load balancing, must pass the session information to another server. Passing session state between servers makes failover and scale out scenarios much harder to implement.

Consider the following guidelines when designing SOAP messages:

- Within a SOAP envelope, the SOAP header is optional but the SOAP body is mandatory. Avoid the use of complex types in all message schemas.
- Consider using SOAP faults for errors instead of relying on the default error handling behavior. When returning error information, the SOAP fault must be the only child element within the SOAP body.

- To force processing of a SOAP header block, set the block's **mustUnderstand** attribute to "true" or "1". Errors that occur when processing the SOAP header should be returned as a SOAP fault in the SOAP header element.

- Research and utilize WS-* standards. These standards provide consistent rules and methods for dealing with the issues commonly encountered in a messaging architecture.

Validation

Designing an effective input validation and data validation strategy is critical to the security of your application. You must determine the validation rules for data you receive from consumers of the service. Consider the following guidelines when designing a validation strategy:

- Validate all data received by the service interface, including data fields associated with the message, and return informative error messages if validation fails. Consider using XML schemas to validate incoming messages.

- Check all input for dangerous or malicious content, and consider the way that data will be used. For example, if the data will be used to initiate database queries you must protect the database from SQL injection attacks. This may be through the use of stored procedures or parameterized queries to access the database.

- Determine your signing, encryption, and encoding strategies.

- Understand the trust boundaries between layers and elsewhere so that you can validate data that crosses these boundaries. However, determine if validation that occurs in other layers is sufficient. If data is already trusted, you might not need to validate it again.

For more information about validation techniques, see Chapter 17, "Crosscutting Concerns."

Technology Considerations

Take into account the following technology considerations when designing a service:

- Consider using ASMX for simplicity, but only when a Web server running IIS is available.

- Consider using WCF services if you require advanced features such as reliable sessions and transactions, activity tracing, message logging, performance counters, and support for multiple transport protocols.

- If you are using ASP.NET Web services, and you require message-based security and binary data transfer, consider using Web Service Extensions (WSE).

- If you decide to use WCF, consider the following:
  - If you want interoperability with non-WCF or non-Windows clients, consider using HTTP transport based on SOAP specifications.
  - If you want to support clients within an intranet, consider using the TCP protocol and binary message encoding with transport security and Windows authentication.
  - If you want to support WCF clients on the same machine, consider using the named pipes protocol and binary message encoding.
  - Consider defining service contracts that use an explicit message wrapper instead of an implicit one. This allows you to define message contracts as inputs and outputs for your operations, which then allows you to extend the data contracts included in the message contract without affecting the service contract.

Deployment Considerations

Services applications are usually designed using the layered approach, where the service interface, business, and data layers are decoupled from each other. You can use distributed deployment for a services application in exactly the same way as any other application type. Services may be deployed to a client, a single server, or multiple servers across an enterprise. However, when deploying a services application, you must consider the performance and security issues inherent in distributed scenarios, and take into account any limitations imposed by the production environment. Consider the following guidelines when deploying a services application:

- Locate the service layer on the same tier as the business layer if possible to improve application performance.
- When a service is located on the same physical tier as the consumer of the service, consider using named pipes or shared memory for communication.
- If the service is accessed only by other applications within a local network, consider using TCP for communication.
- Configure the service host to use transport layer security only if consumers have direct access to the service and requests do not pass through intermediaries.
- Disable tracing and debug-mode compilation for all services except during development and testing.

For more information on deployment patterns and scenarios, see Chapter 19, "Physical Tiers and Deployment."

Relevant Design Patterns

Key patterns are organized into categories such as Communication, Data Consistency, Message Construction, Message Endpoint, Message Protection, Message Transformation, REST, Service Interface, and SOAP; as shown in the following table. Consider using these patterns when making design decisions for each category.

Category	Relevant patterns
Communication	**Duplex.** Two-way message communication where both the service and the client send messages to each other independently, irrespective of the use of the one-way or Request-Reply pattern. **Fire and Forget.** A one-way message communication mechanism used when no response is expected. **Reliable Sessions.** End to end reliable transfer of messages between a source and a destination, regardless of the number or type of intermediaries that separate the endpoints. **Request Response.** A two-way message communication mechanism where the client expects to receive a response for every message sent.
Data Consistency	**Atomic Transactions.** Transactions that are scoped to a single service operation. **Cross-service Transactions.** Transactions that can span multiple services. **Long-running Transactions.** Transactions that are part of a workflow process.
Message Construction	**Command Message.** A message structure used to support commands. **Document Message.** A structure used to reliably transfer documents or a data structure between applications. **Event Message.** A structure that provides reliable asynchronous event notification between applications. **Request-Reply.** Use separate channels to send the request and the reply.

(continued)

Category	Relevant patterns
Message Endpoint	**Competing Consumer.** Set multiple consumers on a single message queue and have them compete for the right to process the messages, which allows the messaging client to process multiple messages concurrently. **Durable Subscriber.** In a disconnected scenario, messages are saved and then made accessible to the client when it connects to the message channel in order to provide guaranteed delivery. **Idempotent Receiver.** Ensure that a service will handle a message only once. **Message Dispatcher.** A component that sends messages to multiple consumers. **Messaging Gateway.** Encapsulate message-based calls into a single interface in order to separate it from the rest of the application code. **Messaging Mapper.** Transform requests into business objects for incoming messages, and reverse the process to convert business objects into response messages. **Polling Consumer.** A service consumer that checks the channel for messages at regular intervals. **Service Activator.** A service that receives asynchronous requests and invokes operations in business components. **Selective Consumer.** The service consumer uses filters to receive messages that match specific criteria. **Transactional Client.** A client that can implement transactions when interacting with a service.
Message Protection	**Data Confidentiality.** Use message-based encryption to protect sensitive data in a message. **Data Integrity.** Ensure that messages have not been tampered with in transit. **Data Origin Authentication.** Validate the origin of a message as an advanced form of data integrity. **Exception Shielding.** Prevent a service from exposing information about its internal implementation when an exception occurs. **Federation.** An integrated view of information distributed across multiple services and consumers. **Replay Protection.** Enforce message idempotency by preventing an attacker from intercepting a message and executing it multiple times. **Validation.** Check the content and values in messages to protect a service from malformed or malicious content.
Message Transformation	**Canonical Data Mapper.** Use a common data format to perform translations between two disparate data formats. **Claim Check.** Retrieve data from a persistent store when required. **Content Enricher.** A component that enriches messages with missing information obtained from an external data source. **Content Filter.** Remove sensitive data from a message and reduce network traffic by removing unnecessary data from a message. **Envelope Wrapper.** A wrapper for messages that contains header information used, for example, to protect, route, or authenticate a message. **Normalizer.** Convert or transform data into a common interchange format when organizations use different formats.

Category	Relevant patterns
REST	**Behavior.** Applies to resources that carry out operations. These resources generally contain no state of their own, and only support the POST operation. **Container.** Builds on the entity pattern by providing the means to dynamically add and/or update nested resources. **Entity.** Resources that can be read with a GET operation, but can only be changed by PUT and DELETE operations. **Store.** Allows entries to be created and updated with the PUT operation. **Transaction.** Resources that support transactional operations.
Service Interface	**Façade.** Implement a unified interface for a set of operations in order to provide a simplified interface and reduce coupling between systems. **Remote Façade.** Create a high level unified interface to a set of operations or processes in a remote subsystem to make that subsystem easier to use, by providing a course-grained interface over fine-grained operations to minimize calls across the network. **Service Interface.** A programmatic interface that other systems can use to interact with the service.
SOAP	**Data Contract.** A schema that defines data structures passed with a service request. **Fault Contract.** A schema that defines errors or faults that can be returned from a service request. **Service Contract.** A schema that defines operations that the service can perform.

For more information on the Duplex and Request Response patterns, see "*Designing Service Contracts*" at http://msdn.microsoft.com/en-us/library/ms733070.aspx.

For more information on the Request-Reply pattern, see "*Request-Reply*" at http://www.eaipatterns.com/RequestReply.html.

For more information on the Atomic and Cross-service Transaction patterns, see "*WS-* Specifications*" at http://www.ws-standards.com/ws-atomictransaction.asp.

For more information on the Command, Document Message, Event Message, Durable Subscriber, Idempotent Receiver, Polling Consumer, and Transactional Client patterns, see "*Messaging Patterns in Service-Oriented Architecture, Part I*" at http://msdn.microsoft.com/en-us/library/aa480027.aspx.

For more information on the Data Confidentiality and Data Origin Authentication patterns, see "*Chapter 2: Message Protection Patterns*" at http://msdn.microsoft.com/en-us/library/aa480573.aspx.

For more information on the Replay Detection, Exception Shielding, and Validation patterns, see "*Chapter 5: Service Boundary Protection Patterns*" at http://msdn.microsoft.com/en-us/library/aa480597.aspx.

For more information on the Claim Check, Content Enricher, Content Filter, and Envelope Wrapper patterns, see "*Messaging Patterns in Service Oriented Architecture, Part 2*" at http://msdn.microsoft.com/en-us/library/aa480061.aspx.

For more information on the Remote Façade pattern, see "*P of EAA: Remote Façade*" at http://martinfowler.com/eaaCatalog/remoteFacade.html.

For more information on REST patterns such as Behavior, Container, and Entity, see "*REST Patterns*" at http://wiki.developer.mindtouch.com/REST/REST_Patterns.

Additional Resources

To more easily access Web resources, see the online version of the bibliography at: http://www.microsoft.com/architectureguide.

- For more information on distributed systems, see "*Enterprise Solution Patterns Using Microsoft .NET - Distributed Systems Patterns*" at http://msdn.microsoft.com/en-us/library/ms998483.aspx.

- For more information on Enterprise Service Bus scenarios, see "*Microsoft BizTalk ESB Toolkit*" at http://msdn.microsoft.com/en-us/library/dd897973.aspx.

- For more information on integration patterns, see "*Prescriptive Architecture Integration Patterns*" at http://msdn.microsoft.com/en-us/library/ms978729.aspx.

- For more information on service patterns, see "*Enterprise Solution Patterns Using Microsoft .NET - Services Patterns*" at http://msdn.microsoft.com/en-us/library/ms998508.aspx.

- For more information on Web services security patterns, see "*Web Service Security*" at http://msdn.microsoft.com/en-us/library/aa480545.aspx.

26

Designing Hosted and Cloud Services

Overview

This chapter looks at the new and emerging technologies and approaches for building and consuming services and applications that are hosted remotely. These kinds of services and applications are accessed over the Internet and run in what is usually termed *the cloud*, hence the commonly used description *cloud computing*. Cloud solution hosters and vendors will generally provide prebuilt service applications with varying levels of configurability and customization. Alternatively, you may prefer to create your own application in-house and host it either internally on your own systems, or externally in the cloud at a hosting provider.

The concept of building or consuming services and applications that are hosted off-premises is becoming more attractive both to independent software vendors (ISVs) and to enterprises as a way to reduce costs, maximize efficiency, and extend capabilities. This chapter will help you to understand the nature and use of cloud-hosted services and applications. It describes the benefits and the typical design issues, and the constraints and technology considerations often encountered when building and consuming these kinds of applications.

Cloud Computing

In many ways, cloud computing represents the converging evolution of computing infrastructure and application models for building and consuming scalable distributed solutions. As techniques for building these kinds of applications have advanced, so too have the capabilities of the infrastructure on which they run. This synergistic evolution allows the infrastructure to be provisioned and maintained largely independently of the applications that it hosts. This in turn allows applications to take advantage of supporting infrastructure services and capabilities while they focus on their specific business functionality.

Many organizations have been able to realize the joint benefits of scalable application models and supporting infrastructure internally on-premises in their own data centers. However, it is the ability to leverage an off-premises outsourced application hosting infrastructure that is behind much of the excitement around cloud computing. The infrastructure provider focuses on hardware, networking, power, cooling, and the operating environment that supports application manageability, reliability, and scalability; leaving the organization free to focus on their application's business functionality. This provides many benefits in terms of reduced capital outlay and operating costs; and increased capacity, scalability and availability.

To leverage these benefits, cloud-hosted applications typically must be architected to follow a specific application model. This allows the cloud-hosting provider to generalize and optimize their operating environment support for application manageability, reliability, or scalability.

Different cloud-hosting providers have different application model requirements. Some adopt a virtual machine approach, where the application is developed and packaged along with its operating system image and the dependent runtime frameworks. Others utilize an application model that provides higher level abstractions for data access and storage (as described later in this chapter), and for computation and communication. Still others provide higher level application models based on highly configurable applications that focus on specific vertical application functionality, such as Enterprise Resource Planning (ERP) or Customer Relationship Management (CRM). Each of these approaches provides distinct advantages and disadvantages.

Furthermore, some off-premises hosted applications are self-contained and designed for users who interact with the application through a dedicated UI. Some of these applications are service-enabled, and provide both a UI and expose their functionality through an API (often exposed through standards such as REST or SOAP) so that they can be integrated into other applications, which themselves can be hosted either on-premises or off-premises. Some off-premises hosted services are specifically designed to provide functionality for integration into other applications, and provide no UI at all.

Cloud-based services generally fall into categories such as storage/compute, business services, and retail/wholesale services. Some common examples of these remote services are:

- **Business services** such as stocks and shares information, invoicing and payment systems, data interchange facilities, merchant services, and business information portals.
- **Retail/wholesale services** such as catalogues, stock query and ordering systems, weather and traffic information, mapping services, and shopping portals.
- **Storage/compute services** such as data storage and processing, data backup, source control systems, and technical or scientific processing services.

These remote services can be consumed by software that runs on-premises, in an organization's data center or on a user's machine, which may be a desktop computer or any other Internet-enabled device. This typically involves a mix of technologies and techniques that are referred to as Software plus Services (S+S). S+S refers to an approach to application development that combines hosted services with locally executed software. The combination of the remote services and the software running locally, with rich seamlessly integrated interfaces and user experience, can provide a more comprehensive and efficient solution than traditional on-premises silo applications. S+S is an evolution of several other technologies including Service Oriented Architecture (SOA), Software as a Service (SaaS), Platform as a Service (PaaS), and Web 2.0 community-oriented architectural approaches.

Note: Cloud computing is an emerging area. This chapter outlines some of the benefits of cloud computing and the high level architectural considerations that you must take into account when building or consuming cloud-hosted applications and services. It is likely that frameworks, tools, and hosting environment improvements will become increasingly available in the near future, which will help to addresses these challenges.

Common Vocabulary for Hosted and Cloud Services

Some of the terms commonly encountered in this chapter and in cloud and hosted service scenarios are the following:

- **Building block service.** A service designed to be consumed by or integrated with other applications or services. An example is a storage service or a hosted Security Token Service (STS) such as the Access Control Service in the Azure Services Platform.

- **Cloud-hosting environment.** An environment that provides a core runtime for hosting applications; and, optionally, building block services, business services, social network services, and hosting services such as metering, billing, and management.

- **Home-built application.** An application that you create in-house, usually specifically targeted at some task, scenario, or process you require; it will often address a need that cannot be sourced from a third party.

- **Hosted application.** An application (packaged or home-built) hosted as a service. It may be hosted internally on your own system, or hosted externally by a partner or hoster.

- **Packaged application.** An application created by a third party or vendor that may provide only limited customization capabilities based on configuration or plug-ins.

- **Platform as a Service (PaaS).** A core hosting operating system, and optional plug-in building block services, that allow you to run your own applications or third-party applications obtained from vendors, in a remote cloud hosting environment.

- **Software as a Service (SaaS).** Applications that perform comprehensive business tasks, or accomplish business services, and allow you to consume them as services with no internal application requirements other than composition and UI.

Benefits of Cloud Applications

Cloud-hosted applications and services may be very beneficial to ISVs, and to service delivery or hosting companies that build, host and deliver services. They also offer benefits to large enterprises that generally consume hosted and cloud-based solutions.

Benefits for ISVs and Service Hosts

The key advantages for ISVs and service hosting companies building and offering cloud-based solutions are the following:

- **Architectural Flexibility.** Vendors can offer their customers a range of deployment options, including hosting for the services they require, and allow users to choose from a range of prebuilt features or choose which features of the application they will implement themselves. This can reduce the architectural liabilities for end users who are developing services.

- **Rich User Experience.** ISVs and service providers can offer richer experiences to their customers by leveraging existing specialized services (such as Virtual Earth). Hosters can combine their offerings with other cloud services obtained elsewhere to offer additional value propositions, and make it easier for end users to integrate services.

- **Ubiquitous Access.** Services in the cloud persist user data and state, and resynchronize when the user reconnects from any location. This supports both offline and occasionally connected scenarios, which is especially useful for mobile devices where a constant connection or bandwidth cannot be guaranteed.

ISVs and service hosts may also consider entering the market for commercial reasons to take advantage of monetization opportunities. The following are some examples:

- Vendors may wish to take advantage of an untapped market opportunity by offering a product that is not currently or easily available elsewhere, or use the cloud to offer lower end versions of their products to protect a high end franchise.

- Startup companies may use the cloud-hosted approach to minimize initial capital expenditure, and to take advantage of properties of the cloud such as elasticity (the capability to grow as required without high initial cost commitment).

- Vendors and users can create applications that generate income more quickly by taking advantage of ancillary services that are already available. For example, they can take advantage of payment and accounting systems in the cloud. Users can even build virtual stores without requiring large investments in IT equipment and networking capabilities.

Benefits for Enterprise Service Consumers

The key advantages for enterprises that consume cloud-based solutions are the following:

- **Architectural Flexibility.** In-house developers can create complete solutions that compose services in the cloud with local application code and their own services. IT departments can choose which features of the application they will implement themselves, and buy in other services that they require.

- **Cost and Time Savings.** IT departments can select the best cloud-based service for each task, and combine them to expose fully functional applications with shorter development times, and at a reduced cost. In addition, the reduction in the requirements for in-house IT infrastructure simplifies management, security, and maintenance costs.

- **Economies of Scale.** Companies can leverage economies of scale for industry average capabilities, and focus on their core activities. The economies of scale available from hosted applications arise from a range of factors, including reduced in-house infrastructure costs to better utilization of hardware that offers opportunities for reduced running costs. However, the gains in economies of scale must be balanced with the loss of control inherent with moving from on-premises to fully hosted applications.

- **Offline Capability.** The cloud can act as hub for roaming users. User data and state can be stored in the cloud and resynchronized when the user reconnects. Users can move between desktop and mobile clients seamlessly with fewer network configurations.

Design Issues

Several common issues are of concern to both ISVs and enterprise customers. While they cover a range of different aspects of hosted and cloud-based scenarios, these issues can be categorized into specific areas. Consider the following as your develop your strategy for hosted and cloud-based services:

- Data Isolation and Sharing
- Data Security
- Data Storage and Extensibility
- Identity Management
- Multi-tenancy
- On-premises or Off-premises, Build or Buy
- Performance
- Service Composition
- Service Integration
- Service Management

Data Isolation and Sharing

Hosters can implement isolation and sharing for databases and for database schemas. There are three basic models:

- **Separate Databases.** Each tenant has a separate database containing their own data schemas. This has the advantage of being easy to implement, but the number of tenants per database server might be relatively low, with subsequent loss of efficiency, and the infrastructure cost of providing services can rise rapidly. It is most useful when tenants have specific data isolation or security requirements for which you can charge a supplement.

- **Shared Databases, Separate Schemas.** All tenants use the same database, but have separate sets of predefined fields available. This approach is also easy to implement, maximizes the number of tenants per database server, and improves database efficiency. However, it usually results in sparsely populated tables in the database. It is most useful when storing data for different tenants in the same tables (commingling) is acceptable in terms of security and isolation, and when you can anticipate the predefined custom fields that will be required.

- **Shared Databases, Shared Schema.** All tenants use the same database and special techniques are used to store data extensions. This approach has the advantage that the number of custom fields you can offer is practically unlimited. However, indexing, searching, querying, and updating processes are more complex. It is most useful when storing data for different tenants in the same tables (commingling) is acceptable in terms of security and isolation but it is difficult to predict the range of predefined custom fields that will be required.

The following table illustrates the benefits and liabilities for the three isolation and sharing models described above. Rows nearer the top of the table imply higher cost and lower development and operational effort. Rows nearer the bottom of the table imply lower cost and higher development and operational effort.

	Benefits	Liabilities
Separate Databases	Easy to implement. Easy to move the application from on-premises to a hosted environment. Simpler back up, restore, and monitoring as most existing tools operate at a database level. High data isolation.	Common tables in the domain model are duplicated across tenant databases. Higher hardware costs.
Shared Database, Separate Schemas	Lower memory consumption. Higher density of tenants per server. Common tables are shared across tenants. Requires a data access component that intercepts table names. Requires tenant-level authorization to access data.	Lower isolation. Backup and restore is a challenge that requires a custom solution. Monitoring tenant activity is a challenge.
Shared Database, Shared Schemas	Least memory consumption (fewer database objects). Highest density of tenants per server.	Least isolation—requires additional development effort to ensure high isolation. Tenant's data is shared amongst tenants. Back up and restore is a challenge that requires a custom solution. Monitoring tenant activity is a challenge.

Applications optimized for a shared database approach may be more complex and involve higher development cost and effort. However, they will generally support more tenants per server, and may have lower operational costs. Applications optimized for a shared schema approach are simpler, and will generally reduce operational costs in the long term, though this reduction is likely to be less than the shared database approach.

If you must create applications quickly, consider the Separate Databases approach by configuring each tenant with their own database. Using this approach no special design is required. Also, consider this approach if your individual tenants have particularly high data security requirements, or will store very large volumes of data, or have a very large number of concurrent end users. The Separate Databases approach is also appropriate if you require the application to be easy to move from on-premises to hosted, or from hosted to on-premises, and it can allow you to more easily scale out if the need arises.

Higher isolation is also useful if you expect to offer per tenant value-added services, where you should consider the Separate Databases or the Shared Database, Separate Schemas approach. However, if you expect to have a very large number of tenants, each with relatively small amount of data, consider a less isolated approach such as Shared Database, Separate Schemas or Shared Database, Shared Schemas.

Data Security

Cloud-hosted applications must implement strong security, using multiple defense levels that complement one another to provide data protection in different ways, under different circumstances, and against both internal and external threats. When planning a security strategy, consider the following guidelines:

- **Filtering.** Use an intermediate layer between a tenant and a data source that acts as a sieve so that it appears to the tenant that theirs is the only data in the database. This is especially important if you use a shared database instance for all of your tenants.
- **Permissions.** Use access control lists (ACLs) to determine who can access data in the application, and what they can do with it.
- **Encryption.** Obscure every tenant's critical data so that it will remain unreadable to unauthorized parties, even if they manage to access it.

Data Security Patterns

Depending on the multi-tenant model you adopt, consider the following security patterns:

- **Trusted Database Connections** (applies to all three multi-tenant models). The application always connects to the database using its own application process identity, independent of the identity of the user, and the server grants the application access to the database objects that it can read or manipulate. Additional security must be implemented within the application itself to prevent individual end users from accessing any database objects that should not be exposed to them. Each tenant (organization) that uses the application has multiple sets of credentials associated with their tenant account, and must grant their end users access to the application using these credentials. These end users access the application using their individual credentials associated with the tenant account, but the application accesses the database using the single set of credentials associated with that application. This means that a single database access account is required for each application (one for each tenant). Alternatively, you can use an STS to obtain encrypted login credentials for the tenant irrespective of the individual user, and use security code in the application to control which data individual users can access.
- **Secure Database Tables** (applies to the Separate Database model and the Shared Database, Separate Schema model). Grant a tenant user account access to a table or other database object. In the Separate Database model, restrict access on a database-wide level to the tenant associated with that database. In the Shared Database, Separate Schema model, restrict access on a per table basis to the tenant associated with specific tables.
- **Tenant Data Encryption** (applies to all three multi-tenant models). Secure the data using symmetric encryption to protect it, and secure the tenant's private key using asymmetric (public/private key pair) encryption. Use impersonation to access the database using the tenant's security context, and use the tenant's

private key to decrypt the data in the database so that it can be used. The disadvantage is that you cannot index encrypted columns, which means that there is a tradeoff between data security and performance. Try to avoid using index fields that contain sensitive data.

- **Tenant Data Filter** (applies to the Shared Database\Shared Schema model). Use SQL views to select subsets of data from tables based on the tenant or user ID, or the tenant account's security identifier. Grant tenants access to only their views, and not to the underlying tables. This prevents users from seeing or accessing any rows belonging to other tenants or users in the shared tables.

Data Storage and Extensibility

Hosted data may be stored in variety of ways. Two different approaches are emerging for implementing data storage in hosted applications: hosted relational database management systems (RDBMS) and nonrelational cloud-based storage. Relational database systems provide storage for structured data, and are more suited to transactional systems or applications that are I/O intensive; they also typically provide lower latency and advanced query capabilities. In contrast, cloud storage refers to any type of data storage that resides in the cloud; including services that provide database-like functionality, unstructured data services (for example, file storage for digital media), data synchronization services, and network-attached storage (NAS) services. Data services are often consumed in a pay as you go model, or in this case a pay per GB model (including both stored and transferred data).

Cloud storage offers a number of benefits, such as the ability to store and retrieve large amounts of data in any location at any time. Data storage services are fast, inexpensive, and almost infinitely scalable; however, reliability can be an issue as even the best services do sometimes fail. Applications that are sensitive to high latency might also be affected as each interaction with the storage service requires network transversal. Finally, transaction support can be an issue with cloud-based storage systems.These systems generally focus heavily on partitioning and availability, and consistency cannot always be guaranteed.

Microsoft Azure storage (in an early preview release at time of writing) comprises a number of services that span different storage needs, which you can access using a REST API:

- **Table Storage Services** provide structured storage in the form of tables, but these tables have no defined schema; instead, they contain entities, each of which holds a number of properties. Popular APIs such as LINQ can be used over any combination of properties. Table Storage Services focuses on providing massively scalable tables at a very low cost. However, it is not a relational database and lacks many of the features you would expect to find in an RDBMS such as joins and foreign keys across multiple tables.

- **Blob Storage Services** offers storage for binary data stored in user-defined containers, which organize sets of blobs within a storage account.

- **Queue Services** store messages that may be read using queuing semantics by any client that has access to the storage account.

A key challenge to solve when using an RDBMS is schema extensibility. This is the ability to extend a table with custom fields without recompiling or rebuilding the application. There are four approaches to extending the schemas at runtime:

- **Fixed Columns.** This pattern models the extension fields as a set of fixed named columns for each extensible entity (each table). The number of fixed columns will depend on the nature of the entity and its usage pattern. It requires a data access layer that encapsulates and abstracts the named fixed columns and metadata tables. Consider the following factors for the Fixed Columns approach:

  - Filtering based on extensible columns is a challenge due to the predefined data types. For example, using variable length data types such as varchar for all the extensible columns limits the capability to filter numerically using the <, >, and = operators. Possible solutions are to allocate a fixed number of fields of each common data type, or to allow the user to mark columns as searchable and use a separate table to store data type specific fields.

  - While this is one of the fastest and more scalable approaches to extensibility, it generally requires a solution for indexed columns that are not string-based.

  - The way that the database treats null values may result in sparse data distribution and wasted space. If a tenant extends only one field, while another extends 20 fields, the database and pages in memory will grow. Microsoft SQL Server 2008 provides a modifier for columns named SPARSE that helps to mitigate this issue.

- **Custom Schemas.** This pattern is used in conjunction with the Separate Schemas multi-tenancy pattern. Each schema belongs to a tenant, and contains a different set of extensible strongly typed columns. Consider the following factors for the Custom Schemas approach:

  - It requires encapsulation and abstraction of the data access layer, and a query processor; though O/RM Frameworks such as Microsoft Entity Framework (EF) or the open source NHibernate framework can assist in implementation. For more information, see Additional Resources at the end of this chapter.

  - Each tenant has their own table, and the table schema will change every time they add or remove a field. The queries will work against the real data type (the columns are not all string types). However, rolling up database schema updates will be non-trivial due to excessive duplication between the tenants' shared fields (as opposed to the Fixed Columns approach, where one or more tables exist for all tenants).

  - This approach is faster than the Fixed Columns pattern when filtering based on extended columns because it uses the primitive data types.

- **Name Value Extension Table.** This pattern allows customers to extend the data model arbitrarily (with an unlimited number of columns), storing custom data in a separate table and using metadata to define labels and data types for each tenant's custom fields. Consider the following factors for the Name Value Extension Table approach:

  - It adds a level of complexity for database functions, such as indexing, querying, and updating records. For example, retrieving data requires multiple joins, and filtering and grouping is a challenge.

  - There is only a single database to manage. However, if a growing user base causes the database to grow, it could be scaled horizontally with tenant partitioning to use separate databases.

  - This approach will be slower than the other approaches because data retrieval requires multiple joins.

- **XML Columns.** This pattern allows customers to extend the data model arbitrarily with an unlimited number of extensions by storing the extension data in an XML column. Consider the following factors for the XML Columns approach:

  - While this approach may seem to be a natural choice for extensibility, it has lower scalability (the capability to add more records) and lower performance (query response time) compared to other approaches.

  - While the use of XML columns in the database leads to relatively simple implementations, ISVs and developers will require additional skills to manipulate XML in the database.

  - It is possible to define indexes for XML columns, but this adds additional complexity and requires extra storage space.

Identity Management

All applications and services must manage user identity. This is particularly important in hosted and cloud-based scenarios that can potentially serve a very large number of customers, and each of these customers may have their own identity framework. A common approach is for the hoster to delegate the responsibility for managing its own user accounts to each customer. The ideal is a solution that takes advantage of the customer's existing on-premises or federated directory service to enable single sign on (SSO) across their local and all external hosted services. This reduces the development effort of building individual and separate identity management systems. Customers can configure access to the application using familiar tools, and SSO allows users to access the application or service using their existing credentials.

To enable such a scenario, you must adopt a solution based on industry standards that interoperate across platforms and organizational boundaries. In general, you should consider a claims-based identity model based on a federated identity service, as illustrated in Figure 1. This helps to decouple applications and services from the authentication mechanism.

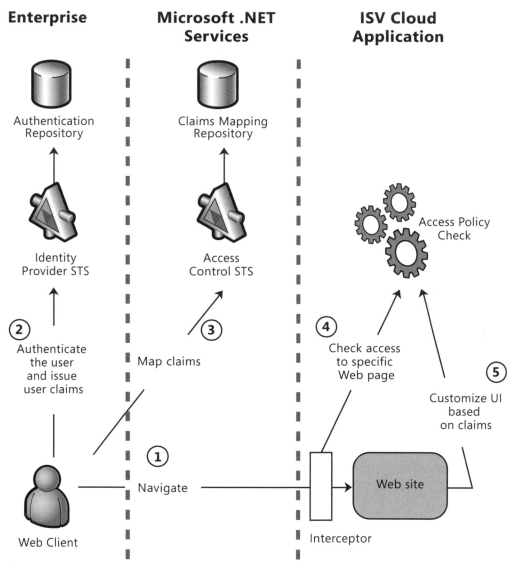

Enterprise

Microsoft .NET Services

ISV Cloud Application

Authentication Repository

Identity Provider STS

(2) Authenticate the user and issue user claims

Web Client

Claims Mapping Repository

Access Control STS

(3) Map claims

(1) Navigate

Access Policy Check

(4) Check access to specific Web page

(5) Customize UI based on claims

Interceptor

Web site

Figure 1

Claims-based identity model based on a federated identity service

The customer's existing identity system sends a cryptographically signed security token that contains a set of claims about each user with every request they make to an application. Hosting companies that trust the customer's identity system can design applications and services to focus just on authorizing relevant claims. The customer identity system must implement an STS that authenticates users, creates and signs security tokens using a standard format, and exposes a service to issue these tokens based on industry standards such as WS-Trust and WS-Federation. The Microsoft Geneva Framework and Geneva Server provide much of the infrastructure required to implement these requirements. When implementing a claims-based identity model, consider the following issues:

- If there is a suitable identity store available, consider using this to provide a single sign on experience across local applications, hosted Web applications, and other hosted services.

- For small or consumer-focused applications where there is no existing identity store available, consider using a service such as .NET Services Access Control federating against Windows Live, or an online solution from a third party.

- You may need to perform transformations on claims generated from a local STS to match the requirements of the hoster. Alternatively, hosters may need to implement transformation systems for different customer STS mechanisms. Consider using the .NET Access Control Service to provide a transformation layer or use the Geneva Framework for implementing your own. For more information about the Geneva Framework, see http://msdn.microsoft.com/en-us/security/aa570351.aspx.

- There may be minor differences in the way that standards-based products from different vendors are implemented. Compatibility and interoperability issues may arise if these products do not strictly adhere to the complex standards, or they provide a slightly different implementation.

- If you decide to design your own STS, ensure that it is secure against attack. As it contains all of the authentication information, vulnerabilities could leave all applications open to exploit. Also, ensure that your STS implementation is robust and reliable, and can serve all foreseeable volumes of requests. Failure of the STS will prevent users accessing all of the applications that depend it.

Multi-tenancy

Individual tenants share the use of the hoster's hardware and infrastructure, as well as sharing databases and database systems (each tenant is an organization that may each have more than one user). Service suppliers must provide a platform with appropriate capacity and performance for hosted services. They must also consider how to keep the cost structure under control, and how they will provide customization through configuration. There are four common stages in moving towards an efficient multi-tenancy architecture with user-enabled configuration. The following sections describe these stages.

- **Custom.** Each customer runs a separate copy of the software assigned only to that customer, and the only way to support multiple customers is to serve them with different copies of the software. Furthermore, because little is done to allow customization through configuration, each copy includes specific customer customizations in the form of custom extension code, custom processes, and/or custom data extensions. Although the software is, technically, delivered as a service (it does not run on the customer's premises), economy of scale cannot be achieved because each customer runs a different instance of the software. Although this could be a useful starting point to validate the business model, it must be avoided once the volume of customers increases. It is impractical to manage thousands of customers using this model.

- **Configurable.** The software can be tailored for each tenant through configuration and by avoiding the use of custom code. All the tenants run the same code; however, the architecture is still not multi-tenant and each customer runs their own copy of the code, even though the copies are identical. The separation can be either virtual (virtual machines on a same server) or physical (running on separate machines). Although this model is a considerable improvement over the custom model described above, the architecture still allows customization through configuration, and the computing power is not shared among the instances. Therefore, the provider cannot achieve economy of scale.

- **Multi-tenant.** The UI can be customizable per tenant, as can the business rules and the data model. The customization per tenant is entirely through configuration using a self service tool, which removes the requirement for the service provider to perform configuration. This level is almost the SaaS perfect case; the exception is any capacity to scale out. At this level, data partitioning means that growth can only be achieved by scaling up.

- **Scalable.** The architecture supports multi-tenancy and configuration, plus the capability to scale out the application. New instances of the software can be transparently added to the instance pool to dynamically support the increasing load. Appropriate data partitioning, stateless component design, and shared metadata access are part of the design. At this level, a Tenant Load Balancer (implemented using a *round robin* or a rule based mechanism) is introduced, maximizing the utilization of hosting resources such as CPU and storage. This means that the total load is distributed across the entire available infrastructure. The data is also reorganized periodically in order to average the data load per instance. The architecture is scalable, multi-tenant, and customizable through configuration.

On-premises or Off-premises, Build or Buy

Cloud-hosted applications allow ISVs and hosters to realize economies of scale; and, in a competitive market, they will tend to pass these saving on to enterprise customers. However, the move to off-premises and hosted scenarios means that enterprises must accept some loss of control of applications, data, and service levels. Enterprises must consider the tradeoffs for moving to such services, in addition to deciding whether to build their own applications or buy them from a third party. The following table illustrates the differences between the build and buy scenarios for hosted applications.

	On-premises	**At Hoster**	**Cloud Service**
Build	An application that is developed in-house and runs in your data center.	An application that is developed in-house and runs at a hosting company.	A vendor-hosted development and runtime environment.
Buy	A packaged application that is bought off the shelf and runs in your data center.	A packaged application that is bought off the shelf and runs at a hosting company.	A hosted application that is bought from a vendor, who also hosts the application.

Gains from economies of scale must be balanced with the reduction in control inherent with moving from on-premises to fully hosted applications. Consider the following guidelines when deciding whether to move to a cloud-based solution, what type of application development approach to follow, and where to host your application:

- Consider **on-premises** hosting if you require full control of your application and data, you have security requirements that prevent you from using hosted services, or laws or national policies prohibit you from using hosted services. When hosting applications internally on your own infrastructure, you may:

  - Choose to develop an in-house application when you cannot source a suitable prebuilt application, or when you want to retain full control of the application feature set.

  - Choose a prebuilt packaged application when one is available that is cost effective and meets all of your requirements.

- Consider **at hoster** hosting if you are considering optimizing your operations but still want to retain control of the software. For example, you might decide to deploy a heavily customized Enterprise Resource Planning (ERP) package at a hoster and offload to them the management of power, hardware, network, and the operating system. Typically, a hoster will accommodate very specific requirements of your organization; for example, setting up a Virtual Private Network (VPN), adding specialized hardware, and more. When hosting applications at an external hosting company, you may:
  - Choose one of the hoster's prebuilt packaged applications if it can meet your requirements. The availability of prebuilt packaged applications may influence your choice of hoster.
  - Choose a home-built application where you cannot locate a hoster that offers a suitable prebuilt application. In this case, you must factor in the cost and time required to develop your own application.
- Consider the **cloud service** (vendor-hosted) approach if you are buying an SaaS application from a hoster or an ISV; you can provide a specification of the required application; you do not have the resources, time, or in-house skills to build the application; or you require an existing standard or customized application at short notice. Another reason is to take advantage of the intrinsic properties of cloud based building block services (such as elasticity) if you are building an application yourself. When purchasing cloud application services from a vendor:
  - Choose a prebuilt packaged application created by a vendor if it can meet your short term and long term requirements. This is the SaaS approach.
  - Choose a vendor-supplied hosting platform to run your home-built application where you cannot source a suitable prebuilt application. You must factor in the cost and time required to develop your own application. This is the PaaS approach.

Performance

Cloud-hosted applications must be scalable to support increasing numbers of services, and increasing load for each service and tenant. When designing services, consider the following guidelines for scaling applications:

- Design services and components to be stateless where possible. This minimizes memory usage for the service, and improves the opportunity to scale out and load balance servers.
- Use asynchronous input and output calls, which allow the applications to do useful work while waiting for I/O to complete.

- Investigate the capabilities of the hosting platform that can improve performance. For example, in Microsoft Azure, use queues to manage requests and worker processes to carry out background processing.
- Use resource pooling for threads, network, and database connections.
- Maximize concurrency by using locking only where absolutely necessary.

When scaling data storage and applications, consider the following guidelines:

- When scaling the data partition, divide subscriber data into smaller partitions to meet performance goals. Use schemes such as Hashing (to subdivide content) and Temporal (based on the time or date range in which the data is valid).
- Consider implementing dynamic repartitioning to repartition the data automatically when the database size reaches a specific maximum size.
- When scaling data storage and applications investigate standard patterns, and the specific techniques and implementations provided by the hosting platform—some examples are data partitioning, load balancing, failover, and geographical distribution.

Service Composition

Users in enterprise-level organizations require access to many different document repositories, types of data, sources of information, and applications that perform specific functions. Traditionally, users interacted directly with each store or application, often using specific isolated applications. However, over time, enterprises have attempted to consolidate systems; often using intranet Web portals or façade-style applications that connect to the appropriate downstream applications.

With the advent of services and SOA applications, IT departments can expose applications and data as services, either hosted in-house or bought in as SaaS. The service portfolios can still expose the combination of traditional local applications, internally hosted services, and remote services through portals, which hide the user from the implementations and allow IT departments to adapt the ranges of services quickly and easily. However, S+S and SaaS designs and technologies allow IT departments and enterprise customers to integrate services fully. Service integration can help to achieve the goal of a *many to one* model where all applications and services are available to the user through a composition architecture that effectively exposes them as a single application, as shown in Figure 2. A service integration mechanism combines the groups of applications in the portfolios and exposes them though a rich client that can interact with any service or application.

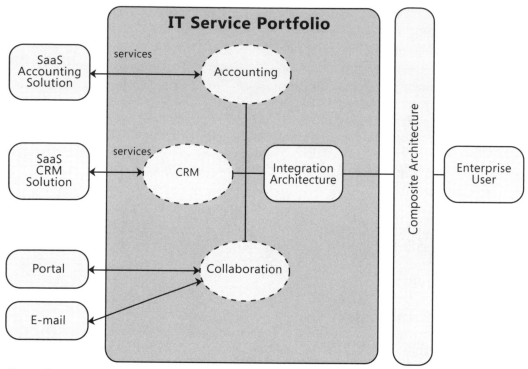

Figure 2
A service integration mechanism can compose multiple services into a single interface

Enterprise consumers of cloud-hosted services will usually need to create composition systems that use the raw services exposed by hosters, and expose them through in-house portals and portfolios. Effective consumer composition architecture can integrate information from many sources for end users; which reduces redundant data entry, enhances human collaboration, and heightens awareness of outstanding tasks and their status. It also improves the visibility of interrelated business information and help users to make informed business decisions. Composition of a unified solution that uses cloud-hosted services usually incorporates the following three layers:

- **Input source layer.** The input sources include cloud-hosted services, internal applications, internal databases, Web services, flat files, and more. Internal resources may be exposed though IT service portfolios.

- **Composition layer.** This is where the raw data is aggregated and provided to the user in a new, unified form. Its function is to transform data into business information and process intelligence. This layer will usually incorporate the following:
  - Components that manage access, data, workflow, and rules.
  - Service agents that negotiate and exchange messages with applications, databases, Web services, and other resources.

- Identity management components that authenticate and authorize users, and manage credentials for Web service communication.
- Data aggregation components that transform data to match the application entity model.
- **User-centric layer.** This layer presents the composite data to the user in a central, integrated, task-focused user interface.

Consuming cloud-hosted services as part of a composite user interface usually requires workflow or step-by-step processes to achieve integration of external and internal services. A common solution is an integration broker that consists of a modularized pluggable pipeline and associated metadata services to control message movement and routing. Typical operations in an integration broker pipeline include the following:

- **Security.** A security module authenticates the data source or digital signature, decrypts the data, and examines it for security risks such as viruses. Security operations can be coordinated with existing security policies to control access.
- **Validation.** A validation module compares the data to relevant schemas and rejects non-conforming data.
- **Transformation.** A transformation module converts the data to the correct format.
- **Synchronization workflow.** A synchronization module uses workflows and rules to determine the logical destinations and order for propagating messages to the appropriate destinations. It can also manage workflow process transactions to guarantee data consistency.
- **Routing.** A routing module uses routing rules that define the physical destinations, and transmits the data messages to the specific target. It may use information in the message to determine destinations based on the content.

Service Integration

Cloud-hosted solutions can help to mitigate some of the challenges encountered with traditional software, but add new and different challenges for the consumer of these services. Consider the following the challenges when moving to hosted cloud services and applications:

- **Identity Management.** Enterprise procedures for adding, updating, and removing users must be extended to the remote services. If the external service depends on user identity, which is very likely for SaaS and for S+S, the provisioning and deprovisioning processes must be extended. In addition, translation of in-house user identity into specific roles may be required, possibly through a federated service, to minimize the migration or duplication of individual user identities at the remote service host. Enterprise user account policies such as password complexity and account lockouts must also be compatible with those of the remote service supplier. If no SSO facility is available, there can be increased liabilities, maintenance costs, and operational inefficiencies.

- **Data.** Requirements of data operations, such as Extract, Transform, and Load (ETL) and data integration, must be analyzed for compatibility with service capabilities. Hosted services may not support complex data storage patterns, which may affect the design of data entities and application architecture. In addition, data may need to be protected more securely to counterbalance the lack of physical security available when hosting in-house. However, applications can store sensitive or private data locally, and use the cloud services only for nonsensitive data. You must also plan for how you will migrate data to the service provider, and how you will migrate it away and to a different provider should the need arise.

- **Operations.** In-house integration services and client applications may not be compatible with services exposed by the service supplier, even when using industry standard protocols. You must also ensure that the service provider can generate appropriate reporting information, and determine how you will integrate this with your own management and reporting systems. In terms of service levels, Service Level Agreements (SLAs) may require revision to ensure that they can still be met when depending on the service provider for escalated support. Enterprises must also be prepared to implement help desk facilities that act as the first contact point for users, and define procedures for escalating issues with the service provider.

- **Security.** Enterprise privacy policies must be compatible with those of the service provider, and rules for actions that users can execute, such as limits on transaction size and other business rules, must be maintained—even if these are not part of the remote service capabilities. This may make the service integration infrastructure more complex. Procedures and policies for maintaining the security and integrity of data in the event of service or interconnectivity failure will also be required. Authentication, encryption, and the use of digital signatures will require the purchase of certificates from certified providers, and may require implementation of a Public Key Infrastructure (PKI). In addition, integration may require changes to firewall rules, and updates to firewall hardware and software may need to be required to provide filtering for application data and XML Schema validation.

- **Connectivity.** Some types of cloud-based applications rely on good quality broadband Internet connections to function well. Examples are online transaction processing and real time services such as voice over IP (VoIP) and Microsoft Office Communications Server. In some areas and some countries, this may not be available. In addition, services that require large data transfers such as backup services and file delivery services will generally run more slowly over an Internet connection compared to a local or in-house implementation, which may be an issue. However, messaging and other similar services may not be as dependent on connection bandwidth or severely affected by occasional loss of connectivity.

- **Service Level Agreements.** Skills and expertise will be required to assess suppliers more comprehensively, and make choices regarding service acquisition and contracts. SLAs may also require revision to ensure that they can still be met when depending on the services hosted by a remote provider.

- **Compliance and Legal Obligations.** Compliance with legal and corporate directives may be affected by the performance of the service supplier, or these compliance directives and legal obligations may conflict if the service provider is located in another country or region. There may also be costs associated with obtaining compliance reports from the service supplier. Local laws and policies may prevent some types of applications, such as banking applications, from running in hosted scenarios.

Service Management

Cloud service providers face certain challenges when hosting and offering services that run in the cloud, specifically around service delivery and support. Some ISVs may build applications that are hosted elsewhere while others may build and host their applications themselves, and there are several challenges that you must consider when contemplating developing hosted services. Some will apply to ISVs that host their own services, while others apply only to hosting companies. The following sections summarize these challenges:

- **Service Level Management.** Enterprise users may each demand variations to the hoster's standard SLAs, with can make it difficult to meet all demands for all customers. Customers may choose a cloud-hosted solution as a way of increasing availability and performance, and so expectations may generally be higher than for an in-house application. Managing and satisfying these expectations could be a complex task because it usually demands managing dependencies (such as network and power providers) and different demands from geographically distributed customers. Maintenance and service downtime should also be carefully planned when hosting services for many different enterprises, especially if they are located in different time zones or have usage that peaks at different times during the day or week.

- **Capacity and Continuity Management.** Service providers will not have the same insight into upcoming changes to customer's capacity requirements as in-house teams will, which may result in unexpected peaks in usage that require extra capacity to be available. Advance planning is difficult as each customer's growth and usage patterns will differ with little or no advance warning. Implementing and adapting services that match customer requirements is more difficult when there are many customers to satisfy. Short term decisions on capacity are likely to prove more expensive in the long run than a staged capacity growth plan, but long term planning without growth estimates from consumers is more difficult.

- **Customer Support.** Help desk staff may need to be aware of and take into account the requirements and usage scenarios of customers to offer optimum support. With many customers for each service, failures or issues with that service will prompt large volumes of calls that may overload the help desk. Help desk staff may need to be able to quantify incurred costs on a per user basis, especially for models where support is a chargeable extra. Ideally, the hosted cloud solution should offer proactive support where the provider will be made aware of issues by monitoring the health of the solution and proactively initiate resolution of the problem with the customer. Self-service support mechanisms may also be utilized to provide the customer with a streamlined, dedicated issue tracking system.

Relevant Design Patterns

Key patterns are organized into categories such as Data Availability, Data Transfer, Data Transformation, Integration and Composition, Performance and Reliability, and User Experience; as shown in the following table. Consider using these patterns when making design decisions for each category.

Category	Relevant patterns
Data Availability	**Polling.** One source queries the other for changes, typically at regular intervals. **Push.** A source with changed data communicates changes to the data sink every time data in a data source changes, or only at regular intervals. **Publish/Subscribe.** A hybrid approach that combines aspects of both polling and pushing. When a change is made to a data source, it publishes a change notification event, to which the data sink can subscribe.
Data Transfer	**Asynchronous Data Transfer.** A message-based method where the sender and receiver exchange data without waiting for a response. **Synchronous Data Transfer.** An interface-based method where the sender and receiver exchange data in real time.
Data Transformation	**Shared Database.** All applications that you are integrating read data directly from the same database. **Maintain Data Copies.** Maintain copies of the application's database so that other applications can read the data (and potentially update it). **File Transfer.** Make the data available by transporting a file that is an extract from the application's database so that other applications can load the data from the files.
Integration and Composition	**Broker.** Hide the implementation details of remote service invocation by encapsulating them into a layer other than the business component itself. **Composition.** Combine multiple services, applications, or documents into an integrated interface while performing security, validation, transformation, and related tasks on each data source. **Portal Integration.** Create a portal application that displays the information retrieved from multiple applications within a unified UI. The user can then perform the required tasks based on the information displayed in this portal.

Performance and Reliability	**Server Clustering.** Design your application infrastructure so that your servers appear to users and applications as virtual unified computing resources to enhance availability, scalability, or both. **Load-Balanced Cluster.** Install your service or application onto multiple servers that are configured to share the workload. The load-balanced hosts concurrently respond to different client requests, even multiple requests from the same client. **Failover Cluster.** Install your application or service on multiple servers that are configured to take over for one another when a failure occurs. Each server in the cluster has at least one other server in the cluster identified as its standby server.
User Experience	**Universal Web.** Maximum reach combined with deployment simplicity, and works on Web browsers with the commonly installed extensions. **Experience First.** Maximize the quality of the user experience by taking advantage of optimized computer and device capabilities.

Additional Resources

To more easily access Web resources, see the online version of the bibliography at: http://www.microsoft.com/architectureguide.

For more information on Microsoft Azure, see *"Azure Services Platform"* at http://www.microsoft.com/azure/default.mspx.

For more information on Microsoft "Geneva" identity management, see *"Geneva Simplifies User Access to Applications and Services"* at http://msdn.microsoft.com/en-us/security/aa570351.aspx.

For more information on Software plus Services, see the following *MSDN Developer Center* resources:

- *"Multi-Tenant Data Architecture"* at http://msdn.microsoft.com/en-us/architecture/aa479086.aspx.
- *"Software + Services (S+S)"* at http://msdn.microsoft.com/en-us/architecture/aa699384.aspx.
- *"Software + Services for Architects"* WebCast by Gianpaolo Carraro at http://www.microsoft.com/feeds/msdn/en-us/architecture/media/SaaS/ssForArchitects.asx.

For more information on Software plus Services architecture, see the following resources from the MSDN *Architecture Journal*:

- *"A Planet Ruled by Software Architectures"* at http://msdn.microsoft.com/en-us/architecture/bb906059.aspx.

- *"Head in the Cloud, Feet on the Ground"* at http://msdn.microsoft.com/en-us/library/dd129910.aspx

- *"Enterprise Mash Ups"* at http://msdn.microsoft.com/en-us/architecture/bb906060.aspx.

- *"Implications of Software + Services Consumption for Enterprise IT"* at http://msdn.microsoft.com/en-us/architecture/bb906061.aspx.

- *"Microsoft Office as a Platform for Software + Services"* at http://msdn.microsoft.com/en-us/architecture/bb906062.aspx.

- *"The Internet Service Bus"* at http://msdn.microsoft.com/en-us/architecture/bb906065.aspx.

For more information on the open source NHibernate framework, see *"NHibernate Forge"* at http://nhforge.org/Default.aspx.

27
Designing Office Business Applications

Overview

This chapter introduces Office Business Applications (OBAs), and shows a typical OBA architecture with the relevant components. It also describes typical scenarios where OBAs are a suitable choice, and provides guidance on design considerations and important patterns for OBAs. Additionally, it provides information on integration of OBA with Microsoft Office SharePoint Server (MOSS) and line-of-business (LOB) applications.

OBAs are a class of enterprise composite application. They provide solutions that integrate the core capabilities of networked business systems with the widely deployed and widely used business productivity services and applications that constitute the Microsoft Office System. OBAs implement business logic that is maintained through end user forms, providing a rich user experience that can help to improve business insight and assist in integrating existing internal or external systems.

OBAs usually integrate with new and existing LOB applications. They leverage the rich UI and automation capabilities of the Office clients to simplify complex processes that require user interaction, and help to minimize errors and improve processes. Effectively, OBAs use the Office client applications to fill the gaps between existing LOB systems and users. Figure 1 illustrates the key components and layers of an OBA. One thing to note is that this diagram includes a layer named Productivity between the Presentation and Application Services Layers. The Productivity layer contains components used to store and manage collaborative work streams in a document-centric manner.

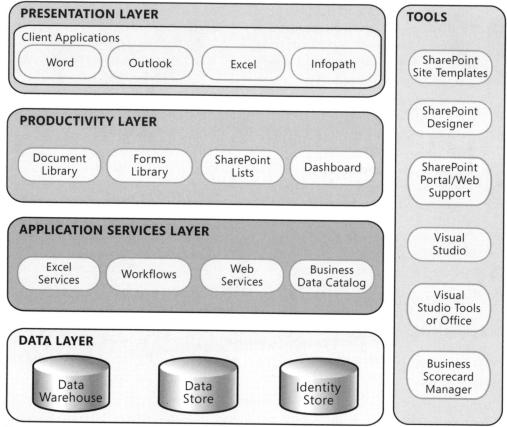

Figure 1
Key components of an OBA

Components of an Office Business Application

An OBA is made up of a variety of applications and services that interact to provide an end-to-end solution to a business problem. It may contain or be created using any or all of the following items:

- **Microsoft Office client applications.** The client applications include Outlook® messaging and collaboration client, Word, Excel, InfoPath® information gathering program, and PowerPoint® presentation graphics program. Custom forms in Outlook can be used to host UI controls with the ability to integrate business logic and data from various sources. Word and Excel offer programmability in the form of the Task Pane, Smart Tags, and the Ribbon. This makes it possible to combine natural document interactions with structured business data and processes. Smart Tags use regular expression pattern matching to recognize identifiers such as telephone numbers, government identification numbers, or custom account numbers within the text of a document. Relevant actions can be presented in the document alongside the data.

- **Windows SharePoint Services (WSS).** Built upon Windows Server, WSS provides content management and collaboration features that can help to improve business processes and team productivity. OBAs can use WSS to store and share documents, forms, and lists; and support offline synchronization and task management.

- **MOSS.** MOSS extends the capabilities provided by WSS to offer enterprise-wide functionality for content management, workflow, search, portals, and personalized sites. OBAs can use MOSS for these features, as well as using Excel Services for reporting, the Business Data Catalog (BDC) for LOB access, and a security framework for single sign on (SSO) capabilities.

- **Technologies and services.** Excel Services allow documents to be authored by clients using Excel in the usual way, and then saved to SharePoint Server. End users can view and interact with the documents in a Web browser, and software developers can programmatically invoke business logic stored within the documents. OBAs can also use Windows Workflow Foundation (WF) functionality that is built into MOSS to capture a process, such as a purchase order approval, and reduce user errors and associated delays. In addition, they can use ASP.NET Web Page and Web Part rendering to create customized Web sites that reflect the company's requirements.

- **Collaboration features.** Collaboration can be managed by Microsoft Office Communications Server (OCS), Microsoft Office Groove® software, and Microsoft Exchange Server.

- **Development tools.** These include SharePoint Central Administration, SharePoint Designer, Visual Studio, and Visual Studio Tools for Office.

Key Scenarios for Office Business Applications

OBAs are designed to interoperate using open standards, standard file formats, and Web services. The metadata definitions of OBA solution objects are based on XML schemas. All Microsoft Office products are service-enabled at all levels, and use interoperable OpenXML file formats as the default schemas for business documents they create. OBAs generally fall into one of three categories that implement key scenarios. These categories, described in the following sections, are:

- **Enterprise content management**, which allows people to find and use information based on their role.

- **Business intelligence**, which enables business insight through capabilities such as server-based Excel solutions.

- **Unified messaging**, which enables communication and collaboration to simplify team management.

Enterprise Content Management

Enterprise content management scenarios allow people to find and use information based on their business role or task requirements by using Office client applications. These applications may interact directly with the LOB system that provides the data. However, as shown in Figure 2, one of the more common scenarios in business environments is the use of MOSS or WSS as a content-management tool for Office client documents.

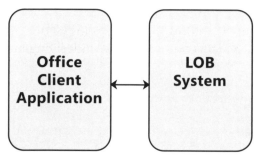

Figure 2a
Office client interacting directly with a LOB system

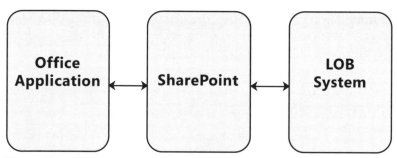

Figure 2b
Office client interacting with LOB system through a SharePoint intermediary

With the SharePoint solution, you can implement versioning and workflow on the files associated with Office client applications. In addition, many of the files can be modified within the SharePoint environment, and features included with MOSS use Excel to create and display reports. As a result, many of the key scenarios are based on using SharePoint with Office client applications. The following OBA patterns, described in detail later in this chapter, are useful for implementing enterprise content management scenarios:

- The Extended Reach Channel pattern extends LOB application functionality to a broader user base using Office applications as the channel.

- The Document Workflow pattern enables control and monitoring of document-centric processes, and can infuse best practices and enhance underlying business processes.

- The Collaboration pattern augments structured business processes with unstructured human collaboration.

Business Intelligence

Business intelligence scenarios enable business insight through capabilities such as server-based Excel solutions. The following OBA patterns, described in detail later in this chapter, are useful for implementing business intelligence scenarios:

- The Document Integration pattern enables the generation of Office documents from LOB applications; enables information workers to embed LOB data in Office documents by interacting with LOB data while authoring the document; and enables server-side processing of documents containing LOB data.

- The Composite UI pattern supports composition of multiple application UIs in an Office document or a SharePoint Web page.

- The Data Consolidation pattern enables a more natural way of interacting with LOB data by allowing users to discover data using searches across multiple LOB applications, and then act on the results. Data Consolidation uses the Discovery Navigation pattern.

Unified Messaging

Unified messaging scenarios support communication and collaboration, which simplifies team management. The Notification and Tasks pattern, described in detail later in this chapter, is useful for implementing unified messaging scenarios. The Notification and Tasks pattern uses Outlook as a primary UI to receive and act on LOB application–generated tasks and alerts.

Common OBA Patterns

OBAs can vary from the very simple to extremely complex custom solutions. OBAs generally incorporate one or more of the common patterns, which are described in the following sections:

- Extended Reach Channel
- Document Integration
- Document Workflow
- Composite UI
- Data Consolidation (Discovery Navigation)
- Collaboration
- Notifications and Tasks

Extended Reach Channel

Extended Reach Channel applications extend LOB application functionality to a broader user base using Office applications as the channel. The Extended Reach Channel pattern is useful for implementing the following scenarios:

- Eliminating duplication of effort that currently exists in your enterprise, such as an Outlook feature for consultants to assign time for meetings to billable projects.
- Extending LOB functionality to a broader set of end users, such as a self-service application that allows employees to update their personal information.
- Improving the use of an existing system that users currently avoid because of duplication of effort or lack of training.
- Collecting information from users through e-mail and automatically updating the system.

The Extended Reach Channel approach supports two different integration patterns: the Direct Integration pattern and the Mediated Integration pattern. The following sections describe these patterns.

Direct Integration Pattern

The Direct Integration pattern describes how Office client applications can expose LOB functionality directly to a broader set of users. In this pattern, access to LOB interfaces is projected directly into an Office client or is extended to an existing behavior such as calendaring. The client application may access the LOB data through a Web service, or may simply display output (such as HTML) generated by the LOB system, as shown in Figures 3a and 3b.

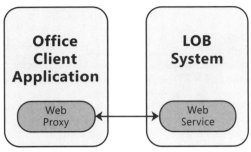

Figure 3a
The Direct Integration pattern using Web services

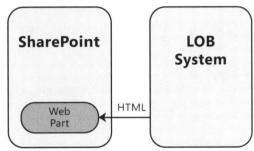

Figure 3b
The Direct Integration pattern using HTML

Mediated Integration Pattern

The Mediated Integration pattern describes how metadata stores such as the BDC can be used to provide an additional level of abstraction that provides common approaches to managing LOB documents, including security with a SSO mechanism based on a credentials mapping. This pattern provides more opportunities for composing services and data into a composite UI. A mediator, which could be the BDC, collects data from disparate sources and exposes it in Office-compatible formats and services that client applications can consume. Figure 4 illustrates the Mediated Integration pattern.

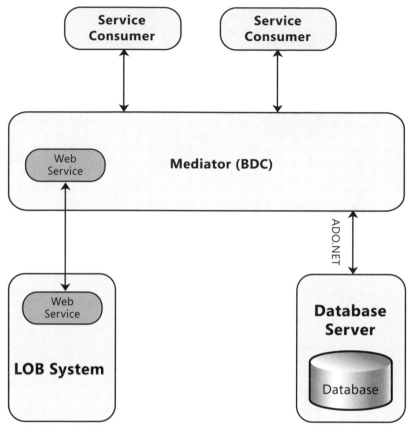

Figure 4
The Mediated Integration pattern

Document Integration

Document Integration applications enable the generation of Office documents from LOB applications; enable information workers to embed LOB data in Office documents by interacting with LOB data while authoring the document; and enable server-side processing of documents containing LOB data. The Document Integration pattern is useful for implementing the following scenarios:

- Reducing duplication of LOB data that is stored in individual Office documents located on user desktop systems.

- Exposing specific subsets of LOB data to Office applications for tasks such as mail merge or reporting.

- Generating Office documents that include items of LOB data in the appropriate format, automatically refreshed as the data changes. Manual creation of common layouts should be avoided; the Office applications should create them using templates where applicable.

- Generating documents that require custom server-side processing of LOB data. Open standards should be used for embedding this data.
- Accepting inbound documents, processing the embedded data, and applying it to the LOB system.

The Document Integration approach supports four different integration patterns that use XML to pass information to and from LOB systems. The simplest is the Application Generated Documents pattern. In addition, there are three intelligent document integration patterns: the Embedded LOB Information pattern, the Intelligent Documents/ Embedded LOB Template pattern, and the Intelligent Documents/LOB Information Recognizer pattern. The following sections describe these patterns.

Application Generated Documents Pattern

The Application Generated Documents pattern describes how the LOB system can merge business data with an Office document using batch-oriented server-side processing, although client-side generation is also feasible. Common examples include exporting data to Excel spreadsheets, or generating reports and letters in Word. This is the most commonly used pattern for document data integration.

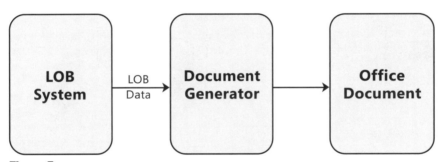

Figure 5
The Application Generated Documents pattern

Intelligent Documents/Embedded LOB Information Pattern

The Intelligent Documents/Embedded LOB Information pattern describes how LOB data can be embedded directly within the body of an Office document, or embedded as an XML document part and exposed through a content control. Alternatively, the Office application can use the Office Custom Task Pane (CTP) to display LOB data that an information worker can browse or search, and embed into a document. Figure 6 illustrates the Embedded LOB Information pattern.

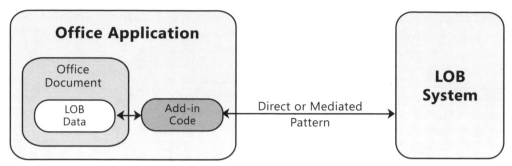

Figure 6
The Intelligent Documents/Embedded LOB Information pattern

Intelligent Documents/Embedded LOB Template Pattern

The Intelligent Documents/Embedded LOB Template pattern describes how a template can be used to combine metadata from a LOB system with document markup, such as content controls, XML schemas, bookmarks, named ranges, and smart tags. At run time, the template is merged with appropriate instances of the LOB data to create a document. The merging can take place through an add-in within the Office client application, or on the server.

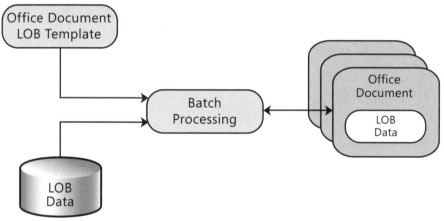

Figure 7
The Intelligent Documents/Embedded LOB Template pattern

Intelligent Documents/LOB Information Recognizer Pattern

The Intelligent Documents/LOB Information Recognizer pattern describes how metadata and document markup, such as content controls, XML schemas, bookmarks, named ranges, or smart tags can contain data recognized by the LOB system. The application can use this data to update the LOB system, or to provide extra functionality for users. On the server side, the application may start a workflow using the information. On the client, the application might present context-sensitive information, such as the details of a customer whose name is recognized in a Word document.

Document Workflow

Document Workflow applications enable control and monitoring of document-centric processes, and can infuse best practices and enhance underlying business processes. The Document Workflow pattern is useful for implementing the following scenarios:

- Applications that exchange information, often via e-mail, to perform multistep tasks such as forecasting, budgeting, and incident management.

- Applications where specific legal or corporate compliance procedures must be followed, and audit information maintained.

- Applications that carry out complex document handling and conditional routing tasks, or must implement best practice-based on rules.

You must consider workflow requirements when implementing this pattern. However, avoid building custom workflow components where possible; instead use the workflow capabilities within SharePoint. The Document Workflow approach supports two different integration patterns that initiate workflows:

- **LOB Initiated Document Workflow pattern.** Documents are passed to a SharePoint document workflow automatically by an action such as saving them to a SharePoint document library or submitting an InfoPath form. The workflow might send the document to the next recipient in a list, store copies, or perform processes on the document depending on the requirements of the application.

- **Cooperating Document Workflow pattern.** There may be a series of interactions between documents and LOB systems that must follow certain rules or prevent certain actions; for example, preventing edits to a submitted document at a specific stage of the process, extracting specific information, and publishing this information back to the LOB system. This pattern will usually use a SharePoint cooperating workflow that provides the flow logic, while the intelligent document provides the LOB interaction mechanisms. In complex scenarios, the LOB system may also update the document as it passes through the workflow.

Composite UI

Composite UI applications support composition of multiple application UIs within an Office document or a SharePoint Web page. The Composite UI pattern is useful for implementing the following scenarios:

- Applications that collect and display several different types of information in a single UI page or screen.
- Applications that use data exposed by multiple networked systems, and display it in a single UI page or screen.
- Applications that must provide a customizable composite interface that users modify to best suit their requirements.

When implementing this pattern, ensure you follow Office standards, and avoid creating custom components when Web Parts that provide the required functionality are available. The Composite UI approach supports several different integration patterns that combine information into a composite UI:

- **Context Driven Composite User Interface pattern.** Contextual information determines the UI composition. The contextual information can be static (such as the application configuration, or a tab added to an Outlook view) or dynamic (such as hiding or showing tab-based data in the source document). Each region of the composite UI presents information through an Office client component. However, users cannot dynamically change the linking at run time between the document components and the source data located in the LOB system.

- **Mesh Composite View pattern.** The UI contains components such as ASP.NET Web Parts or MOSS components that cooperatively interact to expose data from the same or different LOB systems. For example, a part that represents a view of a customer from a customer relationship management (CRM) system might be connected at the time the view is constructed to a part that represents a list of open orders in an enterprise resource planning (ERP) system. When a customer is selected in the CRM part, it raises an event and provides the information on the selected customer identity to the open orders part so that it can show the status of that order.

- **RSS and Web Services Composition pattern.** A specialized version of the Mesh Composite View pattern that combines data published as RSS feeds or through Web services. Multiple SharePoint Data View Web Parts (or custom parts) format and present the published data within the UI. An example is a composite view of the catalogs of several suppliers, where each published item provides a link to a page on the supplier's Web site that contains extra information.

- **Analytics pattern.** A specialized version of the Mesh Composite View pattern that presents a data analysis dashboard to the end user. It can use Excel Services and the Excel Services Web Part provided by MOSS 2007 to display data and charts, or other parts to display custom data and information from the LOB system, and from other sources, within the composite UI. A useful part provided by MOSS for dashboards is the Key Performance Indicator (KPI) Web Part that allows users to define KPIs based on data in any SharePoint list, including a BDC list.

Data Consolidation (Discovery Navigation)

Data Consolidation applications enable a more natural way of interacting with LOB data by allowing users to discover data using searches across multiple LOB applications, and then act on the results. They rely on sufficient LOB entity data being available for the Office applications to act upon. Data Consolidation uses the Discovery Navigation pattern, and is useful for implementing the following scenarios:

- Applications that provide search capabilities for a single LOB system.
- Applications that provide search capabilities across multiple LOB systems.
- Applications that provide search capabilities across a diverse range of LOB systems and other data sources.

Data Consolidation Pattern

The Data Consolidation pattern provides a consistent search experience for information workers by combining the results of searches over one or more sources into a single result set, and presenting not only Uniform Resource Identifiers (URIs) that link to the results, but also actions associated with the found items. Figure 8 illustrates the Data Consolidation pattern creating a content index.

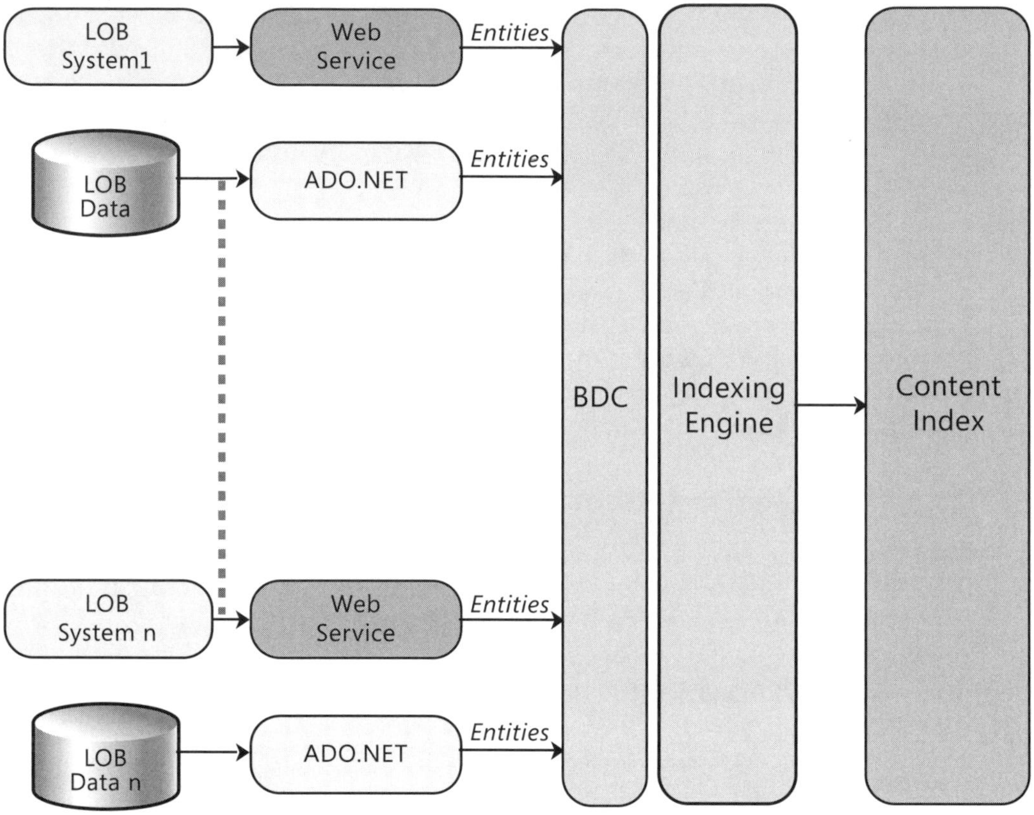

Figure 8

The content index contains information collated from a range of sources

Launching a LOB Process

A subpattern of the Data Consolidation pattern uses action links that can initiate a LOB operation, such as starting a workflow or performing a process on a document, as illustrated in Figure 9.

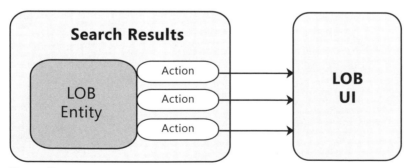

Figure 9

Launching a LOB process based on an action for an item in the search results

Collaboration

Collaboration applications augment structured business processes with unstructured human collaboration. The Collaboration pattern is useful for implementing the following scenarios:

- Applications that involve human interaction that leads to interaction with a LOB system, such as discussion of a sales opportunity before committing an order.
- LOB applications that collate content and user contributions in an unstructured form, and the later must expose it in a structured format.
- Applications that provide information in an unstructured form that users may be able to edit, such as a wiki or discussion site.

The Collaboration pattern uses MOSS Team Site templates that allow users to collaborate around a specific business problem using document libraries, discussion and task lists, team calendars, and simple project management features. The site can be provisioned and populated using LOB data, and exposes links to LOB processes within the appropriate libraries and lists. Access can be through Office documents, or a Web browser.

Notifications and Tasks

Applications that must support notifications and tasks can use Outlook as a primary UI to receive and act upon LOB application-generated tasks and alerts. In addition to Outlook, SharePoint provides notification and task services that can interact with most e-mail systems using the Simple Mail Transfer Protocol (SMTP). The Notifications and Tasks pattern is useful for implementing the following scenarios:

- Applications that assign tasks and generate notifications for end users.
- Applications that integrate multiple LOB operations and must notify users of status or process requirements.

The e-mail–based Notifications and Tasks approach supports several different integration patterns that can notify users of tasks and status:

- **Simple Task and Notification Delivery pattern.** The LOB system delivers tasks and notifications to users as Outlook tasks and e-mail messages in a one-way flow of information. Details of the task or the notification are embedded in the body of the task and e-mail message, but changes are not reflected back in the LOB system. Options for delivering tasks and notifications include delivering them to Microsoft Exchange Server (the push model), using an add-in on Outlook that fetches them (the pull model), or publishing an RSS feed to which users can subscribe.
- **Direct Task Synchronization pattern.** The LOB system sends tasks to users via Exchange or Outlook in a synchronized bidirectional flow of information. Users and the LOB can update tasks at any time, and the changes are propagated to the LOB system. The task may be part of a LOB workflow.

- **Mediated Task Synchronization pattern.** A variant of the Direct Task Synchronization pattern, where MOSS acts as a mediator between the LOB system and Outlook in order to synchronize tasks. The LOB system publishes tasks to a SharePoint Task List, which is synchronized with Outlook Tasks by using Outlook's native synchronization mechanism. Updates to the task in Outlook are automatically pushed back to SharePoint, which raises an event indicating that the change has occurred and allows custom code to update the LOB system.

- **Intelligent Tasks and Notifications pattern.** Action links located in the Outlook CTP allow users to initiate specific actions based on the tasks or notifications sent by the LOB system. Common tasks involve automatically logging on to the LOB system, finding the right information, and updating it. An example is a manager viewing an e-mail message sent by Human Resources to approve a vacation request for an employee, where the CTP contains action links that allow the manager to approve or reject the request by updating the LOB system.

- **Form-based Tasks and Notifications pattern.** A variant of the Intelligent Tasks and Notification pattern, where the e-mail message contains an attached InfoPath form prepopulated by the LOB system. The user can open the e-mail message, fill out the form, and submit it to the LOB system. InfoPath provides data validation, custom calculations, and logic to assist the user when filling out the form. The InfoPath CTP can provide additional information, extracted from the LOB system, to assist the user. A variant of this pattern uses MOSS InfoPath Forms Services to allow users to fill out forms in a Web browser without requiring InfoPath to be installed.

General Design Considerations

The design of a suitable OBA is based on the scenarios you must support, and the types of Office client applications suitable for those scenarios. In addition to considering the base patterns shown in the previous section, consider the following guidelines when designing your OBA:

- **Consider using a mediated integration pattern over direct integration.** When designing an OBA as an extended reach channel, you can implement interfaces directly within documents. For example, an Excel spreadsheet can contain custom input forms. However, this approach requires custom code and limits your ability to reuse functionality. With a mediated integration pattern, you can take advantage of applications such as SharePoint and the Business Data Catalog to decouple the interfaces from the physical documents.

- **Use OpenXML-based schemas for embedding LOB data in documents.** OpenXML is a European Computer Manufacturers Association (ECMA) international standard that is supported by Office 2007 applications, as well as by many independent vendors and platforms. By using OpenXML, you can share data between Office applications and applications developed for other platforms.

- **Create LOB document templates for common layouts that will be reused.** A LOB template contains markup and metadata associated with the LOB that can be bound to specific LOB data instances at a later time. In other words, new documents can be generated by merging LOB data with document templates. End users can create custom documents without developer involvement, and complex documents can be generated using server-side batch processing.

- **Use MOSS to control the review and approval process for documents.** MOSS provides out of the box features that support a basic workflow process for the review and approval of documents. For more complex processing requirements, WF can be used to extend the workflow capabilities found in SharePoint.

- **Use the Collaboration pattern for human collaboration.** Most LOB applications are good at handling structured business processes. However, they are not good at handling the unstructured nature of human interaction with business processes. A site implementing the collaboration pattern addresses this issue by providing an interface geared toward collaboration with other users. The SharePoint Team Site template implements this pattern.

- **Consider remote data synchronization requirements.** Documents that are created, updated, or distributed should be synchronized with the LOB system and then stored for future use. Even though LOB systems are quite useful for handling transaction oriented activities, they are not suited to capturing the significant work that occurs between activities.

Security Considerations

Security is important in Office Business Applications that expose data and functionality through several types of client applications, and have access to corporate LOB data. It is important to secure all access to resources, and to protect data passing over the network. Consider the following guidelines for security when creating OBAs:

- Consider implementing SSO so that users access the client applications and the networked functionality using their current logon credentials, or credentials validated through a federated service such as Active Directory or SharePoint.

- Consider encrypting messages that pass outside of your secure network where possible. You can use channel encryption mechanisms such as Internet Protocol Security (IPSec) to protect the network connection between servers and clients.

- Consider using the trusted subsystem model for data access using role credentials to minimize the number of connections required. See Chapter 19, "Physical Tiers and Deployment" for more information about the trusted subsystem model.

- Consider filtering data at the server to prevent exposure of sensitive data in client applications where this is not necessary.

Deployment Considerations

You can deploy OBA solutions using either a Windows Installer package or the Click Once technology:

- **Click Once** installation requires little user interaction, provides automated updates, and requires little effort for the developer. However, it can only be used to deploy a single solution that is not part of a larger solution; it cannot deploy additional files or registry keys; it cannot interact with the user to configure the installation; and it cannot provide a branded installation.

- **Windows Installer** installation can deploy additional components and registry settings; can interact with the user to configure the installation; and supports custom branding of the installation. However, it requires advanced configuration, more developer effort, and cannot provide automated updates.

Relevant Design Patterns

Key patterns are organized into categories such as Collaboration, Composite UI, Data Consolidation Document Integration, Document Workflow, Extended Reach Channel, and Tasks and Notifications; as shown in the following table. Consider using these patterns when making design decisions for each category.

Category	Relevant patterns
Collaboration	**Collaboration.** Use unstructured human collaboration to augment structured business processes.
Composite UI	**Analytics.** A specialized version of the Mesh Composite View pattern that presents a data analysis dashboard to the end user. **Context Driven Composite User Interface.** Use contextual information to determine the composition of the UI. **Mesh Composite View.** Use components in the UI, such as ASP.NET Web Parts or MOSS components, which cooperatively interact to expose data from the same or different LOB systems. **RSS and Web Services Composition.** A specialized version of the Mesh Composite View pattern that combines data published as RSS feeds or through Web services.
Data Consolidation	**Discovery Navigation.** Allow users to discover data by searching across multiple LOB applications, and then act on the results.

Category	Relevant patterns
Document Integration	**Application Generated Documents.** The LOB system merges business data with an Office document using batch oriented server-side processing. **Embedded LOB Information.** LOB data is embedded directly in the body of the Office document, or embedded as an XML document part and exposed through a content control. **Embedded LOB Template.** A template combines metadata from a LOB system with document markup, such as content controls, XML schemas, bookmarks, named ranges, and smart tags. **LOB Information Recognizer.** Metadata and document markup—such as content controls, XML schemas, bookmarks, named ranges, or smart tags—contain data recognized by the LOB system.
Document Workflow	**Cooperating Document Workflow.** A series of interactions between documents and LOB systems that must follow certain rules or prevent certain actions. LOB Initiated Document Workflow. Documents are passed to a SharePoint document workflow automatically by an action such as saving them to a SharePoint document library, or submitting an InfoPath form.
Extended Reach Channel	**Direct Integration.** Access to LOB interfaces is projected directly into an Office client, or is extended to an existing behavior such as calendaring. **Mediated Integration.** A mediator, which could be the BDC, collects data from disparate sources and exposes it in Office-compatible formats and services that client applications can consume.
Tasks & Notifications	**Direct Task Synchronization.** The LOB system sends tasks to users via Exchange or Outlook as a synchronized bidirectional flow of information. **Form-based Tasks and Notifications.** A variant of the Intelligent Tasks and Notification pattern, where the e-mail message contains an attached InfoPath Form prepopulated by the LOB system. **Intelligent Tasks and Notifications.** Action links located in the Outlook CTP allow users to initiate specific actions based on the tasks or notifications sent by the LOB system. **Mediated Task Synchronization.** A variant of the Direct Task Synchronization pattern, where MOSS acts as a mediator between the LOB system and Outlook in order to synchronize tasks. **Simple Task and Notification Delivery.** The LOB system delivers tasks and notifications to users as Outlook tasks and e-mail messages in a one-way flow of information.

For more information on OBA patterns, see Barker, Rob, Joanna Bichsel, Adam Buenz, Steve Fox, John Holliday, Bhushan Nene, and Karthik Ravindran. *6 Microsoft® Office Business Applications for Office SharePoint® Server 2007*. Microsoft Press, 2008. Additionally, you can refer to the excerpt from the book "*Getting Started with Office Business Applications*" at http://msdn.microsoft.com/en-us/library/bb614539.aspx

Additional Resources

To more easily access Web resources, see the online version of the bibliography at: http://www.microsoft.com/architectureguide.

- *"Automating Public Sector Forms Processing and Workflow with Office Business Application"* at http://blogs.msdn.com/singaporedpe/archive/tags/OBA/default.aspx.

- *"Getting Started with Office Business Applications"* at http://msdn.microsoft.com/en-us/library/bb614538.aspx.

- *"OBA (Reference Application Pack) RAP for E-Forms processing"* at http://msdn2.microsoft.com/en-us/architecture/bb643796.aspx.

- PowerPoint slides and source code at http://msdn2.microsoft.com/en-us/architecture/bb643796.aspx.

- "OBA Central" at http://www.obacentral.com/.

- *"Integrating LOB Systems with the Microsoft Office System"* at http://msdn.microsoft.com/en-us/architecture/bb896607.aspx.

- *"Understanding Office Development"* at http://msdn.microsoft.com/en-us/office/aa905371.aspx.

28
Designing SharePoint LOB Applications

Overview

In this chapter, you will learn about the architecture for a typical SharePoint line-of-business (LOB) application, and the components it contains. You will see the key scenarios and the important design considerations for SharePoint LOB applications. You will also learn about deployment, key patterns, and the technology considerations for designing SharePoint LOB applications.

Microsoft Windows Server® is the core operating system on which SharePoint LOB applications run. SharePoint integrates tightly with the broader Microsoft platform, using Internet Information Services (IIS) as a front-end Web server to host Web sites, and SQL Server as the networked store for site definitions, content type definitions, published content, and configuration data. SharePoint LOB applications can be configured to publish Internet-facing content through Web sites that can scale out with Web farm deployment to service large numbers of users, and integrate with ASP.NET to provide LOB data presentation for these sites. They can use ASP.NET Web Parts, styles, themes, templates, server controls, and user controls for the UI. Figure 1 shows the key features and layers of a SharePoint LOB application.

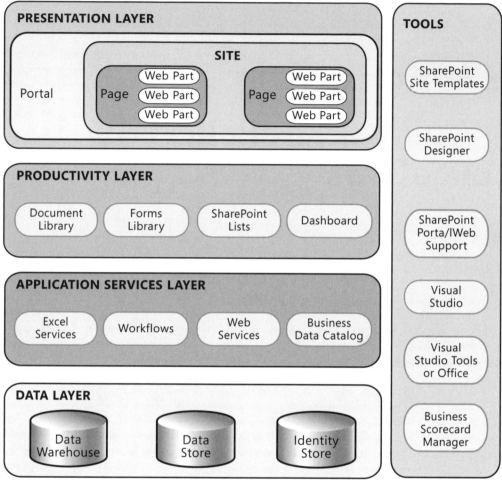

Figure 1
Key features of a SharePoint LOB application

Office Business Applications (OBAs), described in Chapter 27, can also integrate LOB processes to provide rich user experiences for data access, data analysis, and data manipulation by using role tailored business portals built on top of Windows SharePoint Services (WSS) and the Microsoft Office SharePoint Server (MOSS).

Logical Layers of a SharePoint LOB Application

The following list describes each of the layers of a SharePoint LOB application:

- **Presentation layer.** This is the UI of the application. Users connect through a Web browser to the SharePoint Server Portal, which is composed of Web pages. These Web pages can be assembled by using Web Parts, which provide rich composition at the presentation level. Web Parts for Office client applications are also available, and you can build custom Web Parts to implement application-specific functionality.

- **Productivity layer.** Office documents, such as Excel spreadsheets, are stored in document libraries. Forms that automate tasks in the Office applications are stored in forms libraries. The productivity layer also implements features for creating and publishing reports, in the form of either SharePoint lists or Excel spreadsheets. It can also generate output in the form of a dashboard composed of information drawn from multiple services. In addition, as described in previous chapter, Office client applications can be used for information processing and collaboration.

- **Application services layer.** This is a reusable layer within the application that exposes services used by the productivity and presentation layers. It includes Excel Services for reporting, workflows that use Windows Workflow Foundation (WF) to implement business processes or document life-cycle management, and other business Web services. Additionally, clients can access data using the Business Data Catalog (BDC).

- **Data layer.** This layer encapsulates the mechanisms for storing and accessing all of the different types of data required by the application. This includes roles and identities, as well as the operations data and data warehouses that contain the LOB data.

Physical Tier Deployment

The previous section describes the logical grouping of components or functionality of a SharePoint LOB application into separate layers. You must also understand the physical distribution of components on separate servers of your infrastructure. The following list describes the common scenarios and guidelines:

- Deploy the databases for SharePoint on a separate database server or database cluster for maximum reliability and performance.

- In a nondistributed scenario, deploy the presentation, productivity, and application services layers on the same Web server or a Web farm.

- In a distributed scenario, you can deploy the components of the presentation layer (portals, sites, pages, and Web Parts) on a Web server or a Web farm, and the remaining layers and components on a separate application server or application farm.

- For maximum performance under severe load, you might decide to deploy the components for the application services layer on a separate application server or application farm.

Key Scenarios and Features

SharePoint LOB applications are designed to interoperate using open standards, standard file formats, and Web services. The metadata definitions of SharePoint LOB solution objects are based on XML schemas. All Office System products are service enabled at all levels, and use interoperable OpenXML file formats as the default schemas for business documents they create.

MOSS assists in providing content management features and implementing business processes in SharePoint LOB applications. SharePoint sites support specific content publishing, content management, records management, and business intelligence requirements. You can also conduct effective searches for people, documents, and data; participate in forms-driven business processes; and access and analyze large volumes of business data. The following list describes the features of SharePoint LOB applications:

- **Workflow.** MOSS is integrated with WF, and allows developers to create simple workflows and attach them to the document libraries in SharePoint. Users can also create custom workflows using the SharePoint designer.

- **Business intelligence.** MOSS provides users with interactive Business Intelligence portals that support substantial data manipulation and analysis. Users can create dashboards from multiple data sources without writing code. Key Performance Indicators (KPIs) can be defined from Excel Services, SharePoint lists, SQL Server Analysis Services cubes, and a variety of other sources. Because this data is hosted within SharePoint, it can be an active participant in other SharePoint services such as search and workflow.

- **Content management.** Functionality from Microsoft Content Management Server (MCMS) has been rolled into MOSS, allowing it to take advantage of comprehensive Web content management features available directly from the SharePoint platform.

- **Search.** Enterprise Search in MOSS is a shared service that provides extensive and extensible content gathering, indexing, and querying facilities, and supports full text and keyword searches.

- **Business Data Catalog.** The BDC allows enterprise data to be exposed to Web Parts, InfoPath Forms Server, and search functions. Developers can use the BDC to build applications that allow users to interact with LOB data using familiar interfaces.

- **OpenXML file format.** Adoption of the OpenXML file format across the Office System applications facilitates rich server-side document manipulation.

General Design Considerations

While SharePoint provides many of the basic features you will use when interfacing with a LOB application, there are several key design issues that you must consider. These include user experience and the choice of client interface, as well as operational and maintenance issues. Consider the following guidelines when designing a SharePoint LOB application:

- **Enable a user experience tailored to the user's role.** Provide different UI options based on the user's role. SharePoint contains functionality that allows you to automatically tailor the display based on user roles and groups. Utilize security groups or audience targeting to provide only the relevant options to users.

- **Integrate LOB systems with Office client applications.** Choose patterns, such as the Direct Access pattern or Mediated pattern, to integrate LOB systems with Office client applications that are specific to the solution and the functional requirements. Consider ADO.NET or Web services for the Direct Access pattern. Consider using MOSS as a middle-tier application server for the Mediated pattern. For details of these patterns, see Chapter 27, "Designing Office Business Applications."

- **Avoid tight coupling between layers.** Use Web services to resolve dependencies and avoid tight coupling between the layers.

- **Consider remote data synchronization requirements.** All documents that are created, updated, or distributed should be synchronized with the LOB system and then stored for future use. Even though LOB systems are quite useful for handling transaction-oriented activities, they are not suited to capturing the significant work that occurs between activities.

- **Expose back-end LOB data through services for use in SharePoint and OBAs.** Exposing your networked data system via services allows SharePoint and OBA extensions to request, manipulate, and reformat data for the user. In this way, SharePoint can be used to extend networked system behavior without extensive code development.

Specific Design Issues

There are several common issues that you must consider as you develop your design. These issues can be categorized into specific areas of the design. The following sections contain guidelines to help you resolve the common issues in each area:

- Business Data Catalog
- Document and Content Storage
- Excel Services
- InfoPath Form Services
- SharePoint Object Model
- Web Parts
- Workflow

Business Data Catalog

The BDC allows enterprise data to be exposed to Web Parts, InfoPath Forms Server, and search functions. Developers can use the BDC to build applications that allows users to interact with LOB data using familiar interfaces. Consider the following guidelines when developing BDC-based applications:

- Review the structure of data sources to ensure that they are suitable for direct consumption by the BDC, and determine how the data will be used; for example, search, user profiles, or simple display. Ensure that you define an appropriate search scope to avoid over exposing data. Also, check that you are using the most recent data access drivers for the data sources to maximize performance.

- Ensure that you authenticate users, and authenticate processes when connecting to data sources. Consider using the enterprise single sign on (SSO) features provided by SharePoint to authenticate to networked data sources.

- Consider using the BDC Definition Editor from the Office Server SDK to minimize errors when creating the Application Definition File (ADF). If you manually edit the ADF, consider loading the BDCMedata.xsd schema into Visual Studio to minimize errors.

- Consider using the BDC Security Trimmer for custom security trimming of entity instances, if required.

- Avoid overloading the staging area.

Document and Content Storage

Office documents, such as Excel spreadsheets, are stored in document libraries. You can use Office desktop applications to consolidate diverse content from multiple data sources. Consider the following guidelines when storing content in SharePoint:

- When storing documents in document libraries, use content types and their inheritance capabilities to define additional centralized metadata for each document type. Content types created at root sites can be used in child sites automatically. In addition, new content types can be derived and extended, starting from existing content types. Rather than manage each content type individually, use this behavior to simplify the maintenance of content types.

- Identify and plan the content types you will need, and define unique metadata field names and their associations, document templates, and custom forms with the content types. Create the content type at the site level if it must be available on any child site. Create the content type at the list level only if it must be available to just that list.

- Consider customizing the Document Information Panel to collect content type metadata in order to track and edit metadata for documents. You can add business logic or data validation to the Document Information Panel.

- Consider storing user-configurable reference data or nontransient data in lists. However, do not treat SharePoint Lists as database tables. Use a database to store transient or transactional data. Consider caching the contents of a list in a **DataTable** or **DataSet** if the list will be queried multiple times in your application.

- Do not replace file systems with SharePoint document libraries, or attempt to use SharePoint document libraries as a source code control mechanism or as a platform for development team members to collaborate on source code. Use a document library only to store documents that require collaboration and management.

- Consider the restriction of a maximum of 2000 items per list container in document libraries and lists. Consider writing your own UI to retrieve items in lists when the list container exceeds 2000 items.

- Consider organizing documents into folders as opposed to using filtered views. This can provide faster retrieval.

Excel Services

Excel Services consists of three main components: Excel Calculation Services loads the workbook, performs calculations, refreshes external data, and maintains sessions. Excel Web Access is a Web Part that displays and enables interaction with the Excel workbook in a browser. Excel Web Services is a Web service hosted in SharePoint that provides methods that developers can use to build custom applications based on the Excel workbook. Consider the following guidelines when designing to use Excel Services:

- Ensure that you authenticate all users, and secure your Open Data Connection files. Consider configuring Kerberos authentication or SSO for Excel Services to authenticate to SQL Server databases located on other servers.

- Configure the trusted file locations and trusted data connection libraries before publishing workbooks, and publish only the information that is required.

- Ensure that the Excel workbooks are saved to the trusted file locations before publishing, and ensure that Office Data Connection files are uploaded to the trusted data connection libraries before publishing workbooks.

InfoPath Form Services

InfoPath Form Services provides users with the capability to use browser-based forms built on templates stored in SharePoint and exposed to the user through InfoPath. When deployed to a server running InfoPath Form Services, forms based on browser-compatible templates (.xsn) can be opened in a Web browser from computers that do not have Office InfoPath 2007 installed, but they will open in Office InfoPath 2007 when it is installed. Consider the following guidelines when designing to use InfoPath Forms for Form Services:

- Consider creating symmetrical forms, which look and operate exactly the same way whether they are displayed in the SharePoint Server Web interface, or within an Office system client application such as Word, Excel, or PowerPoint.

- Use the Design Checker task pane of InfoPath to check for compatibility issues in browser forms. Also, consider selecting the "Enable browser-compatible features only" option when designing forms for the browser in order to hide unsupported controls.

- Consider using multiple views, instead of a single view with hidden content, to improve the performance and responsiveness of your forms. However, do not rely on the apparent security obtained by hiding information using views.

- Consider enabling protection to preserve the integrity of form templates and to prevent users from making changes to the form template. When exposing forms to public sites, ensure that form templates cannot be accessed by scripts or automated processes in order to prevent Denial of Service (DoS) attacks. Also, ensure that public forms do not include sensitive information such as authentication information, or server and database names.

- Do not use InfoPath Form Services when designing reporting solutions that require a large volume of data.
- Consider submitting the form data to a database when reporting is required, and store any sensitive information that is collected by the forms in a database.
- Consider using Universal Data Connection (UDC) files for flexible management of data connections and reusability.
- Consider using Form View when configuring session state for InfoPath Forms Services.

SharePoint Object Model

SharePoint exposes an object model that allows you to write code that automates processes. For example, you can implement custom versioning for documents, or enforce custom check-in policies. Consider the following guidelines when writing custom code using the SharePoint object model:

- Dispose of the SharePoint objects that you have created after use to release unmanaged resources. Also, ensure that you dispose of the SharePoint objects appropriately in exception handlers.
- Choose an appropriate caching approach, and avoid caching sensitive or volatile data. Consider loading the data from SharePoint objects into a **DataSet** or **DataTable** if caching is required. However, you must consider thread synchronization and thread safety if you do cache SharePoint objects.
- When elevating privileges, note that only new SharePoint objects created after elevation will use the elevated privileges.

Web Parts

Web Parts allow you to provide rich composition at the presentation level. You can build custom Web Parts to implement application-specific functionality, and use Web Parts provided with SharePoint and other environments such as ASP.NET. You can use Web Parts to interact with networked LOB applications or Web services, and to create composite customizable interfaces that support personalization in your SharePoint LOB applications. If you must provide extra permissions for your Web Parts over and above the permissions available to ASP.NET, consider creating a custom code access security policy. Consider the following guidelines when developing Web Parts:

- Identify suitable functionality that you would like to implement in Web Parts, and identify any data sources with which the Web Parts will interact. Consider using Web Part verbs to allow users to perform discrete actions, and categorize your properties to distinguish them from Web Part properties.
- Design Web Parts using layering guidelines to partition your presentation, business, and data logic in order to improve maintainability. Design each Web Part to perform only a single function in order to improve reuse, and design them to be configurable or customizable by users where this is appropriate.

- Implement suitable security measures in Web Parts. Only deploy Web Parts to the global assembly cache where individual user security is not required.

- Use Web Part Zones to host Web Parts that users can manage themselves at run time. If you are using an ASP.NET Master Page, include a Web Part Manager in master pages that Web Part pages will use. Avoid specifying style attributes directly on controls contained within Web Parts.

- Properly dispose any SharePoint objects and unmanaged resources that you create in your Web Parts.

Workflow

SharePoint allows developers to create simple workflows and attach them to the document libraries in SharePoint. Users can also create custom workflows using the SharePoint Designer, or you can create custom workflows using Visual Studio. Consider the following guidelines when designing workflows:

- Be clear on what business process or part of a business process is being automated. Ensure that existing business processes are accurate and documented before physically implementing the workflows, and consider consulting a subject matter expert or business analyst to review existing business processes.

- Choose the appropriate workflow technology to meet the business requirements. For example, use out of the box SharePoint workflows if business requirements are simple; such as document approval. Consider using the SharePoint Designer to create workflows when out of the box workflows cannot fulfill business requirements.

- Consider using Visual Studio to develop custom workflows when business requirements require complex workflows or integration with LOB systems, or to create workflow activities that can be registered with SharePoint Designer in order to empower information workers.

- When developing custom workflows, choose the workflow type that is appropriate for your scenario. Consider state-based and sequential models. Also, consider implementing comprehensive instrumentation within your code to aid debugging.

- When debugging custom workflows, consider setting the logging level to verbose.

- Consider versioning your workflow assemblies and changing the solution Globally Unique Identifier (GUID) when upgrading your old workflows. Also, consider the effect on existing workflow instances that are running when deploying newer versions.

- Consider creating separate workflow history lists and tasks list for workflows created by end users.

- Consider assigning workflows to content types in order to improve manageability. Assigning a workflow to a type means that you can use the workflow in many different content libraries, but you need to maintain it in only one place (this functionality is available for out of the box and Visual Studio workflows, but not for

SharePoint Designer workflows). Bear in mind that there can only be one running workflow instance of the same type per list item; and that workflow instances will only start on list items, and not the list itself.

Technology Considerations

The following guidelines will help you to choose an appropriate implementation technology for your SharePoint workflow, and provide guidance on creating Web Parts for custom SharePoint interfaces:

- If you require workflows that automatically support secure, reliable, transacted data exchange, a broad choice of transport and encoding options, and that provide built-in persistence and activity tracking, consider using WF.
- If you require workflows that implement complex orchestrations and support reliable store and forward messaging capabilities, consider using BizTalk Server.
- If you must interact with non-Microsoft systems, perform electronic data interchange (EDI) operations, or implement Enterprise Service Bus (ESB) patterns, consider using the Microsoft BizTalk ESB Toolkit.
- If your business layer is confined to a single SharePoint site and does not require access to information in other sites, consider using MOSS. MOSS is not suitable for multiple-site scenarios.
- If you create ASP.NET Web Parts for your application, consider inheriting from the class **System.Web.UI.WebControls.WebParts.WebPart** unless you require backward compatibility with SharePoint 2003. If you must support SharePoint 2003, consider inheriting from the class **Microsoft.SharePoint.WebPartPages.WebPart**.

Deployment Considerations

SharePoint LOB applications rely on SharePoint itself to provide much of the functionality. However, you must deploy the additional artifacts, such as components, in such a way that SharePoint can access and use them. Consider the following guidelines when designing a deployment strategy for your SharePoint LOB applications:

- Determine the scope for your features, such as farm, Web application, site collection, or site.
- Consider packaging your features into solutions.
- Consider deploying your assemblies to the BIN folder instead of the global assembly cache in order to take advantage of the low level code access security mechanism.
- Test your solution after deployment using a nonadministrator account.

Relevant Design Patterns

Key patterns are shown in the following table. Consider using these patterns when making design decisions for your SharePoint L OB applications.

Category	Relevant patterns
Workflows	**Data-driven Workflow.** A workflow that contains tasks whose sequence is determined by the values of data in the workflow or the system. **Human Workflow.** A workflow that involves tasks performed manually by humans. **Sequential Workflow.** A workflow that contains tasks that follow a sequence, where one task is initiated after completion of the preceding task. **State-driven Workflow**. A workflow that contains tasks whose sequence is determined by the state of the system.

For more information on the Data-Driven Workflow, Human Workflow, Sequential Workflow, and State-Driven Workflow patterns, see:

- *"Windows Workflow Foundation Overview"* at http://msdn.microsoft.com/en-us/library/ms734631.aspx.

- *"Workflow Patterns"* at http://www.workflowpatterns.com/.

Additional Resources

To more easily access Web resources on using MOSS and WSS to build SharePoint LOB Applications, see the online version of the bibliography at: http://www.microsoft.com/architectureguide.

- *"Developing Workflow Solutions with SharePoint Server 2007 and Windows Workflow Foundation"* at http://msdn.microsoft.com/en-us/library/cc514224.aspx.

- *"Best Practices: Common Coding Issues When Using the SharePoint Object Model"* at http://msdn.microsoft.com/en-us/library/bb687949.aspx.

- *"Best Practices: Using Disposable Windows SharePoint Services Objects"* at http://msdn.microsoft.com/en-us/library/aa973248.aspx.

- *"InfoPath Forms Services Best Practices"* at http://technet.microsoft.com/en-us/library/cc261832.aspx.

- *"White paper: Working with large lists in Office SharePoint Server 2007"* at http://technet.microsoft.com/en-us/library/cc262813.aspx.

Appendices

This section of the guide contains appendices that provide an overview of the Microsoft application platform; and technology matrices covering topics such as presentation, data access, integration, and workflow that will help you evaluate and choose appropriate technologies for your application scenario. Additionally, it walks you through the features in the Microsoft patterns & practices Enterprise Library, which can help to accelerate the design and creation of application by addressing common crosscutting concerns. The appendices also include the Microsoft patterns & practices pattern catalog, which lists key patterns that you will find useful when designing your architecture.

The appendices included in this guide are:

- Appendix A: The Microsoft Application Platform
- Appendix B: Presentation Technology Matrix
- Appendix C: Data Access Technology Matrix
- Appendix D: Integration Technology Matrix
- Appendix E: Workflow Technology Matrix
- Appendix F: patterns & practices Enterprise Library
- Appendix G: patterns & practices Pattern Catalog

Appendix A

The Microsoft Application Platform

Overview

This appendix starts with a summary of the features of the Microsoft platform that will help you to find your way around the technologies if you are not familiar with building applications that target the .NET Framework and Microsoft server technologies. The next section, "Finding Information and Resources," will help you to find information more easily when visiting the many sites that make up Microsoft's vast Web presence.

Next are an overview of the .NET Framework and the Common Language Runtime (CLR), followed by a series of sections that discuss the range of Microsoft application platform technologies available for a range of application types, collaboration, integration, data access, and workflow. Then the chapter provides an overview of several product technologies such as SQL Server, IIS (Web server) and development tools such as Visual Studio, and external libraries.

The Microsoft application platform is composed of products, infrastructure components, run-time services, and the .NET Framework, as detailed in the following table.

Category	Technologies
Application Infrastructure	Common Language Runtime (CLR) .NET Framework
Collaboration / Integration / Workflow	Windows Workflow Foundation (WF) Microsoft Office SharePoint Server (MOSS) Microsoft BizTalk Server
Data Access	ADO.NET Core ADO.NET Data Services Framework ADO.NET Entity Framework ADO.NET Sync Services Language Integrated Query (LINQ)
Database Server	Microsoft SQL Server
Development Tools	Microsoft Visual Studio Microsoft Expression® Studio design software
Mobile	.NET Compact Framework ASP.NET Mobile Silverlight Mobile
Rich Client	Windows Forms Windows Presentation Foundation (WPF)
Rich Internet Application (RIA)	Microsoft Silverlight
Services	ASP.NET Web Services (ASMX) Windows Communication Foundation (WCF)
Web	ASP.NET
Web Server	Internet Information Services (IIS)

Finding Information and Resources

This guide provides a road map for architecture, and describes the best practices you should consider when designing applications for the .NET Framework and Microsoft application platform. While the guide contains a wealth of information, including step-by-step topics for many of the most common scenarios, it cannot provide full details of every conceivable topic. However, Microsoft maintains a library of wide ranging yet deep guidance on all of its technologies, products, and services as described in the following section.

How Microsoft Organizes Technical Information on the Web

If you are just starting out trying to navigate Microsoft's rather large collection of technical documentation, there are a few things that you need to know, which will help to find what you are looking for more quickly.

First, Microsoft has several large Web sites, each with a different function. First Microsoft's corporate Web site (http://www.microsoft.com) contains all of Microsoft's product marketing information, including a substantial amount of technical marketing. For example, if you want to know what Microsoft's official position is on a topic such as Service Oriented Architecture (SOA), you could find that by simply navigating to Microsoft.com and searching for "SOA." In general, Microsoft tries to keep Microsoft. com focused on presenting the corporate image and explaining the benefits of the products, and locates technical information on other dedicated Web sites.

While the technical content is kept elsewhere, you can easily find the links to it from the Microsoft.com home page. If you examine the home page, you will notice categories of content such as *"Highlights," "Latest Releases," "Using Your Computer," "For Business,"* and two categories of technical content, *"For IT Professionals"* and *"For Developers."* Microsoft makes a distinction between software developers, and all other types of IT Professionals. This is primarily because there is so much content for developers, and because developers have significantly different information needs than, say, network administrators or operations personnel. While many of the links in these categories change frequently, the primary Web sites for technical information do not change. Technical information for developers is found on the Microsoft Developer Network (MSDN) site at http://msdn.microsoft.com. The primary site for technical information for all other IT professionals is Microsoft TechNet found at http://technet.microsoft.com.

Microsoft Developer Network

Once on MSDN, you will notice that it is divided into several areas including Developer Centers (typically one for each major development tool, language, technology, and technical domain), the Library (a huge repository of searchable content), Downloads, Support Forums, and Communities (where you can see what others are thinking and writing about, and participate should you choose).

There are also a couple of other important special subsites. Channel9 (http://channel9.msdn.com) features informal videos, usually of Microsoft product group software engineers or architects explaining the technologies they are working on, and often discussing the future plans of developer tools or technologies. CodePlex (http://codeplex.com) is Microsoft's open source project hosting site. There you can browse projects that other people are working on in public communities, or even spin up your own project. The Microsoft patterns & practices team develops all of their offerings in public CodePlex communities, providing the community at large to provide feedback on the project throughout the development cycle.

MSDN also provides technical chats and events such as Webcasts that can be very helpful in learning about a new technology area, or emerging technology.

Microsoft TechNet

Likewise, Microsoft TechNet offers a similar set of information and opportunities. On TechNet, not surprisingly, you will find TechCenters instead of Developer Centers. Other than that, the only significant difference is that TechNet contains the technical content for topics such as network infrastructure design, deployment, operations, and guidance for installing and managing Microsoft's products.

The .NET Framework

At a high level, the .NET Framework is composed of a virtual run-time engine, a library of classes, and run-time services used in the development and execution of .NET applications. The .NET Framework was initially released as a run-time engine and core set of classes used to build applications.

The Base Class Library (BCL) provides a core set of classes that cover a wide range of programming requirements in a number of areas, including UI, data access, database connectivity, cryptography, numeric algorithms, and network communications.

Overlaying the BCL are core technologies for developing .NET applications. These technologies include class libraries and run-time services that are grouped by application features, such as rich client and data access. As the Microsoft .NET Platform evolves, new technologies are added on top of the core technologies, such as WCF, WPF, and WF.

Common Language Runtime

The .NET Framework includes a virtual environment that manages the program's run-time requirements. This environment is called the CLR and provides the appearance of a virtual machine so that programmers do not need to consider the capabilities of the specific CPU or other hardware that will execute the program. Applications that run within the CLR are referred to as *managed applications*. Microsoft .NET Framework applications are developed using managed code (code that will execute within the CLR), although some features (such as device drivers that need to use kernel APIs) are often developed using unmanaged code. The CLR also provides services such as security, memory management, and exception handling.

Data Access

The following data access technologies are available on the Microsoft platform:

- **ADO.NET Core.** ADO.NET Core provides facilities for the general retrieval, update, and management of data. It includes providers for SQL Server, OLE DB, Open Database Connectivity (ODBC), SQL Server Compact Edition, and Oracle databases.

- **ADO.NET Data Services Framework.** This framework exposes data from any Linq enabled data source, typically an Entity Data Model, through RESTful Web services accessed over HTTP. The data can be addressed directly using Uniform Resource Identifiers (URIs). The Web service can be configured to return the data as plain Atom and JavaScript Object Notation (JSON) formats.

- **ADO.NET Entity Framework.** This framework gives you a strongly typed data access experience over relational databases. It moves the data model from the physical structure of relational tables to a conceptual model that accurately reflects common business objects. The Entity Framework introduces a common Entity Data Model within the ADO.NET environment, allowing developers to define a flexible mapping to relational data. This mapping helps to isolate applications from changes in the underlying storage schema. The Entity Framework also supports LINQ to Entities, which provides LINQ support for business objects exposed through the Entity Framework. When used as an Object/Relational Mapping (O/RM) product, developers use LINQ to Entities against business objects, which Entity Framework will convert to Entity SQL that is mapped against an Entity Data Model managed by the Entity Framework. Developers also have the option of working directly with the Entity Data Model and using Entity SQL in their applications.

- **ADO.NET Sync Services.** ADO.NET Sync Services is a provider included in the Microsoft Sync Framework, and is used to implement synchronization for ADO.NET-enabled databases. It enables data synchronization to be built into occasionally connected applications. It periodically gathers information from the client database and synchronizes it with the server database.

- **Language Integrated Query (LINQ).** LINQ provides class libraries that extend C# and Visual Basic with native language syntax for queries. It is primarily a query technology supported by different assemblies throughout the .NET Framework; for example, LINQ to Entities is included with the ADO.NET Entity Framework assemblies, LINQ to XML is included with the System.Xml assemblies, and LINQ to Objects is included with the .NET Framework core system assemblies. Queries can be performed against a variety of data formats, including DataSet (LINQ to DataSet), XML (LINQ to XML), in-memory objects (LINQ to Objects), ADO.NET Data Services (LINQ to Data Services), and relational data (LINQ to Entities).

- **LINQ to SQL.** LINQ to SQL provides a lightweight, strongly typed query solution against SQL Server. LINQ to SQL is designed for easy, fast object persistence scenarios where the classes in the mid-tier map very closely to database table structures. Starting with .NET Framework 4.0, LINQ to SQL scenarios will be integrated and supported by the ADO.NET Entity Framework; however, LINQ to SQL will continue to be a supported technology. For more information, see the ADO.NET team blog at http://blogs.msdn.com/adonet/archive/2008/10/31/clarifying-the-message-on-l2s-futures.aspx.

Mobile Applications

The .NET platform provides the following technology options for mobile applications:

- **Microsoft .NET Compact Framework.** This is a subset of the Microsoft .NET Framework designed specifically for mobile devices. Use this technology for mobile applications that must run on the device as a stand-alone or occasionally connected application.

- **ASP.NET for Mobile.** This is a subset of ASP.NET, designed specifically for mobile devices. ASP.NET Mobile applications can be hosted on a normal IIS Web server. Use this technology for mobile Web applications when you must support a large number of mobile devices and browsers that can rely on a guaranteed network connection.

- **Silverlight for Mobile.** This subset of the Silverlight client requires the Silverlight plug-in to be installed on the mobile device. Use this technology to port existing Silverlight applications to mobile devices, or if you want to create a richer UI than is possible using other technologies.

Rich Client

Windows-based applications are executed by the .NET Framework. The .NET Framework provides the following technology options for rich client applications:

- **Windows Forms.** This is the standard UI design technology for the .NET Framework. Even with the availability of WPF, Windows Forms is still a good choice for UI design if your team already has technical expertise with Windows Forms, and the application does not have a requirement for a highly graphical or streaming media UI.

- **Windows Presentation Foundation (WPF) application.** WPF applications support more advanced graphics capabilities, such as 2-D and 3-D graphics, display resolution independence, advanced document and typography support, animation with timelines, streaming audio and video, and vector-based graphics. WPF uses Extensible Application Markup Language (XAML) to implement the UI, data binding, and event definitions. WPF also includes advanced data binding and template capabilities. WPF applications can be deployed to the desktop or within a browser using a XAML browser application (XBAP). WPF applications support developer/designer interaction—developers can focus on the business logic, while designers can control the appearance and behavior.

- **Windows Forms with WPF user controls.** This approach allows you to take advantage of the more powerful UI capabilities provided by WPF controls. You can add WPF to your existing Windows Forms application. Keep in mind that WPF controls tend to work best on higher-powered client machines.

- **WPF with Windows Forms User Controls.** This technology allows you to supplement WPF with controls that are not provided with WPF. You can use the **WindowsFormsHost** control provided in the **WindowsFormsIntegration** assembly to add Windows Forms controls. However, there are some restrictions and inconsistencies related to overlapping controls, interface focus, and rendering techniques used by the different technologies.

- **XAML Browser Application (XBAP) using WPF.** This technology hosts a sandboxed WPF application in Microsoft Internet Explorer or Mozilla Firefox on Windows. Unlike Silverlight, you can use most of the WPF framework, but there are some limitations related to accessing system resources from the partial-trust sandbox. XBAP requires Windows Vista or both .NET Framework 3.5 and the XBAP browser plug-in on the client desktop. XBAP is a good choice when the required features are not available in Silverlight, and you can specify the client platform and trust requirements.

Rich Internet Application

The Microsoft application platform includes the Silverlight technology for building rich Internet applications. RIAs must be hosted on a Web server such as Windows Server Internet Information Services (IIS). The following options are available for building RIAs:

- **Silverlight.** This is a browser-optimized subset of WPF that works cross-platform and cross-browser. Compared to XBAP, Silverlight is a smaller, faster install but does not support 3-D graphics and text-flowable documents. Due to its small footprint and cross-platform support, Silverlight is a good choice for WPF applications that do not require premium WPF graphics support.

- **Silverlight with AJAX.** Silverlight natively supports Asynchronous JavaScript and XML (AJAX) and exposes its object model to JavaScript located in the Web page. You can use this capability to allow background interaction between your page components and the server to provide a more responsive user interface.

Services

The .NET platform provides the following technologies for creating service-based applications:

- **Windows Communication Foundation (WCF).** WCF is designed to offer a manageable approach to distributed computing and provide broad interoperability, and includes direct support for service orientation. It supports a range of protocols including HTTP, TCP, Microsoft Message Queuing, and named pipes.

- **ASP.NET Web services (ASMX).** ASMX offers a simpler approach to distributed computing and interoperability, but supports only the HTTP protocol.

Workflow

The .NET platform provides the following technology options for implementing workflows:

- **Windows Workflow Foundation (WF).** WF is a foundational technology that allows you to implement workflow. A toolkit for professional developers and independent software vendors (ISVs) who want to build a sequential or state-machine based workflow, WF supports the following types of workflow: Sequential, State-Machine, Data Driven, and Custom. You can create workflows using the Windows Workflow Designer in Visual Studio.

- **Workflow Services.** Workflow Services provides integration between WCF and WF to provide WCF-based services for workflow. Starting with Microsoft .NET Framework 3.5, WCF has been extended to provide support for workflows exposed as services and the ability to call services from within workflows. In addition, Visual Studio 2008 includes new templates and tools that support workflow services.

- **Microsoft Office SharePoint Services (MOSS).** MOSS is a content-management and collaboration platform that provides workflow support based on WF. MOSS provides a solution for human workflow and collaboration in the context of a SharePoint server. You can create workflows for document approval directly within the MOSS interface. You can also create workflows using either the SharePoint Designer or the Windows Workflow Designer in Visual Studio. For workflow customization, you can use the WF object model within Visual Studio.

- **Microsoft BizTalk Server.** BizTalk currently has its own workflow engine that is geared toward orchestration, such as enterprise integration with system-level workflows. A future version of BizTalk may use WF as well as XLANG (an extension of the Web Service Definition Language used to model service orchestration and collaboration), which is the existing orchestration technology in BizTalk. You can define the overall design and flow of loosely coupled, long-running business processes by using BizTalk Orchestration Services within and between applications.

Note: MOSS and BizTalk server are not part of the .NET Framework or Visual Studio; these are independent products, but part of the overall Microsoft platform.

Web Applications

The .NET platform includes ASP.NET for building Web applications and simple Web services. ASP.NET applications must be hosted within a Web server such as IIS. The following technologies are available for building Web applications using ASP.NET:

- **ASP.NET Web Forms.** This is the standard UI design and implementation technology for .NET Web applications. An ASP.NET Web Forms application needs only to be installed on the Web server, with no components required on the client desktop.

- **ASP.NET Web Forms with AJAX.** Use AJAX with ASP.NET Web Forms to process requests between the server and client asynchronously to improve responsiveness, provide richer experience to the client, and reduce the number of post backs to the server. AJAX is an integral part of ASP.NET in .NET Framework 3.5 and later.

- **ASP.NET Web Forms with Silverlight Controls.** If you have an existing ASP.NET application, you can use Silverlight controls to improve the user experience and avoid the requirement to write a whole new Silverlight application. This is a good approach for creating islands of Silverlight content in an existing application.

- **ASP.NET MVC.** This technology allows you to use ASP.NET to build applications based on the Model-View-Controller (MVC) pattern. ASP.NET MVC supports test-driven development and clear separation of concerns between UI processing and UI rendering. This approach helps to avoid mixing presentation information with logic code.

- **ASP.NET Dynamic Data.** This technology allows you to create data-driven ASP.NET applications that leverage LINQ to Entities functionality. It provides a rapid development model for line-of-business (LOB)-style data-driven applications, supporting both simple scaffolding and full customization capabilities.

Web Server – Internet Information Services

The Microsoft platform includes IIS, which provides full-scale support for Internet publishing, including transport services, client applications, administrative tools, database and application connectivity, and encrypted communication. IIS supports the following services:

- **World Wide Web Service.** This service provides all the features required for hypertext document publishing, and delivering other types of content that use HTTP. It provides high performance, compression, extensive configurability, and supports a range of security and authentication options.

- **File Transfer Protocol (FTP) Service.** This service allows you to receive and deliver files using FTP. However, authentication is limited to the Basic method.

- **Gopher Service.** This service supports a distributed document search and retrieval network protocol. It is rarely used today.

- **Internet Database Connector.** This is an integrated gateway and template scripting mechanism for the World Wide Web service to access Open Database Connectivity (ODBC) databases. Generally superseded by new data-access and scripting technologies such as ASP.NET and ASP.NET Data Services.

- **Secure Sockets Layer (SSL) Client/Server.** This provides a mechanism to support encrypted communication over HTTP, allowing clients and servers to communicate more securely than when sending content as plain text.

- **Internet Service Manager Server.** This is an administration console and associated tools that provide local and remote administration features for IIS.

- **Integration with ASP.NET.** IIS 7.0 and later is specifically designed to integrate closely with ASP.NET to maximize performance and minimize server load when using ASP.NET to create and deliver content.

Database Server – SQL Server

A relational database is a common approach for storing and accessing data in an enterprise application. The Microsoft application platform provides SQL Server as the database engine for your applications. SQL Server is available in several variants, from a single-instance, local database (SQL Server Express) scaling to enterprise-level applications through SQL Server Enterprise Edition.

The data access technologies that are part of the .NET Framework allow you to access data in any version of SQL Server, so you do not need to modify your application if you want to scale up to a more powerful version.

Visual Studio Development Environment

The .NET platform provides a comprehensive development environment known as the Visual Studio Team System. Microsoft Visual Studio is the primary environment for developing .NET applications, and is available in several different versions that target specific groups involved in the full life cycle of application development.

You can use the language of your choice within Visual Studio Team System to write applications that target the .NET Framework. As an integrated development environment (IDE), it provides all the tools you require to design, develop, debug, and deploy rich client, RIA, Web, mobile, services, and Office-based solutions. You can install multiple versions side by side to obtain the required combination of features.

Other Tools and Libraries

In addition to Visual Studio, other tools and frameworks are available to speed development or facilitate operational management. Examples are:

- System Center, which provides a set of tools and environments for enterprise-level application monitoring, deployment, configuration, and management. For more information, see the *"Microsoft System Center"* at http://www.microsoft.com/systemcenter/en/us/default.aspx.

- Expression Studio, which provides tools aimed at graphical designers for creating rich interfaces and animations. For more information, see *"Microsoft Expression"* at http://www.microsoft.com/expression/products/Overview.aspx?key=studio.

patterns & practices Solution Assets

For more information on solution assets available from the Microsoft patterns & practices group, see the following resources:

- **Composite Client Application Guidance for WPF** for both desktop and Silverlight makes it easier to create modular applications. For more information, see *"Composite Client Application Guidance"* at http://msdn.microsoft.com/en-us/library/cc707819.aspx.

- **Enterprise Library** contains a series of application blocks that address crosscutting concerns. For more information, see *"Enterprise Library"* at http://msdn.microsoft.com/en-us/library/cc467894.aspx.

- **Software Factories** speed development of specific types of application such as Smart Clients, WPF applications, and Web Services. For more information, see *"patterns & practices: by Application Type"* at http://msdn.microsoft.com/en-gb/practices/bb969054.aspx.

- **Unity Application Block** for both enterprise and Silverlight scenarios provides features for implementing dependency injection, service location, and inversion of control. For more information, see *"Unity Application Block"* at http://msdn.microsoft.com/en-us/library/dd203101.aspx.

- **Detailed guidance** for a wide range of enterprise architecture, design, development, and deployment scenarios. These include scenarios such as solution development fundamentals, client development, server development, and services development. For more information, see the patterns & practices home page at http://msdn.microsoft.com/en-us/library/ms998572.aspx.

Additional Resources

To more easily access Web resources, see the online version of the bibliography at: http://www.microsoft.com/architectureguide.

For more information about the .NET Framework, see the following resources:

- *".NET Framework 3.5 Overview"* at http://msdn.microsoft.com/en-us/library/a4t23ktk.aspx.
- *"Overview of the .NET Framework"* at http://msdn.microsoft.com/en-us/library/zw4w595w(VS.71).aspx.
- *"Overview of the .NET Compact Framework"* at http://msdn.microsoft.com/en-us/library/w6ah6cw1(VS.80).aspx.

For more information about Web services, see the following resources:

- *"Windows Communication Foundation"* at http://msdn.microsoft.com/en-us/library/ms735119.aspx.
- *"XML Web Services Using ASP.NET"* at http://msdn.microsoft.com/en-us/library/ba0z6a33.aspx.

For more information about workflow services, see the following resources:

- *"Microsoft BizTalk ESB Toolkit"* at http://msdn.microsoft.com/en-us/library/dd897973.aspx.
- *"Workflows in Office SharePoint Server 2007"* at http://msdn.microsoft.com/en-us/library/ms549489.aspx.
- *"Windows Workflow Foundation (WF)"* at http://msdn.microsoft.com/en-us/netframework/aa663328.aspx.

For more information about other features of the Microsoft platform, see the following resources:

- For more information on data access, see *"Data Platform Development"* at http://msdn.microsoft.com/en-gb/data/default.aspx.
- For more information about the IIS Web server, see *"A High-Level Look at Microsoft Internet Information Server"* at http://msdn.microsoft.com/en-us/library/ms993571.aspx.
- For more information about SQL Server, see *"SQL Server"* at http://msdn.microsoft.com/en-gb/sqlserver/default.aspx.
- For more information about Visual Studio Team System, see *"Visual Studio 2008 Overview"* at http://msdn.microsoft.com/en-us/vstudio/products/bb931331.aspx.

Appendix B
Presentation Technology Matrix

Overview

This appendix will help you to understand the tradeoffs you must make when choosing a presentation technology. It will help you to understand the design impact of choosing a particular technology, and assist when choosing a presentation technology for your scenario and application type.

Your choice of presentation technology will be related to both the application type you are developing and the type of user experience you plan to deliver. Use the Presentation Technologies Summary to understand the technology choices available for each application type. Use the Benefits and Considerations Matrix to make an informed choice of presentation technology based on the advantages and considerations of each one. Use the Common Scenarios and Solutions to map your application scenario to common presentation technology solutions.

Presentation Technologies Summary

The following sections describe the Microsoft technologies available for each of the four basic application archetypes: mobile, rich client, rich Internet application (RIA), and Web.

Mobile Applications

The following presentation technologies are suitable for use in mobile applications:

- **Microsoft .NET Compact Framework.** This is a subset of the Microsoft .NET Framework designed specifically for mobile devices. Use this technology for mobile applications that must run on the device as a stand-alone or occasionally connected application.

- **ASP.NET for Mobile.** This is a subset of ASP.NET, designed specifically for mobile devices. ASP.NET Mobile applications can be hosted on a normal Web server. Use this technology for mobile Web applications when you must support a large number of mobile devices and browsers that can rely on a guaranteed network connection.

- **Microsoft Silverlight for Mobile.** This subset of the Silverlight client requires the Silverlight plug-in to be installed on the mobile device. Use this technology to port existing Silverlight applications to mobile devices, or if you want to create a richer UI than is possible using other technologies.

Rich Client Applications

The following presentation technologies are suitable for use in rich client applications:

- **Windows Forms.** This is the standard UI design technology for the .NET Framework. Even with the availability of WPF, Windows Forms is still a good choice for UI design if your team already has technical expertise with Windows Forms, and the application does not have a requirement for a highly graphical or streaming media UI.

- **Windows Presentation Foundation (WPF) application.** WPF applications support more advanced graphics capabilities, such as 2-D and 3-D graphics, display resolution independence, advanced document and typography support, animation with timelines, streaming audio and video, and vector-based graphics. WPF uses Extensible Application Markup Language (XAML) to implement the UI, data binding, and event definitions. WPF also includes advanced data binding and template capabilities. WPF applications can be deployed to the desktop or within a browser using a XAML browser application (XBAP). WPF applications support developer/designer interaction—developers can focus on the business logic, while designers can control the appearance and behavior.

- **Windows Forms with WPF user controls.** This approach allows you to take advantage of the more powerful UI capabilities provided by WPF controls. You can add WPF to your existing Windows Forms application. Keep in mind that WPF controls tend to work best on higher-powered client machines.

- **WPF with Windows Forms User Controls.** This technology allows you to supplement WPF with controls that are not provided with WPF. You can use the WindowsFormsHost control provided in the WindowsFormsIntegration assembly to add Windows Forms controls. However, there are some restrictions and inconsistencies related to overlapping controls, interface focus, and rendering techniques used by the different technologies.

- **XAML Browser Application (XBAP) using WPF.** This technology hosts a sandboxed WPF application in Microsoft Internet Explorer or Mozilla Firefox on Windows. Unlike Silverlight, you can use most of the WPF framework, but there are some limitations related to accessing system resources from the partial-trust sandbox. XBAP requires Windows Vista or both .NET Framework 3.5 and the XBAP browser plug-in on the client desktop. XBAP is a good choice when the required features are not available in Silverlight, and you can specify the client platform and trust requirements.

Rich Internet Applications

The following presentation technologies are suitable for use in RIAs:

- **Silverlight.** This is a browser-optimized subset of WPF that works cross-platform and cross-browser. Compared to XBAP, Silverlight is a smaller, faster install but does not support 3-D graphics and text-flowable documents. Due to its small footprint and cross-platform support, Silverlight is a good choice for WPF applications that do not require premium WPF graphics support.

- **Silverlight with AJAX.** Silverlight natively supports Asynchronous JavaScript and XML (AJAX) and exposes its object model to JavaScript located in the Web page. You can use this capability to allow interaction between your page components and the server, and provide a more responsive and interactive user interface.

Web Applications

The following presentation technologies are suitable for use in Web applications:

- **ASP.NET Web Forms.** This is the standard UI design and implementation technology for .NET Web applications. An ASP.NET Web Forms application needs only to be installed on the Web server, with no components required on the client desktop.

- **ASP.NET Web Forms with AJAX.** Use AJAX with ASP.NET Web Forms to process requests between the server and client asynchronously to improve responsiveness, provide richer experience to the client, and reduce the number of postbacks to the server. AJAX is an integral part of ASP.NET in .NET Framework 3.5 and later.

- **ASP.NET Web Forms with Silverlight Controls.** If you have an existing ASP.NET application, you can use Silverlight controls to improve the user experience and avoid the requirement to write a whole new Silverlight application. This is a good approach for creating islands of Silverlight content in an existing application.

- **ASP.NET MVC.** This technology allows you to use ASP.NET to build applications based on the Model-View-Controller (MVC) pattern. ASP.NET MVC supports test-driven development and clear separation of concerns between UI processing and UI rendering. This approach helps to avoid mixing presentation information with logic code.

- **ASP.NET Dynamic Data.** This technology allows you to create data-driven ASP.NET applications that leverage Language-Integrated Query (LINQ) to Entities functionality. It provides a rapid development model for line-of-business (LOB)-style data-driven applications, supporting both simple scaffolding and full customization capabilities.

Benefits and Considerations Matrix

The following tables contain lists of benefits and liabilities for each of the presentation technologies described in the previous sections.

Mobile Applications

Technology	Benefits	Considerations
.NET Compact Framework	Runs on the client machine for improved performance and responsiveness. Does not require 100% network connectivity. Has a familiar programming model if you are used to Windows Forms. Visual Studio provides designer support. Is usually installed in ROM on the device.	Has a limited API compared to a desktop Windows Forms application. Requires more client-side resources than an ASP.NET for Mobile application. Is not as easy to deploy over the Web as an ASP.NET for Mobile application.
ASP.NET Mobile	Supports a wide range of devices, including anything that has a Web browser. Does not have a footprint on the device because no application must be installed. Has a familiar programming model if you are used to ASP.NET Web Forms. Templates for designer support in Visual Studio can be downloaded from the Web.	Design support has been removed from Visual Studio 2008, but the controls will still render on devices. Requires 100% network connectivity to run. Performance and responsiveness are dependent on network bandwidth and latency. Many devices now support full HTML support, so standard ASP.NET applications may be suitable.
Silverlight Mobile	Offers rich UI and visualization, including 2-D graphics, vector graphics, and animation. Silverlight code running on desktops can run on Silverlight for Mobile. Isolated storage is available to maintain objects outside of the browser cache.	Uses more device resources than a Web application. Desktop Silverlight applications running on mobile may require optimization to account for reduced memory and slower hardware. Requires the Silverlight plug-in to be installed. May not run on as many types of devices as Web applications because of plug-in installation requirement.

Rich Client Applications

Technology	Benefits	Considerations
Windows Forms	Has a familiar programming model. Microsoft Visual Studio provides designer support. Offers good performance on a wide range of client hardware.	Does not support 3-D graphics, streaming media, flowable text; or other advanced UI features available in WPF such as UI styling and templates. Must be installed on the client.
Windows Forms with WPF User Controls	Allows you to add a rich UI to existing Windows Forms applications. Provides a transition strategy to full WPF applications.	Depending on the complexity of your UI, it may require higher powered graphics hardware. You cannot overlay Windows Forms and WPF controls.
WPF application	Provides rich UI and visualization including 2-D and 3-D graphics, display resolution independence, vector graphics, flowable text, and animation. Supports variable-bandwidth streaming media (Adaptive Media Streaming). XAML makes it easier to define the UI, data binding, and events. Supports separate developer/designer integration.	Depending on the complexity of your UI, it may require higher powered graphics hardware. Your design team may be less familiar with Expression Blend compared to Visual Studio. WPF ships with fewer built-in controls than Windows Forms.
WPF with Windows Forms Controls	Allows you to supplement WPF with controls that are not provided with WFP; for example, WPF does not provide a grid control.	Requires a **WindowsFormsHost**. It may be difficult to get focus and input to transition across boundaries. You cannot overlap WPF and Windows Forms controls. WPF and Windows Forms controls use different rendering techniques, which can cause inconsistencies in how they appear on different platforms.
XBAP using WPF	Allows you to deploy a WPF application over the Web. Provides all the rich visualization and UI benefits of WPF. Is easier to deploy and update than a WPF or Windows Forms application.	Only works on Vista or on a client with .NET Framework 3.5 and the XBAP browser plug-in installed. Only works in Internet Explorer and Mozilla Firefox browsers, and there may be some limitation on resource access on the client.

Rich Internet Applications

Technology	Benefits	Considerations
Silverlight	Provides a lightweight install for client machines. Provides most of the UI and visualization power of WPF, such as media streaming, 2-D graphics, vector graphics, animation, and resolution independence. Isolated storage provides an application cache independent from the browser cache. Supports high definition video. Client-side processing provides improved user experience and responsiveness compared to a Web application. Supports a wide variety of languages such as C#, Visual Basic .NET, Ruby, and Python. Supports windowless background processing as a replacement for JavaScript. Provides cross-platform support, including Mac and Linux. Provides cross-browser support, including Firefox and Safari.	Requires a Silverlight plug-in to be installed on the client. Your team may be less familiar with Expression Blend compared to Visual Studio. Lacks the advanced 3-D graphics and flowable text support of WPF. Is not easy to transition from WPF or XBAP due to differences in the XAML and controls.
Silverlight with AJAX	Allows you to use existing AJAX libraries and routines from your Silverlight application. Allows Silverlight objects to be dynamically created and destroyed through communication with the server as the user interacts with the application, which can provide additional opportunities for responsive and interactive interfaces.	May be an unfamiliar programming model if your team is used to pure ASP. NET or Silverlight.

Web Applications

Technology	Benefits	Considerations
ASP.NET Web Forms	Brings a development experience similar to Windows Forms to the Web. Has no client dependency. Requires no installation on the client. Provides cross-platform and cross-browser support. Provides Visual Studio design support. A wide range of controls are available.	UI is limited to HTML and Dynamic HTML (DHTML) support. Client-side storage is limited to cookies and View state. Updating page contents requires a full postback and page refresh. Has limited UI responsiveness because all processing occurs on the server.
ASP.NET Web Forms with AJAX	Provides improved UI responsiveness and a richer experience. Supports lazy loading. Allows partial page refreshes. An integral part of ASP.NET 3.5.	May be an unfamiliar programming model if your team is used to pure ASP.NET. Does not work if JavaScript is disabled on the client.
ASP.NET Web Forms with Silverlight Controls	Allows you to add Silverlight rich visualization and UI to existing ASP.NET applications. Provides a strategy for transition to full Silverlight applications.	Requires the Silverlight plug-in to be installed on the client. Your team may be less familiar with Expression Blend compared to Visual Studio.
ASP.NET MVC	Supports test-driven development. Enforces separation between UI processing and UI rendering. Allows you to create user friendly and search engine friendly URLs. Provides full control over markup. Provides full control over how content is rendered. Navigation is controlled by configuration to greatly reduce the amount of code required.	Does not support View state. No support for control events.
ASP.NET Dynamic Data	Allows the creation of fully data-driven sites that render automatically. Has built-in support for LINQ querying languages. Has built-in support for the ADO.NET Entity Framework. LINQ allows you to model your database to create object-to-data mappings.	Currently there are only a few controls that support the technology.

Common Scenarios and Solutions

The following sections provide guidance on choosing the appropriate type of presentation technology for the four basic application archetypes: mobile, rich client, RIA, and Web.

Mobile Applications

For mobile applications, consider the following guidelines when choosing a presentation technology:

Consider using the **.NET Compact Framework** if:

- You are building a mobile application that must support occasionally connected or offline scenarios.
- You are building a mobile application that will run on the client to maximize performance and responsiveness.

Consider using **ASP.NET for Mobile** if:

- Your team has ASP.NET expertise and you want to target the widest possible range of devices.
- You are building an application that must have no client-side installation or plug-in dependencies.
- You are building an application that can rely on 100% network connectivity.
- You must use as few device resources or have the smallest footprint on the device as possible.

Consider using **Silverlight for Mobile** if:

- You are building a mobile Web application and want to leverage the rich visualization and UI capabilities of Silverlight.
- The devices you are targeting have easy access to or already have the Silverlight plug-in installed.

Rich Client Applications

For rich client applications, consider the following guidelines when choosing a presentation technology:

Consider using **Windows Forms** if:

- Your team already has experience building Windows Forms applications and you cannot afford to change to another technology.
- You are extending or modifying an existing Windows Forms application.
- You do not require rich media or animation support.

Consider using **WPF** if:

- You are building a rich client application and want to leverage the rich visualization and UI capabilities of WPF.
- You are building a rich client application that you may want to deploy to the Web using XBAP.

Consider using **Windows Forms with WPF user controls** if:

- You already have a Windows Forms application and want to take advantage of WPF capabilities such as advanced graphics, flowable text, streaming media, and animations.
- Consider using WPF with Windows Forms controls if:
- You are building a rich client application using WPF and want to use a control not provided by WPF.

Consider using **XBAP** if:

- You already have a WPF application that you want to deploy to the Web.
- You want to leverage rich visualization and UI capabilities of WPF that are not available in Silverlight.

Rich Internet Applications

For RIA implementations, consider the following guidelines when choosing a presentation technology:

Consider using **Silverlight** if:

- You want to leverage the rich visualization, streaming media, and UI capabilities of Silverlight.
- You are building an application that requires seamless deployment and the capability to delay load the individual modules it uses.
- You are targeting a range of browsers across different platforms.

Consider using **Silverlight with AJAX** if:

- You want to be able to dynamically manage the object instances in the Silverlight object model from your Web page.
- You want to manipulate Silverlight controls based on user interaction within your Web page.

Web Applications

For Web applications, consider the following guidelines when choosing a presentation technology:

Consider using **ASP.NET Web Forms** if:

- Your team already has experience building ASP.NET Web Forms.
- You have an existing ASP.NET Web Forms application that you want to extend or modify.
- You want to run on the widest possible range of client machines.
- You do not want to install anything on the client.
- You want to design simple functionality such as Create, Read, Update, and Delete (CRUD) operations without a rich UI or animation.

Consider using **ASP. NET Web Forms with AJAX** if:

- You want to create ASP.NET Web Forms with a more responsive and richer user experience.
- You want to support lazy loading and partial page refreshes.

Consider using **ASP.NET Web Forms with Silverlight controls** if:

- You already have an ASP.NET Web Forms application and want to leverage the rich visualization and UI capabilities of Silverlight.
- You are planning to transition your Web application to Silverlight.

Consider using **ASP.NET MVC** if:

- You want to implement the Model-View-Controller (MVC) pattern.
- You want full control over the markup.
- You want to implement a clear separation of concerns between UI processing and UI rendering.
- You want to follow test-driven development practices.

Consider using **ASP.NET Dynamic Data** if:

- You want to build a data-driven application rapidly.
- You want to use the LINQ query language or the Entity Framework data model.
- You want to use the built-in modeling capabilities of LINQ to map your objects to data more easily.

Additional Resources

To more easily access Web resources, see the online version of the bibliography at: http://www.microsoft.com/architectureguide.

- For information on Silverlight, see the official Silverlight Web site at http://silverlight.net/default.aspx.
- For information on "Islands of Richness", see http://blogs.msdn.com/brada/archive/2008/02/18/ islands-of-richness-with-silverlight-on-an-asp-net-page.aspx.

Appendix C
Data Access Technology Matrix

Overview

This appendix will help you to understand the tradeoffs you have to make when choosing a data access technology. It will help you to understand the design impact of each technology, and assist when choosing a data access technology for your scenario and application type.

Your choice of data access technology will be related to both the application type you are developing and the type of business entities you use. Use the Data Access Technologies Summary to review each technology and its description. Use the Benefits and Considerations Matrix to understand the range of technologies available for data access. Use the Common Scenarios and Solutions section to map your application scenarios to common data-access technology solutions.

Data Access Technologies Summary

The following data access technologies are available on the Microsoft platform:

- **ADO.NET Core.** ADO.NET Core provides facilities for the general retrieval, update, and management of data. It includes providers for SQL Server, OLE DB, Open Database Connectivity (ODBC), SQL Server Compact Edition, and Oracle databases.

- **ADO.NET Data Services Framework.** This framework exposes data using the Entity Data Model, through RESTful Web services accessed over HTTP. The data can be addressed directly using Uniform Resource Identifiers (URIs). The Web service can be configured to return the data as plain Atom and JavaScript Object Notation (JSON) formats.

- **ADO.NET Entity Framework.** This framework gives you a strongly typed data access experience over relational databases. It moves the data model from the physical structure of relational tables to a conceptual model that accurately reflects common business objects. The Entity Framework introduces a common Entity Data Model within the ADO.NET environment, allowing developers to define a flexible mapping to relational data. This mapping helps to isolate applications from changes in the underlying storage schema. The Entity Framework also supports LINQ to Entities, which provides LINQ support for business objects exposed through the Entity Framework. When used as an Object/Relational Mapping (O/RM) product, developers use LINQ to Entities against business objects, which Entity Framework will convert to Entity SQL that is mapped against an Entity Data Model managed by the Entity Framework. Developers also have the option of working directly with the Entity Data Model and using Entity SQL in their applications.

- **ADO.NET Sync Services.** ADO.NET Sync Services is a provider included in the Microsoft Sync Framework, and is used to implement synchronization for ADO.NET-enabled databases. It enables data synchronization to be built into occasionally connected applications. It periodically gathers information from the client database and synchronizes it with the server database.

- **Language Integrated Query (LINQ).** LINQ provides class libraries that extend C# and Visual Basic with native language syntax for queries. It is primarily a query technology supported by different assemblies throughout the .NET Framework; for example, LINQ to Entities is included with the ADO.NET Entity Framework assemblies, LINQ to XML is included with the System.Xml assemblies, and LINQ to Objects is included with the .NET Framework core system assemblies. Queries can be performed against a variety of data formats, including DataSet (LINQ to DataSet), XML (LINQ to XML), in-memory objects (LINQ to Objects), ADO.NET Data Services (LINQ to Data Services), and relational data (LINQ to Entities).

- **LINQ to SQL.** LINQ to SQL provides a lightweight, strongly typed query solution against SQL Server. LINQ to SQL is designed for easy, fast object persistence scenarios where the classes in the mid-tier map very closely to database table structures. Starting with .NET Framework 4.0, LINQ to SQL scenarios will be integrated and supported by the ADO.NET Entity Framework; however, LINQ to SQL will continue to be a supported technology. For more information, see the ADO.NET team blog at http://blogs.msdn.com/adonet/archive/2008/10/31/clarifying-the-message-on-l2s-futures.aspx.

Benefits and Considerations Matrix

The following tables contain lists of benefits and liabilities for the data access technologies described in the previous sections. The individual tables cover a range of usage scenarios: object-relational data access, disconnected and offline data access, SOA and service scenarios, and n-tier and general scenarios. Some general recommendations for the data access technologies discussed in this appendix follow the tables.

Object-Relational Data Access

Technology	Benefits	Considerations
ADO.NET Entity Framework (EF)	Decouples the underlying database structure from the logical data model. Entity SQL provides a consistent query language across all data sources and database types. Separates metadata into well-defined architectural layers. Allows business logic developers to access the data without knowing database specifics. Provides rich designer support in Visual Studio to visualize data entity structure. Use of a provider model allows it to be mapped to many databases.	Requires you to change the design of your entities and queries if you are coming from a more traditional data access method. Uses separate object models. Has more layers of abstraction than LINQ to **DataSet**. Can be used with or without LINQ to Entities. If your database structure changes, you must regenerate the Entity Data Model and re-deploy the EF libraries.
LINQ to Entities	A LINQ-based solution for relational data in the ADO.NET Entity Framework. Provides strongly typed LINQ access to relational data. Supports LINQ-based queries against objects built on top of the EF Entity Data Model. Processing occurs on the server.	Requires the ADO.NET Entity Framework.
LINQ to SQL	Simple way to read/write objects when the data object model matches the physical database model. Provides strongly typed LINQ query access to SQL data. Processing occurs on the server.	Functionality integrated into the Entity Framework as of .NET Framework 4.0. Maps LINQ queries directly to the database instead of through a provider, and therefore works only with Microsoft SQL Server.

Disconnected and Offline

Technology	Benefits	Considerations
LINQ to DataSet	Allows full-featured queries against a **DataSet**.	All processing occurs on the client.
ADO.NET Sync Services	Enables synchronization between databases, collaboration, and offline scenarios. Synchronization can execute in the background. Provides a hub-and-spoke type of architecture for collaboration between databases.	You must implement your own change tracking. Exchanging large chunks of data during synchronization can reduce performance.

SOA/Service Scenarios

Technology	Benefits	Considerations
ADO. NET Data Services Framework	Data can be addressed directly via a URI using a REST-like scheme. Data can be returned in either Atom or JSON formats. Includes a lightweight versioning scheme to simplify the release of new service interfaces. The .NET Framework, Silverlight, and AJAX client libraries allow developers to work directly with objects and provide strongly typed LINQ access to ADO.NET Data Services. The .NET Framework, Silverlight, and AJAX client libraries provide a familiar API surface to Windows Azure Tables, SQL Data Services, and other Microsoft services.	Is only applicable to service-oriented scenarios.
LINQ to Data Services	Allows you to create LINQ-based queries against client-side data returned from ADO.NET Data Services. Supports LINQ-based queries against REST data.	Can only be used with the ADO.NET Data Services client-side framework.

N-Tier and General

Technology	Benefits	Considerations
ADO.NET Core	Includes .NET managed code providers for connected access to a wide range of data stores. Provides facilities for disconnected data storage and manipulation.	Code is written directly against specific providers, thereby reducing reusability. The relational database structure may not match the object model, requiring you to create a data-mapping layer.
ADO. NET Data Services Framework	Data can be addressed directly via a URI using a REST-like scheme. Data can be returned in either Atom or JSON formats. Includes a lightweight versioning scheme to simplify the release of new service interfaces. Provider model allows any **IQueryable** data source to be used. The .NET Framework, Silverlight, and AJAX client libraries provide a familiar API surface to Windows Azure Tables, SQL Data Services, and other Microsoft services.	Is only applicable to service-oriented scenarios. Provides a resource-centric service that maps well to data-heavy services, but may require more work if a majority of the services are operation-centric.
ADO.NET Entity Framework	Separates metadata into well-defined architectural layers. Supports LINQ to Entities for querying complex object models. Use of a provider model allows it to be mapped to many database types. Allows you to build services that have well defined boundaries, and data/ service contracts for sending and receiving well defined entities across the service boundary. Instances of entities from your Entity Data Model are directly serializable and consumable by Web services. Full flexibility in structuring the payload— send individual entities, collections of entities, or an entity graph to the server. Eventually will allow for true persistence-ignorant objects to be shipped across service boundaries.	Requires you to change the design of your entities and queries if you are coming from a more traditional data access method. Entity objects can be sent across a network, or you can use the Data Mapper pattern to transform entities into objects that are more generalized **DataContract** types. The planned POCO support will eliminate the need to transform objects when sending them over a network. Building service endpoints that receive a generalized graph of entities is less service oriented than endpoints that enforce stricter contracts on the types of payload that might be accepted.

(continued)

Technology	Benefits	Considerations
LINQ to Objects	Allows you to create LINQ-based queries against objects in memory. Represents a new approach to retrieving data from collections. Can be used directly with any collections that support **IEnumerable** or **IEnumerable<T>**. Can be used to query strings, reflection-based metadata, and file directories.	Works only with objects that implement the **IEnumerable** interface.
LINQ to XML	Allows you to create LINQ-based queries against XML data. Is comparable to the Document Object Model (DOM), which brings an XML document into memory, but is much easier to use. Query results can be used as parameters to **XElement** and **XAttribute** object constructors.	Relies heavily on generic classes. Is not optimized to work with untrusted XML documents, which require different security mitigation techniques.
LINQ to SQL	Provides a simple technique for retrieving and updating data as objects when the object model and the database model are the same.	As of .NET Framework 4.0, the Entity Framework will be the recommended data access solution for LINQ-to-relational scenarios. LINQ to SQL will continue to be supported and will evolve based on feedback received from the community.

General Recommendations

Consider the following general recommendations when choosing a data access technology:

- **Flexibility and performance.** If you need maximum performance and flexibility, consider using ADO.NET Core. ADO.NET Core provides the most capabilities and is the most server-specific solution. When using ADO.NET Core, consider the tradeoff of additional flexibility versus the need to write custom code. Keep in mind that mapping to custom objects will reduce performance. If you require a thin framework that uses the ADO.NET providers and supports database changes through configuration, consider the Enterprise Library Data Access Application Block.

- **Object relational mapping (O/RM).** If you are looking for an O/RM-based solution and/or must support multiple databases, consider the Entity Framework. This is ideal for implementing Domain Model scenarios.

- **Offline scenario.** If you must support a disconnected scenario, consider using DataSets or the Sync Framework.

- **N-Tier scenario.** If you are passing data across layers or tiers, available options include passing entity objects, Data Transfer Objects (DTO) that are mapped to entities, DataSets, and custom objects. If you are building resource-centric services (REST), consider ADO.NET Data Services. If you are building operation-centric services (SOAP), consider Windows Communication Foundation (WCF) services with explicitly defined service and data contracts.

- **SOA and services scenarios.** If you expose your database as a service, consider ADO.NET Data Services. If you want to store your data in the cloud, consider SQL Data Services.

- **Microsoft Windows Mobile.** Many data technologies are too heavy for the limited memory capabilities of most Windows Mobile devices. Consider using SQL Server Compact Edition database and ADO.NET Sync Services to maintain data on a mobile device and synchronize it with a server-based database system. Features such as merge replication can also be useful in Windows Mobile scenarios.

Common Scenarios and Solutions

The following sections provide guidance on choosing the appropriate type of data access technology for your application.

Consider using **ADO.NET Core** if:

- You must use low-level APIs for full control over data access in your application.
- You want to leverage the existing investment in ADO.NET providers.
- You are using traditional data access logic against the database.
- You do not need the additional functionality offered by the other data access technologies.
- You are building an application that must support a disconnected data access experience.

Consider using **ADO.NET Data Services Framework** if:

- You want to access data that is exposed as a service using REST-like URIs.

Consider using **ADO.NET Entity Framework** if:

- You must share a conceptual model across applications and services.
- You must map a single class to multiple tables via inheritance.
- You must query relational stores other than the Microsoft SQL Server family of products.
- You have an object model that you must map to a relational model using a flexible schema.
- You need the flexibility of separating the mapping schema from the object model.

Consider using **ADO.NET Sync Services** if:

- You must build an application that supports occasionally connected scenarios.
- You are using Windows Mobile and want to synchronize with a central database server.

Consider using **LINQ to Data Services** if:

- You are using data returned from ADO.NET Data Services in a client.
- You want to execute queries against client-side data using LINQ syntax.
- You want to execute queries against REST data using LINQ syntax.

Consider using **LINQ to DataSets** if:

- You want to execute queries against a **Dataset**, including queries that join tables.
- You want to use a common query language instead of writing iterative code.

Consider using **LINQ to Entities** if:

- You are using the ADO.NET Entity Framework.
- You must to execute queries over strongly typed entities.
- You want to execute queries against relational data using the LINQ syntax.

Consider using **LINQ to Objects** if:

- You must execute queries against a collection.
- You must execute queries against file directories.
- You must execute queries against in-memory objects using the LINQ syntax.

Consider using **LINQ to XML** if:

- You are using XML data in your application.
- You want to execute queries against XML data using the LINQ syntax.

LINQ to SQL Considerations

LINQ to Entities is the recommended solution for LINQ to relational database scenarios. LINQ to SQL will continue to be supported but will not be a primary focus for innovation or improvement. If you are already relying on LINQ to SQL, you can continue using it. For new solutions, consider using LINQ to Entities instead. For more information, see the ADO.NET team blog at http://blogs.msdn.com/adonet/.

Mobile Considerations

A number of the technologies listed above are not available on the Windows Mobile operating system. The following technologies are not available on Windows Mobile at the time of publication:

- ADO.NET Entity Framework
- ADO.NET Data Services Framework
- LINQ to Entities
- LINQ to SQL
- LINQ to Data Services
- ADO.NET Core; Windows Mobile supports only SQL Server and SQL Server Compact Edition

Be sure to check the product documentation to verify availability for later versions.

Additional Resources

To more easily access Web resources, see the online version of the bibliography at: http://www.microsoft.com/architectureguide.

- *"ADO.NET"* at http://msdn.microsoft.com/en-us/library/e80y5yhx(vs.80).aspx.
- *"ADO.NET Data Services"* at http://msdn.microsoft.com/en-us/data/bb931106.aspx.
- *"ADO.NET Entity Framework"* at http://msdn.microsoft.com/en-us/data/aa937723.aspx.
- *"Language-Integrated Query (LINQ)"* at http://msdn.microsoft.com/en-us/library/bb397926.aspx.
- *"SQL Server Data Services (SSDS) Primer"* at http://msdn.microsoft.com/en-us/library/cc512417.aspx.
- *"Introduction to the Microsoft Sync Framework Runtime"* at http://msdn.microsoft.com/en-us/sync/bb821992.aspx.

Appendix D
Integration Technology Matrix

Overview

This appendix will help you to understand the tradeoffs you must make when choosing an integration technology. It will help you to understand the design impact of choosing a particular technology, and assist when choosing an integration technology for your scenario and application type.

Your choice of integration technology will be related to the kinds of applications you are developing. Use the Integration Technologies Summary to review each technology and its description. Use the Benefits and Considerations Matrix to understand the range of technologies available for integration. Use the Common Scenarios and Solutions to map your application scenario to common integration technology solutions.

Integration Technologies Summary

The following list describes the Microsoft technologies available for application integration:

- **Microsoft BizTalk® Server.** BizTalk Server provides a complete stack of adapters, orchestration, messaging, and protocols for building Enterprise Application Integration (EAI)–enabled systems.

- **Microsoft Host Integration Server.** Host Integration Server provides a platform for connecting applications with IBM zSeries and iSeries applications. In addition, Host Integration Server supports data connections between Microsoft Message Queuing and IBM WebSphere MQ.

- **Microsoft Message Queuing.** Message queuing allows you to connect applications using queued messaging. Message queuing provides guaranteed message delivery, priority-based messaging, and security. It can support integration with systems that may be occasionally connected or temporarily offline. Message queuing also supports both synchronous and asynchronous messaging scenarios.

- **Microsoft BizTalk ESB Toolkit.** This is a series of entities that provides a loosely-coupled messaging architecture built on top of the services provided by BizTalk Server. It exploits the underlying BizTalk Server features to provide a flexible and extensible architecture that includes capabilities such as transformation, delivery assurance, message security, service registry, intelligent routing, and unified exception handling.

Benefits and Considerations Matrix

The following table lists the benefits and considerations for each integration technology.

Technology	Benefits	Considerations
BizTalk Server	Enables electronic document exchange relationships between companies using Electronic Data Interchange (EDI) and/or Extensible Markup Language (XML) formats. Integrates with non-Microsoft systems. Easily extended to provide ESB capabilities. Windows Communication Foundation (WCF) line-of-business (LOB) adapters enable development of custom adapters for use inside or outside BizTalk. Includes adapters for integration with systems such as SAP, Oracle, and SQL databases. Provides a SOAP adapter to help you to work with Web services.	Might lead to a tightly-coupled infrastructure. Requires customization to achieve ESB capabilities.

Technology	Benefits	Considerations
Host Integration Server	Supports network integration between Windows Server and IBM mainframe or AS/400 computers. Provides secure host access and identity management with support for Secure Sockets Layer (SSL)/Transport Layer Security (TLS), single sign on (SSO), and password synchronization. Provides data integration with support for Message Queuing and XML-based Web services. Includes a data access tool for creating and managing connections with IBM DB2 databases. Supports enterprise scalability and performance with simultaneous host sessions, load balancing, and hot failover. BizTalk adapters for Host Systems are available to support BizTalk integration with DB2, IBM WebSphere MQ, Host Applications, and Host Files.	Must be installed in a Windows Server environment. Requires Microsoft Visual Studio 2005 or greater. Requires Message Queuing with routing support.
Microsoft Message Queuing	Enables applications to communicate with each other across heterogeneous networks using message-based methods. Supports reliable messaging between applications inside and outside of an enterprise. Supports transactional capabilities, such as ensuring that messages are only delivered once, that messages are delivered in order, and confirmation that messages were retrieved from destination queues. Provides message routing based on network topology, transport connectivity, and session concentration needs. Allows message delivery over HTTP transport with support for SOAP Reliable Messaging Protocol (SRMP). Supports the distribution of a single message to multiple destinations. Is included with Windows Server 2003 and later. Supports two deployment modes: domain mode with access to the Active Directory, and Workgroup mode. Includes WCF-provided endpoints for Message Queuing.	Deployment mode should be considered prior to installing and configuring Message Queuing. When using the Workgroup deployment mode, messages cannot be encrypted, internal certificates cannot be used, and cross-platform messaging is not supported. Independent clients should be used instead of dependent clients. Message Queuing is optimized for sending remotely and receiving locally. As a result, you should avoid remote queue reads. You should avoid functions that query Active Directory. Asynchronous notifications using events can become lost. WCF endpoints require Microsoft .NET Framework 3.0 or later.

(continued)

Technology	Benefits	Considerations
Microsoft BizTalk ESB Toolkit	Provides dynamic resolution of service end-points at run time, which abstracts endpoint definition. Decouples the message transformation from the application. Integrates closely with WCF to provide secure and reliable messaging. Provides fault detection and reporting, through unified exception handling for both system and business exceptions. Includes resolvers for communicating with service registries such as Universal Description, Discovery and Integration (UDDI). Supports an itinerary-based approach for routing and transformation. Supports client-side and server itineraries. Supports resolver extensibility for creating custom resolvers. Supports the BizTalk designer for itinerary creation. Provides an exception management portal. Exposes all key features such as exception handling, routing, resolution, and more as Web services. Provides itinerary tracking using Business Activity Monitoring (BAM).	Requires BizTalk Server 2006 R2 or later. May require customization for specific business scenarios. By default, there is no tracking display for ESB Itinerary Tracking data.

Common Scenarios and Solutions

The following sections provide guidance on choosing the appropriate type of integration technology for your applications:

Consider using **BizTalk Server** if:

- You want interaction with multiple Web services via an orchestrator as part of a Service Oriented Architecture (SOA).
- You want to support business-to-business processes, including industry standards such as EDIFACT, ANSCI X12, HL7, HIPAA, or SWIFT.
- You want parallel execution of services.
- You need a solution that is highly reliable and requires a dedicated scalable server infrastructure with no code changes required.

- You must be able to measure business Key Performance Indicators (KPIs) by configuring a BAM solution to provide near real time visibility into your application's process data.
- You must abstract your application business logic into declarative rule policies that can be changed easily to match dynamic changes of business requirements.

Consider using **Host Integration Server** if:

- You must support interaction with IBM zSeries or iSeries applications.
- You want to integrate BizTalk with DB2, WebSphere MQ, Host Applications, or Host Files.
- You want to integrate Message Queuing with WebSphere MQ.

Consider using **Microsoft Message Queuing** if:

- You must support message-based interaction between applications.
- You want to integrate with non-Microsoft platforms.
- You must support SRMP.

Consider using the **Microsoft BizTalk ESB Toolkit** if:

- You must support an itinerary-based approach.
- You must support dynamic resolution and routing.
- You want to use dynamic transformations.
- You must support robust and unified exception management for your EAI system.

Additional Resources

To more easily access Web resources, see the online version of the bibliography at: http://www.microsoft.com/architectureguide.

- For more information on BizTalk, see "*BizTalk Server*" at http://msdn.microsoft.com/en-us/biztalk/default.aspx.
- For more information on Host Integration Server, see "*Host Integration Server*" at http://www.microsoft.com/hiserver/default.mspx.
- For more information on MSMQ, see "*Microsoft Message Queuing*" at http://www.microsoft.com/windowsserver2003/technologies/msmq/default.mspx.
- For best practice information on MSMQ, see "*Programming Best Practices with Microsoft Message Queuing Services (MSMQ)*" at http://msdn.microsoft.com/en-us/library/ms811053.aspx.
- For more information, see "*Microsoft BizTalk ESB Toolkit*" at http://msdn.microsoft.com/en-us/library/dd897973.aspx.

Appendix E
Workflow Technology Matrix

Overview

This appendix will help you to understand the tradeoffs you have to make when choosing a workflow technology. It will help you to understand the design impact of each technology, and assist when choosing a workflow technology for your scenario and application type.

Your choice of workflow technology will be related to the type of workflow you are developing. Use the Workflow Technologies Summary to review each technology and its description. Use the Benefits and Considerations Matrix to understand the range of technologies available for workflow. Use the Common Scenarios and Solutions to map your application scenario to common workflow technology solutions.

Workflow Technologies Summary

The following workflow technologies are available on the Microsoft platform:

- **Windows Workflow Foundation (WF).** WF is a foundational technology that allows you to implement workflow. A toolkit for professional developers and independent software vendors (ISVs) who want to build a sequential or state-machine based workflow, WF supports the following types of workflow: Sequential, State-Machine, Data Driven, and Custom. You can create workflows using the Windows Workflow Designer in Visual Studio.

- **Workflow Services.** Workflow Services provides integration between Windows Communication Foundation (WCF) and WF to provide WCF-based services for workflow. Starting with Microsoft .NET Framework 3.5, WCF has been extended to provide support for workflows exposed as services and the ability to call services from within workflows. In addition, Visual Studio 2008 includes new templates and tools that support workflow services.

- **Microsoft Office SharePoint Services (MOSS).** MOSS is a content-management and collaboration platform that provides workflow support based on WF. MOSS provides a solution for human workflow and collaboration in the context of a SharePoint server. You can create workflows for document approval directly within the MOSS interface. You can also create workflows using either the SharePoint Designer or the Windows Workflow Designer in Visual Studio. For workflow customization, you can use the WF object model within Visual Studio.

- **Microsoft BizTalk Server.** BizTalk currently has its own workflow engine that is geared toward orchestration, such as enterprise integration with system-level workflows. A future version of BizTalk may use WF as well as XLANG (an extension of the Web Service Definition Language used to model service orchestration and collaboration), which is the existing orchestration technology in BizTalk. You can define the overall design and flow of loosely coupled, long-running business processes by using BizTalk Orchestration Services within and between applications.

Human Workflow vs. System Workflow

The term *workflow* applies to two fundamental types of process:

- **Human workflow.** This is a type of workflow in which a process that includes human intervention is broken down into a series of steps or events. These events flow from one step to the next based on conditional evaluation. The majority of the time, workflow is composed of activities that are carried out by humans.

- **System workflow.** Sometimes called *orchestration*, this a specific type of workflow that is generally used to implement mediation between business services and business processes. Orchestration does not include any human intervention.

Benefits and Considerations Matrix

The following table lists the key benefits and considerations for each of the workflow technology.

Technology	Benefits	Considerations
Windows Workflow Foundation (WF)	A developer-centric solution for creating workflows. Supports sequential, state-machine, and data-driven workflows. Designer support available in Visual Studio. Includes protocol facilities for secure, reliable, transacted data exchange. Supports long-running workflows that can persist across system restarts.	Custom code is required if you want to host the designer in your application. Does not provide true parallel execution support.

Technology	Benefits	Considerations
Workflow Services	Provides integration between WCF and WF. Allows you to expose workflows to client applications as services. Supports coordination across multiple services to complete a business process. When calling Workflow Services, the WF runtime is automatically engaged for new or existing workflow instances. Provides developer support in Visual Studio 2008, with new templates and tools for Workflow Services.	Requires .NET Framework 3.5 or higher. Extra coding is required when not using default security credentials.
MOSS 2007 Workflow	The workflow engine is based on WF. Approval-based workflow can be defined using the Web interface. SharePoint Designer can be used to define conditional or data-driven workflows. Visual Studio can be used to create custom workflows using WF components and services. Integrates with applications in the Microsoft Office suite.	Workflows are bound to a single site, and cannot access information in other sites. Not well suited for complex line-of-business (LOB) integrated workflow solutions.
BizTalk	Provides a single solution for business process management. Enables electronic document exchange relationships between companies using Electronic Data Interchange (EDI) and/or Extensible Markup Language (XML) formats. Contains orchestration capabilities for designing and executing long-running, loosely coupled business transactions. Integrates with non-Microsoft systems. Easily extended to provide Enterprise Service Bus (ESB) capabilities. WCF LOB adapters enable development of custom adapters for use inside or outside BizTalk.	Saves the orchestration state to SQL Server, which can introduce latency while executing the orchestration. Current version does not use WF. However, a future version may support WF.

Common Scenarios and Solutions

The following sections provide guidance on choosing the appropriate type of workflow technology for your application.

Consider using **WF** if:

- You must build a custom workflow solution.
- You need workflow designer support in Visual Studio.
- You want to host the WF designer in your application.

Consider using **Workflow Services** if:

- You must expose workflows as services.
- You must call services from within a workflow.
- You must coordinate calls across multiple services to complete a business process.

If you are already using SharePoint, consider using **MOSS 2007** workflow if:

- You must enable workflow for human collaboration.
- You must enable workflow on a SharePoint list or library; for example, to support an approval process.
- You need to extend SharePoint workflow to add custom tasks.
- You want to use the workflow designer in Visual Studio.

Consider using **BizTalk Server** if:

- You need a workflow solution that works across different applications and systems.
- You want a server-hosted system workflow product that enables enterprise integration.
- You are developing an application that must gather data from multiple Web services as part of a Service Oriented Architecture (SOA).
- You are developing an application that has long-running business processes that may take many days to complete.
- You must support business-to-business processes based on industry standards.
- You need parallel execution of services.
- You must abstract your application business logic into declarative rules that can be changed easily to match changing business requirements.

Additional Resources

To more easily access Web resources, see the online version of the bibliography at: http://www.microsoft.com/architectureguide.

- For more information on MOSS 2007 workflows, see *"Workflows in Office SharePoint Server 2007"* at http://msdn.microsoft.com/en-us/library/ms549489.aspx.

- For more information on WF, see *"Windows Workflow Foundation"* at http://msdn.microsoft.com/en-us/netframework/aa663328.aspx.

- For more information on Workflow Services, see *"Workflow Services"* at http://msdn.microsoft.com/en-us/library/cc825354.aspx.

- For more information on BizTalk, see *"BizTalk Server"* at http://msdn.microsoft.com/en-us/biztalk/default.aspx.

- For more information on enterprise workflows, see *"Architecting Enterprise Loan Workflows and Orchestrations"* at http://msdn.microsoft.com/en-us/library/bb330937.aspx.

Appendix F

patterns & practices Enterprise Library

Overview

This appendix describes the patterns & practice Enterprise Library, and explains how you can use it in your applications to quickly and simply implement crosscutting concerns such as logging, exception handling, and data access.

Goals of Enterprise Library

The goals of Enterprise Library are the following:

- **Consistency.** All Enterprise Library application blocks feature consistent design patterns and implementation approaches.
- **Extensibility.** All application blocks include defined extensibility points that allow developers to customize the behavior of the application blocks by adding their own code.
- **Ease of use.** Enterprise Library offers numerous useful features that include a graphical configuration tool, a simple installation procedure, and clear and complete documentation and samples.
- **Integration.** Enterprise Library application blocks are designed to work well together and are tested to make sure that they do. It is also possible to use the application blocks individually.

What's Included in Enterprise Library

Enterprise Library contains:

- Application blocks that consist of reusable code you can use to implement solutions for crosscutting concerns such as logging, exception handling, validation, and data access.

- Configuration tools that make it easy to add Enterprise Library blocks to an application and specify configuration information. The configuration tools include a stand-alone configuration editor and a configuration tool that integrates with Visual Studio.

- Common utility functions for tasks such as serialization, used in many places throughout the library and the application blocks and available for developers to use in their code.

- Instrumentation features that allow developers and administrators to monitor the behavior and performance of the application blocks at run time.

- Batch files that build the Enterprise Library source code and copy the assemblies to the appropriate locations.

- Utilities to install the events and performance counter instrumentation exposed by Enterprise Library.

- Utilities to create the sample databases used by the Enterprise Library examples and QuickStarts.

- A full set of QuickStart applications, one for each application block, which demonstrate how you can use the application blocks. They implement common scenarios from each application block and provide links to the relevant sections of the guidance documentation.

- Full source code for Enterprise Library, including Visual Studio projects and unit tests that developers can use to extend and modify the library and the application blocks. Developers make sure applications still meet the design requirements by running the unit tests and writing new tests.

Application Blocks

The following table lists and describes the application blocks designed to assist developers solve common enterprise development challenges.

Application Block	Description
Caching Application Block	Helps developers to incorporate a local cache in their applications. It supports both an in-memory cache and, optionally, a backing store that can either be a database or isolated storage. The block provides all the functionality needed to retrieve, add, and remove cached data, and supports configurable expiration and scavenging policies.
Cryptography Application Block	Simplifies how developers incorporate cryptographic functionality in their applications. Applications can use the application block for a variety of tasks, such as encrypting information, creating a hash from data, and comparing hash values to verify that data has not been altered.
Data Access Application Block	Simplifies development tasks that implement common data access functionality, such as reading data for display, passing data through application layers, and submitting changed data back to the database system. The block includes support for both stored procedures and in-line SQL, and provides access to the most often used features of ADO.NET in simple to -use classes.
Exception Handling Application Block	Helps developers and policy makers to create a consistent strategy for processing exceptions that occur in all architectural layers of an enterprise application. It can log exception information, hide sensitive information by replacing the original exception with another exception, and maintain contextual information for an exception by wrapping the original exception inside another exception.
Logging Application Block	Simplifies the implementation of common logging functions. The block can write information to the Windows Event Log, an e-mail message, a database, Windows Message Queuing, a text file, a WMI event, or a custom location.
Policy Injection Application Block	Helps developers to better manage crosscutting concerns, maximize separation of concerns, and encapsulate behavior by automatically applying policies to object instances. Developers define the set of policies for the target classes and their members through configuration or by applying attributes to individual members of the target class.
Security Application Block	Helps developers implement common authorization-related functionality in their applications and cache a user's authorization and authentication data. Together with the Microsoft .NET Framework 2.0 features, developers can easily implement common security-related functionality.
Unity Application Block	Provides a lightweight, extensible dependency injection (DI) container with support for constructor, property, and method call injection. Developers can use it with Enterprise Library to generate both Enterprise Library objects and their own custom business objects, or as a stand-alone DI mechanism.
Validation Application Block	Provides useful features that allow developers to implement structured and easy to maintain validation scenarios in their applications. It includes a library of validators for validating .NET Framework data types, such as null string and number range validators. It also includes composite validators and support for rule sets.

Caching Application Block

The Caching Application Block lets you incorporate a local cache in your applications that uses an in-memory cache and, optionally, a database or isolated storage backing store. The block provides all the functionality needed to retrieve, add, and remove cached data, and supports configurable expiration and scavenging policies. You can also extend it by creating your own pluggable providers or using third party providers; for example to support distributed caching and other features. Caching can give considerable improvements in performance and efficiency in many application scenarios.

Key Scenarios

The Caching Application Block is suitable if you encounter any of the following situations:

- Repeatedly accessing static data or data that rarely changes.
- Performing data access that is expensive in terms of creation, access, or transportation.
- Working with data must always be available, even when the source, such as a server, is not available.

When to Use

The Caching Application Block is optimized for high performance and scalability. Furthermore, it is both thread safe and exception safe. You can extend it to include your own expiration policies and your own backing store. It is designed to work in the most common data caching situation, which is when the application and the cache exist on the same system. This means that the cache is local and should be used only by that application. When it operates within these guidelines, the application block is ideal for addressing the following requirements:

- You need a consistent and simple interface and implementation for cache functionality across different application environment, which does not change irrespective of the caching store being used. For example, developers can write similar code to implement caching in application components hosted in Internet Information Services (IIS), Enterprise Services, and smart client environments. Also, the same cache configuration options exist for all environments.
- You need a configurable and persistent backing store. The block supports both isolated storage and database backing stores. Developers can create additional backing store providers and add them to the block using its configuration settings. The application block can also symmetrically encrypt a cache item's data before it is persisted to a backing store.

- Changes to the cache configuration settings must not require application source code changes. Developers first write the code that uses one or more named caches. System operators and developers can then configure each of these named caches differently using the Enterprise Library configuration tools.
- Cache items require any of the following expiration settings: absolute time, sliding time, extended time format (for example, every evening at midnight), file dependency, or never expired.
- You want to modify the block source code for extensibility or customization.
- You need to use multiple types of cache store (through different cache managers) in a single application.

You can use the Caching Application Block with any of the following application types:
- Windows Forms
- Console application
- Windows service
- COM+ server
- ASP.NET Web application or Web service if you need features not included in the ASP.NET cache

Considerations

The following considerations apply to using the Caching Application Block:
- You should deploy the block within a single application domain. Each application domain can have one or multiple cache stores, either with or without backing stores.
- Cache stores cannot be shared among different application domains.
- Although you can encrypt data cached in the backing stores, the block does not support encryption of data that is cached in memory.
- The block does not support tamper proofing (signing and verifying items in the cache).

Cryptography Application Block

The Cryptography Application Block makes it easy to incorporate cryptographic functionality such as encrypting information, creating a hash from data, and comparing hash values to verify that data has not been altered.

Key Scenarios

The Cryptography Application Block is suitable if you encounter any of the following situations:

- Quickly and easily encrypting and decrypting information.
- Quickly and easily creating a hash from data.
- Comparing hash values to verify that data has not been altered.

When to Use

The Cryptography Application Block is ideal for addressing the following requirements:

- You need to reduce the requirement to write boilerplate code to perform standard data encryption, decryption, and hashing tasks.
- You need to maintain consistent cryptography practices, both within an application and across the enterprise.
- You need to simplify learning for developers by using a consistent architectural security model across the various areas of functionality.
- You need to add or extend implementations of cryptography providers.
- You need a customizable Key Protection Model.

Considerations

The following considerations apply to using the Cryptography Application Block:

- The block supports only symmetric algorithms that use the same key for both encryption and decryption.
- The block does not automatically manage encryption keys and key storage.

Data Access Application Block

The Data Access Application Block simplifies many common data access tasks such as reading data for display, passing data through application layers, and submitting changed data back to the database system. It includes support for both stored procedures and in-line SQL, and provides access to the most often used features of ADO.NET in simple-to-use classes.

Key Scenarios

The Data Access Application Block is suitable if you encounter any of the following situations:

- Using a **DataReader** or **DataSet** to retrieve multiple rows of data.
- Executing a command and retrieve the output parameters or a single-value item.
- Performing multiple operations within a transaction.
- Retrieving XML data from a SQL Server.
- Updating a database with data contained in a **DataSet** object.
- Adding or extend implementations of database providers.

When to Use

The Data Access Application Block is ideal for addressing the following requirements:

- You need simplicity and convenience while helping developers use the functionality provided by ADO.NET with best practices.
- You need to reduce the requirement for boilerplate code to perform standard data access tasks.
- You need to maintain consistent data access practices, both within an application and across the enterprise.
- You need to make it easy to change the target database type through configuration, and reduce the amount of code that developers must write when they port applications to different types of databases.
- You need to relieve developers from learning different programming models for different types of databases.

Considerations

The following considerations apply to using the Data Access Application Block:

- The Data Access Application Block is a complement to ADO.NET; it is not a replacement. If your application must retrieve data in a specialized way, or take advantage of features specific to a particular database, consider using ADO.NET directly.

Exception Handling Application Block

The Exception Handling Application Block lets you quickly and easily design and implement a consistent strategy for processing exceptions that occur in all architectural layers of your application. It can log exception information, hide sensitive information by replacing the original exception with another exception, and maintain contextual information for an exception by wrapping the original exception inside another exception.

Key Scenarios

The Exception Handling Application Block allows developers to encapsulate the logic contained in catch statements in application components as reusable exception handlers. It is suitable if you encounter any of the following requirements:

- Wrapping an exception. Use the Wrap handler to wrap an exception with a new exception.
- Replacing an exception. Use the Replace handler to replace one exception with another.
- Logging an exception. Use the Logging handler to format exception information, such as the message and the stack trace, and pass it to the Enterprise Library Logging Application Block so that it can be published.
- Shielding an exception at a WCF service boundary. Use the Fault Contract Exception handler, which is designed for use at Windows Communication Foundation (WCF) service boundaries, to generate a new Fault Contract from the exception.
- Propagating an exception, displaying user friendly messages, notifying the user, and assisting support staff. Use a combination of handlers from the block to handle specific exception types and rethrow them if required.
- Localization of exception messages. Use the handlers and their configuration to specify localized message text for exceptions.

When to Use

The Exception Handling Application Block is ideal for addressing the following requirements:

- You must support exception handling in all architectural layers of an application, not just at service interface boundaries.
- You need exception handling policies to be defined and maintained at the administrative level through configuration, and the ability to maintain and modify the rules that govern exception handling without changing the application block code.
- You need to provide commonly used exception handling functions, such as the ability to log exception information, the ability to hide sensitive information by replacing the original exception with another exception, and the ability to maintain contextual information for an exception by wrapping the original exception inside another exception.

- You need to combine exception handlers to produce the desired response to an exception, such as logging exception information followed by replacing the original exception with another.
- You need to invoke exception handlers in a consistent manner so that you can handlers can use them in multiple places within and across applications.
- You need to add or extend implementations of exception handlers.
- You need to handle exceptions via policies as opposed to simply logging them.

Logging Application Block

The Logging Application Block simplifies the implementation of common logging functions such as writing information to the Windows Event Log, an email message, a database, Windows Message Queuing, a text file, a WMI event, or a custom location.

Key Scenarios

The Logging Application Block is suitable if you encounter any of the following situations:

- Populating and logging event information to Windows Event log, an e-mail message, a database, a message queue, a text file, a Windows Management Instrumentation (WMI) event, or a custom location.
- Modifying and formatting context information within the event using templates.
- Tracing application activities and providing identities that can be used to combine event information.
- Preventing unauthorized access to sensitive information using access control lists (ACLs) to restrict access to flat files, or creating a custom formatter that encrypts log information.

When to Use

The Logging Application Block is ideal for addressing the following requirements:

- You must maintain consistent logging practices, both within an application and across the enterprise.
- You need to ease the learning curve for developers by using a consistent architectural model.
- You need to provide implementations that you can use to solve common application logging tasks without repeatedly writing custom or boilerplate code.
- You need to add or extend logging implementations and targets.

Considerations

The following considerations apply to using the Logging Application Block:

- The block logging formatters do not encrypt logging information.
- Trace listener destinations receive logging information as cleartext.
- Some of the Logging Application Block listeners fail while running under partial trust.

Policy Injection Application Block

The Policy Injection Application Block provides a mechanism for automatically applying policies to object instances; this helps developers to better manage cross-cutting concerns, maximize separation of concerns, and encapsulate behavior. Developers define the set of policies for the target classes and their members through configuration of the Policy Injection Application Block or by applying attributes to individual members of the target class.

Key Scenarios

The Policy Injection Application Block is suitable if you encounter any of the following situations:

- Building applications from objects that require encapsulation and separation to provide the most benefit from independence in operation, and provide the maximum capability for reuse.
- Allowing developers, operators, and administrators to create, modify, remove, and fine tune interception policies though configuration, generally without requiring any changes to the code or recompilation of the application. This reduces the chance of introducing errors into the code, simplifies versioning, and reduces downtime.
- Reusing existing object instances. This reduces the requirement for code to generate new object instances and prepare them by setting properties or calling methods, while still allowing handler pipelines to be used for specific members or all members of that class.
- Minimizing the work required and the code that the developer must write to perform common tasks within an application, such as logging, validation, authorization, and instrumentation.

When to Use

The Policy Injection Application Block is ideal for addressing the following requirements:

- You need a ready-built solution that is easy to implement in new and existing applications, particularly in applications that already take advantage of the features of the Enterprise Library.

- You need to manage crosscutting concerns that may otherwise affect the independence of objects that require access to common features (such as logging or validation).

- You need to allow the developer and administrator to configure the behavior of objects in an application through configuration, by adding or removing handlers that execute common tasks or add custom features.

- You need to make it easy for developers to take advantage of features within the Enterprise Library Core and individual application blocks that implement tasks commonly required in enterprise applications.

- You need to reduce development time and cost, and minimize bugs in complex applications that use common and shared tasks and services.

Considerations

The following considerations apply to using the Policy Injection Application Block:

- It uses interception to enable only preprocessing handlers and post-processing handlers, rather than inserting code directly into methods.

- It does not provide interception for class constructors.

- Like all interception technologies, it imposes some extra processing requirements on applications—although the design of the block minimizes these as much as possible.

- Call handlers only have access to the information within the call message, and cannot maintain internal state.

- Policy injection can only take place for public members of the target class.

Security Application Block

The Security Application Block lets you easily implement common authorization-related functionality, such as caching user's authorization and authentication data and integrating with the Microsoft .NET Framework security features.

Key Scenarios

The Security Application Block is suitable if you encounter any of the following situations:

- Caching security-related credentials that you use to perform authorization.
- Obtaining a temporary token for an authenticated user, and authenticating a user using a token.
- Terminating a user session (expire the token).
- Determining whether a user is authorized to perform a task.

When to Use

The Security Application Block is ideal for addressing the following requirements:

- You must reduce the requirement for boilerplate code to perform standard security-related tasks such as caching credentials, and checking authentication.
- You must maintain consistent security practices, both within an application and across the enterprise.
- You want to ease the learning curve for developers by using a consistent architectural model across the various areas of functionality provided.
- You need to use custom implementations of security providers.

Considerations

The following considerations apply to using the Security Application Block:

- The default store for cached security-related information is the Caching Application Block. Although the Caching Application Block can be configured to encrypt cache data in backing stores, the application block does not support encryption of cache data stored in memory. If this threat is significant for your application, you can use an alternate custom caching store provider that supports in-memory encryption.
- The authorization manager is not supported under partial trust.

Unity Application Block

Unity is a lightweight, extensible dependency injection container that supports object interception, constructor injection, property injection, and method call injection. You can also use it with Enterprise Library to generate both Enterprise Library objects and your own custom business objects.

Key Scenarios

The Unity Application Block is suitable if you encounter any of the following situations:

- Performing dependency injection through a container that supports constructor, property, and method call injection, and can manage the lifetime of object instances.
- Performing dependency injection for classes that have dependencies on other objects or classes, and these dependencies are complex or require abstraction.
- Configuring and changing the dependencies at run time.
- Caching or persisting the container across post backs in a Web application.

When to Use

The Unity Application Block is ideal for addressing the following requirements:

- You need simplified object creation, especially for hierarchical object structures and dependencies, which simplifies application code.
- You need to abstract requirements by specifying dependencies at run time or in configuration to simplify management of crosscutting concerns.
- You need to increase flexibility by deferring component configuration to the container.
- You need a service location capability where clients can store or cache the container. This is especially useful in ASP.NET Web applications where the developers can persist the container in the ASP.NET session or application.

You should not use the Unity Application Block in the following situations:

- Your objects and classes have no dependencies on other objects or classes, or your dependencies are very simple and do not require abstraction.

Considerations

The following considerations apply to using the Unity Application Block:

- Dependency injection may have a minor impact on performance.
- Dependency injection can increase complexity where only simple dependencies exist.

Validation Application Block

The Validation Application Block provides a range of features for implementing structured and easy-to-maintain validation mechanisms using attributes and rule sets, and integrating with most types of application interface technologies.

Key Scenarios

The Validation Application Block is suitable if you encounter any of the following situations:

- Implementing structured and easy to maintain validation code to validate fields, properties, and nested objects, and prevent the injection of malicious data into your application.
- Enforcing business rules and to providing responses to user input.
- Validating data several times within the same application using the same rules.
- Combining the wide range of prebuilt validators to support complex scenarios and a wide range of capabilities.

When to Use

The Validation Application Block is ideal for addressing the following requirements:

- You need to maintain consistent validation practices for almost all standard .NET data types in ASP.NET, Windows Forms, and WCF applications.
- You need to create validation rules using configuration, attributes, and code.
- You need to associate multiple rule sets with the same class and with members of that class.
- You need to apply one or more rule sets when you validate an object, and reuse business validation logic.

Considerations

The following considerations apply to using the Validation Application Block:

- Some technologies such as ASP.NET and Windows Forms provide built-in validation features. Therefore, if your validation logic only needs to be applied within these technologies you may not need to use the application block unless you need to reuse the validation logic.
- WCF and other applications that use XML data can use XML Schemas to validate messages at the XML level. If your validation logic only needs to be applied within these technologies you may not need to use the application block unless you need to reuse the validation logic.
- In very simple cases, when you only need to validate a few objects, you may not want to incur the overhead of adding the application block.

Additional Resources

To more easily access Web resources, see the online version of the bibliography at:
http://www.microsoft.com/architectureguide.

- *"Enterprise Library"* at
  http://msdn.microsoft.com/en-us/library/cc467894.aspx.

- *"The Caching Application Block"* at
  http://msdn.microsoft.com/en-us/library/cc511588.aspx.

- *"The Cryptography Application Block"* at
  http://msdn.microsoft.com/en-us/library/cc511721.aspx.

- *"The Data Access Application Block"* at
  http://msdn.microsoft.com/en-us/library/cc511547.aspx.

- *"The Exception Handling Application Block"* at
  http://msdn2.microsoft.com/en-us/library/aa480461.aspx.

- *"The Logging Application Block"* at
  http://msdn.microsoft.com/en-us/library/cc511708.aspx.

- *"The Policy Injection Application Block"* at
  http://msdn.microsoft.com/en-us/library/cc511729.aspx.

- *"The Security Application Block"* at
  http://msdn.microsoft.com/en-us/library/cc511928.aspx.

- *"The Unity Application Block"* at
  http://msdn.microsoft.com/en-us/library/cc511654.aspx.

- *"The Validation Application Block"* at
  http://msdn.microsoft.com/en-us/library/cc511802.aspx.

- *"Enterprise Library Frequently Asked Questions"* at
  http://www.codeplex.com/entlib/Wiki/View.aspx?title=EntLib%20FAQ.

Appendix G
patterns & practices Pattern Catalog

Composite Application Guidance for WPF and Silverlight

Category	Patterns
Modularity	**Service Locator.** Create a service locator that contains references to the services and encapsulates the logic to locate them. In your classes, use the service locator to obtain service instances. See *"Service Locator"* at http://msdn.microsoft.com/en-us/library/dd458903.aspx.
Testability	**Dependency Injection.** Do not instantiate the dependencies explicitly in your class. Instead, declaratively express dependencies in your class definition. Use a Builder object to obtain valid instances of your object's dependencies and pass them to your object during the object's creation and/or initialization. See *"Dependency Injection"* at http://msdn.microsoft.com/en-us/library/dd458879.aspx.
	Inversion of Control. Delegate the function of selecting a concrete implementation type for the classes' dependencies to an external component or source. See *"Inversion of Control"* at http://msdn.microsoft.com/en-us/library/dd458907.aspx.
	Separated Presentation. Separate the presentation logic from the business logic into different artifacts. The Separated Presentation pattern can be implemented in multiple ways, such as **Supervising Presenter** or **Presentation Model**, etc. See *"Separated Presentation"* at http://msdn.microsoft.com/en-us/library/dd458859.aspx.
	Presentation Model. Separate the responsibilities for the visual display and the user interface (UI) state and behavior into different classes named, respectively, the view and the presentation model. The view class manages the controls on the UI, and the presentation model class acts as a façade on the model with UI-specific state and behavior, by encapsulating the access to the model and providing a public interface that is easy to consume from the view (for example, using data binding). See *"Presentation Model"* at http://msdn.microsoft.com/en-us/library/dd458863.aspx.
	Supervising Presenter (or Supervising Controller). Separate the responsibilities for the visual display and the event-handling behavior into different classes named, respectively, the view and the presenter. The view class manages the controls on the UI and forwards user events to a presenter class. The presenter contains the logic to respond to the events, update the model (business logic and data of the application), and, in turn, manipulate the state of the view. See *"Supervising Presenter"* at http://msdn.microsoft.com/en-us/library/dd490821.aspx.

Data Movement Patterns

Category	Patterns
Data Movement Patterns	**Data Replication.** Create a replication set and replication link that move data between two locations. A high-level pattern that describes the general process of the more detailed Data Movement Patterns described in this table. See *"Data Replication"* at http://msdn.microsoft.com/en-us/library/ms978671.aspx.
	Master-Master Replication. Copy data from the source to the target and detect and resolve any update conflicts that have occurred since the last replication (due to changes to the same data on the source and target). The solution consists of a two replication links between the source and the target in opposite directions. Both replication links transmit the same replication set in both directions. Such a pair of replication links is referred to as *related links*. See *"Master-Master Replication"* at http://msdn.microsoft.com/en-us/library/ms978735.aspx.
	Master-Subordinate Replication. Copy data from the source to the target without regard to updates that may have occurred to the replication set at the target since the last replication. See *"Master-Subordinate Replication"* at http://msdn.microsoft.com/en-us/library/ms978740.aspx.
	Master-Master Row-Level Synchronization. Use a pair of related replication links between the source and target and a synchronization controller to manage the synchronization in both directions. To synchronize more than two copies of the replication set, create the appropriate replication link pair for each additional copy. See *"Master-Master Row-Level Synchronization"* at http://msdn.microsoft.com/en-us/library/ms998434.aspx.
	Master-Subordinate Snapshot Replication. Make a copy of the source replication set at a specific time (this is known as a snapshot), replicate it to the target, and overwrite the target data. In this way, any changes that might have occurred to the target replication set are replaced by the new source replication set. See *"Master-Subordinate Snapshot Replication"* at http://msdn.microsoft.com/en-us/library/ms998430.aspx.
	Capture Transaction Details. Create additional database objects, such as triggers and (shadow) tables, and record changes of all tables belonging to the replication set. See *"Capture Transaction Details"* at http://msdn.microsoft.com/en-us/library/ms978709.aspx.
	Master-Subordinate Transactional Incremental Replication. Acquire the information about committed transactions from the source and replay the transactions in the correct sequence when they are written to the target. See *"Master-Subordinate Transactional Incremental Replication"* at http://msdn.microsoft.com/en-us/library/ms998441.aspx.
	Master-Subordinate Cascading Replication. Increase the number of replication links between the source and target by adding one or more intermediary targets between the original source and the end target databases. These intermediaries are data stores that take a replication set from the source, and thus act as a target in a first replication link. They then act as sources to move the data to the next replication link and so on until they reach the cascade end targets. See *"Master-Subordinate Cascading Replication"* at http://msdn.microsoft.com/en-us/library/ms978712.aspx.

Category	Patterns
Pattlets	**Maintain Data Copies.** Synchronously write to the data copies from the originating application, or synchronously post data to a local cache for later movement by an asynchronous service. See *"Patterns and Pattlets"* at http://msdn.microsoft.com/ en-us/library/ms998465.aspx. **Application-Managed Data Copies.** When a particular application makes a change to its copy of the data, it should then also make changes to the other copies. The application should ensure that copies of the data and/or derived data are updated in the same transaction that changed the original data. See *"Patterns and Pattlets"* at http://msdn.microsoft.com/en-us/library/ms998465.aspx. **Extract-Transform-Load.** A type of data movement that may execute complex queries to acquire data from heterogeneous sources, may apply complex manipulation that includes aggregation and cleansing, but always makes a simple write that replaces any changes on the target. See *"Patterns and Pattlets"* at http://msdn.microsoft.com/ en-us/library/ms998465.aspx. **Topologies for Data Copies.** The architectural approaches to deploying data copies on several platforms. See *"Patterns and Pattlets"* at http://msdn.microsoft.com/ en-us/library/ms998465.aspx.

Enterprise Solution Patterns

Category	Patterns
Deployment Patterns	**Deployment Plan.** Create a deployment plan that describes which tier each of the application's components will be deployed to. While assigning components to tiers, if it is found that a tier is not a good match for a component, determine the cost and benefits of modifying the component to better work with the infrastructure, or of modifying the infrastructure to better suit the component. See *"Deployment Plan"* at http://msdn.microsoft.com/en-us/library/ms978676.aspx. **Layered Application.** Separate the components of your solution into layers. The components in each layer should be cohesive and at roughly the same level of abstraction. Each layer should be loosely coupled to the layers underneath. See *"Layered Application"* at http://msdn.microsoft.com/en-us/library/ms978678.aspx. **Three-Layered Services Application.** Base your layered architecture on three layers: the presentation, business, and data layers to provide decoupling and increase cohesiveness. See "Three-Layered Services Application" at http://msdn.microsoft.com/ en-us/library/ms978689.aspx. **Tiered Distribution.** Structure your servers and client computers into a set of physical tiers and distribute your application components appropriately to specific tiers. See "Tiered Distribution" at http://msdn.microsoft.com/en-us/library/ms978701.aspx. **Three-Tiered Distribution.** Structure your application around three physical tiers: the client, application, and database tiers. See "Three-Tiered Distribution" at http://msdn.microsoft.com/en-us/library/ms978694.aspx.

(continued)

Category	Patterns
Distributed Systems	**Broker.** Use the Broker pattern to hide the implementation details of remote service invocation by encapsulating them into a layer other than the business component itself. See *"Broker"* at http://msdn.microsoft.com/en-us/library/ms978706.aspx. **Data Transfer Object.** Create a data transfer object (DTO) that holds all data that is required for the remote call. Modify the remote method signature to accept the DTO as the single parameter and to return a single DTO parameter to the client. After the calling application receives the DTO and stores it as a local object, the application can make a series of individual procedure calls to the DTO without incurring the overhead of remote calls. See *"Data Transfer Object"* at http://msdn.microsoft.com/en-us/library/ms978717.aspx. **Singleton.** Singleton provides a global, single instance by making the class create a single instance of itself, allowing other objects to access this instance through a globally accessible class method that returns a reference to the instance. Additionally declare the class constructor as private so that no other object can create a new instance. See *"Singleton"* at http://msdn.microsoft.com/en-us/library/ms998426.aspx.
Performance and Reliability	**Server Clustering.** A *server cluster* is the combination of two or more servers that are interconnected to appear as one, thus creating a virtual resource that enhances availability, scalability, or both. See *"Server Clustering"* at http://msdn.microsoft.com/en-us/library/ms998414.aspx. **Load-Balanced Cluster.** Install your service or application onto multiple servers that are configured to share the workload. This type of configuration is a load-balanced cluster. Load balancing scales the performance of server-based programs, such as a Web server, by distributing client requests across multiple servers. Load-balancing technologies, commonly referred to as load balancers, receive incoming requests and redirect them to a specific host if necessary. The load-balanced hosts concurrently respond to different client requests, even multiple requests from the same client. See *"Load-Balanced Cluster"* at http://msdn.microsoft.com/en-us/library/ms978730.aspx. **Failover Cluster.** A *failover cluster* is a set of servers that are configured so that if one server becomes unavailable, another server automatically takes over for the failed server and continues processing. Each server in the cluster has at least one other server in the cluster identified as its standby server. See *"Failover Cluster"* at http://msdn.microsoft.com/en-us/library/ms978720.aspx.
Services Patterns	**Service Interface.** Create a component that provides an entry point through which consumers of the application can interact with the service, and exposes a coarse-grained interface while decoupling the implementation from the business logic. See *"Service Interface"* at http://msdn.microsoft.com/en-us/library/ms998421.aspx. **Service Gateway.** Encapsulate the code that implements the consumer portion of the contract into its own Service Gateway component that acts as a proxy to other services, encapsulating the details of connecting to the source and performing any necessary translation. See *"Service Gateway"* at http://msdn.microsoft.com/en-us/library/ms998420.aspx.

Category	Patterns
Web Presentation Patterns	**Model-View-Controller.** The Model-View-Controller (MVC) pattern separates the data in the domain, the presentation, and the actions based on user input into three separate classes. The Model manages the behavior and data of the application domain, responds to requests for information about its state (usually from the View), and responds to instructions to change state (usually from the Controller). The View manages the display of information. The Controller interprets the mouse and keyboard inputs from the user, informing the model and/or the view to change as appropriate. See *"Model-View-Controller"* at http://msdn.microsoft.com/en-us/library/ms978748.aspx. **Page Controller.** Use the Page Controller pattern to accept input from the page request, invoke the requested actions on the model, and determine the correct view to use for the resulting page. Separate the dispatching logic from any view-related code. Where appropriate, create a common base class for all page controllers to avoid code duplication and increase consistency and testability. See *"Page Controller"* at http://msdn.microsoft.com/en-us/library/ms978764.aspx. **Front Controller.** The Front Controller pattern solves the decentralization problem present in Page Controller by channeling all requests through a single controller. The controller itself is usually implemented in two parts: a handler and a hierarchy of commands. The handler receives the HTTP Post or Get request from the Web server and retrieves relevant parameters from the request. The handler uses the parameters from the request first to choose the correct command and then to transfer control to the command for processing. The commands themselves are also part of the controller. The commands represent the specific actions as described in the Command pattern. See *"Front Controller"* at http://msdn.microsoft.com/en-us/library/ms978723.aspx. **Intercepting Filter.** Use the Intercepting Filter pattern to create a chain of composable filters to implement common preprocessing and post-processing tasks during a Web page request. See *"Intercepting Filter"* at http://msdn.microsoft.com/en-us/library/ms978727.aspx. **Page Cache.** Cache the output generated by the server for pages that are accessed frequently but change less often in order to reduce the processing load on the server. See *"Page Cache"* at http://msdn.microsoft.com/en-us/library/ms978759.aspx. **Observer.** Use the Observer pattern to maintain a list of interested dependents (observers) in a separate object (the subject). Have all individual observers implement a common Observer interface to eliminate direct dependencies between the subject and the dependent objects. See *"Observer"* at http://msdn.microsoft.com/en-us/library/ms978753.aspx.

Integration Patterns

Category	Patterns
Integration Layer	**Entity Aggregation.** Introduce an Entity Aggregation layer that provides a logical representation of the entities at an enterprise level, with physical connections that support the access and that update to their respective instances in back-end repositories. See *"Entity Aggregation"* at http://msdn.microsoft.com/en-us/library/ms978573.aspx.
	Process Integration. Define a business process model that describes the individual steps that make up the complex business function. Create a separate process manager component that can interpret multiple concurrent instances of this model and that can interact with the existing applications to perform the individual steps of the process. See *"Process Integration"* at http://msdn.microsoft.com/en-us/library/ms978592.aspx.
	Portal Integration. Create a portal application that displays the information retrieved from multiple applications in a unified UI. The user can then perform the required tasks based on the information displayed in this portal. See *"Portal Integration"* at http://msdn.microsoft.com/en-us/library/ms978585.aspx.
Integration Topologies	**Message Broker.** Extend the integration solution by using the Message Broker pattern. A *message broker* is a physical component that handles the communication between applications. Instead of communicating with each other, applications communicate only with the message broker. An application sends a message to the message broker, providing the logical name of the receivers. The message broker looks up applications registered under the logical name and then passes the message to them. See *"Message Broker"* at http://msdn.microsoft.com/en-us/library/ms978579.aspx.
	Message Bus. Connect all applications through a logical component known as a message bus. A *message bus* specializes in transporting messages between applications. A message bus contains three key elements: a set of agreed upon message schemas, a set of common command messages, and a shared infrastructure for sending bus messages to recipients. See *"Message Bus"* at http://msdn.microsoft.com/en-us/library/ms978583.aspx.
	Publish/Subscribe. Enable classes to publish events that other applications can subscribe to in order to receive specific messages. A Publish\Subscribe mechanism sends events or messages to all interested subscribers. See *"Publish/Subscribe"* at http://msdn.microsoft.com/en-us/library/ms978603.aspx.

Category	Patterns
System Connections	**Data Integration.** Integrate applications at the logical data layer by allowing the data in one application (the source) to be accessed by other applications (the target). See *"Data Integration"* at http://msdn.microsoft.com/en-us/library/ms978572.aspx. **Functional Integration.** Integrate applications at the business logic layer by allowing the business function in one application (the source) to be accessed by other applications (the target). See *"Functional Integration"* at http://msdn.microsoft.com/en-us/library/ms978578.aspx. **Service-Oriented Integration.** To integrate applications at the business logic layer, enable systems to consume and provide Extensible Markup Language (XML)-based Web services. Use Web Services Description Language (WSDL) contracts to describe the interfaces to these systems. Ensure interoperability by making your implementation compliant with the Web Services (WS-*) family of specifications. See *"Service-Oriented Integration"* at http://msdn.microsoft.com/en-us/library/ms978594.aspx. **Presentation Integration.** Access the application's functionality through the UI by simulating a user's input and by reading data from the screen display. See *"Presentation Integration"* at http://msdn.microsoft.com/en-us/library/ms978588.aspx.
Additional Integration Patterns	**Pipes and Filters.** Implement the transformations by using a sequence of filter components, where each filter component receives an input message, applies a simple transformation, and sends the transformed message to the next component. Conduct the messages through pipes that connect filter outputs and inputs and that buffer the communication between the filters. See *"Pipes and Filters"* at http://msdn.microsoft.com/en-us/library/ms978599.aspx. **Gateway.** Abstracts the access to an external system to a single interface. The pattern eliminates the need for multiple systems to understand how to connect to the external system. Therefore, the Gateway pattern simplifies the development and maintenance processes that are related to accessing external systems. See *"Additional Integration Patterns"* at http://msdn.microsoft.com/en-us/library/ms978722.aspx.

Web Services Security Patterns

Category	Pattern
Authentication	**Brokered Authentication.** The Web service validates the credentials presented by the client, without the need for a direct relationship between the two parties. An authentication broker that both parties trust independently issues a security token to the client. The client can then present credentials, including the security token, to the Web service. See *"Brokered Authentication"* at http://msdn2.microsoft.com/en-us/library/aa480560.aspx. The following three patterns describe specific implementations of the Brokered Authentication pattern. **Brokered Authentication: Kerberos.** Use the Kerberos protocol to broker authentication between clients and Web services. See *"Brokered Authentication: Kerberos"* at http://msdn2.microsoft.com/en-us/library/aa480562.aspx. **Brokered Authentication: X509 PKI.** Use brokered authentication with X.509 certificates issued by a certificate authority (CA) in a public key infrastructure (PKI) to verify the credentials presented by the requesting application. See *"Brokered Authentication: X509 PKI"* at http://msdn2.microsoft.com/en-us/library/aa480565.aspx. **Brokered Authentication: STS.** Use brokered authentication with a security token issued by a Security Token Service (STS). The STS is trusted by both the client and the Web service to provide interoperable security tokens. See *"Brokered Authentication: STS"* at http://msdn2.microsoft.com/en-us/library/aa480563.aspx. **Direct Authentication.** The Web service acts as an authentication service to validate credentials from the client. The credentials, which include proof of possession that is based on shared secrets, are verified against an identity store. See *"Direct Authentication"* at http://msdn.microsoft.com/en-us/library/aa480566.aspx.
Authorization	**Trusted Subsystem.** The Web service acts as a trusted subsystem to access additional resources. It uses its own credentials instead of the user's credentials to access the resource. See *"Trusted Subsystem"* at http://msdn2.microsoft.com/en-us/library/aa480587.aspx.
Exception Management	**Exception Shielding.** Sanitize unsafe exceptions by replacing them with exceptions that are safe by design. Return only those exceptions to the client that have been sanitized, or exceptions that are safe by design. Exceptions that are safe by design do not contain sensitive information in the exception message, and they do not contain a detailed stack trace, either of which might reveal sensitive information about the Web service's inner workings. See *"Exception Shielding"* at http://msdn2.microsoft.com/en-us/library/aa480591.aspx.
Message Encryption	**Data Confidentiality.** Use encryption to protect sensitive data that is contained in a message. Unencrypted data, which is known as *plaintext*, is converted to encrypted data, which is known as *ciphertext*. Data is encrypted with an algorithm and a cryptographic key. Ciphertext is then converted back to plaintext at its destination. See *"Data Confidentiality"* at http://msdn.microsoft.com/en-us/library/aa480570.aspx.
Message Replay Detection	**Message Replay Detection.** Cache an identifier for incoming messages, and use message replay detection to identify and reject messages that match an entry in the replay detection cache. See *"Message Replay Detection"* at http://msdn2.microsoft.com/en-us/library/aa480598.aspx.

Category	Pattern
Message Signing	**Data Origin Authentication.** Use data origin authentication, which enables the recipient to verify that messages have not been tampered with in transit (data integrity) and that they originate from the expected sender (authenticity). See *"Data Origin Authentication"* at http://msdn2.microsoft.com/en-us/library/aa480571.aspx.
Message Validation	**Message Validator.** The message validation logic enforces a well-defined policy that specifies which parts of a request message are required for the service to successfully process it. It validates the XML message payloads against an XML schema (XSD) to ensure that they are well-formed and consistent with what the service expects to process. The validation logic also measures the messages against certain criteria by examining the message size, the message content, and the character sets that are used. Any message that does not meet the criteria is rejected. See *"Message Validator"* at http://msdn2.microsoft.com/en-us/library/aa480600.aspx.
Deployment	**Perimeter Service Router.** Design a Web service intermediary that acts as a perimeter service router. The perimeter service router provides an external interface on the perimeter network for internal Web services. It accepts messages from external applications and routes them to the appropriate Web service on the private network. See *"Perimeter Service Router"* at http://msdn2.microsoft.com/en-us/library/aa480606.aspx.

Additional Resources

To more easily access Web resources, see the online version of the bibliography at: http://www.microsoft.com/architectureguide.

- For information on patterns in the Composite Application Library, see Composite Application Guidance for WPF and Silverlight.
- For information on data patterns, see Data Patterns.
- For information on enterprise solution patterns, see Enterprise Solution Patterns Using Microsoft .NET.
- For information on integration patterns, see Integration Patterns.
- For information on Web Service Security, see Web Service Security Guidance: Scenarios, Patterns, and Implementation Guidance for Web Services Enhancements (WSE) 3.0.

Index